WHOLE-FACULTY STUDY GROUPS

3rd Edition

WHOLE-FACULTY STUDY GROUPS

**Creating Professional Learning Communities
That Target Student Learning**

3rd Edition

Carlene U. Murphy   Dale W. Lick

Foreword by Shirley M. Hord

CORWIN PRESS
A Sage Publications Company
Thousand Oaks, California

For information:

Corwin Press
A Sage Publications Company
2455 Teller Road
Thousand Oaks, California 91320
www.corwinpress.com

Sage Publications Ltd.
1 Oliver's Yard
55 City Road
London EC1Y 1SP
United Kingdom

Sage Publications India Pvt. Ltd.
B-42, Panchsheel Enclave
Post Box 4109
New Delhi 110 017 India

Printed in the United States of America

Library of Congress Cataloging-in-Publication Data

Murphy, Carlene U.
Whole-faculty study groups: Creating professional learning communities that target student learning / by Carlene U. Murphy and Dale W. Lick.— 3rd ed.
        p. cm.
Includes bibliographical references and index.
ISBN 1-4129-0893-0 (cloth) — ISBN 1-4129-0894-9 (pbk.)
    1. Teacher work groups—United States. 2. Teachers—In-service training—United States.
3. School improvement programs—United States. 4. Academic achievement—United States.
I. Lick, Dale W. II. Title.
LB1731.M865 2005
370'.71'55—dc22   2004015943

This book is printed on acid-free paper.

06 07 08 10 9 8 7 6 5 4 3

Acquisitions Editor:	Rachel Livsey
Editorial Assistant:	Phyllis Cappello
Production Editor:	Julia Parnell/Diane S. Foster
Copy Editor:	Dan Hays
Typesetter/Designer:	C&M Digitals (P) Ltd.
Proofreader:	Scott Oney
Indexer:	Pamela Van Huss
Cover Designer:	Tracy E. Miller

Contents

Tables
and Figures

Foreword

It just keeps getting better! And better!

For anyone who missed the first edition (1998), Carlene Murphy and Dale Lick gave us the definition, descriptions, and applications of Whole-Faculty Study Groups (WFSGs). The second edition (2001) brought additional information, understanding, and insights about the processes and outcomes of WFSGs in schools. Now, more time and experience of the authors and the model in the field have produced highly credible results—staff and student learning outcomes.

In this third edition, Murphy and Lick express WFSGs as professional learning communities. They point out how groups of teachers come together to

use reliable assessments to identify strong areas and weak spots in their curriculum and instruction that do not result in desired gains for students;

specify what they should modify or change in their teaching to gain increased student results;

determine what and how they need to learn to become more effective with students;

deliver their new strategies or program and monitor implementation; and

check consistently on student results to track how teachers' work is benefiting students.

These steps are those employed by professional learning communities whose undeviating focus is on student gains and on how what teachers and administrators do supports those gains. Thus, this is the connection of WFSGs to professional learning communities.

In this era of highly promoted collaboration and democratic participation, WFSGs show us a way to express and demonstrate collaboration and democracy in professional teachers' work. These groups provide the opportunity for those closest to the work of students to use their expertise to guide that work. Furthermore, WFSGs provide the possibility for those who have learned their art and craft through training and experience to share their knowledge and skills with those who are in their early professional years. Together, experts and novices learn with and from each other, and they make important decisions about how they will design and deliver a high-quality, intellectually stimulating instructional program for students.

This way of working is particularly significant because the profession, particularly those members who research and write about it, has widely proclaimed the importance and value of functioning professional learning communities in schools. Sadly, there has been limited experience and study of how to create professional learning communities, and Murphy and Lick have gone a long way to filling this gap with their specific and concrete directions about constructing WFSGs. To them, we are indebted.

We know that when professionals have the power and authority to make decisions about their work, they are more stimulated and challenged to do their best work and to take the risks that are part of that work. In the company of like-minded professionals, they assume the responsibility and accountability that have been placed on them, and through the creation of collaboratively created tasks for students, they enhance their students' chances for successful high-quality learning.

It is not only teachers who play an important role in the creation and operationalization of WFSGs. The principal is a major player, and Murphy and Lick describe this role carefully and in detail so that administrators can take guidance from their writing. For years, principals were not considered in the instructional process, but effective schools and effective districts have shown that administrators have a significant role to play in the nurture and development of faculty. Administrators do this not only by making the resources of time and material available but also by providing human resources and their own personal attention. Making time for teachers to meet in WFSGs is a critical factor that principals and other administrators can support with creative scheduling and other arrangements. The authors give suggestions for how this can be done. This volume has abundant suggestions and ideas for how logistical and managerial issues may be handled as well as how the content and substantive work of WFSGs may be supported successfully.

This third edition from Murphy and Lick is a superb resource and a must read for all educators involved in the improvement of education. It should be in the hands of individuals from the state department of education to the classroom teacher because it speaks to all layers of the system and to the role that each person must play to ensure successful learning for all students.

—*Shirley M. Hord*
Scholar Emerita
Southwest Educational Development Laboratory
Austin, Texas

Preface

THE NEW EDITION

Whole-Faculty Study Groups: Creating Professional Learning Communities That Target Student Learning is a new edition of our earlier books. The titles of the first edition, *Whole-Faculty Study Groups: A Powerful Way to Change Schools and Enhance Learning* (1998), and the second edition, *Whole-Faculty Study Groups: Creating Student-Based Professional Development* (2001), reflect the shift in focus. In the first edition, we were not as clear as we are now in how Whole-Faculty Study Groups (WFSGs) change schools and what types of learning are enhanced for students. In the second edition, we presented a much more coherent picture of how WFSGs are implemented and maintained. In this new edition, 4 more years of experiences in many very different schools bring more clarity to all three phases of the change process: initiation, implementation, and institutionalization. On the basis of practice, in this edition, there is more focus on assessment of student results, and the action-research cycle that WFSGs experience is described in more detail. A major change from the earlier editions is that this edition views WFSGs as a system rather than simply as a model or a design for professional development. We are taking the view, as seen in Figure 2.1, that when implemented as described in this book, WFSGs represent a systemic change system. The theory that supports professional learning communities has remained constantly supportive; however, we have tried to more directly connect theory and research to the WFSG practice. In the first two editions, we did not use the term *professional learning communities*, assuming that readers would connect the term to what we were describing. We realized that we may not have made the connection, however, when principals asked, "Now that we have Whole-Faculty Study Groups in place, when do we begin implementing professional learning communities?" This new edition also uses the National Staff Development Council's staff development standards to illustrate how the WFSG system continues to use the context-process-content framework for its basic design. Although the three books are similar, many important modifications and significant additions have been included in this new edition.

The WFSG system has spread to school systems across the country, and the implementation and work of study groups has become a daily occurrence in many schools, districts, and school systems. Because such work is continuous in these schools, the process and its refinement are constantly evolving. What one study group does has the potential to affect others, not only in that school but also in other schools that use the WFSG system.

In addition, as Murphy and other consultants travel from school to school throughout the country in their consulting role and Lick continues to research the theoretical basis for study groups, new ideas are generated that help strengthen the WFSG system. These changes accumulate over time and lead to major adjustments that make the process even more effective.

In the 6 years since the first edition was written, several hundred schools have implemented the WFSG system, which translates to more than 2,000 individual study groups. From these and continuing groups, new insights into the WFSG approach have created a wealth of new and helpful material.

If the study group model were a "paper-and-pencil" design, it might remain in a fixed or rigid state. Because the model continually evolves from how teachers actually work together in schools, it is fluid, flowing, and readjusting itself. As leaders in schools chronicle the movement of study groups, we examine why some are high-performing groups and others struggle. What we learn is shared with continuing schools and those that are considering or just beginning the process. This edition of our book is how we keep schools up to date with our findings on what is working best.

Included in this edition of the book are the following major changes we have made during the past 4 years:

- An updating of every chapter
- The addition of three new chapters to make the book more effective and usable
- A reorganization of chapters to allow the book to flow more usably for the reader
- An expansion of the discussion of practical approaches and processes that will help the user and reflect "what works most effectively" in difficult situations
- New materials on key and timely topics, such as "learning communities" and "learning teams"
- Fourteen new and important "lessons learned"
- Completely revised and updated sets of practical and concrete resources
- Illustrations in the appendix

NEED AND PURPOSE

Staff development, school reform, and the improvement of schools are not as simple as the general and educational rhetoric of the past decade would imply. Well-intentioned societal leaders and school personnel have talked about the necessity to change and improve, and schools and their personnel have attempted a wide variety of what appeared to be logical and progressive solutions. Unfortunately, most of these have failed or, at best, been only partially successful. This failure or limited success happened because change, even positively perceived change, is difficult to bring about in long-standing, well-established organizations. Like other organizations, schools are not naturally open or amenable to major change.

To successfully reform, improve, and transition schools to meet tomorrow's needs will require approaches and processes that are different than most attempted during the past decade. We must not only decide what changes or reforms are required but also put in place meaningful staff development and significant transition processes to help negotiate the societal, organizational, cultural, and people barriers in and affecting schools.

One of the most successful and exciting new approaches to staff development, reform, and change in education today is that involving professional WFSGs, as discussed in detail in this book. A key element in these efforts and unique to this book is "whole-faculty" involvement, not just study groups but WFSGs, in which all members of the faculty are committed to the effort, actively involved in it, and responsible for an important part of the total effort. Where WFSGs have been properly implemented, they have been unusually successful. The WFSG system is a holistic, practical process for facilitating major staff development and schoolwide change and for enhancing student learning and school improvement. This book presents a detailed discussion of WFSGs, their step-by-step application, and the underlying change principles necessary for such study groups to be successful in the school environment.

A second key element is that WFSGs are a student-based approach to professional development, and they rest on the basic question, "What do students need for us, the teachers, to do?" Using this focus radically changes the tone and dynamics of professional development for teachers, and brings it right to the heart of the matter. Based on our work in leading and managing major change and our experiences in hundreds of schools and more than 2,000 WFSGs in those schools, this book provides (a) the practical knowledge required to implement and successfully use the WFSG approach in schools and (b) the theoretical foundation to understand the key change elements involved and how these can be applied to facilitate staff development and schoolwide change, enhance student learning, and improve schools. Furthermore, the book contains a generous collection of relevant and illustrative examples of real-world situations and a detailed, step-by-step practical methodology for the development of successful professional WFSGs in schools.

In particular, this book grew out of a wide array of real-world, Whole-Faculty Study Group efforts and experiences, it encompasses the existing relevant literature on study groups, and it significantly expands this knowledge base through (a) new up-to-date information and refinements of processes, procedures, and approaches; (b) new experiences and applications from user schools throughout the country; and (c) a unique integration and use of practical and theoretical change-knowledge concepts and change-management approaches.

WHO SHOULD READ AND USE THIS BOOK?

This book should be read and used by anyone who is interested in facilitating important staff development and change in schools and increasing student learning. A primary audience for the book should be the personnel in K–12 schools—all teachers, administrators, and staff.

For schools that choose to introduce the WFSG approach, all school personnel will be involved in their schoolwide effort. Consequently, in such schools, each faculty member, administrator, and staff member should have a copy, or many copies should be shared with school personnel, allowing full and convenient access across the school.

In addition, the book holds special potential for individual teachers and administrators and groups of teachers and administrators who are considering new options for seriously improving their schools. Other important audiences for this book include the following:

- Central office personnel in school systems, especially for consideration and possible implementation of study groups in their school system
- College of education faculty in colleges and universities for understanding this new and successful process for schoolwide change and enhanced student learning, as well as for possible use as a textbook or reference book in classes relating to teacher training and school enhancement
- Community college faculty and administrators for consideration of study groups and their application in their institutions for collegewide change and improving student learning
- School, community college, college, and university libraries
- Individuals and groups in national and international workshops on study groups and their application in education, from small seminars to large groups
- Individuals and groups in corporate, community, and governmental organizations involved with schools, education, and training

ORGANIZATION AND CONTENTS

The book is organized so that its chapter contents logically build on each other, with each laying a foundation for those that follow. The contents include the key elements in the WFSG and change processes and their implementation along with a large number of real-world examples and illustrative cases. The book is written so that it can serve as a textbook, a detailed reference book, or a stand-alone guide for the effective initiation, comprehensive implementation, and successful completion of the WFSG approach to staff development and major improvements in schools.

Chapter 1 discusses the school reform environment and the potential of the WFSG approach, serving as a major change process to improve schools, enhance student learning, and move schools toward becoming learning organizations.

The concept and nature of study groups, their strengths and perceived weaknesses, their purposes, and their ability to serve as vehicles for staff development and change and the creation of collaborative work cultures are described in Chapter 2.

Chapter 3 provides an overview discussion of relevant research findings relating to school change and improvement, including professional learning communities, staff development and training, the change process, school cultures, and leadership.

Chapter 4 sets the framework for the three components of the WFSG approach: context, process, and content. Key among the context-related topics discussed are roles and responsibilities of school personnel, school district influence, importance of leadership, power of a shared vision, time and resource requirements, school data and student needs, organizational structure, and capacity building.

Critically important issues of school culture are discussed in Chapter 5, including the change concepts of building commitment, effective leadership and sponsorship, human change and resistance, roles of change, assimilation capacity, modification of school-related cultures, and the overarching universal change principle.

The process for the WFSG system, including the 15 study group process guidelines for success, is unfolded in Chapter 6, helping educators acquire and develop the knowledge and skills necessary to increase student performance and improve schools.

Chapter 7 introduces the seven steps of the WFSG decision-making cycle, which provide the mechanisms for decision making involving data collection and analysis; critical student needs; study group organization around student needs; and plans of action, implementation, and evaluation.

The heart of the study group process, the content, detailed in Chapter 8, is what teachers study; investigate; add to their strategies, repertoires, and resource bank; do to become more skillful in the classroom with students; and use when study groups meet.

Chapter 9 describes how to use the study group process to build synergistic groups, which are "authentic teams," and how to turn such teams into highly productive and successful learning teams and learning communities in schools.

Chapter 10 reviews, in the WFSG process, the stages of change, concerns and practices related to change, questions that leaders must answer for study groups, and sets of practical, concrete approaches to help study groups become fully successful.

Chapter 11 discusses "learning experiences" from the "educational field of practice," including key local school, regional, state, and national WFSG initiatives.

Chapter 12 presents 14 reflective "lessons learned" from the authors' extensive work and study of WFSGs, which should be helpful to readers of this book.

Finally, the appendixes contain a plethora of helpful nuts-and-bolts information, forms, guides, and illustrations for the effective application of the WFSG approach, including study group action plans, study group logs, and artifacts from WFSG schools.

We hope that the material in this book will inspire and help you understand and use WFSGs in your work to produce especially meaningful staff development, create more effective schools, and generate learning environments that significantly enhance student learning and improve schools in the 21st century.

Acknowledgments

We acknowledge Joe Murphy for the care and love he has given to the family he inherited when he married Carlene in 1978, especially to her children, Laura and Douglas, and, later, to Laura's daughters, Sarah and Allison, and to Douglas's son, Joshua. We also acknowledge the love and care Joe gives to Carlene's grandniece, Toni Carrington, who, through adoption, is the child of Carlene and Joe. Not only has Joe been a personal source of comfort and joy but also he is Carlene's professional partner. The work described in this book has been done in partnership with Joe. He is the silent partner but powerful thinker and critical friend. In the past 15 years, there have been only a handful of training sessions that Carlene has conducted that Joe did not patiently attend.

Through the writing of these acknowledgments, Carlene is especially mindful of what her children Laura and Douglas may have, unintentionally, not had so that unknowingly, the foundations of this book could be laid. The foundations of this book are rooted in Carlene's early teaching and work experiences in the 1960s and 1970s that most often meant spending precious time away from her young children.

We acknowledge Marilyn Lick for her patience, understanding, and continuous support and encouragement of Dale and his work on the book.

We express deep appreciation for Rachel Brown, a dear friend and colleague of Carlene's, who started working with Carlene in 1977 and continues today. The Carlene-Rachel professional partnership exhibits all the characteristics of other great and well-known partnerships: loyalty, dedication, dependability, sincerity, and generosity of time, energy, and brain power.

We acknowledge all the faculties that have implemented and sustained Murphy's Whole-Faculty Study Groups (WFSGs) since 1987. We continue to marvel at the richness of learning at the original sites in Augusta, Georgia, with Bruce Joyce and Beverly Showers as our teachers. The sites that followed the Augusta schools taught us many lessons that greatly influenced and shaped the current work. We give special recognition to schools in Americus and Marietta, Georgia; San Diego, California; Round Rock, Texas; and Greeley, Colorado. There were many more schools; however, these may well be considered the WFSG "laboratory" schools.

We acknowledge ATLAS Communities, a national comprehensive school reform design, and the public schools in school districts that have implemented and are currently implementing the ATLAS design. We especially appreciate Linda Gerstle, the executive director of ATLAS Communities, for her untiring and generous support to Carlene and to all the WFSG work. We especially acknowledge the professionals who support the schools at the ATLAS sites—the site developers who have supported all the study groups, taken the major role in assisting the work of study groups, and cared deeply about the work of the study groups. They have not only elevated the work of individual study groups but also enhanced the thinking about all aspects of WFSGs.

We acknowledge Carlene's colleagues who are assuming more of the responsibilities for assisting schools in the initiation and maintenance of WFSGs. Karl Clauset, in addition to being a supportive colleague, provided invaluable feedback on several chapters, especially Chapter 7. Karl is a thoughtful, generous friend with great expertise and knowledge of the WFSG process. Lynn Baber and Terri Jenkins, friends and colleagues in Augusta, are dedicated and tireless in their efforts to train and assist faculties. Anita Kissinger, Director of Staff Development, is doing stellar work in the schools in Springfield, Missouri, leading an entire district toward institutionalizing WFSGs in a majority of its schools. Emily Weiskopf is providing strong leadership to a number of districts whose leaders want WFSGs to become a routine practice in schools. Enough cannot be said about Janet Langlois at the Louisiana Department of Education and the regional Learning-Intensive Networking Communities for Success coordinators in Louisiana. They have marshaled an entire state in their belief that WFSGs will contribute to an increase in student achievement in Louisiana.

We acknowledge a large group of Georgians who have provided consistent and sustained leadership in the field of staff development to Georgia's schools. Among these are Fulton Stone, who coordinated staff development efforts at the Georgia Department of Education for 20 years, and Steve Preston, who continues to keep the focus on staff development at the department; Gale Hulme, who excels in everything she does and especially in providing statewide leadership training and opportunities for Georgia's educators at all levels; and Kathy O'Neil, who keeps the Georgia Staff Development Council on a steady course through her service to the council.

We applaud the teachers in all the schools in which WFSGs have been implemented. Teachers have done stellar work and have exemplified the meaning of professionalism, student-based decision making, risk taking, perseverance, and unselfish giving. Teachers in all circumstances have given their energy, time, expertise, and heart in abundance.

The contributions of the following reviewers are gratefully acknowledged:

Anita Kissinger
Staff Development Director
Springfield Public Schools
Springfield, MO

Allan Alson
Superintendent, Evanston Township High School
Founder and president, governing board
Minority Student Achievement Network
Evanston, IL

Judith Davidson
Assistant Professor
Leadership in Schooling, Graduate School of Education
University of Massachusetts–Lowell
Lowell, MA

Karl Clauset
Independent Education Consultant
Clauset Consulting
Bellingham, WA

About the Authors

**Carlene U. Murphy** began her 47th consecutive year of work in public schools in September 2004. She is Director of the National WFSG Center in Augusta, Georgia. She began her teaching career as a fourth-grade teacher in August 1957 in her hometown of Augusta. After 1 year of living at home and teaching, she decided to spread her wings and went to Memphis, Tennessee, where she would teach the fourth grade for 13 years. It is the children she taught in Memphis that she sees in her mind's eye today as giving her the energy and love for what she continues to do. Returning to Augusta to begin the 1971–1972 school year, she was a classroom teacher for 2 more years before moving into administrative positions. She developed the programs for gifted children in the Richmond County school system and administered those programs for 5 years before becoming director of staff development in 1978. During the 15 years as director of staff development, she also designed and administered the district's Adopt-A-School program that received national recognition, and she assumed responsibilities for the district's public relations functions, including publications and coordinating special events.

The 15 years (1978–1993) as the Richmond County (Augusta) School District's director of staff development brought many accolades to the district and to Murphy. In 1991, Richmond County received the Award for Outstanding Achievement in Professional Development from the American Association of School Administrators. The district also received Georgia's Outstanding Staff Development Program Award for 2 consecutive years. In 1992, she was awarded the National Staff Development Council's Contributions to Staff Development Award, one of the organization's highest honors. She was the first practitioner to receive that honor. Her personal service to the National Staff Development Council included serving as chairperson of the annual national conference in Atlanta in 1986, as president in 1988, and on the board of trustees from 1984 to 1990.

After retiring from the Richmond County schools in 1993, she worked through 1997 as a private consultant for the schools and districts that wanted to implement the process that she would name Whole-Faculty Study Groups (WFSGs). She has written extensively about her work in *Educational Leadership* and the *Journal of Staff Development*.

From the summer of 1997 to December 2002, Murphy worked as a full-time consultant with ATLAS Communities. She worked with all ATLAS schools in the implementation of WFSGs. She also continued to work with schools not associated with the national comprehensive school reform design.

 **Dale W. Lick** is past president of Georgia Southern University, the University of Maine, and Florida State University, and he is currently a university professor in the Learning Systems Institute at Florida State University. He teaches in the Department of Educational Leadership and Policy Studies and works on educational and organizational projects involving transformational leadership, change creation, leading and managing change, learning teams, learning organizations, distance learning, new learning systems (e.g., the HyLighter Learning and Assessment Systems), strategic planning, and visioning.

A mathematician by academic training, Lick previously held administrative and faculty positions at the Port Huron Junior College, University of Redlands, University of Tennessee, Drexel University, Russell Sage College, and Old Dominion University. He also served as a visiting research mathematician at Brookhaven National Laboratory, an adjunct professor of biomathematics at Temple University, and a scientific consultant to the U.S. Atomic Energy Commission.

Included in 45 national and international biographical listings, Lick is the author of four books; more than 60 book chapters, professional articles, and proceedings; and 285 original newspaper columns. His recent books are *Whole-Faculty Study Groups: A Powerful Way to Change Schools and Enhance Learning* and *Whole-Faculty Study Groups: Creating Student-Based Professional Development* (both with Carlene Murphy), and *New Directions in Mentoring: Creating a Culture of Synergy* (author and coeditor with Carol Mullen). Recent publications are "Mega-Level Strategic Planning: Beyond Conventional Wisdom" and "Change Creation: The Rest of the Planning Story" (both with Roger Kaufman), Chapters 1 and 2 in the book *Technology-Driven Planning: Principles to Practice*; "Whole-Faculty Study Groups: Facilitating Mentoring for School-Wide Change," *Theory Into Practice*; "Leadership and Change," Chapter 3 in *A Field Guild to Academic Leadership* (edited by Robert Diamond); and "Medieval Scholarship Meets 21st Century Learning Technology, Part One: The Collaborative Annotation Model" and "Part Two: The Interactive Annotation Model" (both with David Lebow), *Online Classroom*.

Lick received both bachelor's and master's degrees from Michigan State University and a Ph.D. from the University of California at Riverside. He holds all three levels of formal training and certification for Leading and Managing Organizational Change: Change Knowledge, Instructor/Trainer, and Consultation Skills, from the international change research and development organization, Conner Partners (formerly ODR, Inc.), Atlanta, Georgia. He also completed formal programs on *The Seven Habits of Highly Effective People* (Stephen Covey) and *Learning Organizations* (Peter Senge).

For
Laura Louise Brown Wilson and Douglas Gordon Brown,
with a mother's unconditional love.

The 1958–1959, 1959–1960, and 1960–1961 Fourth Grade Classes
Oakhaven Elementary School
Memphis, Tennessee
with remembrance and appreciation for what you taught a teacher.

and
Dale and Marilyn's parents
John R. and Florence M. Lick
E. Merril and Beatrice O. Foster

1

Introduction

The past several years have helped us see more clearly than ever before that staff development, school reform, and the improvement of schools are complicated and challenging undertakings. As discussed in the Preface, change, even positively perceived change, is difficult to bring about in long-standing, well-established organizations. Our schools are clearly among such organizations, and their cultures, the ones that have given us so much success and stability in the past, are deeply ensconced and rigid. Like all other such organizations, they are not naturally open or amenable to major change. Can we bring about meaningful reform and major change in our schools? The answer is "absolutely yes," and many such changes will be essential in the future! To do so, however, will require approaches and processes that are different from most of those attempted during the past decade. We must not only decide what change or reform is required but also put in place a significant transition process to help us negotiate the societal, organizational, cultural, and people barriers in and affecting the schools.

Major change in our schools, as is true in other types of organizations, requires active and effective sponsorship—support, encouragement, pressure, and accountability—from the leadership (e.g., boards, superintendents, and principals). With strong sponsorship at each level in the school, teachers and other school personnel feel a greater sense of empowerment and are more comfortable with change and more willing to seriously attempt new major projects and processes.

If genuine reform is to come from within our schools, then teachers and school personnel must be importantly and intimately involved. In particular, teachers must be perceived, treated, and held accountable as educational professionals. To treat them as such requires that teachers enjoy the latitude to invent local solutions and to discover and develop practices that embody central values and principles rather than to implement, adopt, or demonstrate practices thought to be universally effective (Little, 1993).

THE WHOLE-FACULTY STUDY GROUP SYSTEM

One of the most exciting new approaches to staff development, school improvement and reform, enhancement of student learning, and change in education is Murphy's Whole-Faculty Study Groups (WFSGs).

The Whole-Faculty Study Group system is a job-embedded, self-directed, student-driven approach to professional development. It is a professional development system designed to build communities of learners in which professionals continuously strive to increase student learning. This is accomplished by practitioners (a) deepening their own knowledge and understanding of what is taught, (b) reflecting on their practices, (c) sharpening their skills, and (d) taking joint responsibility for the students they teach.

"Whole-Faculty" means that every faculty member at the school is a member of a study group focusing on data-based student instructional needs. In such a context, a study group is a small number of individuals, three to five, joining together to increase their capacities to enable students to reach higher levels of performance. The collective synergy of all the study groups advances the whole school.

The essence of the WFSG system resides in the following four grounding or fundamental questions.

- What do students need for teachers to do so that teachers will have a deeper understanding of what they teach?
- What do students need for teachers to do so that teachers will be more skillful in how they teach?
- What do students need for teachers to do so that teachers will challenge students to learn difficult and fundamental concepts?
- What do students need for teachers to do so that teachers will give students skills to be deep thinkers and problem solvers?

The WFSG system has all the teachers on a faculty actively involved in study groups addressing student needs. WFSGs are student based! Consequently, the essential or overarching question that guides the WFSG system is as follows.

What are our students learning and achieving as a result of what we are learning and doing in our study group?

A properly implemented model encompasses the change characteristics discussed previously as well as several others, including collaboration and synergy; comentoring; individual, team, and organizational resilience; elements of learning organizations; and culture modification.

WFSGs allow teachers the freedom and flexibility to explicate, invent, and evaluate practices that have the potential to meet the needs of their students and the community their schools serve. As teachers work together in study groups, they alter their practices to provide new and innovative opportunities for their students to learn in challenging and productive new ways.

Effective WFSGs are a complex mixture of many activities occurring simultaneously. This model is a holistic, practical process for facilitating major schoolwide change and for enhancing learning outcomes in the schools. In particular, Murphy's WFSGs include the following:

- Giving teachers in schools a structure for collaboration and school improvement
- Supporting each other and, together, planning, learning, testing ideas, and sharing and reflecting on classroom practice
- Grappling with broad principles of teaching, learning, and practice
- Engaging in the pursuit of genuine questions, problems, and curiosities in ways that alter perspectives, policies, and practices
- Constructing subject matter knowledge versus merely consuming it
- Immersing in sustained work with ideas, materials, and colleagues
- Experiencing the frustrations of dealing with "what is" while envisioning "what could be"
- Functioning not only as consumers of research but also as critics and producers of research
- Contributing to knowledge and practice
- Struggling with the fundamental questions of what teachers and students must learn and know

WFSG: WHEN, WHERE, AND HOW IT BEGAN

In December 1986, Carlene Murphy, Joseph Murphy, Bruce Joyce, and Beverly Showers had their first conversation about how to increase student achievement through staff development in the Richmond County School District in Augusta, Georgia. Carlene Murphy was director of staff development in the public school district, which comprised 60 schools, and Joseph Murphy was dean of the School of Education at Augusta State University. Bruce Joyce and Beverly Showers, authors of a then newly published book titled *Increasing Student Achievement Through Staff Development,* were and still are nationally and internationally known scholars in the fields of staff development and models of teaching. This conversation led to a 3-year working relationship and an intense focus on (a) the culture of the school and the process of innovation, (b) ways teachers learn new teaching strategies, and (c) ways teachers transfer new skills into the classroom.

One of the first decisions the foursome made was that their work would involve whole schools. This meant that the staff development program would be offered only to whole faculties, and every teacher in such a school would participate in all phases of the program. The program was voluntary for a school, but if at least 80% of the teachers voted to support the program, all teachers would be expected to participate. This decision, whole-faculty participation, later became the central feature of what is today called the WFSG approach.

During the next 5 years, after discussions among the superintendent, principals, and faculties, 12 schools chose to become a part of the whole-school improvement program. The content of the improvement program was several models of teaching (Joyce & Weil, 2003) or approaches to teaching designed to bring about particular kinds of learning and help students become more effective learners. The models selected also helped students acquire information, ideas, skills, ways of thinking, and means of expressing themselves.

The whole-school improvement, called the Models of Teaching (MOT) program, put emphasis on content and on what teachers would be learning to do.

The skill development phase of Richmond County's program was two-pronged. One prong had teachers attending training sessions to learn the theory that supported the selected models while providing them with many opportunities for demonstrations and practice strategies with other teachers in a risk-free environment. The other prong involved using the models of teaching focused on redesigning the workplace, including having all the teachers on a faculty in small groups focusing on the implementation of the teaching strategies in their classrooms. Without the work that occurred in the small groups, the level of use of the models of teaching would not have had such a profound impact, and cultural norms would not have shifted from teacher isolation to teacher collaboration. Murphy discovered that in doing the work, one cannot separate the content (MOT) from the process (study groups). If the program had not had powerful content, it would not have mattered what processes were used.

It took a powerful process, however, to push high levels of application of the models of teaching to result in significant student learning. This very important understanding is the foundation of Chapters 6 through 8.

From 1987 to 1993, seven articles were published in professional journals and chapters in two books were written about the work in Richmond County. These publications are listed in the references and recommended reading list.

GOING NATIONAL WITH WFSGs

In January 1993, Murphy retired from the Richmond County Public Schools and began working with schools at the national level. She designed a process through which each school would identify its own required staff development content. The procedure required the faculty, in conjunction with the administration, to identify the priority academic needs of its students and specify the content that would enable teachers to address identified student needs.

In terms of support and resources, Murphy recognized that most districts had valuable resources and support personnel who had expertise in different academic areas, such as reading, mathematics, and science. University personnel, textbook representatives, and private consultants also could provide services and resources to schools in curriculum content and in effective teaching practices.

After working with schools for several years and trying various procedures for identifying the student's study groups and how study groups could be organized,

Murphy designed the decision-making cycle (DMC) described in Chapter 7. From these varied practical experiences over several years (e.g., responding to different school contexts), the procedural guidelines given in Chapter 6 evolved from Murphy's work.

In 1994, Murphy called the work she was doing "whole-faculty study groups." This title emerged as a result of the types of requests she was receiving. When school and district leaders began contacting Murphy about working with their school or district using study groups, she would ask, "A whole faculty?" Most often, the answer was "No. Any teacher who wants to be in a study group." Murphy's response was "My work is with whole schools, not setting up independent, stand-alone study groups." Over time, Murphy found it necessary to call her work whole-faculty study groups to distinguish it from other types of collegial arrangements. The first time this term appeared in a publication was in the article, "Whole-Faculty Study Groups: Doing the Seemingly Undoable," in the *Journal of Staff Development* (Murphy, 1995).

The WFSG approach has evolved dramatically since it began in 1986. Nonetheless, the heart of the WFSG process rests with Joyce and Showers from the early days in the schools in Augusta.

ATLAS COMMUNITIES

In 1997, Murphy became associated with ATLAS Communities, one of the national comprehensive school reform designs. Starting with Murphy's involvement, the WFSG system became the centerpiece of professional development in all ATLAS Communities' schools. ATLAS had previously strongly encouraged schools to organize faculty into study groups; WFSG became the standard for ATLAS schools, however. The Murphy-ATLAS relationship greatly increased the number of schools implementing WFSGs and expanded its knowledge base. Through spring 2004, 135 schools had chosen ATLAS Communities as their change model knowing that one nonnegotiable aspect of ATLAS is that all faculty would be members of study groups.

As indicated previously, ATLAS Communities is a comprehensive design. The ATLAS design or framework includes four key elements. The goal is to fully integrate the four elements during a 3-year period. The elements are

- Teaching, learning, and assessment: The central academic purpose of ATLAS is to help students understand important ideas and concepts and to challenge students to apply their knowledge in new situations.
- Professional development: ATLAS asserts that professional development is the cornerstone of the change effort and WFSGs are the cornerstone of professional development.
- Family and community: In ATLAS Communities, schools, families, and the communities have reciprocal relationships in which families and communities contribute to the school and the school values their voices.
- Management and decision making: Management structures are in place and involve all stakeholders.

When we refer to ATLAS Communities, readers should keep in mind that the reference is to more than schools implementing WFSGs; ATLAS is an integrated

approach to the change process. For more information about ATLAS, see www
.atlascommunities.org. There is no measure to accurately determine the impact
ATLAS Communities has had on the ongoing development and evolution of the
WFSG system. The ATLAS-Murphy partnership greatly increased the number of
schools, the demographics of the schools, and the scope of geographic locations of
schools to implement WFSGs. From 1997 to 2002, Murphy exclusively worked with
ATLAS, with the exception of the Louisiana Department of Education and
Springfield, Missouri, public schools.

LOUISIANA'S STATEWIDE LEARNING-INTENSIVE NETWORKING COMMUNITIES FOR SUCCESS PROCESS

In 2000, Murphy began working with the Louisiana Department of Education in
relation to its Learning-Intensive Networking Communities for Success (LINCS),
a statewide English language arts, mathematics, science, and social studies initiative.
LINCS is a multidimensional professional development partnership in association
with the Louisiana Department of Education, the Louisiana Systemic Initiatives
Program, and the Southern Regional Education Board. The purpose of the LINCS
process is to establish professional learning communities in which classroom teachers
build content knowledge and strengthen the ability to design and implement
standards-based, content-rich, technology-enhanced lessons into their daily instruction to improve student achievement. This program requires a 5-year commitment
from a school and integrally involves the WFSG process.

Continuous communication between Murphy and the LINCS staff has contributed to the history and the effectiveness of the WFSG process. In Chapter 11, data
from the LINCS schools are discussed.

SPRINGFIELD PUBLIC SCHOOLS

A partnership was forged in 2001 between Murphy and the Springfield public schools
(SPSs). After attending a national institute on WFSGs, Director of Staff Development
Anita Kissinger presented the WFSG system to her supervisors and colleagues. As
a result, six district instructional specialists have been trained in WFSGs and have
conducted orientations and trainings for SPS faculties. As of September 2003, 55 of the
61 SPSs were using WFSGs as the vehicle for implementing school improvement
plans. The Springfield schools continue to add to the data on the effects of WFSGs.

In Chapter 11, more information is given about specific results. It should be
noted that the good results from the WFSG process have been obtained in conjunction with other critical variables for creating this positive change, including the hard
work of district and school administrators, the time allocated to WFSG meetings,
and the substantive content that teachers do in their study group meetings.

AUTHORS' COLLABORATION

In spring 1997, Dale W. Lick contacted Murphy after reading about her work. Lick
was intrigued with the idea that all faculty at a school were members of teams or

small groups focusing on the goal of the organization—student achievement. Lick commented that the model was as close to a synergistic organizational development model as anything he had seen in public schools. The two decided that Murphy's public school experience and Lick's organizational and change experience from his more than 25 years of administrative work should be integrated. Lick would integrate his theoretical and practical knowledge of organizations and change and his experience in working with teams into Murphy's work. Two major results of the Murphy and Lick collaboration were the two books, *Whole-Faculty Study Groups: A Powerful Way to Change Schools and Enhance Learning* (1998) and *Whole-Faculty Study Groups: Creating Student-Based Professional Development* (2001).

THE WFSG NATIONAL CENTER

The WFSG National Center is in Augusta, Georgia. The vision of the center is to be "the exemplary learning organization that provides systemic support for creating collaborative cultures ensuring student success." Its mission is to "ensure student achievement through the authentic application of the WFSG system in schools worldwide." The Web site, www.MurphysWFSG.org, gives contact, schedule, and other information about the center. The center sponsors the National WFSG Conference in February each year, including general and concurrent sessions presented by individuals and teams concerning WFSGs in schools. In conjunction with the conference, preconference workshops (institutes) are offered on skill building: the Level I institute for representatives from schools who are planning or just beginning WFSGs, the Level II institute for representatives from schools who are interested in maintenance and continuation strategies for WFSGs, and the Looking at Student Work (LASW) institute. Each summer, the center also sponsors Level I, Level II, and LASW institutes in June and July. In addition, the center offers a range of services directly to state and regional agencies and districts and schools.

THE VIDEO JOURNAL OF EDUCATION

The Video Journal of Education has produced a program titled "Whole-Faculty Study Groups: Collaboration Targeting Student Learning," which is presented by Carlene Murphy. The first video, "A Catalyst for Change," discusses the context that supports WFSG and the 15 process guidelines. The second video, "A Structure for Collaboration," discusses the DMC and the four guiding principles. Both tapes include interviews with teachers and principals and study groups' meeting and classroom work. (For additional information, see www.TeachStream.com.)

THE IMPORTANCE OF HISTORY

People often say to Murphy, "WFSG is such a good idea. How did you come up with it?" In her mind in response, she reflects on her and Lick's two previous WFSG books and their development and the numerous presentations that she, Lick, and others have made throughout the country on WFSGs and how important it is for others to understand that a major part of the success of the WFSG system is the years of work with it by real people, in real schools, in many very different places, and in all kinds of circumstances. The history of the WFSG system illustrates an evolutionary, purposeful work by many dedicated professional educators over more than 20 years. From this history, our readers and implementers should take comfort in knowing that (a) the WFSG system is a valuable part of the work today leading to the advancement of our schools and enhanced student learning, and (b) this WFSG book is the result of a long and fruitful period of progressive and accountable development.

2

Enabling Faculties to Become Professional Learning Communities

We can not longer afford to be innocent of the fact that "collaboration" improves performance. . . . It is stunning that for all the evidence and consensus of expert opinion, such collaboration—our most effective tool for improving instruction—remains exceedingly, dismayingly rare. It continues to be crowded out by our persistent but unexamined addiction to complex, overhyped planning and improvement modules. Though such terms as "learning communities" and "lesson study" are heard more than ever, we hardly acknowledge their central importance in actual practice: It is a rare school that has established regular times for teachers to create, test, and refine their lessons and strategies together.

—Mike Schmoker as quoted in National
Staff Development Council (2004, p. 5)

rganizing teachers into small groups or study groups to promote collegial interchange and action is not a new idea. Individuals have formed such study groups since at least Aristotle's time. The study group concept is an important approach to learning. Teachers who take courses or workshops together often form study groups. Across a school district, they may form a study group to dig deeper into new content areas. Teachers may also share a common interest or need, study for an exam together, discuss a book they have all read, research a problem, or pursue a project of common interest.

Although teachers working together in small groups or study groups is common, organizing the entire school faculty into study groups to bring about schoolwide improvement is unusual. *Whole-Faculty Study Groups* (WFSGs) is a term used when each faculty member at a given school is a member of a study group. In this context, a *study group* is three to five individuals joining together to increase their capacities through new learning for the direct benefit of students. It is a job-embedded, self-directed, data-based professional development strategy. As the study group process increases in complexity, such groups may function in a way that enables members to actually implement new practices, change behaviors, and demonstrate new skills and knowledge in the classroom. WFSGs could be described as a whole-school professional learning community that is composed of smaller professional learning communities.

In WFSG-approach schools, the faculty, through a consensus process, decides that the WFSG structure will enable every faculty member to collaboratively address student needs at the school, and therefore each certificated staff member will be a member of a study group to support whole-school improvement. In these schools, study groups become part of a schoolwide design and are regular and legitimate entities of the school organization. The structure gives teachers the responsibility for designing their own professional development. The whole faculty has a voice in deciding if the WFSG structure becomes a part of a schoolwide design. No one tells a study group what to do, however. What study groups do is determined through a whole faculty decision-making process. Teachers select instructional needs of their students. Members decide how they will address the needs.

WFSG: A PROFESSIONAL DEVELOPMENT SYSTEM

WFSGs are seen as a professional development system in Figure 2.1. The system is contained within a school's improvement plan. The instructional council, focus team, and principal keep the whole school focused on all the students and keep improvement targets visible to the whole school. The individual study groups are at the center of the system. Whole faculty training for district initiatives, new curriculums, and new instructional strategies feed the study groups. Individuals in the study groups attend workshops, courses, summer institutes, and conferences sponsored by the district, regional agencies, state departments, and national organizations. In WFSG, these learning opportunities converge, and implementation for the benefit of students is the focus. The system is maintained with student data.

WFSGs: *WHOLE* MEANS *ALL*

By *whole faculty*, we mean all classroom teachers, all resource teachers, all special area teachers, librarians, counselors, and anyone else holding professional certification.

The WFSG System:
Where professional development activities converge and classroom implementation
for the benefit of students is the focus.
The School Improvement Plan encircles the work.

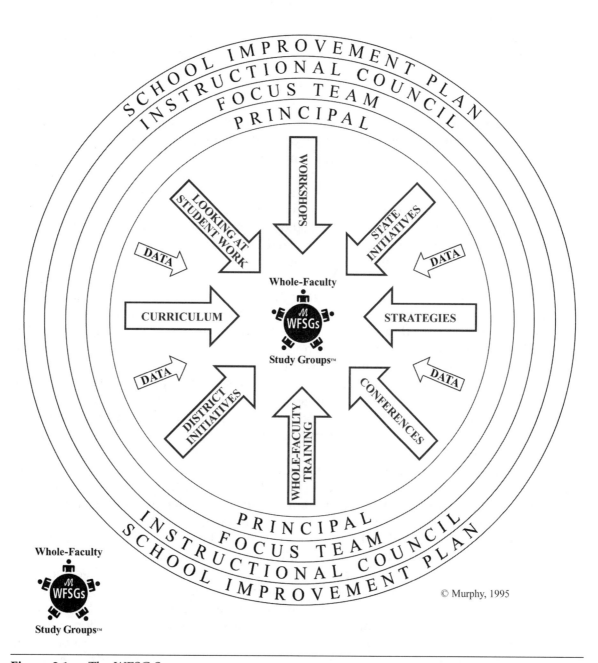

Figure 2.1 The WFSG System

Usually, administrators will form a study group of administrators within the school or will be in a study group with administrators across the district. Some of the schools that have teaching assistants will include the assistants in the study groups with the professionally certificated personnel; most, however, will have study groups with only teaching assistants. In many schools, nonteaching personnel form study groups that focus on the role they have in supporting instruction. All study groups within the context of the WFSG approach follow the same procedural guidelines, which means, for instance, that the groups have action plans and keep logs.

Making the school better for all students is a constant function of every study group in the school. It is the collective energy and synergy generated from the study groups that propel the school forward. In particular, a student does not excel as a middle-school student because he or she had a great fourth-grade teacher. The more likely reason is because the student had outstanding learning opportunities as a kindergartner and first through fifth grader. Similarly, the middle school continues to excel because the student's teachers have an extensive repertoire and are masters of their content. The cumulative effect of good teaching over years of schooling produces a graduate who does well and can be expected to continue as a learner. When every teacher in a school is in a study group that targets effective teaching practices, an important range of schoolwide needs will be met. To focus on a schoolwide need, data and the effectiveness of curricula must be examined from all grades. For example, the fourth grade is not singled out because it is the grade in which the state tests are administered. If the standardized tests administered in the fourth grade indicate that reading comprehension is a problem, then that is a problem for all grades in the school.

In forming WFSGs, the faculty goes through a process of analyzing student and school data to identify student needs that study groups will address. When the needs are determined, groups form based on these needs. Each group then determines what its teachers will do when the group meets to address a specific student need. Often, this means examining what will enable teachers to effectively use new and refined instructional practices and materials in the classroom. Each group of teachers also decides how they will support each other and the use, at the impact level, of new practices and materials. As study groups implement new and more effective practices and materials, each classroom improves, resulting in improvement in the whole school.

The goal of WFSGs is to focus the entire school faculty on creating, implementing, and integrating effective teaching and learning practices into school programs that will result in an increase in student learning and a decrease in negative behaviors of students, as reflected in related, relevant data sources.

WFSGs bring individual needs and institutional needs together in an organizational setting. Teachers become more skillful, knowledgeable, and confident as their study groups progress and gain competence and as their students become more skillful, knowledgeable, and confident. The power in the WFSG process rests in the promise that teachers will become more knowledgeable and skillful at doing what will result in higher levels of student learning. Study groups that function simply to satisfy interests of group members often lack adequate content focus to boost the goal of the school. The primary goal of schools is to meet student needs; therefore, it is the collective energy and synergy from the study groups and the whole faculty that propels the effectiveness of the school forward.

To our knowledge, the documented effects of study groups on students and the learning environment are limited to situations involving WFSGs focusing on instruction. Schools that have successfully implemented the WFSG approach have many differences, such as those reflected in student age and level, location (e.g., rural vs. urban), socioeconomic circumstances, and size. Even with the many demographic differences in schools, we have not seen that demographic factors make significant differences in how the adults in the schools work together in study groups.

WFSGs: THE GUIDING QUESTION

The WFSG system is guided by one question that must be kept in front of the faculty at all times. There is one question that leaders ask over and over again. There is one question that should be on a large poster and placed where it can be seen at all times by the faculty. (One faculty taped such posters to the faculty restroom doors.) There is one question that sets WFSGs apart from other collegial arrangements. That one essential question is the following:

> *What are students learning and achieving as a result of what teachers are learning and doing in study groups?*

Figure 2.2 illustrates the relationship between student needs and what teachers do in the study groups. Student needs are identified. In study groups, teachers design lessons together using strategies that target those needs. In classrooms, teachers use the new or refined teaching strategies. The teaching strategies become learning strategies for the students, and when students use the strategies appropriately, student learning increases.

WFSGs: THE GUIDING PRINCIPLES

How we act and what we do are most often based on our principles. A principle is defined as a fundamental truth, a rule of conduct, integrity. The WFSG system is based on the following five guiding principles:

- Students are first.
- Everyone participates.
- Leadership is shared.
- Responsibility is equal.
- The work is public.

The First Principle: Students Are First

WFSG is an approach to staff development that overtly puts the needs of students first. The theme "what do students need for us to do" runs throughout the book and throughout the WFSG process. Teachers in WFSG schools routinely examine student work collaboratively, listen to students, observe students in each other's

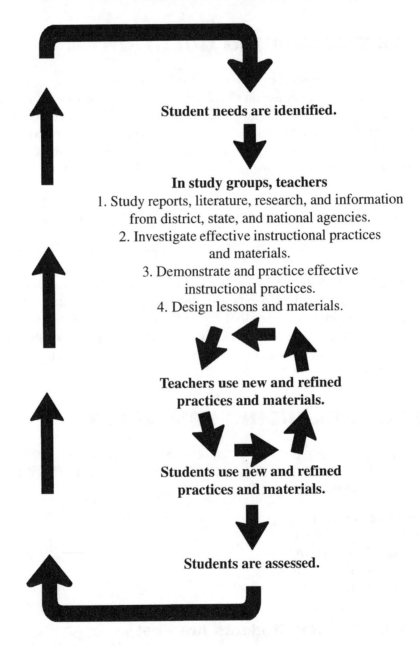

Whole-Faculty

Study Groups™

Whole-Faculty Study Groups' Impact on Student Performance

Student needs are identified.

In study groups, teachers
1. Study reports, literature, research, and information from district, state, and national agencies.
2. Investigate effective instructional practices and materials.
3. Demonstrate and practice effective instructional practices.
4. Design lessons and materials.

Teachers use new and refined practices and materials.

Students use new and refined practices and materials.

Students are assessed.

© Murphy, 1995

Figure 2.2   WFSG's Impact on Student Performance

classrooms, and pay attention to a wide variety of student data. The student voice is heard and is the factor that makes what teachers do in study groups authentic.

The Second Principle: Everyone Participates

Every certificated person is a member of a study group having from three to five members. Members of a study group may teach at the same grade level or at different grade levels, teach in the same department or in different departments, and be special area teachers and regular classroom teachers. If teaching assistants have instructional responsibilities, they may also be members of study groups with the teachers, or they may form study groups that have only teaching assistants as members. In some schools, nonteaching personnel form study groups to investigate ways they can support the instructional programs. Principals most often are members of study groups with other principals.

The Third Principle: Leadership Is Shared

Every member of the study groups serves as leader on a rotating basis. The instructional council consists of a representative from each study group and meets every 4 to 6 weeks as the primary study group communication network. Members of study groups also rotate attending the council meetings.

The Fourth Principle: Responsibility Is Equal

No one person in a study group is more responsible for the work than any other person. Everyone is equally responsible for every aspect of the group's work. Group norms are established at the first meeting, and every member holds every other member responsible for respecting and adhering to the norms.

The Fifth Principle: The Work Is Public

All the work that study groups do is public. Action plans are posted in the school on clipboards or electronically. This is also true for the study group logs. Any teacher can ask a teacher in another study group about the work of that group. There are whole faculty sharing times and printed summaries of what every group is doing. Sharing study group work is on the agendas of faculty meetings, grade-level meetings, and department meetings.

WFSGs: IDENTIFY STUDENT NEEDS

The WFSG system is grounded in student instructional needs. The system is governed by the WFSG decision-making cycle (DMC; see Chapter 7). The DMC is a seven-step process. In Steps 1 through 4, the whole faculty meets to analyze student data and to specify student needs that study groups will address. Steps 5 through 7 occur after the study groups are formed and work begins.

WFSGs: PROCEDURAL GUIDELINES

The WFSG system is a framework or structure consisting of 15 procedural or process guidelines. The guidelines are described in Chapter 6 and make the expectations clear. The guidelines also manage the group dynamics, defining relationships and behavioral norms. Study groups that routinely use the Checklist for Procedural Guidelines in Resource A to confirm adherence to the operational rules are much less likely to go astray.

WFSGs: THE RUBRIC

The WFSG rubric is divided into three components: context, process, and content. The context component is shown in Table 4.1, the process component is shown in Table 6.1, and the content component is shown in Table 8.1. The rubric describes what each of the components of the WFSG system look like in practice. A rubric is similar to an innovation configuration (Hall & Hord, 2001; Hall & Loucks, 1981). Both identify and describe, in operation, the major components of a new practice when the innovation is in use. Both represent the patterns of innovation use, usually on a scale using specific descriptors of behavior. The scale on the WFSG rubric is as follows: not yet, beginning implementation, developing implementation, and advanced implementation. A more in-depth discussion of the WFSG rubric is provided in Chapter 10.

WFSGs: FUNCTIONS

WFSGs serve many functions and purposes, including the major ones in the following list; often, these functions occur simultaneously:

- Developing a deeper understanding of academic content
- Supporting the implementation of curricular and instructional initiatives
- Integrating and giving coherence to a school's instructional programs and practices
- Targeting a schoolwide instructional need
- Studying the research on teaching and learning
- Monitoring the impact or effects of instructional initiatives on students
- Providing a time when teachers can examine student work together

Developing a Deeper Understanding of Academic Content

At ATLAS Communities' March 2000 Principals' Institute, Murphy had a conversation with Howard Gardner, author of *Frames of Mind: The Theory of Multiple Intelligences* (1983). Gardner stated that from his perspective, the reason for having teacher study groups is to discuss for understanding, to reconnect to ideas, to make greater use of the mind. Gardner went on to say that understanding is to take something new and apply it to something you already know. He added that disciplinary understanding is why we have schools. As Murphy thought about this conversation, she searched for a definition of understanding that she thought would apply to teaching. In Blythe (1998), she found the following definition: "Understanding is a matter of being able to do a variety of thought-provoking things with a topic, such as explaining, finding evidence and examples, generalizing, applying, analogizing, and representing the topic in new ways" (p. 12). Wow! If teachers did these in study groups and with students so that students could do them, what remarkable outcomes would happen in schools. The most serious need that we see in schools is that many teachers do not have a deep understanding of what they teach. When this is true, teachers cannot expect students to understand what teachers teach. If students do not understand what they have been taught, they cannot be successful on assessments that require students to take their knowledge and use it in new ways. If teachers do not understand what they teach, they cannot design a variety of thought-provoking activities with a topic. In the WFSG approach, teachers select a student need and convert that need into a topic or an area of study. In study groups, teachers talk to each other to build their own and each other's understanding. They explain to one another what they know about a topic to deepen their understanding and search for new ways to apply what they know to enable them to explain it to their students in different ways. Also, they develop analogies of an idea or concept so they can help students develop analogies.

Reconnecting to ideas with colleagues is a luxury that teachers often have not had. To make greater use of the mind is a notion that only Howard Gardner would put into words. As a fourth-grade teacher for 15 years, Murphy relates that during those years she frequently felt as if she could only think on the fourth-grade level. Teachers must be challenged in their thinking and to go beyond the obvious. Study groups help teachers "push the envelope," to stay on the cutting edge of their disciplines.

In Ted and Nancy Sizer's (1999) book, *The Students Are Watching: Schools and the Moral Contract*, we gleaned an idea that fits this purpose for having study groups. Study group members tend to want to stay within their area of comfort and not to reach for the unknown. The Sizers challenge us to grapple, to do something that is more difficult for us. The opposite of grappling is boring. Substantive work challenges and excites teachers. Developing deeper understanding and grappling put study groups in a context that accelerates learning for teachers and, as a result, accelerates learning for students.

Supporting the Implementation of Curricular and Instructional Initiatives

The implementation of new learning is affected by the fact that our individual abilities to understand and use new curricular and instructional ideas frequently encountered in courses and workshops vary considerably, as do our personal assumptions, values and beliefs, and experiences. By providing teachers of varying attitudes, understandings, knowledge, and skills with the opportunity for support of each other, new learning will more likely be used in the workplace. Study groups create such opportunities, increasing the implementation of new practices learned in courses and workshops and the effectiveness of new curricula and educational materials.

For instance, teachers are trained to use new instructional strategies that are backed by a strong research base and apply to a wide variety of curriculum areas. Such strategies or models may include cooperative learning, inductive thinking and concept attainment, and mnemonics. These strategies are often categorized as higher-order thinking skills. The expectation is that all the teachers in a school are to reach high levels of appropriate use of these strategies in their classrooms. This is not likely to happen if the workplace is not designed to prepare teachers to support each other in the immediate and sustained use of the new practices. The leaders of such a training effort might ask study groups to do the following:

- Share lessons and materials already used so others can use the plans or materials and thus reduce preparation time
- Observe students in each other's classrooms to learn from student responses to the strategies
- Plan future applications of the strategies within their curriculum areas in an attempt to integrate new strategies with existing repertoires and instructional objectives

If teachers do not have a schoolwide, structured support system, they will often delay using the new practices. When they do use them and a lesson goes poorly, it will be an even longer time before they try again. If there is any fear or skepticism about the new procedure, delay gives anxiety time to develop and practice will not ensue. Thus, a major training effort fails to achieve its intended results.

If the school has a schoolwide design that encourages sharing successes and failures, however, there will be a high degree of comfort in practicing lessons together and doing joint work in preparing lessons. As a teacher's comfort level increases, so does the level of use with students and the assurance that new strategies and new materials will have a positive impact on the students in the school.

Integrating and Giving Coherence to a School's Instructional Programs and Practices

A study group addresses data-based student needs (see Chapter 7). After analyzing data, student needs are listed and subsequently grouped and placed into categories. For example, based on the needs of the students currently taught, a study group may target a specific need, such as synthesizing, that is in a group of needs (i.e., category) that the faculty called "critical thinking skills." Most likely, there are a number of instructional programs with an array of accompanying materials, textbook series in all the content areas, and learning strategies that all target critical thinking skills. Typically, the materials and strategies used in one program are not integrated into another area of the curriculum. A learning strategy used in science may not be applied to language arts. A study group would determine what materials and training programs are available and develop lessons integrating the content and processes. This analysis would minimize or avoid the traditional layering of initiatives, bringing coherence to disjointed efforts, which happen all too often. For example, various reading and writing programs, cooperative learning, and higher-order thinking skills are typically perceived as three separate strategies or programs because they are usually introduced to teachers in three separate and distinct packages or by three different trainers. Frequently, it is left to the teacher to try to figure out relationships and common attributes of the three strategies. A group of teachers that regularly meet over a period of time can synthesize the new information and innovations and together develop lessons that incorporate all three strategies to increase the critical thinking skills that the study group is targeting.

Targeting a Schoolwide Instructional Need

After the whole faculty analyzes information about the whole school and its students, the faculty has a list of specific student needs and the needs have been categorized or grouped (see Chapter 7, Step 3). Most often, when a list of student needs is categorized or grouped, a need will appear in several categories. For example, on a list of student needs, the need "increase vocabulary" is frequently listed and is evidenced in several data sources. "Increase vocabulary" could go in a reading category, a writing category, a mathematics category, a science category, a project learning category, a critical thinking skills category, or almost any other category or grouping of needs. Once categories are formed from the list of student needs, teachers select the category that contains the needs most representative of the students they teach. If "increase vocabulary" is in every category, all study groups will most likely address that need. One study group may be addressing the need through "mathematics," another may be targeting the need through "writing," and another may be working on the same through "study skills." The difference will be in how they approach the need or personalize the need in terms of the grade level or content area they teach. In this way, across the school there will be an increase in vocabulary development. Figure 7.2 refers to these different perspectives as "doors," indicating that a study group may enter any one of several doors to the room of whole-school improvement carrying the same student need with them. When individuals look at the list of categories a faculty is addressing, their first response is, "Wouldn't it be more effective if all the study groups were addressing the same needs?" Most often, they are targeting the same schoolwide student needs but from different perspective or through different lenses. Categories give teachers choice—choice in how they will address the same needs.

Studying the Research on Teaching and Learning

An important aspect of the study group process is the reflection on research that describes effective teaching and effective schools, allowing the faculty to make wiser, research-based decisions. In WFSGs, teachers increase their contact, understanding, and application of new innovations from educational research in the United States and abroad, providing for better use of funds and an improved educational environment. Teaching is often perceived as being so personal to a particular teacher and classroom that the teacher does not believe that what happens with another class has any significance for him or her. This reality was made evident in the work in Augusta, Georgia, where there was a commitment to increasing student achievement through the training of staffs in several models of teaching. At the beginning of the effort, teachers were given examples of successful efforts of schools in other states that used a similar approach for school improvement. The teachers responded, "That's California, not here." The next year, after successful implementation of the program in one middle school in the district, the success was shared with another middle school in the same district. The teachers responded, "That's East Middle School, not here." The school did decide, however, to join the school improvement program. The next year, after successful implementation in most of the classrooms in the new middle school, the success one teacher had in her classroom with her students was shared with another teacher in the same school. The teacher responded, "That's Mrs. Brown's classroom, not mine." It seems no matter how close to home examples of success are, the belief that "my classroom and my students are different from anyone else's" is so pervasive that it is difficult for many teachers to learn from what others have done or are doing. The personalization of teaching is one of the barriers broken when teachers meet routinely in study groups and share teaching practices. As teachers become more open and objective about teaching and learning practices, they feel and become less isolated. Contact with a broad base of relevant research encourages teachers to take more seriously what other districts are discovering about general improvement strategies and to be more actively involved in the collection and analysis of data that come from their own schools and classrooms.

Monitoring the Impact or Effects of Instructional Initiatives on Students

WFSGs form around a general category of student needs that the teachers recognize as needs their students have. After student needs are identified and listed, the listed needs are categorized. Teachers choose a category (e.g., writing) they believe represents the needs of the students they teach. When groups meet for the first time, they will examine more specific data regarding their category of choice. Their study group will list in their action plan the specific needs in the category that members will target. Step 6 in the DMC (see Chapter 7) is a series of action research cycles. In each cycle, the group does the following:

- Assesses the current status of the targeted need of the students in the members' classrooms
- Identifies strategies and materials to use in the classrooms (interventions)
- Plans lessons together using the new strategies or materials
- Teaches the lessons to students
- Reflects on student responses and examines student work from the lesson
- Repeats the cycle

The collection and analysis of information over a period of time will indicate to teachers in the study group whether the interventions are making a difference in student learning. If a study group is targeting mathematics needs, the basic resource will be the mathematics textbook the teachers use. Many of the strategies and materials identified for classroom use will be from the textbook and supplementary materials. In this way, the impact of a new mathematics program or textbook series can be monitored and evaluated.

Providing a Time When Teachers Can Examine Student Work Together

Teachers rarely meet together to examine student work. Examining student work in a study group gives teachers the opportunity to benefit from multiple perspectives. Because teachers in study groups routinely meet together, each is familiar with what the others are doing in the classroom. Examining the student work from their classrooms is like looking through a special window. Through the student's work, they can see the teacher's work. Much of the student work that teachers bring to the study group is work the teachers have jointly developed. The student work gives the study group more information about the student needs that the group is addressing. If the study group is addressing mathematics, the student work would be in mathematics.

Most often, study groups use a protocol for conversation around the work. Chapter 8 provides a more complete description of how to collaboratively examine student work.

When speaking to groups about her teaching experiences, Murphy remembers that as a classroom teacher she spent hours each day looking at student work. She says that this was something she did alone or with a student or maybe with a parent; it is something she never did with another teacher or with a group of teachers, however. Teachers often view the work of their students as private. In a study group, with the name of the student removed from the work, teachers learn from the work of each other's students how to better meet the needs of the students.

WFSGs: WHAT THEY ARE NOT

Stand-Alone Study Groups

Most independent or stand-alone study groups do not depend on organizational support. They are groups of individuals that have a common interest and will consider themselves a study group until, as individuals, they satisfy their need for the group. There are unlimited possibilities for professional study groups to function other than in an organizational setting. Study groups may form within or outside the context of a school or school district. Study groups emerge as a result of individuals' interests or needs and are usually less structured. Independent or stand-alone study groups serve a very important role in the growth of individuals, and their importance should not be minimized.

Committees

Study groups are vehicles for self-improvement for the benefit of the individual and the whole organization. A study group is not an appointed group with an assigned job or task. Committees have appointed or elected leaders who usually assume the major responsibility for the success of the committee. Study groups generally focus on professional development issues and not administrative issues. Committees are often larger than study groups, and an end point is assumed. Generally, committees develop recommendations for someone else to implement. Study groups implement and try out perceived solutions to a problem, collect information about the degrees of change, and share their information with the whole faculty.

A comparison highlighting the key characteristics of WFSGs, independent study groups, and committees is given in Table 2.1.

Traditional Meetings

Similar to the differences shown in Table 2.1 is the way study groups differ from the usual grade-level meetings in elementary schools, team meetings in middle schools, and department meetings in high schools. The following lists distinguish the differences.

Grade-level and departmental meetings generally

- Focus on managerial or logistical directives from the school, district, or state
- Have an agenda that is determined by directives from the school, district, or state
- Are leader driven by a grade or department chairperson
- Have a "talk to" format, meaning that the leader presents information and the participants primarily respond to topics generated by the leader

Study group meetings generally

- Are aimed at the professional development of the members
- Focus on "what I need to do and learn to change how I teach and what I teach"
- Have an action plan that is the group's agenda
- Are driven by member needs that are tied to student needs
- Rotate leaders, with the leader not being responsible for the content of the meeting or what the group will do
- Recognize all members as being equal in status and responsibility

STRATEGIES FOR GROUPING TEACHERS FOR COLLABORATION

There are many strategies and combinations of strategies for faculties to use to meet the National Staff Development Council's (NSDC) (2004) staff development standard: "Staff development that improves the learning of all students organizes adults into learning communities whose goals are aligned with those of the school and district" (p. 13).

Table 2.1 lists a few collaborative designs or ways to organize teachers into groups. The listed characteristics or descriptors of the designs or strategies are not meant to be all-inclusive of the collaborative strategy. The intended purpose is to give a general overview so the reader can see some likenesses and differences. A collaborative strategy does not have to have a name; rather, it can simply be a way of having teachers work together. Most of the strategies listed in Table 2.1 have formal structures, meaning a set of procedures that are generally followed. A learning community is more than a group of individuals who meet together. WFSGs are systems within schools composed of small learning communities made up of three to five individuals who join together to collectively become one professional learning community. A principal asked Murphy, "How are WFSGs like professional learning communities?" She answered, "WFSGs are professional learning communities." Another principal said, "We have had WFSGs for 2 years; now we are going to have professional learning communities." Both comments indicate that terms become the problem.

In *Moving NSDC's Staff Development Standards Into Practice: Innovation Configurations* (Roy & Hord, 2003), the NSDC describes the most desired level for "meets regularly with colleagues during the school day to plan instruction" as "meets regularly with learning team during scheduled time within the school day to develop lesson plans, examine student work, monitor student progress, assess the effectiveness of instruction, and identify needs for professional learning" (p. 14).

When selecting a collaborative or learning community strategy, the NSDC standard should be the standard for choosing or designing a strategy. Every aspect of the

Strategies for Grouping Teachers	Distinguishing Characteristics
Action Research Team	• Inquiry based • Individual, small groups, or schoolwide • Uses multiple data sources • Leadership emerges from within the group • Organized around a student learning goal • May have a facilitation team if schoolwide • Draws on current research base • External knowledge creates new knowledge-in-action • Voluntary
Committees	• Usually more administrative in nature • Predetermined purpose • Focused on assigned task • Investigative • Individuals appointed or volunteer • End point • Two or more people • Recommendations made for others to implement • Leader appointed or elected who has primary responsibility for the work
Critical Friends Group	• Voluntary • Usually all teachers not in a group • Up to 12 members • Meet at least monthly • Trained facilitator/coach leads group • Organized according to individual interest or when the group meets • Use protocols • Looking at student work is major focus
Curriculum Committee	• In school or cross district • May include parents • Expands knowledge in the content area • Becomes acquainted with the newest thinking and programs in the field • Develops commitment to new content, materials, strategies • Consists of volunteers and/or appointees • Led by chairperson or cochairs • Usually meets for several months • Align new curriculum with state/district standards and assessments
Department, Team, and Grade-Level Meetings	• Focus on managerial or logistical directives from the school administration, district, or state • Have an agenda that is determined by directives from the school administration, district, or state • Have an agenda that is not usually of a professional development nature • Are leader driven by a grade/team chairperson or department chairperson • Have a "talk to" format, meaning the leader presents information and the participants primarily respond to topics generated by the leader • Have a set schedule • Not voluntary

Table 2.1   Strategies for Grouping for Collaboration

(Continued)

Table 2.1 (Continued)

Strategies for Grouping Teachers	Distinguishing Characteristics
Lesson Study	• Individual or small group • Voluntary • May not be school-based • May not stay together beyond lesson study • Group organized around lesson to be developed • Based on "research lesson" developed by small group • Cycle: goal established, research conducted, lesson planned, lesson taught and observed, lesson evaluated, lesson revised • Schoolwide (Japan) • Affiliated with a university (Japan) • Lessons digitally filed on computer (Lesson Lab, Inc., Los Angeles) • Lessons videoed and critiqued (Lesson Lab, Inc.)
Peer Coaching Team	• Teachers form teams of two or three • Team members plan together and observe each other in classrooms • Members of team have had common training/development experience • Members encourage each other while reflecting on classroom practices
Small Learning Community	• Part of a school or faculty • The part has a common theme, i.e., careers, math and science, performing arts
Study Groups (Independent or Stand-Alone)	• May or may not be tied to an organizational need or to a specific organization • Individuals agree to work together to learn more about a subject or topic • Group members may be within same school, or not within same school • Study usually focused on becoming more knowledgeable about a predetermined need, such as block scheduling • Selective, based on choice of individuals • Has an end point • Leadership often remains with person who initiates group or volunteer • Usually voluntary
Whole-Faculty Study Groups	• Voluntary for school; if consensus among faculty to implement, all faculty are members of a WFSG • Whole school, everyone in a group, impact on all students • Data-based decision-making process to determine student needs • Groups organized around the student needs • Three to five members in each group • Each WFSG designs an action plan for addressing its student needs • Logs are completed after each meeting and are publicly posted • Meet weekly for 1 hour or biweekly for 2 hours • Teachers rotate leadership • Ongoing, legitimate part of the school's routine • Use protocols • Looking at student work is a major focus

REFERENCES

Educational Leadership, March 2002

Journal of Staff Development, Spring 2002

Murphy, C., and Lick, D. (2001). *Whole-Faculty Study Groups: Creating Student-Based Professional Development*. Thousand Oaks, CA: Corwin Press

Wood, F., and McQuarrie, F. (1999). On-the-job learning. *Journal of Staff Development*, Summer 1999 previous descriptor of the standard is built into the WFSG system as described in Chapters 6 through 8.

WFSGs: MAJOR STRENGTHS

The most obvious strength of WFSGs is the support and encouragement teachers give each other. The structure ensures that study group meetings become a routine for the school and for the individual teachers. When professional study groups are part of a schoolwide design, the principal's support and pressure are positive forces for action and success. Pressure is typically perceived as a negative force or pain. Change, however, often occurs because some pressure or pain has built up to the point that it leads to action (Fullan, 2001a).

The way the school is organized so that adults in the school can engage in serious and purposeful learning requires adjustments in scheduling activities. Providing time for study groups to meet weekly is a form of pressure. Allocating resources is a form of support. Fullan (2001a) asserts that it is increasingly clear that both pressure and support are necessary for successful change efforts that alter the fundamental ways an organization works. The WFSG approach fundamentally alters existing structures and roles. The principal, the primary and sustaining sponsor of school change, is the major source of the pressure and support that makes it possible for teachers to have the willingness and skill to establish and maintain collaborative work cultures. Study groups operating outside a schoolwide design seldom have the level of organizational sponsorship that connects teacher learning and student learning. In every school in which WFSGs have become a routine feature of the workplace and in which changes in teacher and student behaviors are evident, the principal, providing effective sponsorship, is the key factor.

WFSGs: MEETING RESISTANCE

We have found that faculties resist beginning "another new thing." The feeling of overload is so strongly felt by teachers that there is an immediate, automatic negative response to WFSG unless the system is presented as a way to facilitate what the teachers are already having to do. Teachers already have to design lessons using new curricula. In study groups, teachers work together on designing lessons using new curricula. The following points combat resistance:

- WFSG is a vehicle to do collaboratively what teachers have been doing alone.
- WFSG is a structure for implementing the school improvement plan or a process for ensuring that targeted school goals are being addressed.
- WFSG is a place to work on the work of teaching and learning.
- WFSG is not another program to be implemented in the classroom.

A point of strong resistance is finding time to do another thing. To most, it seems an impossibility. This point can be tempered by reminding teachers that long after students are dismissed each day, teachers' cars are still in the school's parking lot. During those hours spent after school, teachers are most often working alone in their classrooms preparing for their students. In WFSGs, teachers would spend less time working in isolation and more time collaborating with colleagues.

WFSGs: GETTING STARTED

It is usually the principal who first receives information about WFSGs. The principal has the choice of whether to inform the school's faculty. If the principal chooses to inform the faculty and the faculty is receptive to the WFSG approach, the principal will use some mechanism to establish agreement to begin. Initially, agreement to begin must be realistic. Schools handle this agreement in two ways. One way to reach agreement on study group implementation is to have some form of voting. If the norm at a school is to vote on initiatives, it should be predetermined what the percentage of agreement must be for the study group work to begin. Whatever the agreed-on percentage, however, it must be binding for everyone. If the vote exceeds the predetermined percentage, everyone must be a member of a study group. If the result is less than the predetermined percentage, the question is closed until another time. A second way to begin study group work is for the faculty to engage in a consensus process, meaning working for, at least, some level of agreement from everyone. The following is an example of how one school reached consensus.

The principal and three teachers attended a WFSG institute in February and left the institute with a plan to introduce the faculty to WFSGs. The principal distributed printed information to everyone and posted information on the school's electronic mailing system. The principal and the teachers spoke to faculty members individually, answering questions and elaborating on details. In team meetings and other group meetings, the information about WFSGs was discussed, and if concerns were expressed, they were addressed. In May, each teacher was given the opportunity to meet with the principal or the teachers who had attended the institute to indicate their level of agreement to begin the process. No teacher expressed a desire less than willingness to begin. In June, a WFSG consultant came to the school and worked with those teachers who chose to attend a 2-day training program. In September, the whole faculty experienced the DMC, and by the first of October study groups were meeting.

There are two approaches to getting started after at least one person on the faculty has learned about WFSGs, the faculty has been introduced to the concept, and there is consensus to begin:

1. A focus team, consisting of the principal and several teachers, attends a WFSG institute at the district, regional, state, or national level. The team assumes the responsibility for leading the faculty through the DMC. The team continues to be in contact with a WFSG consultant through at least the first year of implementation.

2. A WFSG consultant leads the faculty through the DMC and continues to work with and support the faculty through at least the first year of the implementation.

Schools begin through the leadership of individuals on the faculty who read this book and follow the directions in Chapter 7. However the process begins, it is the "authentic application" of the WFSG principles and the 15 WFSG process guidelines in Chapter 6 that are required to produce meaningful results.

A MEANS TO AN END

When Murphy is contacted by a principal for assistance relative to getting the WFSG system in place, she asks, "Why?" Typically, the answer is "Because I think that study groups are an excellent approach to staff development." In this case, the principal is focusing on a "means." After more conversation, the principal usually understands that the "end," student learning, should be the reason. One of the confusing problems we face in education is differentiating between means and ends. The WFSG approach is a means to an end: increased student learning. In education, when someone asks about the success of our educational efforts, we often tell them about our teachers, our facilities, our libraries, our technology, and our curricula. What they are really asking about, however, are the outcomes of our efforts, such as percentages of students graduating, levels of student accomplishment, and graduate preparation for college or work. The former (teachers, facilities, libraries, technology, and curricula) are means, the way to deliver ends, whereas the latter (graduation rates, academic accomplishments, and graduate preparation) are ends—the results, consequences, accomplishments, and payoffs of our efforts.

Means and ends are not the same. Means are the ways to deliver ends, including resources (e.g., time, money, students, teachers and administrators, Parent-Teacher Association, the community, technology, and facilities) and methods (e.g., teaching, collaborating, self-study, learning, thinking, planning, and developing).

Some typical means and ends are shown in Table 2.2. The ends are the results, the "what" to be accomplished, whereas the means are the "how" to accomplish the desired results. Unfortunately, in education, we have a tendency to spend most of our resources on the means without first clearly determining the desired ends. If you do not have a target (a desired end), it is difficult to find means that will help you hit it. If you want to enhance success, first clearly determine your desired results (ends), and then select your means based on the ends you wish to achieve.

Starting with means before identifying desired ends is backward and usually ineffective. One of the main reasons for a lack of real success in educational reform during the past decade was that we spent most of our time and money on means without having well-defined goals that the means were to have successfully addressed. Test your own school's record. In your school's educational mission, decide what the means and ends are and observe how much attention has been given to the means.

Means help accomplish ends but are not ends in themselves. The definitions are as follows:

- End: A result, outcome, output, or product
- Means: The tools, methods, techniques, resources, or processes used to achieve an end

Kaufman, Herman, and Watters (1996) remind us that one of the six critical success factors in education is to "differentiate between ends and means" (p. 18)—focus on the "what" (the desired ends) before selecting the "how" (the means).

We often use the term *vehicle* as a synonym for *means*. We say that WFSG is a vehicle (or means) to get to where a school needs to go: higher student achievement.

	Means	Ends
Classrooms and laboratories	X	
Libraries	X	
Financial support	X	
Staff development	X	
Graduation		X
Board of education	X	
Teachers	X	
Study groups	X	
Graduate employment		X
Collaborative learning	X	
Strategic planning	X	
Shared governance	X	
Course grade		X
Technology	X	
Graduate competence		X
Policies	X	
Accountability	X	

Table 2.2   Typical Means and Ends

As Figure 2.3 illustrates, WFSGs are the vehicle, and the vehicle is powered by what the study groups do when the groups meet.

After the WFSG approach has been implemented, someone has to keep reminding the teachers (and others) why the study groups were initiated and implemented in the first place. The ends—student learning—have to be constantly put before the groups and others. When strong advocates of study groups want to organize study groups simply for the sake of having study groups, a disservice is done to WFSGs, the school, and the coerced faculty. Advocates, for example, must understand and share with others that study groups are a means to an end and not an end in and of themselves. The desired end of study groups is positive change in student learning and the learning environment. When increased student success is the vision and guiding principle, individuals and study groups are motivated, work harder, and take responsibility for the successful implementation of the required processes and procedures.

SUMMARY

Best practice is a term often heard in education today. We read, for instance, about what are best practices for teachers to use with their students. In Zemelman, Daniels, and Hyde's (1993) *Best Practice: New Standards for Teaching and Learning in America's Schools*, the authors list the underlying assumptions, principles, and theories that characterize integrated learning (p. 7). Best practice is what we do in the classroom with students that exemplifies those principles, assumptions, and theories.

In WFSGs, the teachers are the students. The same principles that apply to elementary, middle, and high school students also apply to a 30- or 55-year-old student who is learning more about the art of teaching. As a professional development

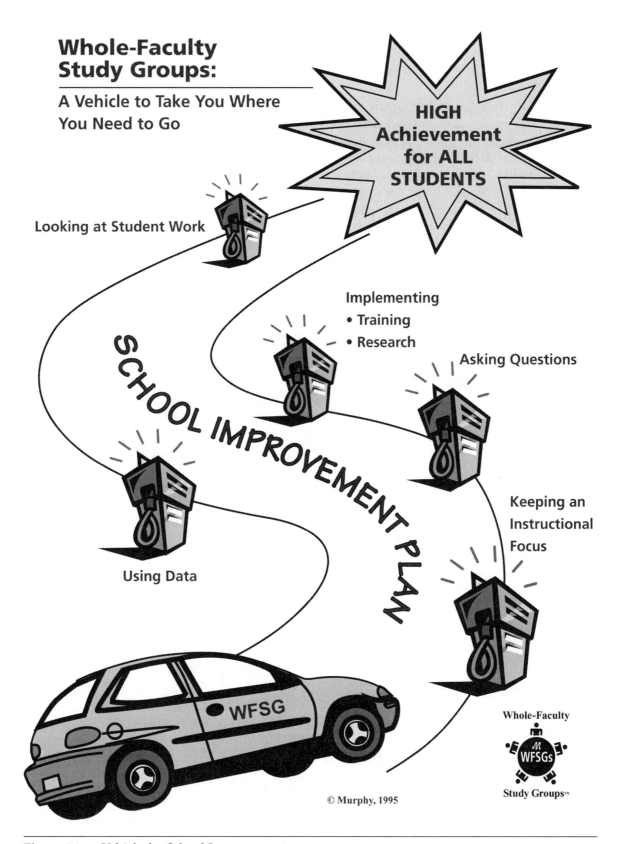

Figure 2.3   Vehicle for School Improvement

model, the WFSG approach presents an integrated learning experience for adult students. It is an approach to learning characterized by the following learning principles for the study group processes:

- They are *student centered*. Teachers in a group determine what they must know and what they must do more skillfully to meet the needs of their students.
- They give teachers the opportunity to *experiment*. In groups, teachers try new materials, new techniques, new strategies, and new technologies.
- They inspire *reflection*. As teachers talk about their practices, they reflect on what works and what does not work and how a critical element for change in practice is to occur and be sustained.
- They provide *authentic learning experiences*. The teachers are not following an instructor's syllabus or set of objectives presented to them. Experiences are designed by the group and tied to the teachers' classrooms and students. Because the group is addressing its students' needs, the work of the group is real and meaningful.
- They focus on the *whole*. The needs of the whole school, the whole class, and the whole art of teaching are brought into focus. Isolation, once the norm, is broken. Not only has isolation from each other been a common work condition but also instructional programs and strategies have often been viewed separately.
- They support *democratic behavior*. All faculty members have an opportunity to decide if having the teachers work together in small groups will benefit their students. All faculty members have a voice in what student needs will be addressed as well as the method that will be used to determine the membership of the study groups. Also, after the study groups are formed, each member of the group has a voice in determining exactly how the group will work and what the group will do.
- They allow teachers to *construct* their own learning and their own meanings in what they read, hear, and see. The process validates a teacher's individuality and empowers a teacher to go beyond the boundaries that are usually set by others.
- They give teachers the *motivation* to establish challenging and rigorous standards for themselves.

3

What the Research Tells Us

Education in the United States is greatly enriched by the work of individuals in universities, school districts, government agencies, and private practice who collect, analyze, and report data about all aspects of education. These individuals, most often called researchers, bring clarity, meaning, and direction to educators at all levels and the general public on the "state of education" in U.S. schools. In this chapter, we highlight the studies that seem to have the greatest impact on the purpose for having and the functioning of Whole-Faculty Study Groups (WFSGs). These studies are in the areas of professional learning communities, staff development and training, the change process, school culture, and leadership.

PROFESSIONAL LEARNING COMMUNITIES

The University of Chicago's Center for School Improvement worked with a number of Chicago elementary schools during a 3-year period. Bryk, Rollow, and Pinnell (1996) reported that there is a need to restructure and renorm teachers' work so that a professional learning community emerges to sustain school improvement.

Professional learning communities are also identified as important in a summary report titled *Successful School Restructuring* (Newmann & Wehlage, 1995). More than 1,500 schools throughout the United States were part of four large-scale studies: the School Restructuring Study, the National Educational Longitudinal Study of 1988, the Study of Chicago School Reform, and the Longitudinal Study of School Restructuring. Results of these studies were combined into summary findings. Newmann and Wehlage reported that the creation of a "professional community not only boosted student achievement gains, it also helped to make the gains more equitable among socioeconomic groups" (p. 37).

Louis, Marks, and Kruse (1996) reported on research from more than 900 teachers in 24 nationally selected restructuring elementary, middle, and high schools. The research hypothesized that how teachers interact when they are not in their classrooms may be critical to the future of school restructuring and its effects on students. Louis et al. found that a strong school-based professional community for teachers is associated with increased engagement and achievement for students. They also found the following five core characteristics of professional school communities:

- Teachers and administrators share basic norms and values about children, learning, and teaching.
- Reflective dialogue, rich and recurring talk about teaching practice and student learning, enlarges the teachers' world and helps them view teaching from one another's perspectives.
- Deprivatization of practice occurs when teachers practice their craft openly and problem-solve together.
- A collective focus on student learning drives decisions.
- Collaboration exists across grade-level groups.

The value of the WFSG approach and other designs that build collaborative cultures is well documented. Lucas (2000) found that the WFSG process had a positive impact on teachers' professional growth and on student learning in the schools.

Sebring and Bryk (2000) reported that schools that are improving are characterized by cooperative work relations among all adults. They state that in schools in which trust and cooperative adult efforts are strong, students report that they feel safe, sense that teachers care about them, and experience greater academic challenge. In contrast, in schools with flat or declining test scores, teachers are more likely to state that they do not trust one another, and both teachers and students report less satisfaction with their experiences.

Rosenholtz (1989) investigated social organizational features in 78 elementary schools in eight school districts in Tennessee. Her investigation included school and classroom observation; interviews with teachers, principals, superintendents, board members, and parents; data collection from 1,213 teachers; and an analysis of student achievement. Rosenholtz concluded that schools could be categorized as moving (i.e., learning-enriched environments) or stuck (i.e., learning-impoverished environments). Table 3.1 summarizes the characteristics of the two categories.

Studies by the federally funded Center for Research on the Context of Secondary School Teaching at Stanford University revealed that teachers' participation in a "professional community" had a powerful effect on how successfully they were able to adapt their instructional strategies to meet students' needs (Bradley, 1993). One such study, by McLaughlin and Talbert (2001), conducted in-depth research in 16 high schools in seven school districts in California and Michigan. One of the cases cited (that of Rothman) was of 2 high schools in the same California district. Both served approximately the same student population and functioned under the same rules and regulations. The study found, however, that one school had high student failure and dropout rates, whereas the other had test scores among the highest in the state and 80% of its students went to college. The difference was reflected in the

Moving	Stuck
Learning was enriched for students and teachers	Learning was impoverished for students and teachers.
Higher levels of student achievement were the norm.	Lower levels of student achievement were the norm.
Teachers worked together.	Teachers worked alone, rarely asking for help.
Teachers shared beliefs about on-the-job learning.	Isolation, self-reliance, and turf issues predominated.
High consensus was shared on the definition of teaching.	Low consensus was shared on the definition of teaching.
Shared instructional goals occupied a place of high significance.	Inertia seemed to overcome teachers' adventurous impulses.
Teachers had a marked spirit of continuous improvement in which no teacher ever stops learning how to teach.	Teachers were less likely to trust, value, and legitimize sharing expertise, seeking advice, and giving help.
80% of the teachers responded that their learning is cumulative and that learning to teach is a lifelong pursuit.	17% of the teachers expressed a sustained view of learning for themselves.

Table 3.1   Characteristics of the Moving and Stuck Schools

professional characteristics of the schools. Table 3.2 provides a summary of the factors associated with student achievement from the work of McLaughlin and Talbert.

Louis et al. (1996) supported the work of Rosenholtz (1989) and McLaughlin and Talbert (as cited in Bradley, 1993), concluding that there are three benefits from promoting structural conditions and social and human resources that support school-based professional communities:

1. Teachers are empowered to work to improve student learning. Their "sense of affiliation with each other and with the school, and their sense of mutual support and individual responsibility for the effectiveness of instruction, is increased by collaborative work with peers" (Louis, Kruse, & Marks, 1996, p. 24).

2. Teachers' sense of personal dignity in their profession is increased. This sense of dignity relates directly to their sense of efficacy, their empowerment to affect student learning.

3. Teachers' collective responsibility increases. Their concern goes beyond the learning of children in their own classes and includes the progress made by students in the entire school. Whole-school improvement becomes the focus.

Linda Darling-Hammond (as cited in Lewis, 1997) of Teachers College, Columbia University, has worked extensively with professional development in schools. In a September 1996 report to the National Commission on Teaching and America's Future, she and her colleagues recommended that new policies be required to accomplish the following:

High Student Achievement	Low Student Achievement
High levels of collegiality	Low levels of collegiality
High levels of innovation	High norms of privacy (no sharing of resources or materials)
High levels of opportunity for adult learning	No support or opportunity for adult learning
Subject matter seen as dynamic	Subject matter seen as static (canons were not to be challenged)
Commitment to success for all students, publicly declared	Large number of students fail
High standards for all students	Low standards for students
High degree of commitment to the school as a whole	Low commitment to the school workplace
More positive views of students	More negative views of students

Table 3.2 McLaughlin and Talbert's (2001) Comparisons

- Redesign school structures to support teacher learning and collaboration, giving serious attention to practice
- Rethink schedules and staffing patterns to create blocks of time for teachers to plan and work together
- Make it possible for teachers to think in terms of shared problems, not "my classroom" or "my subject"
- Organize the school into small, collaborative groups

Darling-Hammond and McLaughlin (1995) identified six characteristics of effective professional development that involves teachers as both teachers and learners. We believe that all six characteristics, as follows, are embedded in the WFSG system:

1. It must engage teachers in concrete tasks of teaching, assessment, observation, and reflection.

2. It must be grounded in inquiry, reflection, and experimentation that are participant driven.

3. It must be collaborative, involving a sharing of knowledge among educators and focus on teachers' communities of practice rather than on individual teachers.

4. It must be connected to and derived from teachers' work with their students.

5. It must be sustained, ongoing, intensive, and supported by modeling, coaching, and the collective solving of specific problems of practice.

6. It must be connected to other aspects of school change.

STAFF DEVELOPMENT AND TRAINING

From the inception of the process that became the WFSG system, the work of Bruce Joyce and Beverly Showers was at the heart of the system. Joyce and Showers (1982, 1995) described five important components of staff development:

1. Presentation of theory or the description of a new skill or behavior

2. Demonstration or modeling of the new strategy or skill by a trainer with no audience action

3. Initial practice in a protected or simulated setting

4. Practice with an audience, providing structured, open-ended feedback

5. Coaching and follow-up help as a skill is being applied and tried in the classroom

In a study of 100 individuals in training, Joyce and Showers (1983) examined the effect (in percentages) that various components contributed toward the transfer of skills or new behaviors in the classroom. The results were as follows:

- Presentation only   10%
- Demonstration   added 2%–3% more
- Protected practice   added 2%–3% more
- Practice with feedback   added 2%–3% more
- With coaching   95% of the participants transferred
                                       the skill to the classroom

In the WFSG system, the components continuously interact in a seamless way. WFSG members are (a) learning about new skills through their own investigations, (b) demonstrating the skills to each other and practicing the skills together when the study group meets, (c) examining student work from the lessons that are taught, (d) coaching each other through all aspects of lesson development and implementation of the new practices in the classrooms, (e) observing each other's students as the skills are being used in the classroom, and (f) collaboratively reflecting on the observations. In the WFSG approach, coaching occurs, for example, when teachers examine student work, when teachers demonstrate and practice lessons in study group meetings, and when teachers observe each other's students in classrooms. Imagine the following situation: During several study group meetings, study group members develop concept attainment lessons. In the study group meetings, they practice the lessons. They then inform each other as to when they will be teaching the lessons during the following week. The teachers pair up and work out a schedule for observing in each other's classrooms. During the next study group meeting, teachers debrief the observed lessons and share how students responded. Data are used in the next round of lesson development. As a result, all the Joyce and Showers components discussed previously are integrated into the WFSG approach.

THE CHANGE PROCESS

In groundbreaking work on the change process in schools, Huberman and Miles (1984), in their book *Innovation Up Close: How School Improvement Works*, established three distinct phases or stages of the change process. Fullan (2001a) has further developed our understanding of the three phases. The stages are initiation, implementation, and institutionalization or continuation. The initiation/implementation/institutionalization schema is how WFSG activities are organized and scheduled. Leaders begin WFSGs with the assumption that the system will be institutionalized or will become a routine practice of the school—that is, that the process will become "how we do business at this school." We believe continuation has to be an assumption in the beginning and into implementation; it is frequently not realized, however.

The initiation phase is called initiation, mobilization, or adoption and consists of the process that leads up to and includes a decision to adopt or proceed with a change (Fullan, 2001a). We usually consider the initiation phrase as being from the time leaders begin to consider the innovation through getting started. It includes gathering information, contacting and contracting with consultants, purchasing materials, meeting with teachers, getting approval from district leaders, budgeting funds, gathering pertinent data, articulating intended results, and deciding to begin. It also includes training that is needed to begin. With WFSGs, the initiation stage includes having the faculty experience the decision-making cycle and the forming of study groups. This phase includes the first two or three study group meetings during which members are adjusting to the logistics of WFSGs. The primary source of support during this phase is the principal and an expert source within or outside of the school.

The implementation phase involves the first experiences of attempting to put an idea or reform into practice (Fullan, 2001a). Implementation of WFSGs actually begins after the study groups are formed and the early work of getting started is complete. By the end of the third study group meeting, the study groups are ready to begin researching and testing ideas.

The institutionalization phase—also called continuation, incorporation, and routinization—refers to whether the change gets built in as an ongoing part of the system or disappears by way of a decision to discard or through attrition (Fullan, 2001a). Institutionalization occurs when practices that were once new are integrated into and become an important part of the fabric of school and teacher structures and routines. Successful institutionalization requires continued support, encouragement, strong sponsorship, and recognition. How long institutionalization takes is unclear. Contextual factors are most often what determine whether a practice is continued and maintained.

Another framework incorporated into the WFSG system is the Concerns Based Adoption Model (Hord, Rutherford, Huling-Austin, & Hall, 1987). Its stages of concern (Figure 3.1) and levels of use (Figure 3.2) provide guidance to leaders in addressing the concerns that individuals express and in making decisions about how to provide technical assistance.

The concerns-based adoption model (CBAM) is a framework and set of tools for understanding and managing change in people. CBAM is about the natural and developmental process that each of us goes through whenever we engage in something new or different. The research was conducted by Shirley Hord, William Rutherford, Leslie Huling-Austin, Gene Hall, Susan Loucks-Horsley, and their colleagues at the Research and Development Center for Teacher Education at the University of Texas at Austin (Hall, George, & Rutherford, 1979; Hall, Loucks, Rutherford, & Newlove, 1975).

The team reached the following conclusions:

- Change is a process, not an event.
- Change is accomplished by individuals.
- Change is a highly personal experience.
- Change involves developmental growth.

STAGES of CONCERN About an Innovation

STAGES OF CONCERN	EXPRESSIONS OF CONCERN
VI REFOCUSING	I have some ideas for how we can get more benefits from it.
V COLLABORATION	How can I relate what I am doing to what others are doing?
IV CONSEQUENCE	How is my use affecting students? How can I refine it to have more impact?
III MANAGEMENT	I seem to be spending all my time getting materials ready.
II PERSONAL	How will using it affect me?
I INFORMATIONAL	I would like to know more about it.
O AWARENESS	I am not concerned about it.

I M P A C T (VI, V, IV)

T A S K (III)

S E L F (II, I, O)

Adapted from: Shirley M. Hord, William L. Rutherford, Leslie Huling-Austin, and Gene E. Hall. The **Concerns-Based Adoption Model (CBAM)** Project. Research and Development Center for Teacher Education, the University of Texas at Austin.

Figure 3.1   Stages of Concern

LEVELS of USE of the Innovation

LEVELS OF USE		TYPICAL BEHAVIORS
VI	**RENEWAL**	Reevaluates the quality of use of the innovation.
V	**INTEGRATION**	Makes deliberate efforts to coordinate with others in using the innovation.
IVB	**REFINEMENT**	Assesses impact and makes changes to increase it.
IVA	**ROUTINE**	Has established a pattern of use and is making few, if any, changes.
III	**MECHANICAL**	Is poorly coordinated, making changes to fit user. Use is disjointed and superficial.
II	**PREPARATION**	Prepares to use the innovation.
I	**ORIENTATION**	Seeks information about the innovation.
O	**NO USE**	Takes no action with respect to the innovation.

The levels VI through III are grouped under **USER**. The levels II through O are grouped under **NONUSER**.

Adapted from: Shirley M. Hord, William L. Rutherford, Leslie Huling-Austin, and Gene E. Hall. The **Concerns-Based Adoption Model (CBAM)** Project. Research and Development Center for Teacher Education, the University of Texas at Austin.

Figure 3.2   Levels of Use

CBAM DEFINITIONS

Concerns-Based Adoption Model (CBAM): A framework and set of tools for understanding and managing change in people. CBAM is about the natural and developmental process that each of us goes through whenever we engage in something new or different.

Innovation or Change: Materials, behaviors, practices, beliefs, understandings, products, structures, or processes that are NEW to an individual.

Concerns: Feelings, reactions, and attitudes that an individual has about something new or different. Concerns are not necessarily anxieties, worries, or fears.

Use: Actions taken in relation to an innovation; the behavioral dimensions of change.

Intervention: An action or event that influences the use of an innovation.

Components: The major elements of an innovation. Critical components are those elements that must be used, the components that define the innovation. Related components are those elements that are not required, the components that enhance or strengthen the innovation.

Variations: The different ways in which the components can be used or operationalized.

Configuration: The patterns that result from different combinations of innovation components and their different variations.

Facilitator: Anyone who has some responsibility for helping people change and for creating a context to support change.

Adapted from: Shirley M. Hord, William L. Rutherford, Leslie Huling-Austin, and Gene E. Hall. The **Concerns-Based Adoption Model (CBAM)** Project. Research and Development Center for Teacher Education, the University of Texas at Austin.

Figure 3.3   Concerns-Based Adoption Model Definitions

- Change is best understood in operational terms.
- The focus on facilitation should be on individuals, innovation, and the context.

The previous conclusions support the WFSG process and have been the guide-posts of the WFSG system. CBAM defines an *innovation* or *change* as materials, behaviors, practices, beliefs, understandings, products, structures, or processes that are new to an individual (see Figure 3.3). The complexity of the WFSG system is that WFSGs are a bundle of innovations, including all those listed previously. Confronting only one, such as new materials, can be daunting. With WFSGs, however, the confrontation is with a collection of new things, such as picking up a bushel basket of fruit instead of reaching for one apple. The WFSG bushel basket has the following in it:

- Having the whole faculty participate
- Adhering to the 15 procedural guidelines
- Learning new content
- Implementing new strategies in the classroom
- Reflecting on teaching practices with colleagues
- Monitoring student effects
- Examining student work in a group setting
- Adjusting to new time requirements or different uses of time
- Understanding and accepting cultural shifts
- Being part of synergistic groups

WFSGs search for and identify interventions that will influence the use of or the adaptability to the innovations. What makes the WFSG system so complex (and powerful) is that each innovation has major elements or components. For example, "implementing new strategies in the classroom" is preceded by (a) identifying one strategy, (b) developing lessons or using that strategy, (c) demonstrating the strategy to each other, (d) using the strategy in the classroom, and (e) reflecting on the outcomes of using the strategy. Each of the components that precede and follow implementing the strategy may be new to one or more members of a study group. When leaders and faculties consider adopting the WFSG system, they usually only consider the structure—that is, the 15 guidelines. What is hidden from view is the bundle of innovations. It is not long into the implementation phase that the bundle begins to unravel, and leaders need to be supported in their efforts to support individuals.

The stages of concern (Figure 3.1) and the levels of use (Figure 3.2) charts are in the WFSG training materials, but, as leaders of change efforts know, "it is not real until it is real"—that is, little attention is paid to the concepts until implementation problems happen. The stages of concern are apparent in WFSG schools as external consultants meet with study groups. It is like individuals have the word "management" imprinted on their foreheads, telling us that management and logistical details are the focus of concern. The setting of norms, rotation of leaders, using the action plan, and completing a log are new procedures that cause members concern. Principals need to be advised that as long as the concerns are focused on personal and management issues, the work is not going to impact students. Principals need to address the concerns in such a way that the study groups can become more concerned about the consequence of the work so that students will benefit from the work. With the strong and constant message of student needs and student impact, the consequence and collaboration stages are obtainable in the first year. In Chapter 6, the developmental stages of groups are described. The developmental stages and the stages of concern correspond. In both, consequence is the stage in which student impact is greatest.

The levels of use have dual implications for WFSGs. First, the levels of use apply to the WFSG process as the innovation. Meeting in a small group with colleagues to work collaboratively on teaching and learning is new. WFSGs begin at the mechanical level. If groups remain at the mechanical level, the work will seem disjointed and superficial to members. At the routine level, the work is smoother; the group continues to do what is comfortable, however, and members do not engage in actions that require them to change how they work with colleagues. For example, the group does much verbal sharing without routinely examining student work using protocols. Second, if the content of a study group is new materials and teaching strategies, the content consists of multiple innovations. If, for example, the content is learning or teaching strategies, each member of the study group may be at a different level of use of a single strategy. If the group is developing skill at using several learning strategies, each member may be on a different level of use of each strategy. When we overlay an individual's stage of concern regarding a specific innovation with the individual's level of use of the innovation, we get some notion of the complexity of innovation. Although it is not realistic to diagnose every faculty member's stage of concern and level of use with a particular innovation, it is helpful for leaders to be aware of the CBAM and the implications it has for providing appropriate and timely technical assistance.

SCHOOL CULTURES

Fullan (2001b) believes that transforming the culture—changing the way we do things around here—is the point in achieving successful change. The point of WFSGs is to change the culture of schools from one of isolation to collaboration; from individual knowledge to group knowledge; from individual work to joint work; from individual responsibility to joint and collective responsibility; and from the teacher as follower to all teachers as leaders. In this book, we discuss in depth the structure of WFSGs. The structure is only a set of tools for reculturing, as Fullan (2001b) calls the work of change. Fullan states,

> It is a particular kind of reculturing for which we strive: one that activates and deepens moral purpose through collaborative work cultures that respect differences and constantly build and test knowledge against measurable results—a culture within which one realizes that sometimes being off balance is a learning moment. (p. 45)

The image of successful change and of reculturing that Fullan (2001a, 2001b) describes is a daunting mission. Such work is not for the fainthearted. Long-standing practices of isolation, traditions of territorial protection, feelings of mistrust, and histories of disillusionment are cultural fortresses. Creating new relationships forged through WFSGs that are built on trust, high expectations, new knowledge and skills, and more coherent instructional programs establish a culture of mutual respect. Saphier and King (1985) identified 12 norms of school culture that should be in place and strong to create a healthy school culture: (a) collegiality; (b) experimentation; (c) high expectations; (d) trust and confidence; (e) tangible support; (f) reaching out to the knowledge base; (g) appreciation and recognition; (h) caring, celebration, and humor; (i) involvement in decision making; (j) protection of what is important; (k) traditions; and (l) honest, open communications. If these norms are in place and strong, then improvements in instruction will be significant, continuous, and widespread, according to Saphier and King. If these norms are weak, however, then improvements will be infrequent, random, and slow. Of the 12 norms, Saphier (as cited in Richardson, 1996) points to three norms—collegiality, experimentation, and reaching out to a knowledge base—that have the highest correlation with changing the school environment and improving student achievement. Saphier (as cited in Richardson, 1996) stated that current data continue to support the 1985 Saphier and King study.

Saphier and Gower (1997) devoted a chapter to the conditions that build a professional development culture that incorporates optimal conditions for teacher learning. One of the conditions that opens wide the gates for improving schools through professional development is for schools to have within them collegial structures and personal support for reflection and study of the knowledge base on teaching. We believe that WFSGs provide this cultural condition of Saphier and Gower as well as the 12 cultural norms presented by Saphier and King (1985).

LEADERSHIP

Michael Fullan lights the torch and leads the way for us to follow. He reminds us that it is the moral purpose of leaders that will enable schools to do the seemingly undoable. As leaders, we must be deeply passionate about improving the quality of life in schools for adults and for students. Fullan (2001b) asserts there are five components to leadership:

1. Moral purpose

2. Understanding the change process

3. Strong relationships

4. Knowledge building

5. Coherence making among multiple priorities

Throughout this book, we assert what we believe to be the moral purpose of the WFSG system and of the leaders who strive to implement and institutionalize the system:

> To determine what students need for us to do and for leaders to do what students need leaders to do is the bedrock of WFSGs.

The system is dedicated to changing the cultures of schools so that all individuals work as one for the betterment of students. The student voice is the voice that gives the system its purpose and its direction. Leaders of schools that implement the WFSG system, if successful over time in establishing and maintaining student-centered professional adult learning communities, are grounded in their commitments, reliability, and steadfast convictions. Fullan (2001b) and Sergiovanni (1999) agree that authentic leaders display character and moral purpose.

The research is clear on the importance of leadership in school reform. According to Spillane, Halverson, and Diamond (1999), who summarize the literature on leadership, leadership is critical to innovation in schools. They wrote,

> We know that schools with shared visions and norms about instruction, norms of collaboration, and a sense of collective responsibility for students' academic success create incentives and opportunities for teachers to improve their practice (Bryk & Driscoll, 1985; Newmann & Wehlage, 1995). Moreover, we know that principal leadership is important in promoting these conditions (Liberman et al., 1994; Louis & Kruse, 1995; Rosenholtz, 1989). (p. 3)

Spillane et al. also developed a distributed theory of leadership: School leadership is constituted in the dynamic interaction of multiple leaders (and followers) and their situation around particular leadership tasks. They stated that "leaders' practice is 'stretched over' the social and situational contexts of the school; it is not simply a function of what a school principal knows and does" (p. 7). This theory of distributed leadership is embedded in the WFSG system. A team, including the principal, receives instruction in how to "roll-out" WFSGs at the school. The team selects data that the faculty will review. The data determine what the faculty will do in study groups. The leadership of each study group is rotated among members. The school's instructional council is composed of representatives from each study group using a rotation system. Study groups make recommendations for inclusion in the school's improvement plan. The principal may distribute the responsibility among other leaders in the school, such as assistant principals, for providing feedback to the study groups. We acknowledge that the theory of distributive leadership is deeper and more extensive than we are able to describe here. One of the statements that Spillane et al. made, however, that "leadership is 'stretched over' the practice of actors within an organization" (p. 15), relates directly to one of the guiding principles of WFSGs: Leadership is shared.

SUMMARY

We believe that the establishment of professional learning communities resulting in higher levels of student success is one of the most important outcomes of the authentic application of the WFSG system. Murphy's research (Murphy & Lick, 1998) validates the positive impact that high norms of collegiality have on student learning. The research cited in this chapter confirms our belief that when WFSGs are implemented properly and are sustained over time, the context of the school will reflect strong professional learning communities that contribute importantly to student learning. The previously discussed research leaves little doubt that effective school-wide change and enhanced student learning require a structure or a process for greater collaboration among teachers. Furthermore, it is unlikely that the desired cultural norms described previously will happen without a deliberate strategy. Knowing general educational research and acknowledging the validity of the research will not by itself change anything. Faculties must be given a framework and process for change that is flexible enough to give them the latitude necessary to transform the research into practice. The WFSG process is such a framework. It provides a structure that creates forward-moving, learning-enriched schools.

Consistent with the previously discussed research, the purpose of this book is to give schools, school leaders, and teachers a practical, proven-in-practice strategy and a step-by-step procedure for doing what researchers conclude that schools should do to improve. The researchers cited, and many not cited, clearly state that collaborative school cultures and effective school leadership enhance student performance. What most researchers do not do is tell schools how to do what they say should be done. Chapters 6 and 7 in this book, however, specifically tell schools how to implement a schoolwide structure that, if sustained over time, provides a process for school improvement and enhanced student learning as well as a process for the school to become a "university" for teachers, in which teachers are committed not only to student success but also to each other's professional growth and success.

4

Context

Conditions That Facilitate Change

A framework for designing professional development has three major components: context, process, and content. Georgia Sparks (1983) introduced the context/process/content schema as a way of organizing research findings. The schema is used by the National Staff Development Council (NSDC) as the organizer for NSDC's Staff Development Standards (2003). Murphy and Lick (1998) used context/process/content as the framework for describing the Whole-Faculty Study Group (WFSG) system. Each of the three components requires thoughtful, deliberate action. Because each component has different characteristics, there are distinct actions that leaders should take when considering and making provisions for each component. These components are equally important and create a seamless whole. In the planning stages, each is given separate consideration; however, in reality, the components are inseparable.

The *context*, the focus of Chapters 4 and 5, addresses the organization, system, or culture in which the study groups exist. It is the organizational or cultural factors that facilitate or impede progress toward the organization's intended results. The context includes how the organization "feels" to the personnel as well as the norms that govern their lives. It is often the informal structure of how things get done. The context will largely determine how psychologically safe individuals feel, how willing they are to take risks, what behaviors are rewarded and punished, and whether it is standard to work in isolation or with peers. The context of an organization is typically the first line of concern for sponsors and change agents.

Process, the focus of Chapter 6, refers to the "how" of staff development. It describes the means for the acquisition of new knowledge and skills. A process is a way of doing something. It is how change happens and continues to develop over the course of time. A process implies that there are steps or procedures that one goes through in the course of accomplishing a goal.

Content, the focus of Chapters 7 and 8, refers to the actual skills and knowledge educators want to possess or acquire through staff development or some other means. In WFSGs, the search for content begins with identifying student instructional needs. The decision-making cycle (DMC) is a step-by-step set of procedures for establishing the student needs that study groups will address. The student needs lead members to what the groups will do. The content of WFSGs is what study groups do to become more knowledgeable and skillful. It is the substance of the WFSG process. For teachers, it is teaching students how to read and the history, English, science, and mathematics that they teach. It is also how to teach for understanding and what brain research tells us about how to meet the needs of students. It is instructional strategies and skills and how to plan and assess instruction. We often refer to content knowledge or what one knows about a subject. When we read a book, the content is the text, what we learn. We could think of the content as the ingredients of a process, what is in the process, what the process holds. Figure 4.1 shows the relationship between context, process, and content. This chapter and Chapter 5 describe the contextual conditions that support WFSGs.

NATIONAL STAFF DEVELOPMENT COUNCIL'S STAFF DEVELOPMENT CONTEXT STANDARDS

The NSDC's staff development standards (NSDC, 2003) are grounded in research that documents the connection between staff development and student learning. The standards are organized into context standards, process standards, and content standards. The context standards recognize that staff development that improves student learning for all students does the following:

- Community: Organizes adults into learning communities whose goals are aligned with those of the school and district
- Leadership: Requires skillful school and district leaders who guide continuous instructional improvement
- Resources: Requires resources to support adult learning and collaboration

The WFSG system meets each of the three standards in the most obvious ways. WFSGs organize all certificated faculty and others directly involved in instructional programs into study groups that meet once a week or every 2 weeks, usually during the school day. The study groups develop lesson plans, examine student work, monitor student progress, assess the effectiveness of instruction, and identify needs for their continuing professional development needs. The key success factor for WFSGs is skillful leadership at the school and district level to continuously guide the process. Each study group identifies the resources it will need, lists the resources in the study group action plan, and secures the resources for its work.

A Framework for Designing Professional Development

CONTEXT: Organizational or cultural factors that facilitate or impede progress toward intended results, such as: a shared vision and norms of continuous improvement and collegiality.

PROCESS: How individuals, groups, and the whole will function, behave, perform; procedures to be followed; the means for the acquisition of new knowledge and skills.

CONTENT: What individuals, groups, and the whole will study, learn, or become skillful in doing to achieve the intended results; skills, attitudes, and knowledge to be acquired.

PROCESS

CONTEXT

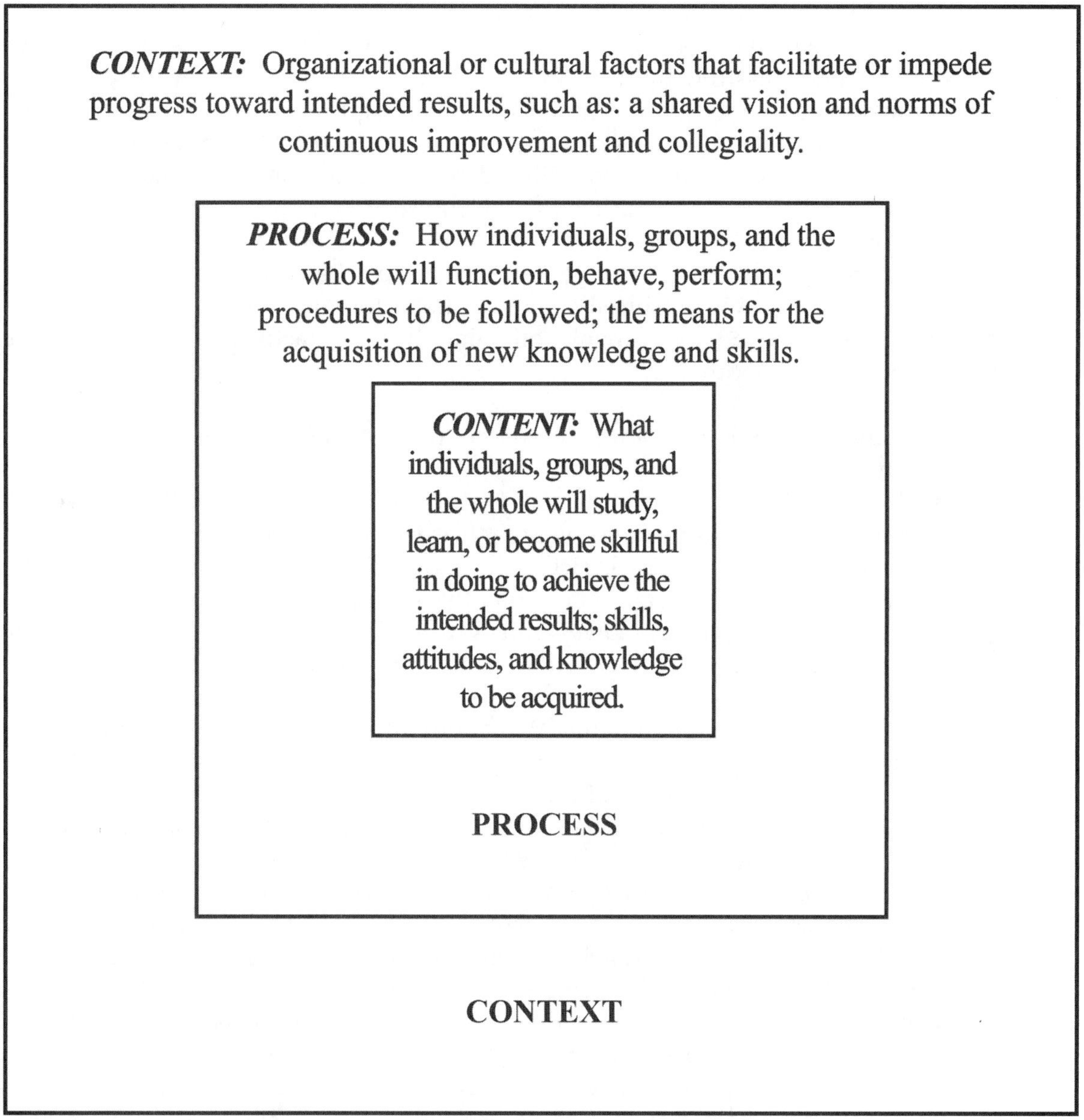

Figure 4.1   A Framework for Designing Professional Development

THE WFSG RUBRIC: CONTEXT

The WFSG rubric has three components: context, process, and content. Table 4.1 shows nine context descriptors and four stages of implementation of each descriptor.

THE CONTEXT FOR WFSGs

There is no one type of context that is an ideal precondition for WFSGs. They have been initiated successfully in different schools where the contexts are very dissimilar. As schools authentically apply the WFSG principles and guidelines, the more similar the contexts become. In great measure, the contextual conditions of a district and school determine what is accomplished and what does not get done. These conditions create the school environment in which progress and change will potentially flourish or be inhibited.

Contextual conditions do have to be considered when major change efforts are initiated. For this reason, we briefly mention the factors that seem to have the greatest impact on the context of a school. Following the list of factors, several of them are discussed in more depth.

- Leadership: School leaders, in large part, create the context for school improvement.
- Vision: A shared vision of success for all students translates into a powerful, compelling, and inspiring contextual feature of the school.
- District influence: The district context or culture has a huge impact on a school. Schools can begin major initiatives without the involvement or direct support of the district. However, it is difficult, if not impossible, to continue and sustain those initiatives without sooner or later gaining the support of the district.
- Nature and needs of students: What students are like at a school establishes the conditions for what needs to happen.
- Roles and responsibilities of faculty members: What individuals are expected to do has a great impact on how they feel about where they work. Individuals tend to feel safe when it is clear what is expected of them.
- Time for professional development: It is commonly believed that we find time for what is important. If leaders truly believe teacher collaboration is directly linked to higher student achievement, time will be found within the school week for teachers to collaborate.
- Resources: The availability of resources to meet the needs of faculty and students is a critical element to successful change.
- Community support: Schools exist within communities, another context. A school community consists of parents, nonparents, businesses, community agencies, churches, and clubs.
- History: All organizations have a history. Even new schools inherit a history from other local schools and their community. For example, a climate of uncertainty is created when a school has had a number of principals within a 5-year period.
- Organizational culture: A staff that operates within the norms of critical inquiry and continuous improvement and exhibits caring and supportive relationships is far more likely to be a successful school.

	Not Yet	Beginning Implementation	Developing Implementation	Advanced Implementation
Context	• Members disregard, resent, or do not receive feedback from the principal.	• Members review principal's feedback with no action.	• Members discuss and follow up on principal's suggestions.	• Members often refer to principal's helpfulness and invite him or her to meetings.
Context	• Members do not utilize feedback given to the group from the principal and/or the instructional council.	• Members pose few questions for feedback and are unsure what to do with the feedback received.	• Members appreciate the feedback they receive, sometimes acting on it, sometimes not.	• Members engage in a rich dialogue with those giving feedback.
Context	• Study group action plans and logs are not posted or have a number of logs missing.	• SGAPs and logs are posted but not immediately upon completion; members often have to be reminded.	• SGAP and all of the group's logs are posted in a timely manner.	• Items promptly posted, members show evidence of reviewing and using the feedback from other groups.
Context	• Members show no awareness of and no interest in what other study groups are doing.	• Members indicate some interest in learning about what others are doing.	• There is evidence in logs that the study group is discussing the work of other groups.	• Members frequently seek out and use work from other study groups at the school.
Context	• Members do not show evidence of their willingness to be vulnerable within the group.	• Members are hesitant but will share what is not working.	• Members accept suggestions and share the results of the revisions.	• Members are genuinely open with one another about their strengths and weaknesses.
Context	• Members rarely, if ever, buy in and commit to decisions.	• Members feign agreement during meetings.	• Members are cautious yet show willingness to confront and be confronted on expected behaviors and actions.	• Members openly call each other on behaviors and actions that aren't consistent with agreed on behaviors and actions.
Context	• Individuals do not connect their work to others in the group.	• Members connect to each other but not to whole school improvement.	• Members talk about whole school but no evidence of tying their work to a school improvement plan (SIP).	• Members continually refer to a SIP and their role in meeting schoolwide goals.
Context	• Members are not focused on results – improving student performance in specific learning needs for their current students.	• Members are easily distracted and express doubt that results are possible.	• Members refer to data, express concern, and desire to attain results.	• Data is always on the table in some form and members hold themselves accountable for attaining results.
Context	• No interest in observing in each other's classrooms.	• Members have invited other members to observe in their classrooms but no action.	• Members are observing in each other's classrooms but not debriefing within the group.	• Members routinely observe in each other's classrooms and pre- and postconference within the group.

Table 4.1   WFSG Rubric: Context

- Assessment of results: Data-based decision making creates a culture that is results oriented.
- Building capacity: Distributing leadership among the faculty and creating internal capacity for continuing effective instructional initiatives create contextual norms that sustain school improvement.
- Organizational structures: There are several structures in schools to get the work of schooling done. It is important that the faculty understands the functions of each structure. For example, it should be clear how WFSG meetings differ from department meetings.
- Equity: Treating all students and adults with respect and dignity is basic to feelings of safety and worth.

In the following sections, we discuss certain key factors in greater depth, including shared vision, leadership, roles and responsibilities, an organizational structure called the instructional council, district influence, and time.

SHARED VISION

Researchers (Hall & Hord, 1987; Hord, Rutherford, Huling-Austin, & Hall, 1987) found five functional categories of interventions for change:

1. Vision clarity is reflected in operational terms.

2. Planning, providing resources, and making organizational arrangements are required.

3. Training and development of skills are provided.

4. Monitoring and evaluation occur.

5. Consultation, reinforcement, and data-driven interventions are evident.

In Chapter 6, the WFSG procedural guidelines are presented and described. In the guidelines, four of the functional categories are evident. The fifth feature, vision clarity, is not evident. Schools that implement WFSGs have a clearly articulated vision that is evidenced in the faculty's commitment to identify and address student needs. Most often, WFSGs are implemented as a result of a school having gone through a process of clearly articulating its vision. The WFSG structure is one tool for achieving the school's vision. For this reason, visioning is not part of the WFSG decision-making cycle as described in Chapter 7.

The decision-making process is rooted in a school's vision that includes success for all students, no matter the wording of the vision statement. There are as many ways to articulate or word a vision as there are schools, most often depending on the consultant hired to facilitate the visioning process.

Visions, missions, and goals should be posted on the walls of most schools, either framed or on banners. Such statements are prominent in school improvement plans and accreditation reports. A school's vision is actualized in how the faculty hears, sees, and interprets the students' voices. If faculties respond to the four fundamental questions at the beginning of Chapter 1, the vision of success for all students will be realized.

It is important to remember that the school's shared vision (a) provides direction to resource allocation and management, (b) indicates how personnel will be deployed, (c) defines how schedules will be organized, (d) indicates what will be the professional development priorities, and (e) provides the guidepost in decision making about teaching and learning.

After the visioning work is done, the WFSG system is a strategy for implementing the school's improvement plan, which is guided by the school's vision. For example, the Springfield, Missouri, public schools utilized the Deming model (Leonard, 1996) and professional learning communities (DuFour & Eaker, 1998) as basic frameworks for their school improvement process. The district initiated this process through presentations to the leadership team (all district and site leaders). Follow-up sessions and ongoing implementation supports were provided for administrators and faculties. Then, the WFSG system was chosen as the design to actualize professional learning communities in the school improvement planning process, essentially putting into practice the Deming, DuFour, and Eaker ideas.

It is unusual for a district or school not to have been engaged in some form of visioning process. On the lighter side, Murphy tells of a conversation she had with Roland Barth in the late 1980s. He said, "At one time if I had said I had a vision, people would have thought I was crazy. Now you can't get a job interview unless you say you have a vision."

LEADERSHIP

School leaders create the context for school improvement. According to the Southwest Educational Development Laboratory (www.sedl.org/pubs/change34/4), the literature on educational leadership and school change recognizes the role and influence of the principal on whether change will occur in the school. It seems clear that transforming the school organization into a learning community can be done only with the leaders' sanction and active nurturing of the entire staff's development as a community. The studies of Kenneth Leithwood (1999) and colleagues have shown that leadership contributes significantly to school conditions fostering organizational learning processes. The WFSG system is a structure for mobilizing the whole school organization for learning.

Ultimately, the principal is the key factor in the initiation, implementation, and continuation of WFSGs. The principal determines what structures are in place, how time is utilized, how resources are distributed and managed, and what behaviors are acceptable. We believe that it is the principal's job to create the conditions that make it possible for all faculty to be members of study groups that meet routinely for the improvement of student learning, including finding the time for study groups to meet once a week. The supportive leadership role of principals is a critical element in the school organization becoming and being sustained as a learning community.

We have found that although culture is the accumulation of many individuals' values and norms, the principal is most often the "keeper" of the norms of the workplace either by facilitating or by impeding the building of community through WFSGs. Kent Peterson, coauthor with Terrance Deal of *Shaping School Culture* (1999), expressed in an interview with Joan Richardson (2001) that

> principals are the primary shapers of school culture, in both large and small ways. Principals send large cultural messages to staff and students with every decision regarding budgets, curriculum, instruction, as well as interactions with central office and community leaders. But principals also send

hundreds of cultural messages to students and teachers every day. In every interaction with a student or teacher, a principal telegraphs a message about his or her expectations for that school. That gives the principal enormous opportunities to shape a school's culture—for good or ill. (p. 1)

Peterson also noted (as cited by Allen, 2003) that the principal's roles include being a "symbol" who supports core values through daily work; a "potter" who builds culture through hiring, budget, and supervisory decisions; a "poet" whose written and oral messages can reinforce a healthy culture; an "actor" on all the "stages" of school events; and a "healer" who can help repair the culture after tragedy, conflict, or loss.

In our work with principals, we see a principal's positive and negative habits magnified through the lens of implementing WFSGs. Dennis Sparks (2003) writes, "The habits that produce significant change in teaching and learning begin with significant change in what leaders think, say, and do. . . . In addition, it requires exposure and risk because new learning will often be public in nature" (p. 2). Most often, principals lead faculties to the decision to begin WFSGs, thinking that they will be observers of the process rather than seeing themselves as an intricate part of the learning process. Teachers, however, want to see the principal engaged in learning more about effective classroom practice, giving feedback to study groups about the work of the groups, and making public what the principal knows about instruction. Providing weekly constructive, helpful feedback is not a habit most principals have nurtured. In WFSG schools, it is a habit that must be developed. The quality and quantity of feedback principals give to study groups help to shape the end results.

A current log from each study group meeting is given to the principal or another leader representing the principal. The study group expects feedback. The feedback motivates group members to more fully implement not only whatever is the work of the group but also the intentions of the WFSG process. A principal's feedback is typically written either directly on the log or in an e-mail to members. This personalized feedback about the group's challenges and successes creates a two-way communication system. In the process, the principal, in areas less familiar, may have to ask for help from local personnel, district support staff, or external consultants. Generally, the principal takes on the role of a learner along with study group members. This activity has a powerful and positive effect on the culture of the school. The more public the work of the principal, the greater the risk and exposure but also the greater the rewards.

Principals are accustomed to giving feedback to individual teachers. Principals foster a culture that is preoccupied with learning when they shift their emphasis from helping individual teachers improve instruction to helping teams of teachers ensure that students achieve the intended outcomes of schooling (Dufour, 2002).

PRINCIPAL STUDY GROUPS

Principals, the leaders of WFSGs in schools, need support and to have opportunities to participate in professional learning communities with colleagues who have similar responsibilities. A contextual condition that enables principals to have the knowledge and skill to do what they are asking others to do is for principals to participate in principal study groups. For this to happen at the organizational level, it has to be a priority of the superintendent and the superintendent's staff. Just as teachers need to feel and see evidence of the active support of the principal, so must principals feel and see evidence of the active support of top district leaders.

During the 2003–2004 school year in Springfield, Missouri, 45 of its 51 schools implemented WFSG. The district implemented a districtwide support system for principals by creating the conditions for all 51 principals to be members of study groups with their principal colleagues. To begin this process, principals were surveyed about their needs as leaders. Unanimously, the greatest need was how to confront mediocre teaching. Thus, the essential question for the year was "How can we effectively confront mediocre teaching?"

Study groups were composed of principals representing all schools. Action plans were developed at the first meeting. The principals met once a month at district-level Job-Alike meetings. At every other Job-Alike meeting, each principal WFSG shared its work. This took the place of a "principal" version of an instructional council.

The majority of the groups also met in between the monthly time provided to them. Meeting twice a month was critical to groups for momentum to be sustained. The groups that met twice a month moved beyond the grumbling stage much quicker than those groups that met only once a month.

District leaders are seeing results from these study groups. Many of the principal study groups have examined the district's teacher evaluation tool, and the consistency of its use has been studied to determine its effectiveness for helping teachers improve their practice. Principals have teamed up and are doing classroom walk-throughs to try to come to consensus on what quality instruction looks like in comparison to mediocre teaching. New interview procedures, including new interview questions and the use of rubrics to score interviewees' responses, are a few of the outcomes of the principal study groups. The most significant result, however, is the creation of a collaborative culture among leaders in the district. Barriers are being broken down, and principals are using each other's skills and expertise to gain insights into how to provide instructional leadership to teachers that will ultimately result in improved student achievement.

Springfield is not the only district in which principal study groups are active. In most districts that have more than one school implementing WFSGs, the principals of the participating schools are members of principal study groups. Many of the groups use the time together to share action plans and logs from the schools and to get ideas for giving feedback.

Principal study groups represent a major strategy for the continuation of WFSGs. The groups provide both support and opportunities to learn more about instructional leadership. Principal study groups use the same procedures and strategies that WFSGs use. The principal groups have action plans, keep logs, maintain a set schedule, have norms, rotate leadership, focus on instruction, and examine "teacher" work using protocols. A consultant or trainer may meet with a group to introduce the members to new knowledge and skills. Principal study groups are an excellent vehicle for introducing principals to new instructional programs and strategies.

FEEDER PATTERN OR PATHWAY STUDY GROUPS

A strategy for supporting and increasing opportunities for teachers and principals to lead is to organize study groups across a feeder pattern of schools. Such a strategy also increases the chances that WFSGs will become institutionalized at the school and district level. ATLAS Communities calls such groups pathway study groups and, therefore, we do the same. The pathway study groups do not replace WFSGs in schools; rather, they support and supplement the study groups in the schools. A feeder pattern, or pathway, is the elementary schools and middle schools that "feed" their students into the same high school. One of the components of the ATLAS Communities design is working with a pathway of schools in a district. A *pathway* is a PreK through 12th-grade configuration of schools.

Pathway study groups are another organizational pattern for study groups. At many ATLAS Communities sites, after the WFSGs are in place at schools for one school year, pathway study groups are formed. Again, the same WFSG guidelines apply. A pathway study group would be composed of elementary, middle, and high school teachers. There are procedures in each pathway for forming the groups. A pathway leadership team (ATLAS Communities, 2000) identifies student needs from needs the schools are addressing. Usually, pathway study groups meet three times during a school year. Pathway study groups focus on the PreK through 12th-grade continuum and the development of meaningful, instructionally focused conversation across the grade levels. The pathway groups support and enhance the work of the WFSGs. All teachers in all the pathway schools may not be expected to be a member of a pathway study group, and these do not take the place of WFSGs in the schools; rather, the pathway groups supplement and enhance the school study groups.

The Everett, Washington, school district has had pathway study groups in place for more than 5 years. Teachers have indicated that the pathway groups have improved grade-level articulation by helping high school teachers learn what is taught at the middle school and vice versa. One of the most exciting outcomes of the pathway study groups in Everett is the "swap days." This is when an elementary teacher and a high school teacher teach each other's classes for a day. In Murphy's observation of a pathway group, she heard a high school teacher ask a primary teacher to spend one meeting giving the high school teachers tips on how to teach high school students to read.

When a district moves to implement the WFSG system, many patterns for organizational development become visible. In such a system, teachers are members of study groups in their schools, principals are in study groups, and, as an option, teachers are also in cross-school study groups. The managers of such a system need to constantly monitor groups to ensure that the groups are focused on instructional improvement, targeting increased student learning.

TIME FOR PROFESSIONAL DEVELOPMENT

There is an old saying that we find time for what is important. How a school structures the school day to include both student and teacher learning is, in our opinion, the most critical contextual condition that makes WFSGs and other professional learning communities possible. If leaders truly believe what research shows (see Chapter 3)—that collaboration is directly linked to higher student achievement—time will be found within the school day for teachers to collaborate. The first NSDC Staff Development Context Standard (2003, p. 13) is that the adults at a school are organized into learning communities whose goals are aligned with those of the school and district. The highest indicator of meeting the standard is the following: "The teacher meets regularly with colleagues *during the school day* [italics added] to develop lesson plans, examine student work, monitor student progress, assess the effectiveness of instruction, and identify needs for professional development" (p. 14). WFSGs do the five activities listed but most often not during the school day. Therefore, WFSG schools easily meet the highest indicator of the standard, except for schools that do not provide the time within the school day for study groups to meet. More schools are seriously exploring options for finding the time within the contract day; however, far too few schools are doing so. In most communities, the public, including parents, does not accept the critical role that professional development plays in more successful learning for students. Districts and schools have not done a sufficient job in making the connection between student learning and teacher learning. Until schools do so, communities will not support releasing students from school for teacher learning. Many superintendents do not support plans for releasing students early or having students arrive late 1 day a week for teacher development because they know that boards of education, in response to their constituents, will most often not support such requests. Schools may go in one of several directions in getting the support of superintendents and boards of education.

In one district, a middle-school faculty made the decision in the spring of a school year to implement WFSGs at the beginning of the next school year if time could be found within the school day for the study groups to meet. The principal met with the superintendent. The superintendent was not in favor of any strategy for releasing students. The middle school was the only school in the 21-school district planning to implement WFSGs for the next school year, meaning whatever was decided would be an exception for one school. The principal was firm in his determination to convince the superintendent that teachers would honor the time for professional learning. The principal collected information linking higher student achievement to professional learning communities and on how WFSGs were a proven practice with a standardized structure. He met with the superintendent again. In fact, it took several meetings before the superintendent agreed on a release time schedule that included 12 days when students would be released 2 hours early, providing a total of 24 hours of study group time. In addition, the principal indicated that teachers would use 2 hours during each of the already scheduled 5 planning days when students would not be present for WFSGs, providing an additional 10 hours for a total of 34 hours for study groups to meet during the school year. The schedule is shown in Resource C. During the first year of implementing WFSGs, the principal sent reports to the superintendent and the assistant superintendent for instruction after each round of study group meetings. The quarterly WFSG newsletter was sent to board members. District leaders were invited to attend all whole-faculty sessions for WFSG sharing, training, and celebrations. During the first year of implementing WFSGs, the faculty demonstrated its integrity to the process, honored all release time expectations, and saw results in both teacher learning and student learning. This demonstrates how the strong sponsorship and advocacy of the principal influenced district leaders to approve strategies for finding time for study groups to meet within the school day.

Several schools have begun WFSGs without release time and after 1 or 2 years obtained the approval of district leaders for different patterns of releasing students for study groups to meet. In all such cases, the secret of success in getting the release time approved after beginning has been the levels and types of communication with district leaders. Data of proven effects are the most powerful piece of evidence.

Schools begin WFSGs by using one or a combination of ways for finding time described in this section. Finding time for study groups to meet is the most important issue for faculties considering WFSGs and those that have adopted WFSGs. It is the common obstacle schools face in the study group process. We state the following with conviction: *There is time in the school week for teachers to collaborate, if the administration and faculty are willing to change other things!* Schools have been most creative in how they have found time to make the WFSG process work in their schools, as the following 22 approaches demonstrate:

1. Release students early 1 day a week. Many schools exceed the minimum number of instructional minutes required by the state. For such schools, releasing students early 1 day a week would not require changing the dismissal time during the other 4 days. For schools that do not exceed the minimum instructional minutes, adding minutes to one or more of the other 4 days would be necessary.

2. Have a "late start" day once a week when students report to school 1 hour later on that morning. This gives the teachers 1 hour for study groups to meet.

3. Have a late start day once a week that begins only 30 minutes later for students than the other 4 days. The teachers report 30 minutes earlier, and the two half-hour blocks are combined for 1 hour of study group time.

4. Use teaching assistants to release teachers for study group meetings. A team of five teaching assistants can release five teachers during the first hour of the school day so that they can have their study group meeting. For the last hour of the day, the team of teaching assistants could cover the classrooms of another five teachers. Each day, two study groups could meet. For schools that have 10 or fewer study groups, this plan has worked.

5. Use teams of parents or business partners to release teachers for the hour that their study groups meet.

6. Pair teachers. Teachers from one study group take students from teachers in another study group for the first or last 30 minutes of 1 day. The next day, the process is reversed. Because teachers arrive at least 30 minutes before students arrive and stay 30 minutes after students leave, a 1-hour block is created for study group meetings at the end of a day or at the beginning of a day. In combined classes, students have individual study, reading, and journal writing time; students work one-on-one with each other; clubs meet; and other types of student-planned activities are initiated.

7. Identify a team of five substitutes that spends 1 day every other week at the school. On that day, the team releases five teachers at 9:00 a.m. to meet as a study group and continues to do this each hour of the day. The team of substitutes moves from class to class. As many as six study groups meet on that day. For schools that have more than six study groups, the team of substitute teachers returns for part of another day. On the weeks that the substitute teachers do not provide released time, study groups meet for 1 hour after school.

8. Limit faculty meetings to one afternoon a month, such as on the second Wednesday. On the other three Wednesdays of the month, study groups meet. Some districts expect teachers to reserve one afternoon a week for faculty or other types of meetings.

9. Use part or all of a daily team planning period once a week. On 1 day a week, the planning period is labeled "study group time." During that hour, teachers meet in their study groups.

10. Permit teachers to use WFSGs to earn compensatory time for their after-school study groups. The 1-hour weekly study group meetings total what 2 full days of staff development time would equal. Therefore, on 2 days designated as staff development days on the school calendar, teachers do not report to school.

11. Dismiss students 2 hours early 1 day a month, and have each study group submit a plan to the principal for an additional 2 hours during each month.

12. Dismiss students 2 hours early on one Wednesday a month. On another Wednesday of the month, teachers meet after school in study groups. On the other two Wednesdays, the principal chairs a faculty meeting.

13. Design an assembly model to give teachers time to collaborate during the school day. This option also provides enrichment opportunities for students. Special assemblies are scheduled every other week at the school. The assemblies are part of a cultural arts enrichment program that is funded by the school's Parent-Teacher Association (PTA) or the school's adopters. Various art groups, such as a theater group, the opera, the symphony, a ballet group, storytellers, dancers, musical groups, drama clubs, and other performing groups, present programs to the students. On assembly day, there are two assembly periods that are 90 minutes in length. Half of the classes in the school are scheduled for each assembly. Each period consists of two 45-minute performances that occur concurrently. Half of the students scheduled for an assembly period go to one of the 45-minute performances, and the other half of the students go to the other performance; then they switch. This creates a 90-minute block of time for the teachers, who attend study group meetings during the time their students are in the assembly. Administrators, paraprofessionals, and parents remain with the students during the two assembly periods. Classroom teachers have the responsibility of delivering and settling the students in the designated area (e.g., cafeteria or gym) and getting students when the two performances are finished. Students know that teachers are meeting in study groups while they are in assemblies. When students return to their rooms, they share with the teachers what they have learned. Likewise, teachers share with students what they learned in study group meetings. Principals have reported that on assembly day parents show up who are not scheduled to assist and ask "May I help?" On alternating weeks, when assemblies are not scheduled, study groups meet for 1 hour after school.

14. Do an analysis of the number of instructional minutes in a regular school day. If it is determined that the school is banking time in terms of instructional minutes, specify the number of minutes. For example, a high school exceeds the minimum number of minutes per day for instruction by 5 minutes daily. To have time in the school day for study groups to meet, take the accumulated 5 minutes and combine it with the time from a staff development day. This means that the school has 26 days on which it may begin classes 45 minutes later. On 1 day a week, study groups meet from 7:30 to 8:15 a.m.,

with classes starting at 8:20 a.m. and all periods shortened. On the other 4 days, classes begin at 7:30 a.m. Students know that on study group day, the bell schedule is not the same as on the other 4 days.

15. Take the holistic approach to when all study groups would meet. All times allocated on district and school calendars for staff development and staff meetings are viewed as one large block of time; this includes full days, half days, and afterschool time. Instead of focusing on the exact weekly clock hours that study groups meet, focus on tasks that must be completed over a period of time. For instance, after examining several databases, one faculty made the decision that all eight study groups would focus on reading instruction. Another understanding was that groups would cover the same material in the same block of time, but how they did so was up to each group. Blocks of time to cover the predetermined content were established. For example, through a whole-faculty consensus process, it was decided that from December 11 to February 12, study groups would cover teaching vocabulary with context clues, word identification and phonics, and comprehension questioning. The groups would look at the calendar and view all segments of time as a whole and decide how they would organize that amount of time to cover the research and shared practice on the predetermined content.

16. Allow teachers to select when their study group will meet once a week. At one school in which this was done, not only did groups meet at different times but also they met on different days. Several study groups met early in the morning, others met during lunchtime or during planning periods, still others met after school, and one met in the evening. Teachers accounted for their professional development time, and on designated staff development days teachers were not expected to attend meetings.

17. Redesign a modified day plan that may have been in place prior to the initiation of the study group process. At one school, the modified day, Monday, was formed by having the school start 5 minutes early and end 5 minutes later on Tuesday through Friday, making the student's day 8:40 a.m. to 3:25 p.m. 4 days a week. On Mondays, the students left at 1:45 p.m., and the teachers left at 4:25 p.m. Prior to study groups, teachers spent that block of time doing individual teacher preparation, meeting in committees, and participating in faculty meetings. Now, 1 hour of that block of time was earmarked for study groups to meet.

18. Reconfigure a modified day. One district had 1 day per week that was modified so that students were dismissed 2 hours earlier than on the other 4 days. Generally, this time was for individual teacher preparation time, faculty meetings, and district meetings. When five elementary schools elected to initiate the study group process, those schools reconfigured the modified day. Four faculties decided to use 1 hour of the 2-hour time block for study groups. The faculty at the fifth school decided that study groups would meet every other week for 1½ hours. On study group day after study group meetings, the whole staff met together for 30 minutes to report on the progress of each group.

19. Schedule weekly common planning periods for teachers in the same study group.

20. Enlist college students who are willing to spend 1 day a week at the school. For example, college students participating in Eco-Watch, an outward-bound environmental leadership program, are expected to do classroom and schoolwide environmental activities with elementary students. This frees teachers to meet in study groups. The college students keep a record of the hours they spend in school, and at the end of the school year the hours are converted into dollars for college tuition.

21. Make allowances for the time teachers spend after school in their study groups. If teachers are expected to stay 45 minutes after students are dismissed and a group of teachers in a study group stays 1½ hours after dismissal time, those teachers will be allowed to leave earlier on the other days of the week. A version of this idea would be for schools in which teachers, by contract, are expected to stay 45 minutes after students are dismissed to shorten the 45 minutes to 30 minutes on 4 days, creating 1 hour for all study groups at the end of 1 day a week.

22. Release teachers from their teaching duties for 1½ hours each week. The students would remain at school, being dismissed at their regular times. Professionals from area universities, health care facilities, community agencies, businesses, and city and county governmental agencies consider how volunteers can provide instruction in foreign languages, physical education, athletics, nutrition, civics, drama, music, art, environmental education, and other areas for the students during that time. Students could be grouped differently than in the regular classes, forming larger and smaller classes across grade levels. PTAs consider budgeting funds for this purpose where funds are required.

All the preceding strategies for finding time for teachers to collaborate require that the time allocated be spent in serious and purposeful work, increasing the teachers' relevant knowledge and skills. Because it may be perceived by the public that time is being taken from students, strategies must be put in place to inform internal and external publics about how students directly benefit from time allocated to this form of teacher development. Communication must be continuous and effective, however. As time passes, information regarding student gains will encourage the community to continue to support the idea that student development is directly linked to teacher development. Teachers should tell their students what they do and learn in their study groups on a regular basis. Soon after a study group meets presents a good learning opportunity for students. Teachers can often say, "Today, we are going to do something that I learned in my study group this week." Many students may go home and tell their parents about what they learned; the parents and students then see the connection, and the idea of how students benefit when time is allocated for teacher learning is no longer an abstract concept. If information about study groups and their effectiveness is meaningfully presented, parents and other groups can become strong advocates for this form of teacher development and school improvement.

An interesting twist on finding time for teachers to meet with colleagues was initiated by the school administration at a high school in Lubbock, Texas. Community businesses were asked to bring their business to school to save teachers time. For example, a local cleaners picked up and delivered cleaning to the school, and an automobile shop did the same when cars needed servicing.

TIME NEEDED FOR OTHER WFSG TASKS

In addition to finding time for WFSGs to meet, there are other time requirements for the WFSG system. First, time is needed to launch WFSGs, most often at the beginning of a school year or within the first half of a school year. Faculties that have not had an orientation to WFSGs that includes a discussion of the principles, functions, and procedural guidelines will need to be informed. This would also be a time to show selected portions of the Video Journal of Education's *Whole-Faculty Study Group* program, which includes an introduction to the 15 procedural guidelines. On the videotapes, real study groups meet and discuss various aspects of WFSGs. An orientation session will take approximately 1 hour.

The next activity for the whole faculty is to go through Steps 1 through 4 of the DMC (Chapter 7), which will take approximately 3 hours. This session should be scheduled as soon as possible after the new school year begins. Schools that have faculty present several days before the students arrive will schedule the DMC for part of one of the planning days. It is not until faculties experience Steps 1 through 4 that study groups are organized, so the quicker the better. Many schools that do not have any time prior to students arriving schedule the DMC for two 90-minute sessions after school. Other schools use part of the first staff development day. It is recommended that before school dismisses in May, principals put the DMC on the schedule for the opening of school events.

On the calendar of events for the school year, the instructional council (IC) should be scheduled for 1 hour every 4 to 6 weeks. Most often, the IC meets for 1 hour after school. As previously discussed, the IC is composed of one person from each study group, with members attending the IC on a rotating basis. Usually, a member of a study group will only attend one IC meeting per school year.

Times to share what groups are doing and to celebrate successes should also be scheduled. These events may be part of other scheduled meetings, such as faculty meetings.

The total amount of time spent in professional learning communities may seem longer than in other forms of professional development. The total amount of time needed for WFSGs, however, is often less than that spent in traditional workshops, courses, and sessions with speakers during a school year. If study groups meet weekly during a school year, excluding holiday weeks, the total time is approximately 30 hours. Most courses and workshops require 10 contact hours for one credit. Many teachers enroll in courses that award three to five credits—that is, 30 to 50 hours of contact time. Also, it is not unusual for principals and district leaders to schedule speakers, trainers, and other consultants to lead all-day sessions (6 hours). WFSG time is spread out over the year so it may seem, on the surface, to be more time-consuming than it is in reality. It is important to remember that in WFSGs, teachers do what they have chosen to do to address the needs of their students. Teachers are not following a syllabus designed by or expectations set by someone who does not know the students they teach.

ROLES AND RESPONSIBILITIES IN WFSGs

With the implementation of WFSGs, new relationships are forged. Everyone in the school must know and understand the roles that support the WFSG system. Roles and responsibilities of individuals and groups within the WFSG system are grounded in the five guiding principles presented in Chapter 2: Students are first, everyone participates, leadership is shared, responsibility is equal, and the work is public.

Table 4.2 is a list of the responsibilities of the principal, study group leader, individual study group members, focus team, IC representatives, and district leaders.

The Principal

The principal creates the conditions for successful initiation, implementation, and continuation of WFSGs. Sebring and Bryk (2000) reported, for example, that principals of improving schools in Chicago skillfully used a combination of support and pressure to promote teacher collaboration and created time for collaboration and allocated school resources to support the improvement efforts. WFSGs will not accomplish intended purposes, increases in student learning, if the principal does not establish the necessary conditions.

The Focus Team

The focus team is composed of the principal and four or five teachers and is the unit that gets WFSGs started. At the beginning of each school year, the focus team leads the whole faculty through the steps in the WFSG DMC (Chapter 7) to review data that provide direction at the beginning of a cycle.

To begin the first year, the focus team needs special instruction or training. The first year may begin at any time from August through February. The special instruction occurs prior to the beginning of WFSGs. The focus team may attend a district, state, regional, or national WFSG institute that is at least a 2-day training experience. The WFSG National Center sponsors training for focus teams in February, June, and July (www.murphyswfsg.org). A WFSG consultant may conduct training at a school, with the school's focus team serving as assistants while learning the process. A focus team may also organize itself for study around this book and, using Resource B, lead the faculty through the DMC. Any of these training avenues should result in an initiation plan—a step-by-step plan of what to do and who will be responsible for each activity in the plan. The end results of the focus team's work with the whole faculty are that the WFSG process is initiated, including an orientation if one has not been conducted, and the faculty experiences Steps 1 through 4 on the DMC, resulting in the identification of student needs and the formation of study groups.

There is a common misunderstanding about the focus team. Faculty members not on the team perceive the focus team to be "experts" in WFSGs because members attended training. It is not generally understood that the team learned only how to get the study groups started, hardly scratching the surface of the complexity of the system. Once study groups are formed, individuals on the focus team are members of study groups with the same status as other study group members. By the time WFSGs get started, all faculty members have the same information. In some situations, if the school or district contracts with the WFSG National Center and a consultant from the center continues to work with the focus team during the school year, members of the focus team will have procedures in place for providing new information to all faculty.

Because of the specificity of the focus team's initial tasks, it is recommended that, regardless of the size of the school, the focus team be limited to four to six members. Just as with study groups, the larger the size, the more difficult it is for members of the focus team to meet for additional planning sessions and equally

Whole-Faculty Study Groups

Roles and Responsibilities

The Principal

- Is the sponsor and the key advocate
- Is an active participant in training and planning sessions
- Receives the action plans and responds to the plans
- Receives the study group logs and responds to the logs
- Ensures that there is time for study groups to meet and guards that time
- Helps to identify expertise, both internal and external, to support study group work
- Assists in making arrangements for teachers to observe students in each other's classes
- Establishes and maintains internal communication networks among study groups
- Puts the monthly meetings of the instructional council on the school calendar and attends the meetings
- Receives the names of the representatives that will attend an IC meeting and confirms logistics with all the representatives, e.g., date, time, location, what to bring
- Uses the study groups as the primary units to implement the school's improvement plan
- Communicates what study groups do to district leaders, parents, and the general community
- Is assertive in providing technical assistance to a study group that loses its momentum or is not doing work that is likely to impact student learning
- Initiates procedures for the study groups to assess results

The Study Group Leader

- Rotates weekly, every 2 weeks, or monthly so that leadership is a shared responsibility among all study group members
- Confirms logistics with study group members (e.g., date, time, location, resources)
- Checks the log from the last meeting to confirm what the focus of the meeting will be
- Checks the logs to see if it is time to revisit the action plan and the group norms, then taking the appropriate action
- Starts and ends the meeting on time
- Reminds members who stray from the focus of the meeting to refocus
- Sees that the study group log is completed and that the members and the principal receive a copy

Individual Study Group Members

- Respect norms established by the study group
- Take turns serving as leader, recognizing that leadership is a shared responsibility
- Take turns representing the study group at an instructional council meeting and bring back to the study group what they have learned
- Commit to the actions on the study group action plan
- Take responsibility for their own learning and for seeking resources
- Take responsibility for regularly bringing student work to the study group meeting
- Bring back to the study group what they have done in the classroom as a result of the study group work

Table 4.2 WFSG Roles and Responsibilities

Whole-Faculty Study Groups

Roles and Responsibilities

The Focus Team

- Is the principal and a representative group of teachers
- Attends training to deepen their understanding of WFSGs and to learn how to lead the faculty through the decision-making cycle
- Leads the whole faculty, if one has not already been done, in an orientation to define WFSGs, review the research supporting WFSGs, develop understanding of the functions of WFSGs, and present the 15 WFSG guidelines
- Leads the whole faculty through the decision-making cycle (Steps 1 – 4) that results in establishing what study groups will do and in the establishment of study groups
- Leads the whole faculty through the decision-making cycle at the beginning of each school year to establish/confirm the work of study groups
- Is represented on the instructional council

Instructional Council Representatives

- Represent each study group (one representative per study group)
- Rotate membership, except for the principal and representation of the focus team
- Meet once every 4 or 5 weeks, dates on school calendar
- Share what each study group is doing
- Share successes and challenges
- Are a training unit for skills that need to be shared with study groups
- Plan celebrations and whole-faculty sharing times
- Make decisions regarding formal procedures for assessing study group work
- Take at least 15 minutes of the next study group meeting to share information
- May need to take one full meeting to teach the study group a protocol or to lead the study group in learning more about a given topic
- Chart changes in student learning and keep student data on the table

District Level Support Staff

- Collect and distribute relevant information to the principal
- Assist the focus team, as needed
- Help identify and make available district resources
- Attend faculty meetings and training sessions, as appropriate
- Are knowledgeable about the study group action plans
- Provide expertise to study groups, as needed
- Are advocates for the school with the superintendent and board of education members
- Speak for the school when district budgets are developed
- Support need for time for study groups to meet with responsible parties
- Communicate with district level staff what the study groups are doing

share responsibility for their tasks. There are no criteria for the selection of the focus team other than that members should represent a cross section of the grades at the school. Before accepting responsibility, prospective members should be given a written description of the team's responsibilities.

The Study Group Leader

The leader of a study group requires no special training. The work of the group gives the group its direction, as per the study group action plan. The focus of a study group is on the work of the group, not on that of any individual member. All members are equal in status and share responsibility for the work and success of their study group. Members of a study group rotate leadership every week or after every 2 weeks.

The Individual Study Group Member

The most important role in study groups is that of the individual member. If the study group is productive, it will be because every single member does his or her part. It will be because each member participates and is willing to give his or her colleagues what they require to be successful. The success of WFSGs rests on the shoulders of each member. WFSGs are only as successful as each member feels them to be. Each member of a study group has students for whom he or she is responsible. The critical end result of WFSGs is that each student learns more. This student focus requires that teachers enable each of their students to learn more.

The Instructional Council

The IC comprises a representative from each study group, the principal, and one or two members of the focus team. The primary purposes of the IC are to communicate among the study groups and to deliver information to each study group (see Figure 4.2). The IC meets every 4 to 6 weeks. The functions of the IC and the focus team are different. The focus team leads the faculty through the DMC at the beginning of a school year to get study groups started, which requires special training. The IC oversees the total process, maintains WFSGs during the school year, and requires no special training for participation. One or two members from the focus team are standing members of the IC, as is the principal. These individuals rotate serving as facilitators of the IC meetings. Other than these individuals, people attending meetings will usually be different each time the IC meets. Members of study groups rotate attending IC meetings. For instance, if there were five members of a study group, each member would attend only one meeting of the IC during a school year. People who attend the IC meetings are referred to as representatives, not members.

The group of representatives may be given any name, such as representative council, that does not conflict with the name of another group at the school. WFSGs are focused on the instructional needs of students; therefore, "instruction" seems to be an appropriate term to use for this representative group. The IC is the logical group to receive special instruction or training during the school year in new skills that study groups need to deepen the work. For example, study groups need to learn how to use protocols for examining student work. Training in how to use protocols

WFSG Instructional Council:
A Network for Communication and Support

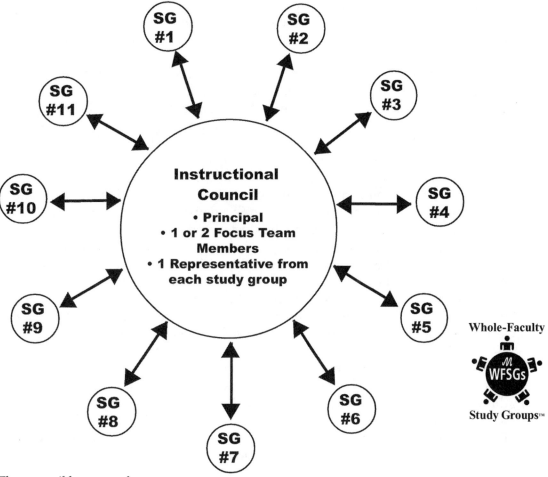

The council has several purposes:

1. To keep communication open among all study groups.
2. To review all action plans and revised plans.
3. For study group representatives to share what the groups are doing.
4. To hear problems groups are experiencing and to have joint participation in how those problems might be solved.
5. To share successes and plan for dissemination of those successes.
6. To determine how groups can share resources.
7. To determine if the whole faculty requires common training.
8. To coordinate events, speakers.
9. To plan whole-faculty sharings and celebrations.
10. To identify common instructional concerns.
11. To set instructional goals.
12. To set limits on instructional initiatives.

The Council meets every 4 to 6 weeks, meeting the first time immediately after all groups have met twice.

Figure 4.2   WFSG Instructional Council Network

appropriately is usually not included in the orientation to WFSGs or in the session on the DMC. A consultant or other experienced leader in the use of protocols can provide instruction to the IC. At the next round of study group meetings, the members who attended the IC meeting would share the information with their study groups. There may be times during the school year when the representatives will need release time, an hour or as long as a day, to receive special instruction. Resource E contains agendas and minutes from IC meetings and strategies for making meetings productive.

The operation and functions of the IC in large schools and small schools are the same. The only factor that may need modification is the number of study group representatives that attend the IC meetings. One large high school had 47 study groups. Obviously, it would be difficult for 47 study group representatives to meet together and accomplish the IC's purposes. This school clustered the study groups, placing 3 study groups in each cluster for a total of 16 clusters. The 3 study groups in a cluster rotated sending a representative. Thus, if the IC met six times during the school year, only two members from each study group would have to have attended an IC meeting during the school year. In September, a schedule was established so everyone would know the rotation. The cluster study groups of three met for approximately 15 minutes during the study group meeting that immediately followed the IC meeting. If more time was needed, study groups in the cluster could meet for the full hour. This would be the case when the representatives must teach study group members how to use a particular protocol or group technique. When clustering is done, it makes sense to cluster study groups that are doing similar work. For instance, technology study groups could be one cluster. Not only does the clustering facilitate communication but also it gives study groups addressing similar student needs the opportunity to share. In large schools, clustering provides a forum to accomplish a number of professional development needs, especially in the area of training. It is difficult to address any type of professional development need with more than 100 teachers in a large room at one time. The high school that had 47 study groups had a faculty of more than 250 teachers. The study group organization and the clustering system helped the school tailor its professional development needs.

DISTRICT INFLUENCES

The literature on school improvement has stressed the important role that districts can play in improving instruction by providing vision, focus, support, and policy coordination and by building commitment at the school level (Bodilly, 1998; Elmore & Burney, 1997; Murray & Hallinger, 1988; Spillane, 1996). Corcoran, Fuhrman, and Belcher (2001) report on a study conducted by the Consortium for Policy Research in Education. The study examined the roles played by central office staff members in shaping instructional reform in three large urban districts. The researchers organized their findings into three broad categories that represent the major strategic decisions that face any organization seeking to improve its performance:

1. Deciding what to do—the problem of design and adoption

2. Determining how to get it done—the problem of support and coordination, which includes the need to focus people's attention on the desired changes,

ensure effective implementation, reduce distractions, and buffer the work from competing agendas

3. Scaling up the reforms if they are successful—the problem of replication

These strategic decisions have major implications for all leaders as everyone struggles with meeting the demands of lawmakers, community leaders, and parents. One of the findings is most aligned with our experience in the continuation of WFSGs. In all three districts in which the study occurred, within 4 years of launching the reforms, the superintendents who had led the design of the initiatives left under pressure from their boards and local political leaders. In our work, we have found that the instability of the tenure of superintendents and principals creates a sense of disbelief in faculties that an initiative will actually "stay the course." A new superintendent or principal most often arrives with his or her own ideas of what works best.

Districts Both Facilitate and Constrain Schools

As we consider the context of schools, we underscore the influence of the school district in which a school is located and the district leaders who are ultimately held responsible for the school. Schools exist within the context of school districts. The school district is in fact the structural organization that typically shapes schools and schooling. It is the central board of education and district administrators who are ultimately responsible for what happens in schools. The district can be one of the most important sponsors of innovation in schools or a serious inhibitor of progress. The district level both constrains and facilitates. It provides a kind of supported enforcement. The culture of the district gives the underlying structure of meaning, and it permeates schools. It facilitates or constrains school administrators' and teachers' perceptions, interpretations, and behaviors. Schools want approval of district leaders and to be consistent and in compliance with district expectations. The district has influence that affects almost every major decision that school personnel make. Districts can reward, censure, or sanction. Often, that influence is invisible, not generally openly discussed. It is there, however. The district office can be a critical sponsor of change; it creates conditions for the process of change, establishes specific district goals, ensures accountability, and sets time lines. It is the district that initiates most of the instructional innovations that confront schools. The district usually sets priorities for budgets. How much money schools have for staff development, heavily influenced by district priorities, determines what schools can do. Districts determine whether consultants are used, what materials are purchased, whether teachers are paid for their involvement in staff development activities, and whether substitutes are obtained to release teachers for study or training.

Schools frequently have building-level responsibility for implementation and staff flexibility to respond to their environment but not at the expense of district goals and priorities. It seems that the matter of school-district balance is not easily solvable. It represents an inherently complex dilemma between autonomy and accountability and variation and consistency.

The major problem faced by school districts and schools is not so much resistance to innovation but the fragmentation, overload, and incoherence resulting from the uncritical and uncoordinated acceptance of too many innovations (Fullan, 2001a; see also the Assimilation Capacity section in Chapter 5). The key role of the district support staff is to help schools sort out and implement correct choices for each school. Many good programs are diffused at the school level simply because schools are unclear as to the district-level priority of the program. A major function of WFSGs is to set school priorities and focus on implementing those priorities to the level that student effects are measurable. The school faculty is asked to identify instructional initiatives and bring coherence to what they and the school are trying to do.

Responses of District Leaders Often Differ

Murphy's work as the administrator of a school district's staff development programs for 15 years gave her an insider's view of the operation of a school district with 60 schools within its jurisdiction. Within the context of WFSGs or any other school initiative, it is appropriate to examine how various district-level leaders respond to innovations that are in various stages of implementation in schools. A district-level leader is defined as a person with a title, such as superintendent, assistant superintendent, director, coordinator, and curriculum specialist. Such individuals are usually not assigned full-time to any particular school and work under the supervision of the superintendent, an assistant superintendent, or a department director. A conversation Murphy had with colleague Mike McMann in Seattle, Washington, added validity to Murphy's experiences. The two agreed that district-level leaders in the same district respond to an initiative in different ways, as do leaders in schools. The response may be to prevent, ignore, permit, acknowledge, expect, or empower. One leader may actually take action to prevent an initiative from happening. Another may simply ignore what is happening or about to happen. A leader with authority may permit an initiative to happen without actually encouraging the initiators or acknowledging work that the faculty has done. This last response makes school leaders uneasy and seems to be the most damaging, especially in the first year of implementation. It is somewhat of a "wait and see" position, and just when the school requires the most visible support, key district support personnel, such as curriculum specialists, are unsure about priorities. As an initiative gets under way, the leader who permitted the work to begin may quickly move to acknowledgment. For example, in Augusta, Georgia, the superintendent, who permitted the Models of Teaching (MOT) program work to begin, started many of the principals' meetings by having a principal of a MOT school share the good work the faculty was doing. This form of acknowledgment is very powerful.

Once an initiative is under way, some leaders will ignore the work or try to prevent it from continuing. Some leaders who once ignored the work or may have even tried to prevent it from happening will come to acknowledge and expect the work to continue and improve. Some leaders who once publicly acknowledged the work or expected the work to begin and continue may at some later time try to prevent it from continuing. Leaders may, in fact, change their positions or attitudes toward an innovation. Teachers in schools find these responses both confusing and disheartening. Teachers may hear rumors one day that the work will continue, and the next day they may hear that continuation is not supported. Teachers may hear that one influential person feels one way and another influential person feels the opposite. The clatter in district offices has a significant influence on how principals and teachers feel and act in schools. It also affects the context of schooling. For a school initiative, such as WFSGs, to have the early momentum required to get

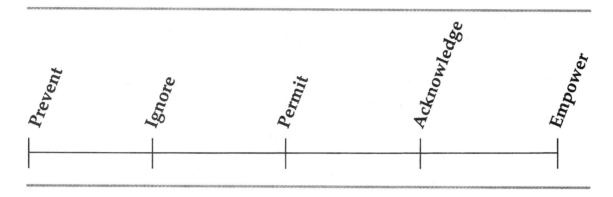

Figure 4.3   Leadership Response to Initiatives

groups moving and for teachers to be willing to spend the extra time and energy on collaborative work, continuous acknowledgment from the district office is essential.

Figure 4.3, which shows leadership responses to initiatives, does not represent a linear movement. A leader may initially respond to an initiative at one point, such as "permit," and over a period of time offer another response, such as to "empower" the initiators or to "ignore" the initiative.

SCHOOLS FOLLOW
THE LEAD OF THE DISTRICT

Schools that have been most successful in initiating and implementing WFSGs are those in districts that value schools as learning communities for the adults in their schools. Most of the initiators of the study group process are district leaders. Districts have used district funds to supplement school funds in efforts to support the study group process. Districts have recognized WFSG schools and asked their principals to speak at meetings of administrators. When districts stop showing signs of approval and support for what schools do, schools become discouraged, regardless of how well the process is going. Schools follow the lead of the district. As district interests shift, so will school interests (Murphy, 1991b).

Everyone must take seriously the sponsorship role that districts play in change at the school level. People often forget that the district, not the schools, employs teachers and administrators. For the vast majority of teachers, districts are unquestionably important organizations. Most teachers, however, especially in large districts, only vaguely perceive district relationships. Districts are often thought of as unpredictable and hostile—the "they" who make ill-informed and unwelcome decisions. If positive change is desired in schools, then there must be as much concern given to the quality of district leadership and sponsorship as there is to the quality of schools.

Districts and Continuation of School Initiatives

As previously discussed, the district culture or context has a huge impact on the school. This is often most evident when a school is in the late stages of implementing an initiative and is moving into the institutionalization stage. Frequently, schools have special funding sources (e.g., grants) to begin an initiative, and after 2 or 3 years the district is expected to "pick up" the funding of the initiative by budgeting funds for continuing costs (e.g., personnel costs and time for professional development). In Murphy's work with ATLAS Communities, a national comprehensive school reform design, she has seen the work diluted or discontinued when full responsibility shifts to the district. One of the most puzzling aspects of the lack of continuation is that success does not guarantee that an initiative will be continued. Most often, in ATLAS Communities' schools there were proven results. Leaders of initiatives in schools and districts assume that if success can be validated through student results, support for the initiative will grow. Because of the organization pattern of many school districts, however, what makes one school or department look good may in fact make another school or department look less than good. If an initiative is primarily sponsored by the staff development department and it is successful, it may make other department heads feel less successful. What we are suggesting here is that power relationships or power struggles are part of the context of districts and schools. Seymour Sarason (1990) wrote, "Schools will remain intractable to desired reform as long as we avoid confronting their existing power relationships" (p. 5). Sarason continues, "Changing power relationships consistent with the goals of the changes is, to indulge understatement, no simple affair. History, tradition, overlearned attitudes, and unrealistic time perspectives ensure turmoil" (p. 64). We mention this only because we do not want initiators and implementers of WFSGs to feel personal defeat if WFSGs do not continue in schools. Continuation is often due to factors over which they have no control. The worth of a program or practice may not be great enough for organizational support to continue. It is difficult for schools to continue an initiative without the ongoing support of district leaders. Likewise, it is difficult for teachers to continue an initiative without the ongoing support of the principal, especially structural changes such as WFSGs. Even with documented student benefits, lack of perceived support within the organization may simply be too great to overcome. As noted previously, initiators of major change often feel that they failed when, after several years, a successful initiative is not continued at the organizational level. If any type of student benefits are evident, however, even after 1 year, we believe the effort had success and should be celebrated.

Using WFSGs as an example, four schools in a district had WFSGs in place for 4 years and student benefits were evident. A new superintendent discontinued the early release for students that had provided the time for study groups to meet in all of the four schools. The superintendent made it clear that the new prescriptive reading series would provide whatever staff development the teachers needed, and that consultants from the publishing company would provide workshops for teachers after school, on Saturdays, and on staff development days. During the first year of the superintendent's tenure, all four schools tried with varying degrees of effort to keep the study groups in place to support the training being provided by the consultants. The teachers, feeling the pressure from all directions in addition to having to spend extra time in workshops, eventually stopped trying to work against what they saw as a lack of organizational support for the study groups. Without ongoing, broad-based pressure and support from the principal for WFSGs, and with new initiatives sponsored by the new superintendent getting the attention, the powerful study group routine was broken. We do not want to leave this example on a negative note. Instead, we ask, does the break discredit WFSGs or cancel out benefits to students and staff when the study groups were in place? No. Students and staff benefited from the work, and those benefits will enhance the future work of the students and teachers.

Moving Schools in Moving Districts

Rosenholtz (1989) defined stuck and moving environments as learning-impoverished and learning-enriched environments for the adults and students, respectively. She found that moving schools (learning-enriched schools) were typically found in moving districts, and stuck schools (learning-impoverished schools) were most often found in stuck districts. Rosenholtz stated that we must examine interorganizational relations and those conditions that drive schools to more or less efficient ends. She suggested that the keys to unlocking sustained commitment and capacity for schools' continuous renewal include the following:

- How districts select principals and teachers
- Whether districts offer them continuous opportunities for learning
- Whether task autonomy is delegated to schools and thereafter monitored

How these three areas are dealt with can greatly facilitate the initiation and continuation of WFSGs or inhibit them. It is almost impossible for schools to redesign themselves without district sponsorship. The role of the district is critical. Individual schools can become highly innovative for short periods of time without the district, but they cannot sustain innovation over time without district action and support to establish conditions for continuous and long-term improvement (Levine & Eubanks, 1989).

SUMMARY

In this chapter, we presented in detail several of the contextual conditions that support WFSG work. We know that the context of school reform offers us the greatest challenge. Where change happens has to be the first consideration of those working with and in schools. We have to know where we are before we can get to where we want to go. Every school is unique. Every school, like every individual, has a personality of its own. Two schools just blocks away from one another, serving the same community and operating under the same policies and procedures, can be as different as night and day. We cannot work in one school like we work in another school. Although all WFSG schools follow the same 15 procedural guidelines, how these guidelines work within the context of a school makes the process different. The individuality of the people in schools, adults and students, makes the difference. Even with WFSG guidelines and other consistent WFSG features, there is no cookie-cutter solution. In the WFSG jar, each cookie is different. The contextual conditions make the difference.

5

Recognizing and Understanding School Culture

School culture is not always visible to outsiders and even to many within it, but it is always there and always powerful and rigid. The culture is the social and normative glue, the common bond, that holds together the educational and educationally related aspects of a school and creates the central features, structures, and approaches that characterize it (Birmbaum, 1988).

The culture is what sets one school distinctly apart from another; it is a school's self-concept, analogous to an individual's personality. The culture of a school, for example, establishes a unique set of ground rules, both stated and unstated, for how people in the school think and behave and for what they assume to be true.

SCHOOL CULTURE IS CENTRAL TO UNDERSTANDING THE CONTEXT

Schools have evolved over a long period of time, and our general approaches to schooling have been in place for centuries. As a consequence, schools have well-established cultures, a part of the context for the study group environment (referred to in Chapter 4). School cultures give schools and their programs stability and govern how issues are addressed and what can happen in schools. School cultures are fairly rigid, however, and make schools far less open to change than might be desirable when trying to introduce new concepts and practices for the enhancement of student learning and school improvement.

Among the best mechanisms for bringing about meaningful cultural change are professional Whole-Faculty Study Groups (WFSGs). When properly supported and applied, study groups have the potential to modify aspects of a school culture to allow for enough change so that educational processes and schools can be improved. Why is this so important? Because school cultures, like many other cultures, are difficult to productively and qualitatively change. Although not all cultural change is valuable, positive school change will occur only when aspects of the school's culture are changed appropriately.

Because our interests in culture focus on its relationship to change (e.g., student learning enhancement and school improvement), we use a definition adapted from Conner (1993) that has been used successfully in organizational change efforts:

> School culture reflects the interrelationship of shared assumptions, beliefs, and behaviors that are acquired over time by members of a school.

BUILDING BLOCKS OF SCHOOL CULTURE

As stated previously, key building blocks of the culture of a school are the assumptions, beliefs, and behaviors of the school and its personnel. To change the culture of the school for its improvement, one must change one or more of the assumptions, beliefs, and behaviors.

Assumptions in a school are the unconscious and therefore unquestioned perceptions concerning what is important and how people and things operate in and relating to the school—that is, the unconscious rationale for people continuing to use certain beliefs and behaviors. For example, teachers often have the unconscious assumption that the lecture approach is a good way to teach, whereas research indicates that, in fact, there may be more effective approaches.

Beliefs are the values and expectations that people hold to be true about themselves, others, their work, and the school. They provide a basis for what people in the school hold to be right or wrong, true or false, good or bad, and relevant or irrelevant about their school and its operation. Belief statements in schools, for instance, relate to such things as the vital role played by the personal interaction of the teachers and students, the importance of lesson plans, and the need for staff development.

Behaviors are the ways people conduct themselves on a day-to-day basis. They are perceptible actions that are based on values and expectations and are ideally aimed at carrying out the school's mission. Whereas assumptions and beliefs often reflect intentions that are difficult to discern, behaviors are observable and can be noted objectively. Behaviors of teachers may include such things as how they teach, prepare lesson plans, and use technology and for administrators may be how they assess teaching, involve faculty in decision making, and encourage innovation.

Teachers in a WFSG school often have had unconscious assumptions about their self-esteem and professionalism. Their WFSG efforts helped them see themselves more like other professionals, changing their unconscious assumptions about their self-esteem and professional outlook dramatically. The changes in these assumptions also brought about changes in the teachers' beliefs and behaviors of themselves, representing positive, major shifts in their effectiveness and in the general faculty and school culture.

School cultures can be realigned through a process called *cultural shift*. Such a cultural transformation requires realigning, in some measure, assumptions, beliefs, and behaviors to make them more consistent with the new directions of the school. One important strength of the study group process is that it has the capability to bring about cultural shifts and, through such shifts, desirable changes in how a school functions, such as follows, with the flow being more like a wave than a sequence:

Study groups → Cultural changes → Student changes

We outline study group processes in later chapters and show how these processes lead to important cultural shifts in schools.

ASSIMILATION CAPACITY

One of the major problems for schools (and most other organizations as well) and their personnel is that they have too many change efforts going on at any one time. People and schools have only so much capacity or resources to deal with change—their *assimilation capacity*. The assimilation capacity is different for different individuals; some individuals have little capacity to deal with change, whereas others may have substantial capacity. The same is true for groups and organizations, with some having limited assimilation capacity and others having much more.

When there is so much change that an individual's assimilation capacity is surpassed, then that individual's efforts are degraded and the individual performs below normal levels of productivity and quality. Such an individual is said to be *dysfunctional*, and his or her actions or feelings divert resources away from meeting the desired productivity and quality standards. Dysfunctional individuals perform below their normal levels of productivity and quality, as do dysfunctional groups and schools. Dysfunctional behaviors in individuals range, for example, from low levels (symptoms: poorer communications, reduced risk taking, and lower morale) to high levels (symptoms: covertly undermining of the leadership, chronic depression, and physical breakdown). Simply stated, if individuals, groups, or schools are asked to handle too much change, they will become dysfunctional and cannot perform optimally. Many schools and faculties today exceed their assimilation capacities and are, in fact, dysfunctional. The following is a three-step process for dealing with such concerns:

1. Leaders should learn about limited assimilation capacities and associated dysfunctions and their serious negative impact on their people and schools.

2. Before initiating new projects, a listing of all existing change projects should be prepared and prioritized, ranging from low priority to high priority or imperatives—those projects that will make significant differences.

3. All but the highest-priority projects should be considered for termination or reduction in scope, and a plan should be implemented to eliminate or reduce as many of the nonimperative projects as is practical and cost-effective.

ROLES OF CHANGE IN SCHOOLS

As schools attempt to build commitment for study group efforts that affect their people, processes, and outcomes, an understanding of the four roles of change—change sponsor, change agent, change target, and change advocate—is critical.

A *change sponsor* or *sponsor* is an individual or group who has the power to sanction or legitimize the change or efforts of the study group. In schools, depending on the specific change effort, a sponsor might be the school board, superintendent, principal, or a combination of these individuals because they typically are the ones, with final authority, who can sanction or legitimize study group efforts and change. Also, in a WFSG situation, in which essentially the whole faculty has endorsed the study group initiative, the faculty becomes an important and potentially effective sponsor.

It is the sponsor's responsibility to (a) decide which initiatives and changes will be authorized; (b) communicate his or her decisions and priorities to the school and its personnel; and (c) provide the appropriate encouragement, pressure, and support for study groups' efforts. Strong sponsors are essential to the building of commitment and can create a school environment that enables study group efforts to be especially productive.

In school districts that seriously choose to participate in study groups, sponsors make the study group process both important to the schools and legitimate for principals, teachers, and others to invest time and serious commitment. A *change agent* or *agent* is an individual or group responsible for implementing a desired change. Teachers and study groups often play the role of change agent, as do various administrators and supervisors. Agents' success depends on their preparation as change agents; relations with others in the school; and ability to diagnose problems, deal with the issues, plan solutions, and implement their plan effectively. A *change target* or *target* is an individual or group who must actually change.

Targets are the people who must change if innovation is to be successful. In school improvement projects, targets typically are students, teachers, and administrators. Targets will be more responsive to our change efforts if we put things in their frame of reference and help them fully understand the desired change, why it is important, what is expected of them, and the impact that the change will have on them and the school. Fullan (2001a) states that people must be able to attach their own personal meaning to the change experiences. The change agent, then, must be alert to how the meaning of change is communicated to the targets of the change. Figure 2.2 illustrates that teachers and students are expected to change with the implementation of WFSGs.

A *change advocate* or *advocate* is an individual or group who desires a change but does not have the authority or power to sanction it. Frequently, faculty study groups, the principal, or nonschool persons or groups, such as parents, play the role of advocate when they want something to happen but do not have the power to approve it. Advocates typically recommend actions to those with the authority to approve or further recommend. For instance, a community person may advocate for a special resolution to the school board, or a department chair may ask the principal for a budget consideration. Note, however, that advocates are not sponsors or effective replacements for sponsors.

In different circumstances, an individual or group may play different change roles. A typical example is when a principal is a change agent to the superintendent but a sponsor to school teachers. The important thing to remember is to determine the role you are playing in the given situation and perform it well.

EFFECTIVE SPONSORSHIP OF CHANGE IN SCHOOLS

All four change roles are necessary for the success of WFSGs. The roles of those in leadership positions are especially critical, however. When the responsibilities of the principal were listed previously, the first item was the sponsor, and for district influence, the district is one of the most important sponsors. For major innovations to be successfully implemented in our schools, sponsors must demonstrate strong, decisive, and visible commitment to those efforts. Simply, significant change will not occur without sufficient commitment and action by sponsors, such as those by a board of education, superintendents, and principals. Sponsors must show strong commitment to ensure that agents and targets are effective in their roles. Often, the difference between success and failure in school efforts comes down to the quality of the sponsorship.

In an excellent book on change, Conner (1993) outlines the characteristics of a good sponsor. An adaptation of these characteristics in the school setting follows:

- Power: Power in the school to legitimize the change with targets
- Pain: Discomfort with some area of the school that makes change there attractive
- Vision: Clear understanding of what change must occur
- Resources: Commitment of school resources (e.g., time, money, and people) necessary for successful implementation
- Long view: Understanding of the effect the change will have on the school
- Sensitivity: Appreciation for the personal issues raised by the change
- Scope: Capacity to understand fully the impact of the change
- Public role: Demonstration of public support to gain others' commitment
- Private role: Capacity to convey strong support to key individuals or groups
- Management: Capacity to reward facilitators and disapprove inhibitors
- Monitor: Capacity to monitor both the progress and the problems of the transition
- Sacrifice: Commitment to pursue the transition, knowing there is a cost for change
- Persistence: Demonstration of consistent long-term support for the change

If most of the above sponsorship criteria are met, there is a high probability for good sponsorship and support. If several of these are not satisfied, however, leaders should work to improve sponsorship for the effort or replace the sponsors with stronger ones.

WFSGs and their schoolwide efforts represent major change in the school. As a result, they will require the same strong and effective sponsorship as that outlined previously. What should be done if sponsorship is weak? When sponsors are not fully committed to the study group process, do not fully understand it, or are unable or unwilling to provide adequate support, there are only three options (Conner, 1993): strengthen sponsorship, find strong alternate sponsorship, or prepare to fail.

Strong sponsorship is absolutely essential to the success of WFSGs and their desired change initiatives!

HUMAN CHANGE AND RESISTANCE IN SCHOOLS

There is one certainty with change: Someone will resist. Why? Because resistance is natural and normal for people. Nonetheless, if there were one point we would like to communicate, it would be this: Do not let resisters stop necessary change. Too often, we let a small, loud percentage of a faculty rule the day. We should listen to concerns of others, try to understand, and take their concerns into consideration. At some point, however, we simply have to get started, include those resisting in study groups, and assume that in a small group with peers, their concerns can be worked out. Murphy often illustrates this point when she tells a story about a teacher in Augusta, Georgia, who initially was very reticent and vocal about her objection and opposition to the whole school improvement program. The teacher did not want to be a member of a study group; like all teachers at the school, however, she was included in a study group. From August through October, she was cool to other members and somewhat reluctant to fully participate. By January, she was demonstrating strategies to her study group colleagues and bringing student work to show how well her students were responding. By April, she was being videotaped as an example of how to effectively use the strategies and study group meetings to fine-tune a lesson. Within 2 years, she was a member of Murphy's staff. Suppose she had been allowed not to participate? The gulf between this teacher and those teachers in study groups would have widened, and her constructive contributions would have been lost.

In their book chapter titled "The States of Growth of People in the Organizations," Joyce and Showers (1995) describe how individuals interact with the environment, drawing conclusions from 300 educators in 21 districts. They relate three prototypes that are useful in helping staff developers understand behaviors of individuals. One prototype is a "gourmet omnivore," those individuals, approximately 20% of the total, who exploit and enrich whatever environment they find themselves in. The next prototype is a "passive consumer," those individuals, approximately 70%, whose degree of activity greatly depends on who they are with—amiable, though unenterprising. The third prototype is a "reticent consumer," those individuals, approximately 10%, who expend energy actually pushing away opportunities for growth. Joyce and Showers state, "The hard-core reticent even rejects opportunities for involvement in decision making, regarding them as co-opting moves by basically malign forces" (p. 179). Knowing that approximately 70% of individuals in schools are passive consumers, we have a better sense for creating the WFSG environment. In particular, WFSGs stimulate passive consumers and cause them to participate more fully. This passive consumer group is the population on which we should focus. What do we do? In WFSG schools, we simply include them. By including them, we gain a chance to have an impact on their attitude and behaviors and to benefit from their input.

We must remember that resisters teach children, too. Philip Schlechty (1993) writes that individuals play different roles in the restructuring process. The five types of roles that are activated are trailblazer, pioneer, settler, stay-at-home, and saboteur. The first three will go where they need to go and do what they need to do, just at different rates. The trailblazers are the first to go, not afraid to venture into the unknown; the pioneers follow, often cutting their own paths before the roads are clear; the settlers wait until they have assurances that roads are clear and some bridges have been built. The settlers go in large groups, believing that there is safety in numbers. This is the largest group, and as with any major movement, it is the settlers that will bring stability. These are the folks who, after they understand and accept what is ahead of them, we know we can depend on. The stay-at-homes will not keep the others from going, but they are simply happy with the way things are and want to stay put. After everyone else has gone, however, they do not want to be alone, and they will come lagging behind and grumbling. The saboteurs do not want to move and are not going to let anyone else move either. They are lone rangers who are not afraid of taking risks and who have many of the same qualities and needs as trailblazers. Leaders are wise to keep the saboteurs in sight.

The foregoing two ways of thinking about individuals make for fun and interesting conversations, putting faces on each type of individual. We do not think one should take this discussion too literally, however, because individuals change roles depending on the issue. Nevertheless, it is good to have some frame of reference when we are initiating and implementing major change efforts, such as WFSGs. When one works with an all-inclusive system, there are all types of individuals within the circle.

We also know that human beings have a strong need for control (Conner, 1993). This is especially true with regard to change. When we have a sense of control over change and its circumstances, we typically feel comfortable. Therefore, the change we initiate, understand, and have a sense of control over is a change with which we are comfortable.

There are actually two types of control we all seek: *direct control*, in which we have the direct ability to request or actually dictate outcomes that usually occur, and *indirect control*, in which we have the ability to at least anticipate the outcomes of a change. People usually have the highest level of comfort when they have a sense of direct control.

Indirect control results in less, but important, comfort with change. For example, if I am not in direct control of some change but understand it and know the implications of it, I then can anticipate what will occur. This, again, is indirect control, and I will feel less threatened by the change than if I had no sense of the possible outcomes.

What all this means is that if leaders of an innovation want people to feel comfortable with a particular change, they must do whatever is appropriate and necessary to give others a sense of control, either direct or indirect, for the change effort. If this can be done, leaders enhance the chances that people will be helpful with the change.

If people are not given some sense of control over the change, however, they may feel threatened. As a result, they will do what comes naturally when people do not understand or appreciate what is going on: They will resist the change either openly and overtly or covertly. Human resistance to change is not an aberration or a reflection that something is wrong with someone. Instead, it is a natural reaction to change when one does not understand the change and its implications. Consequently, if you do not want people to resist, then, very simply, you must help them understand the change and its implications and give them a sense of either direct or indirect control. The major change principle that describes how to do this is discussed in the next section.

UNIVERSAL CHANGE PRINCIPLE FOR SCHOOLS

In this section, we describe a critical principle for dealing with and helping others deal with change. It establishes a contextual condition that prepares others for change. This gives an overarching approach for leading and managing change and is applicable for change virtually everywhere. Thus, we call it the *universal change principle*.

For our discussion of change and the universal change principle, think of *learning* as gaining information, knowledge, or understanding for effective action relative to the change or the implications of the change under consideration in schools.

> *Universal change principle: Learning must precede change.*

That is, if people are to help bring about change, then they must be provided with the appropriate "learning," in advance, so that they understand and appreciate the change and its implications. Providing the appropriate learning allows people to gain a reasonable sense of control with respect to the change.

Appropriate learning may include knowing the theoretical and practical underpinnings that support the proposition that the new process, practice, program, attitude, belief, or material would bring about the desired change in a specific school or with a particular group of students. When initiators or change agents confirm with teachers that there are few clear answers that fit every situation, teachers are more likely to see themselves as experts in their situation, given the latitude to find the answers for their students. Teachers with this attitude and who are part of a strong support system will be less likely to become frustrated and rebellious when the proposed changes hit snags. Learning that precedes the change includes a clarification of the meaning of the change and whatever information is required for the proposed implementers to agree to begin.

For example, a simple illustration of the universal change principle might be that of a driver who wants to make a turn ahead. He provides learning for those behind him by lighting his turn signal a few hundred feet before the turn. As a result, other drivers learn of the first driver's desired change and then have time to make appropriate adjustments. In this case, learning preceded change for the success and safety of all.

A school example might involve a principal who wants the mathematics faculty to use a new approach for teaching basic mathematics. If that principal just announces one day that starting next semester the mathematics faculty will teach by the new method, probably most of the faculty will be unfamiliar with the new approach, not understand its value and implementation, not feel comfortable with this new change, and, as a consequence, resist rather than be helpful with what the principal desires to have happen.

Suppose, instead, that the principal uses the universal change principle to guide the implementation of what he or she desires to have happen. The principal would first ask, "What learning must take place before this change can be successfully implemented?" Then, the principal would most likely involve the mathematics faculty in a series of discussions concerning (a) what he or she is thinking about;

(b) why this is important to improving student learning and to the faculty and school; (c) what the implications are for the students, faculty, and school; (d) what training and support will be provided; (e) how people will be rewarded for participating; and (f) how and when the new approach should be implemented. Doing this does not guarantee that everyone will support the change and that resistance will be averted. It does, however, ensure greater understanding of what is desired, why it is important, and its implications for students, faculty, and the school. It helps the faculty gain a sense of control for the project, making them feel much more comfortable with it and its implementation. As a result, the faculty are far more likely to help with the change rather than resist it. The proper application of the universal change principle does take additional time and effort but generally pays off handsomely in terms of real accomplishment in the end.

This is an excellent example of the concept of "slowing down to speed up"—that is, taking a little longer initially to provide the appropriate learning, and then being able to speed up the process later as a consequence of the learning foundation provided earlier. Notice that the universal change principle also implies "No surprises!" Change surprises only add to the anxiety and fear and increase resistance and reduce others' support of change. Also, the universal change principle implies that if there is to be a lot of change, then there must be a lot of learning taking place first. In fact, if the change is major, then several iterations of learning may be required at different times, depending on the change, circumstances, and people involved. For large school changes, typically there must be several applications of the universal change principle at different times and with different groups of people. In fact, it is helpful, in advance of the announcement of a desired change effort, to develop a relatively detailed plan based on the universal change principle. This means that one must determine the groups that must have additional learning and then provide each of them with the appropriate and necessary learning iterations, specifically designed for each group, to precede the desired change.

SUMMARY

In this and the previous chapter, we presented in detail several of the contextual conditions that support WFSG work. Principals often ask whether they should take a particular action. Our most frequent answer is "it depends on the context." The context determines what can be done and what cannot be done without causing an imbalance in roles and relationships and pressure and support. The current norms of the workplace govern how decisions are made, who is included in the decision-making process, and the benefits for honoring the decisions as well as the penalties for not respecting the decisions. The contextual and cultural norms often determine the level of satisfaction individuals have for where they work. In teaching conditions that seem to be the most challenging, teachers will stay because of the professional norms of the school. In schools with high-achieving students, teachers may request transfers because the culture often promotes lower levels of collaboration at the school. A faculty whose members have respect for each other, mutual trust, a willingness to learn from each other, and a desire to put students first is a faculty that, with adequate support from the district and community, will be successful.

6

Process

A Proven Structure for Collaboration

As previously stated, process refers to a particular method of doing something, generally involving a number of steps or operations. In the context of study groups, it relates to how members work together in a group to acquire new knowledge and skills. The Whole-Faculty Study Group (WFSG) approach is a process through which teachers acquire and develop knowledge and skills in a collaborative setting. Intended results of the work are higher student achievement and performance.

NATIONAL STAFF DEVELOPMENT COUNCIL'S STAFF DEVELOPMENT PROCESS STANDARDS

The National Staff Development Council's (NSDC) staff development standards (NSDC, 2003) are grounded in research that documents the connection between staff development and student learning. The standards are organized into context standards, process standards, and content standards. The process standards recognize that staff development that improves student learning for all students has the following characteristics:

- Data-driven: Uses disaggregated student data to determine adult learning priorities, monitor progress, and help sustain continuous improvement

- Multisourced: Uses multiple sources of information to guide improvement and demonstrate its impact
- Research-based: Prepares educators to apply research to decision making
- Design-based: Uses learning strategies appropriate for the intended goals
- Learning and change-based: Applies knowledge about human learning and change
- Collaborative: Provides educators with the knowledge and skills to collaborate

WFSGs encompass all the process standards. The WFSG decision-making cycle (DMC) (see Figure 7.1) includes the first three standards. In Steps 1 and 2, student data are used to determine adult learning priorities. Step 6 includes continuous cycles of action research to monitor progress and sustain improvement. Guideline 10 covers a range of professional development strategies to reach the intended goals. Critical learning and change process concepts are built into the WFSG system (Chapters 3–5). The 15 WFSG procedural guidelines that are discussed in this chapter provide an operational structure that guides the collaborative process.

THE WFSG RUBRIC: PROCESS

The WFSG rubric has three components: context, process, and content. Table 6.1 shows 10 process descriptors and describes four levels of use of each descriptor.

PROCESS GUIDELINES FOR WFSGs

The 15 process or procedural guidelines of the WFSG system weave in and out of each other. The guidelines are interwoven so as to form a structure through which study groups work. Think of a basket, a basket with great utility. The guidelines are the wooden strips of equal strength and width in the basket. All the guidelines woven together form a basket or process strong enough to hold multicolored stones of substantive content. A guideline that is weakened would be like narrowing one of the wooden strips, causing holes to appear in the basket. A basket (the process) with holes might be too porous to hold the contents. To ignore or omit a guideline altogether would endanger the contents even more. Figure 6.1 is a "process" basket. Each slat in the basket represents one of the guidelines discussed in this chapter. The strong basket represents a strong process, WFSGs, that can carry the weight of strong, substantive content. There may be more attractive baskets, and there may be baskets that are easier to manage. What has been fashioned for WFSGs, however, is a basket that has great utility and, figuratively speaking, takes strong content to and from study group meetings and to and from the classroom.

The 15 guidelines provide the process structure that is required for study groups to achieve their desired results. These process or procedural guidelines are the result of Murphy's work since 1986 with hundreds of schools and thousands of study groups in those schools. The procedures have been standardized to the degree that the benefits of what has been learned can be replicated in any school. Replication is possible because the work has been done in high schools, middle schools, elementary schools, primary schools, and charter schools; schools in large urban cities, such as Detroit, Seattle, San Diego, and New York City; schools in rural communities,

	Not Yet	Beginning Implementation	Developing Implementation	Advanced Implementation
Process	The same person leads the group each time it meets.	Leadership is rotated.	Leadership is rotated and group members feel comfortable with this.	Each member willingly takes his or her turn leading the group.
Process	The group has not agreed on a set of norms.	Norms are written but not honored.	Group norms are written and mostly honored.	All feel responsible for the success of the group and hold each accountable to the group's norms.
Process	The action plan is not complete and/or recommended revisions have not been made.	The action plan is complete. Occasionally the group reviews its action plan and makes minor revisions.	The action plan is complete and is revised, adding and deleting as work progresses.	The action plan is complete and often referred to during meetings. It is a living document and is kept in front of the group at all times.
Process	Logs are not turned in, not complete, or do not accurately describe what the group did.	Logs are turned in but members do not use them as a point of reference for future work.	Logs are helpful reminders of the work of the group.	Logs tell a rich story of dialogue and action around student learning.
Process	The group does not look at student work (LASW) together using a protocol or reflect on their own learning and teaching.	LASW is occasional. Reflection on learning and teaching is practiced as debriefing.	LASW is routine but does not generate reflection on practice.	LASW is the basis of reflection on learning and teaching and guides actions.
Process	There is no instructional council (IC) for members to attend.	Same member of the study group attends every meeting of the IC.	Members rotate attending IC but little, if any, time is spent sharing what took place.	Members rotate attending the IC, discuss and use information from the IC, and tie what the study group is doing to what other groups are doing.
Process	Group size is not within guideline.	Group size is five or fewer but one member dominates.	Group size is five or fewer but several members are not fully engaged.	Group size is five or fewer and all members are fully engaged.
Process	The group meets once a month.	The group meets every other week for an hour.	The group meets three times a month for an hour.	The group meets weekly for at least an hour.
Process	There is a hierarchy within the group.	Some members have more influence than others.	Equality is on the surface but not always evident.	Equality is evident in all behaviors and actions.
Process	The group uses annual district or state assessments to measure changes in student performance on their student learning needs.	Some members use a classroom assessment to assess student results at the end of the year on the study group's chosen student learning needs.	The study group uses a common classroom assessment to collect baseline data and assess student results at the end of the year on the study group's chosen student learning needs.	The study group uses a common classroom assessment to collect baseline data, monitor student progress every 6 to 12 weeks, and assess results at the end of the year on the study group's chosen student learning needs.

Table 6.1 WFSG Rubric: Process

Whole-Faculty Study Groups
why they work...
Strong Process Holds Strong Content

Figure 6.1   Whole-Faculty Study Groups—Why They Work: Strong Process Holds Strong Content

such as south Georgia, upstate New York, and central Kansas; schools in suburban areas, such as those near Atlanta, Miami, and Chicago; schools as large as 3,000 students and 250 faculty members with 47 study groups; schools with as few as 300 students and 10 faculty members and 2 study groups; and schools representing many cultures. Because the work is continuous in these schools, the WFSG process and its refinements are constantly evolving. Murphy has used what has worked for one study group to help another, and as new ideas accumulate, she has made adjustments to the procedures. The procedures have evolved from the actual work of teachers together in schools. For schools that want results, it is strongly recommended that these guidelines not be altered. They form a framework that gives the process an effective, time-proven, reliable operational structure. Within the structure, there is great latitude for deciding what study groups will do and how they will be organized. For schools that use the *Whole-Faculty Study Groups* term to describe the school's collaborative model, the guidelines are nonnegotiable. What is completely open, however, is what student needs a group will target and how the group will address the needs.

A faculty that authentically applies the WFSG guiding principles and the 15 procedural or process guidelines has permission to call what they do Whole-Faculty Study Groups. Because Whole-Faculty Study Groups is a trademarked or registered name for a specific system, faculties that do not follow the guidelines and principles should not use the term. The guidelines are listed here, and a detailed discussion of each guideline follows:

1. Determine study group membership by who wants to address a set of data-based student needs identified through a process that involves the whole faculty.

2. Keep the size of the study group between three and five members.

3. Establish and keep a regular schedule, meeting weekly for approximately 1 hour or every 2 weeks for as long as 2 hours.

4. Establish group norms and routinely revisit the norms.

5. Establish a pattern of study group leadership, rotating among members.

6. Develop a study group action plan (SGAP) by the end of the second study group meeting.

7. Complete a study group log after each study group meeting.

8. Have a curriculum and instructional focus that require members to routinely examine student work and observe students in classrooms engaged in instructional tasks that result from the study group's work.

9. Use a variety of learning resources, both material and human, that serve as the "expert voice" to the learners.

10. Use multiple professional development strategies, such as training, to accomplish the study group's intended results.

11. Reflect on the study group's work and the impact of current practice on student performance.

12. Recognize all study group members as equals.

13. Expect transitions or shifts in the work.

14. Assess study group work to determine the evidence that the targeted student needs have been improved.

15. Establish a variety of communication networks and strategies.

Guideline 1. Determine study group membership by who wants to address a set of data-based student needs identified through a process that involves the whole faculty

The student need that the group will address determines membership. Focus is on the work and not on personal connections of the individuals. It does not matter who is in a group. The homogeneity or heterogeneity of the study group is not a critical element. Study group members may have similar responsibilities (e.g., first-grade teachers, mathematics teachers, or elementary principals) or unlike responsibilities (e.g., across grade level, across subject level, or across schools or districts). A study group is most often composed of those who want to pursue or investigate a set or category (e.g., writing) of specific student needs that has been identified through an analysis of student data. The content of the study, investigation, or training generally determines who will be a member of a study group. The focus is on adult-to-adult relationships in a learning situation. What grade or subject a member teaches is secondary to the adult relationship forged around teaching. For example, a study group focusing on technology may have teachers of kindergartners to 12th graders because the application of computer skills is generic.

The DMC is a step-by-step process to determine what study groups will target and how study groups will be organized. The DMC is presented in Chapter 7. The whole faculty meets to complete Steps 1 through 4. In Steps 1 through 3, specific student needs are identified from data, and a list of student needs is generated. The student needs on the list are grouped into categories (e.g., reading comprehension, vocabulary development, study skills, and mathematics). In Step 4, each faculty member is asked to make personal choices as a leader guides the faculty through a process of self-selection, requiring teachers to develop a personalized or individual action plan. The question is, which category of student needs do your students need for you to target? Teachers are challenged to put more weight on what their students need than on what teachers may want to do or are interested in doing. Student needs drive the decision making. Once a teacher acknowledges, for instance, that his or her students are not performing at an acceptable level in reading comprehension, that acknowledgment becomes a teacher's choice. Once the teachers have set the "student need" priority areas, they are then asked how they would like to see the work organized in a group of which they would be a member and to write an essential question to guide the work of a group. After the teachers have given careful consideration to what their students need for them to do, the leader identifies those who have made similar decisions. Teachers making the same choices are grouped together. Using reading comprehension as the example, all the teachers who see in the data that their students are weakest in this area will be asked to go to a designated area of the meeting room or to another room. If more than five teachers have made the same choice, those teachers use the essential question or other information on their personal preference plan to further group themselves. Once groups are formed with no more than five members, each group becomes an official study group and gives the leader a list of the teachers' names. If all the study groups are not going to meet at the same time, the procedure described will need to be modified. If the teachers are going to meet during planning periods 1 day a week, there is an intermediate step between making the choice and forming a group. The person leading the faculty through the decision-making process will ask all the teachers who plan to go to a designated room during second period, for example. Once all the teachers who have a second period planning time are together, they will share their choices and group themselves into small groups.

Guideline 2. Keep the size of the group between three and five members

It is recommended that groups be no smaller than three and no larger than five members. With small groups, each member will participate more and take greater responsibility. Most study groups schedule 1 hour for a meeting, which means the group will actually have approximately 45 minutes of real work time. With five members, each person has only approximately 10 minutes of "talk time" when he or she is expressing a thought or responding to a colleague. In groups larger than five, individuals can "hide" and not assume their share of the work. The larger the study group, the more likely the group will splinter into two groups. The size of groups affects how comfortable individuals feel about serving as leader. With small groups, rotating leadership is comfortable. An individual does not feel the same sense of pressure with four other individuals as he or she would with a larger number. The intimacy of a smaller group generates such a supportive relationship that when leadership is rotated, an observer of the study group often cannot tell who is the leader. If time is not provided within the school day for groups to meet, the larger the group, the more difficult it is to find a common time when all members can be present.

Guideline 3. Establish and keep a regular schedule, meeting weekly for approximately 1 hour or every 2 weeks for as long as 2 hours

It is strongly recommended that study groups meet weekly for approximately 1 hour; if not weekly, no less than every 2 weeks for approximately 2 hours. There is a direct relationship between the amount of time a study group meets and student effects. Study groups engage in cycles of action research driven by data and supported by ongoing development work. Without frequent, regular meetings, the length of time between the steps in the cycle greatly reduces the power of the actions. The power in action research results from immediate feedback on the effects of an intervention so that modifications can be made for the next round of use. Issues relating to time are often the reason why many faculties do not begin WFSGs and why WFSGs are not continued in schools that do begin them. Once consensus is reached to begin, the first decision that faculties must make is when the study groups will meet. Most often, principals take the responsibility of working with school, district, and community leaders in finding ways for teachers to meet within the contract week. Once a time is identified and set aside, it should be guarded against all encroachments. The major morale buster is for study group time to be taken for purposes other than the group's predetermined agenda. Frequently, there is a set time when all study groups will meet. If groups are going to be meeting at different times, at times not determined by the school schedule, or as arranged by study group members, the groups must set a time and day for the entire year. At the first meeting, members confirm the day and time of their study group meetings and write those times in the first log, such as every Tuesday from 3:00 to 4:00 p.m. or every other Tuesday from 3:00 to 5:00. Weekly meetings for approximately 1 hour keep the momentum at a steady pace and give study group members ongoing learning and support systems. It is better to meet more frequently for shorter periods of time than infrequently for a longer block of time. More than 2 weeks between meetings is too long to sustain momentum and get regular feedback on classroom practice. An hour is the minimum amount of time necessary to accomplish the intent of a given meeting. Also, when groups are between three and five in size, everyone has the opportunity to be an active participant. An unexpected benefit of weekly meetings is less absenteeism, building more commitment to the task of the group.

Meeting once a month works against the process. If a study group meets once a month for 1 hour, the total number of contact hours for the school year will be equal to 8 hours or approximately 1 day. If a study group meets twice a month for 1 hour, that will equal approximately 16 hours or approximately 2 days for the year. If a study group meets weekly, the total time the group will meet during the school year will be approximately 32 contact hours, which is approximately 4 days. Most college and staff development courses are 30 to 50 contact hours. Even weekly meetings will typically not equal the time spent in a college course. When teachers first hear that groups will stay together for a school year, they can usually be heard saying with astonishment, "A year?" An experienced leader of WFSGs, however, will say, "Make that ___ hours" (whatever the total time will be). One action research cycle takes three or four meetings. The power of the WFSG approach is what teachers implement immediately after the meeting and the immediate feedback from classroom use at the next meeting. This important "bouncing ball" or "back-and-forth" progress is less in biweekly meetings and significantly less in monthly meetings.

Guideline 4. Establish group norms and routinely revisit the norms

At the first study group meeting, members should discuss and reach agreement on norms of behavior for the group and then write them in their log. Study group members should collectively agree on what is acceptable and unacceptable behavior in a study group meeting, such as the following:

- Begin and end on time.
- Take responsibility for one's own learning.
- Do what we agree to do.
- Respect all.
- Stay focused.
- Implement what we learn.
- No fault is to be given or taken.

Today, it is common to see "put cell phones away" on a list of norms. If a teacher is expecting an emergency call, that teacher would ask for an exception for that meeting. Otherwise, it is too distracting for an individual to break the rhythm of learning to take or make a call. Norms set the basis for the operation of the group, help create its empowering synergy, and lead to the group's "learning team" success, as discussed in Chapters 9 and 11. Once norms are established and agreed on, members are encouraged to feel comfortable gently reminding each other when a norm is not being respected. It is important to revisit norms frequently.

Guideline 5. Establish a pattern of study group leadership, rotating among members

Shared leadership is a principle of WFSGs. Members share leadership of a study group by rotating the role of leader. Members also share leadership by rotating their representation at instructional council (IC) meetings. When the whole faculty learns how to follow a protocol for examining student work or a protocol that has other functions, any member of a study group can facilitate the protocol. Leadership roles take practice, and the only way to practice is to do leadership tasks. The principle of shared leadership is based on the belief that all teachers are leaders. Unfortunately, the current norm in many schools is not expecting all teachers to be leaders.

At the first study group meeting, members should establish a schedule for the rotation of leadership. The schedule is written in the log. Each member serves as study group leader on a rotating basis. The leadership rotation may occur weekly, biweekly, or monthly. Leadership is shared to avoid having one member become more responsible than other members for the success of the group. All members are equally responsible for obtaining resources and keeping the group moving toward its intended results and desired ends. Individual members should look to themselves and each other for direction, not to a single person. This sense of joint responsibility for the work of the study group builds interdependence and synergy within the group. When every group member feels equally responsible for the success of the group, there is a higher level of commitment and no one leader is to blame for the failure of the group to accomplish its goals. All must share the burden of any failure or joy of accomplishment. The most positive feature arising from the use of the rotation approach is the important assumption that anyone from the study group can represent the group at any point in time, expanding the effective capacity for leadership at the school. When a member serves as leader, this person should do the following:

- Confirm logistics with study group members (e.g., day, time, location, and what to bring)
- Check the log from the last meeting to confirm what the focus of the next meeting should be
- Check to determine if it is time to revisit the action plan and the group norms
- Start and end the meeting on time
- Remind members who stray from the focus of the meeting to refocus
- See that the study group log is completed and members and the principal receive a copy
- Share any comments from the principal or other support persons that may have been made on the log from the last meeting

Guideline 6. Develop a SGAP by the end of the second study group meeting

Before study groups are formed, everyone writes a practice action plan or a "personal preference" action plan in the session when the whole faculty goes through Steps 1 through 4 of the DMC. At this general session, each teacher is given the opportunity to select the general category of student need that he or she will choose when given a choice. Each teacher is then asked to write, with guidance, an action plan that the teacher believes will address the needs of his or her students. This practice gives all teachers an opportunity to learn how to write an action plan before they are expected to write one as part of a study group, and it provides a practice action plan to share later with their study group members. Often, ideas from the individual action plans form the basis for a single action plan for the study group.

By the end of the second study group meeting, each group's action plan should be completed and given to the principal. It is important that a study group develop its own action plan. If there are 10 study groups in the school, then there should be 10 different action plans. Student needs are identified by the whole faculty, but how a study group goes about its investigation is for each group to decide. The action plan sets the common goals for the study group. Every member is given a copy of the group's action plan. The action plan is reviewed and revised approximately every 6 weeks. A study group's action plan should include the following:

- The general category of student need
- The essential question that will guide the study group throughout its work
- The specific student needs to be addressed by the group (see Figure 7.2)
- The actions the teachers will take when the study group meets (see Figure 7.4)
- The resources the study group will use
- The group's norms
- Assessment of evidence that the study group work is having an impact on targeted student needs by specifying (a) specific student needs from the plan, (b) data sources with evidence of improvement, (c) baseline status of needs, and (d) targeted and actual results at the end of a 6- to 12-week period

Study groups usually have to be coached on how to complete the assessment portion of the plan. Because the work begins early in the school year, teachers are guided to use data sources that will provide evidence in 6 to 12 weeks. For example, if a study group is working on vocabulary development, there will be end-of-unit tests and textbook checklists that will give an indication of progress. Every 6 to 12 weeks, groups are encouraged to revise the assessment part of the action plan and reestablish targets. Groups are discouraged from listing the Iowa Test of Basic Skills (ITBS) as a data source because these tests are not given until late in the school year and results are not available until much later. Groups are told that it will be the cumulative effect of the intermediate measures that will impact the ITBS scores.

The part of the action plan that requires careful explanation is what the study group plans to do when it meets. Teachers are inclined to write what they want their students to do. Instead, the members should list the specific actions that they will take when they sit around a table and work together. This portion of the plan serves as the study group's agenda for all its upcoming meetings. Most often, teachers are either told what to do or tell others (e.g., students) what to do. We have found that it is difficult for teachers to focus on themselves and be clear about what they are going to do when their study group meets. This portion of the plan should give the reader a visual image of what the members will be doing when they meet. The principal is alert to verbs that indicate that the actions will be passive, such as discuss, share, read, and explain. The principal should encourage more active verbs, such as modeling, demonstrating, designing, examining, practicing, and constructing.

The study groups should expect the principal and other appropriate leaders to give them feedback on their action plans. Typical feedback includes suggestions regarding resources and questions about the specific actions of the group. The action plan for each group is usually put on a clipboard, and the clipboard is placed where teachers will frequently see it. Plans are posted so that everyone will know what all study groups are doing. Teachers are encouraged to use Post-it notes to ask questions and give suggestions to other study groups. Action plans are also posted on the school's electronic mail system.

The action plan should be revisited at regular intervals and adjusted to be consistent with current actions. A group may initially plan to go in one direction and then, during the study or training program, it will see a different avenue to follow. This takes on a higher level of importance when the group assesses its progress toward its intended results at the end of the school year. If the actions a group takes are not aligned with student needs or results for students are not appropriate or adequate, the assessment will indicate that the group missed its target.

Guideline 7. Complete a study group log after each study group meeting

A study group log is a brief, written summary of what happened at a specific meeting, and collectively they give a group history. The study group log should include the following information:

- Date, time, location, and leader of the meeting
- Group members present and absent
- What happened today? A brief summary of discussions and activities
- Classroom application: What are students learning and achieving as a result of what you are learning and doing?
- Was student work brought to the meeting? If so, who brought it?
- What are you ready to share with other study groups?
- What concerns or questions do you have for school leaders?
- Next meeting (e.g., agenda items and work to prepare)
- Date, time, location, and leader of next meeting

After meetings, members are given a copy of the completed log. Each member keeps a notebook of his or her study group work, including the action plan, the logs, and artifacts from meetings. Using the logs, a group can refer to past meetings and confirm why they decided to take a particular action. Members can see their progress in their relations with one another, their thinking, and their actions. After each meeting, a copy of the log is given to the principal and posted on the same clipboard that has the group's action plan. It is expected that the principal or his or her designee will acknowledge in some way the group's work. Principals use the following types of methods to give feedback:

- Write comments directly on the log
- Use a Post-it note for writing a comment, sticking it to the log
- Write a memo
- Send an e-mail to all members in a study group
- Use the dialogue box for comments if the log is electronically posted

The log is not used in evaluations but as a tool for determining what outside support may be helpful or promptly addressing concerns of the group. Logs may become part of the study group's portfolio or an individual teacher's portfolio. It is usually during the third or fourth meeting when the "classroom applications" section of the log is completed. It takes about that long for the study group to get organized and to do the background work to support classroom use. The study group may collect classroom application information by using the first 5 to 10 minutes of the meeting to go around the table and share, or sharing can be integrated into conversations throughout the meeting. Much of the learning about classroom practice comes from the sharing of what is and is not working in teachers' classrooms. This generates concrete and precise "teacher talk" about teaching, a major outcome or result of study groups.

Guideline 8. Have a curriculum and instructional focus that require members to routinely examine student work and observe students in classrooms engaged in instructional tasks that result from the study group's work

The results of actions taken by study groups should be evidenced in the work students do. Collecting data from student work is the engine that drives the work of teachers in their study groups. The student needs that the faculty identifies in Step 2 of the DMC can be addressed through what and how teachers teach. Results of what and how teachers teach are mirrored in what students do. Students give back to us, in some way, what we have given them or led them to do, or what they have discovered. It is this work that guides teacher work. Teacher action is grounded in student action that is grounded in teacher action. This process is a cycle.

It is helpful if study groups use a protocol for looking at student work. Protocols give teachers guidelines for conversation within a limited amount of time, and they create a structure for speaking, listening, and questioning. In Chapter 8, we discuss in detail the "looking at student work" strategy.

The content of any professional development approach should have promise for positive effects on students. As outlined in Chapter 2, the functions of study groups are to (a) develop a deeper understanding of academic content, (b) support the implementation of curricular and instructional innovations, (c) integrate and give coherence to a school's instructional practices and programs, (d) target a schoolwide instructional need, (e) study the research on teaching and learning, (f) monitor the impact of instructional changes on students, and (g) provide a time when teachers can examine student work together. These seven functions require that members not get sidetracked by administrative issues or issues that have a low instructional impact. WFSGs take on the groups' content curriculum materials, instructional strategies, curriculum designs, use of technologies, standards, and assessment practices. The groups will use a variety of strategies to address the targeted student needs. For example, they may have an external person offer group training, and members may read books and articles, view videotapes, demonstrate strategies to each other, visit classrooms and schools, design materials, view and learn to use computer software, attend a workshop or conference together, and develop lessons that will be taught in classrooms.

Whatever the content, it must be complex and substantive enough to provide a practical vision, not just rhetoric or feelings. It is the content of the study group that will hold the members together while they are gaining trust and rapport with each other and developing skills for working together as a cohesive group. The content takes the focus off the individual. The content supplies a foundation for the process that will lead the group to joint, interdependent work. Through the content, colleagues can share responsibilities; support each other's initiatives; discover their unconscious assumptions; clarify their ideas, beliefs, and professional practices; and ground the group's commitment to serious, professional accomplishment.

Guideline 9. Use a variety of learning resources, both material and human, that serve as the "expert voice" to the learners

A study group designs its curriculum of study to include a comprehensive list of resources. Study groups need to hear an expert voice in person, through the written word, or through video. This expert voice will lead the members of the group to deeper knowledge or higher levels of skill. Resource lists may include trainers, resource people, titles of books, professional journals, videos, audiotapes, computers and software, conferences, and other sources of relevant information. The most accessible sources for materials are the Internet and files of other teachers in the building. Principals often ask teachers in a building to share their files on specific topics or general areas of study to create an enhanced, central resource file for areas of study being pursued by the different groups. The Internet is a powerful resource that connects the school to teachers throughout the nation and the world.

Some schools have had a day proclaimed as Clean Out File Cabinets Day. If there are 10 study groups, 10 cardboard boxes are labeled and put in a central location. Anyone who has anything on the student need that a group is addressing puts materials in the appropriate box. If an item is to be returned to the original owner after a study group finishes with it, then the owner would write on the item "Please return to _____."

Other sources for materials are district offices, other schools, regional service agencies, libraries, colleges and universities, businesses, and professional associations. Also included as learning resources are individuals who have special expertise, such as teachers, school administrators, district administrators and support staff, university professors, independent consultants, parents, and business and community leaders. The foregoing list of learning resources represents a valuable resource base for the learning that must precede the changes that teachers hope to bring about in their classrooms. A more detailed list of such resources is given in Chapter 8.

Guideline 10. Use multiple professional development strategies, such as training, to accomplish the study group's intended results

The WFSG system can include most other professional development designs or strategies. These strategies are described in detail in Chapter 8. Study groups conduct action research and lesson study; teachers most often have to be taught the procedures associated with these. Such training is part of the ongoing development of study groups. The initial training in how to organize and function in study groups is just the beginning of the training in how to initiate, implement, and institutionalize WFSGs. Through whole-faculty meetings, study group meetings, and IC meetings, skills and strategies are presented and expectations for use made clear. Study groups invite people to meet with them to train members to use a particular skill, or the members attend a workshop together. Study groups can form combinations of members for observing each other's students in classrooms. Study group members immerse themselves in the content to gain a deeper understanding of what they teach. Study group members develop curriculum for current use and experiment with it in their classrooms. They listen to students by interviewing them during study group meetings, and they videotape themselves and their students and share what they learn. Study groups actively seek new strategies to deepen their knowledge and develop skills.

Study group members are to be reminded that when we do not know how to do something, we can develop that skill by letting a person who is more knowledgeable in that skill area show us how. The more skillful individual may be in the study group, from elsewhere in the school, or from elsewhere altogether. When skill development is required, inviting a trainer or skilled practitioner to study group meetings to demonstrate effective practices may be necessary. Just reading about how to do something is usually not sufficient. Reading and discussing books and articles and studying relevant research are important because such efforts can affect attitudes, beliefs, and behaviors and can provide an expanded knowledge base for improving classroom practice. At some point, however, individuals must move from the abstract (from what is written, read, and discussed) to the concrete (to what one actually does).

Furthermore, to ensure skill development at a level that gives teachers the confidence to appropriately and effectively use the skill in the classroom, study group members may need to develop a plan that will include several training components. A plan for skill development includes (a) the theory that explains and supports the importance of the skill, (b) opportunities for participants to observe a number of demonstrations of the skill, and (c) opportunities to practice the skill to a reasonable competency level (Joyce & Showers, 1995). The study group provides a safe environment for teachers to practice skills, design lessons together using the skills, observe each other, and feel support in determining why some lessons go well and others do not. The value of ongoing technical training and support of effective classroom practices cannot be overemphasized.

Guideline 11. Reflect on the study group's work and the impact of current practice on student performance

Definitions of *reflection* are "to give back an image; to think seriously on or upon; contemplation; a thoughtful idea." Reflection is an important aspect of both learning and teaching. Study groups give teachers the opportunity for reflection—time and space to consider the impact of decisions, analyze data, and think carefully about next steps. In the plan-act-reflect cycle, reflection is often perceived as "assess." There is assessment in reflection. As one has images of past actions, frequently the individual is looking for what went well and what did not go as well as intended. Outcomes of reflection, for example, could be redesigning a lesson. Precise talk about what occurred during the teaching of a lesson is verbal reflection and is a critical part of study group talk. Without reflection about what occurred, most likely there will be no adjustments or changes in teaching practices. Although on logs reflection may appear to be the most neglected study group practice, it is the most central to the process.

Members of study groups are encouraged to keep personal journals of their reflections about their teaching and learning. Teachers encourage students to write to learn, summarize what they have learned, and make personal sense out of what they are learning. Teachers will benefit from doing the same. Writing what they are thinking helps them construct meaning for themselves from their experiences. In a study group, not only are we thinking about ourselves but also we think about group experiences. As an experience from the classroom is shared, members may write about how others perceive the experience and how they feel about those perceptions. Use of journals is up to the study group. Occasionally, excerpts may be shared. Some study groups set aside time during every third meeting for deliberate and planned reflection. Killion (1999) expands on strategies for journaling. Serious journal writers keep their journals open during a meeting and occasionally make a quick note of key ideas. Specific entries directly related to the work of the study group include the following:

- Date, time, and location of the study group meeting
- Description of what happened
- Individual's analysis of what happened
- How what happened is connected to other experiences
- Interactions with other individuals that may have been especially helpful or bothersome
- Meeting's accomplishments
- What the group did not get done
- What the group should do for the next meeting
- Individual's feelings about what he or she is learning

The journal indicates the individual's learning, reflections, feelings, and reactions. Expressions of frustration, concern, and joy, new insights, and references for the future are important parts of one's own reflections about the process and the content of the study.

Guideline 12. Recognize all study group members as equals

It is more productive if individuals do not feel intimidated, hesitant, or anxious about differences in job titles or certifications, experience, and degree levels among group members. No one is deferred to because of rank or other factors. Contributions from each member are encouraged, expected, and respected. *Comentoring* is a term we use to indicate in the WFSG process that group members all mentor each other. The study group functions under the belief that all members have something valuable to contribute to the group (i.e., empowerment; see Chapter 9) and then provides an opportunity for all to fully share their ideas and experiences (i.e., participative involvement; see Chapter 9). This approach provides an environment for "appreciative understanding" (see Chapter 9), empowering its members and enabling the group to reach a higher level of synergy and meaningful productivity. It is the shared leadership and equal-status principle and strong content focus that lessens the need to train groups in group dynamics. With a strong sense of individual responsibility and an action plan for accomplishing specific results, the focus is on what the group is doing and not on the characteristics of individuals. If the work of the group is substantive enough and tied to what teachers and students are doing in the classrooms, the related dynamics will hold the group together and allow it to function well. As the work progresses, members develop trust and rapport with each other and learn how to work together synergistically within the context of their study. Thus, comentoring becomes a routine activity, as illustrated by the frequency of observing students in each other's classrooms. Through these observations, the teachers learn more about each other's students and can better address the needs of all the students in the members' classrooms. Without the element or condition of equality, comentoring is not possible. Comentoring accepts that one member may be more skillful in one area than another member but that such expertise does not put either person in a privileged position or status.

Equality within the context of the WFSG approach means that all members of a study group equally share the tasks of leadership. Each member of a study group serves as leader and represents the study group at IC meetings. Each member learns to facilitate a protocol, and leadership functions are shared in all aspects of the system. Recognizing all study group members as equals means equal in status, equal in responsibility, and equal in ability to lead.

Guideline 13. Expect transitions or shifts in the work

The definition of *transition* is "passing from one condition, place, or phase to another." For study groups, a transition is when there is or is going to be a change in the current conditions. A transition has occurred when a study group reaches closure on what the group intended to do and is refocusing its work, when a schoolwide instructional need has become so apparent that all groups need to stop/look/listen/ take action, and when there is a break in the school calendar. Transitions are times to reflect, take stock, and celebrate!

A study group is expected to remain a group until the end of a school year. Changing group membership more often is disruptive to the group process because each change in the composition of the group forces the group to repeat the earlier stages of group development. A group may change its action plan at any time when the group believes the plan is not meeting the needs of the students. If an action plan is developed in September, actions have been implemented to the group's satisfaction, and the group wants to develop another plan in February, a transition occurs. The transition is not in group membership but in the content or conditions of the study. If the school receives information from the state or the district that an instructional issue has to be addressed immediately that is within the parameters of study group work, such as trying new materials to determine appropriateness, the work can be done in the study groups. The principal should consider other structures within the school that may be more appropriate, however, such as grade-level or department meetings. At the end of the school year, all groups should bring closure to their work. Even if the study group plans to stay together when the new school year begins and continue the work it is currently doing, it still must formally transition to the next year. Such groups will confirm at the beginning of the new school year that the student needs addressed continue to be a priority. For a study group that wants to stay together for another school year but believes it wants to work on a different set of student needs, a positive transition would be to celebrate its success for the year. At the beginning of the new year when the faculty returns to Steps 1 through 3 on the DMC, the group would reach consensus as to which of the student need categories (e.g., reading) it would now address.

At the end of a school year, study groups typically consider the following choices:

- Stay together as a group and continue current work
- Stay together as a group and address another student need
- Disband and form new groups

If three study groups (15 people) or more out of nine study groups at the school want to disband, at the beginning of the next year, those people wanting to disband will meet together. After experiencing Steps 1 through 3 on the DMC, each would do a personal study group plan, and new groups would form according to student needs preferences.

Guideline 14. Assess study group work to determine the evidence that the targeted student needs have been improved

When considering what and how to assess the effects of study group work, members need to revisit the group's action plan. At the bottom of the plan (see Guideline 6), the members agreed how and what would be assessed to determine the effectiveness of the group's work, and there is a space for indicating the group's targeted results. On the form "Assessment of WFSG Work" (Resource A), the chart is repeated to record what the data indicated at the beginning of the group's work through the ending of the work, including the assessment items in Guideline 6. If the study group has been engaged in ongoing cycles of action research, they will have a clearer notion of progress with supporting data. Within the cycles, there were examinations of student work that, over time, are reliable sources of impact.

In another part of this book, we asked the question, "Will WFSGs increase student achievement?" Our answer, "It depends," often depends on the following:

- The substance of the content of the work and its application to a student need
- The amount of time the group meets
- The principal's willingness and ability to provide the pressure and support that the groups need

When these three conditions are present, student results are documented (see Chapter 11).

Another area to examine is the contextual features of the school. Have there been cultural shifts? Teachers will want to consider the impact of WFSGs on the school's culture—for example, the school's underlying assumptions, beliefs, and behaviors, such as the school's norms of collegiality, faculty and staff learning, a change-adaptable environment, and continuous improvement.

Other assessment questions would focus on the effectiveness of the study group process, especially how each study group functions. Questions should be asked about the rotation of leadership, the size of the group, whether group norms were honored, whether members felt equally valuable in accomplishing the group's work, and whether the meeting day and time facilitated group work. In Chapter 10, additional questions regarding context, process, and content are presented. Study groups whose members are in the lower stages of concern (Hall & Hord, 1987)—that is, they are more concerned about personal and management issues than about collaboration—are less likely to see student impact. Resource A provides additional examples of formats used for assessing progress of study groups.

Guideline 15. Establish a variety of communication networks and strategies

Communication among study groups helps create the context for whole school change. Establishing lines of communication among study groups and with other groups is a critical element to the WFSG approach. An integral part of WFSGs is that every faculty member will be in a study group, and everyone (the whole) will know what all groups are doing and learning. Such effective communication increases the chances that everyone will receive benefit from others' work, as the following examples indicate:

- As discussed in Chapter 4, the IC includes a representative from each study group. The representatives meet every 4 to 6 weeks to share the work of study groups. Resource E contains examples of minutes from IC meetings.
- On agendas for grade-level, department, and team meetings, it is important to include what study groups are doing. When a majority of the study groups at a school have heterogeneous (e.g., across grade levels, departments, and teams) membership, grade-level and department meetings are opportunities for greater communication. For example, if only one fourth-grade teacher is in a particular study group that is addressing listening skills, that teacher could share a listening rubric that his or her study group developed with her fourth-grade colleagues. The other fourth-grade teachers could then give their colleague feedback, which could be shared with the original study group. This creates a powerful feedback and input cycle for all study groups. Teachers do not have to wait for a whole-faculty sharing time to benefit from what other study groups are doing.
- Some schools publish a faculty newsletter that has a brief description of what each study group is doing, including its work or an idea that is exciting.
- In most schools, there is a whole-faculty sharing time at least twice a year—midyear and the end of the school year. Celebrations are very important. These are special times for leaders to let teachers know that they appreciate and recognize the work that study groups are doing. They represent special communication times for groups to have fun and do creative things to inspire others and raise the status of learning at the school.
- Schools should communicate with the board of education, district leaders, parents, students, and the general public about what study groups are doing.
- Students must be told what is taking place in study groups. Teachers are encouraged to tell students that a particular strategy or activity they are using in class is a strategy the teachers learned in their study group. This type of sharing has great influence on students and parents because it is important for them see teachers as learners and understand that learning is a lifelong process.
- SGAPs and study group logs are posted in a public place and electronically. One clipboard for each study group is usually hung in the office area. Each study group puts its action plan on a clipboard, and after each meeting the group's log is added for all to see.
- "Showcase" times are encouraged. When a study group becomes excited about a strategy that produces positive results, the group sends all the teachers an invitation to "come and see it working in our classrooms!"
- Newsletters aimed at specific groups (e.g., faculty and parents) are helpful. In school newsletters sent to parents, one corner should be reserved for "Study Group News."
- Brochures work. A study group investigating motivational strategies for reading created a trifold brochure on blue paper that listed successful ways to motivate students to read and distributed it to all the faculty.
- Videos are powerful. A technology group made a video showing students using a digital camera, scanner, and computer for writing and designing their own books.
- Exhibits and seminars are helpful. Before a PTA meeting, one school had a study group assigned to each classroom for parents to learn more about the activities and contributions of study groups.

- Bulletin boards are used in public places in school to display study group work.

Recapping the Guidelines

Process refers to how individuals work together to acquire new knowledge and skills and usually involves a number of procedures or operations. The process basket has to be strong enough to carry the contents, especially content that has substance. The WFSG basket, properly applied, with its 15 interwoven guidelines as slats of the basket, is sufficient to hold strong content (see Figure 6.1). Only those schools that authentically apply the WFSG guidelines and the WFSG guiding principles, however, are likely to be fully successful and deserve to use the term Whole-Faculty Study Groups as the name of their collaborative improvement design.

DEVELOPMENTAL STAGES OF STUDY GROUPS

The process or procedural guidelines alone will not determine how individuals will function within WFSGs. Leaders and others working with and in study groups must understand that study groups go through developmental stages just like all other types of groups. Study groups in a school will experience each stage to some degree, and some groups will remain in one stage longer than other groups.

We have given names to four growth stages that seem to fit the various study group stages. This approach originated from the book *The One Minute Manager Builds High Performing Teams* (Blanchard, Carew, & Parisi-Carew, 2000). See Table 6.2 for other variations on the names of the four stages. The four stages, which reflect how we have seen them function, are as follows:

Stage 1: Forming

Stage 2: Grumbling

Stage 3: Willingness

Stage 4: Consequence

Stage 1: Forming

The forming stage begins when the faculty is first given information about the WFSG process, and it continues beyond the forming of the study groups. In the

Stages	Blanchard, Carew, & Parisi-Carew	Outward Bound	Author Unknown	Murphy & Lick
1.	Orientation	Forming	Testing	Forming
2.	Dissatisfaction	Storming	Infighting	Grumbling
3.	Resolution	Norming	Getting Organized	Willingness
4.	Production	Performing	Mature Closeness	Consequence

Table 6.2 Synonyms for Names of Developmental Stages

beginning, the whole faculty is considered "the group"; later, the three- to five-member study group is considered the group. During this stage, members may experience the following:

- Become eager to begin
- Have high expectations
- Feel some anxiety
- Have high levels of personal concern
- Need more information
- Wonder about expectations
- Depend on authority
- Feel dependent on what they have heard or read
- Prepare to participate
- Hesitate
- Be polite and guarded
- Fear differences
- Have concern for being a leader

During the forming stage, individuals need much information. They must be able to express themselves and ask many clarifying questions. The principal and the focus team's members should be accessible and open to dissenting voices. Individuals may require one-on-one attention. Members' concerns focus on getting more information and details about expectations of and implications for themselves. In Figure 3.1, the stages of concern show that in the early stages of an innovation, individuals focus on "self" and are at the informational and personal levels of concern. Each individual is interested in substantive aspects of the process, such as the evidence that student learning will improve. Group members, uncertain about the effects of study groups, will see their school as different from any other school, and the fact that many other schools are implementing WFSGs will not soothe their personal concerns. They will want to know what is required of them, if the principal and district leaders are going to support study groups over time, and if teachers will have adequate resources for their groups. Participants want to understand how the process will affect them, how they will be part of the decision-making process, and what the potential conflicts may be with existing structures. In particular, their concerns will be about themselves, financial or status implications, and time for study groups to meet. It is extremely important that school leadership present clear and reasonable options for teachers during this early stage.

The most critical aspect of this early stage is for the whole faculty to work together to make decisions about what study groups will do. Following the steps in the DMC (see Chapter 7) enables group members to feel a part of the effort. Teachers must know that their voices will be heard. When they experience the analysis of student data and see that what study groups do is grounded in student needs, they become more trusting of the process. Additional comfort comes when they realize that it is the study group members who decide exactly what the group will do in relation to student needs.

As individuals move from the whole group to smaller study groups, many of the feelings of concern will be transferred to and expressed in their study group. Consequently, it is important that study groups are given clear and concise instructions as to what to do during their first two study group meetings. It is helpful for them to have materials with tangible information describing precisely what they are to do. During these first two meetings, groups establish norms and leadership rotation schedules and begin developing the action plan. These expectations keep the group members focused on tasks and not on themselves and each other.

Stage 2: Grumbling

It is usually during the grumbling stage that there is a dip in morale and commitment as the group comes to realize its tasks are more difficult than it initially expected. The saying "It isn't real until it's real" is true. Fullan (2001a) refers to this dip as the "implementation dip." In the context of study groups, this dip usually occurs when the initial energy wanes and the group is faced with the logistical aspects of the process. Using Figure 3.1, we see that these individuals are at the management level of concern, focusing on the tasks required of WFSGs. In Figure 3.2, these same individuals are at the mechanical level of use in that the tasks seem disjointed and superficial. During this stage, members actually see that no one outside their group is going to tell them what to do, and this reality becomes something to grumble about. A fly on the wall might hear, "Why don't they just tell us what to do?" The interesting aspect of this stage is that individuals can become quite contented and comfortable grumbling. It appears that as long as they can grumble, usually complaining about forces outside of themselves and their group, they can easily become complacent. These individuals need to feel some discomfort to move beyond this stage.

During the grumbling stage, study group members may experience the following:

- Feel dissatisfied with past decisions
- Sense a discrepancy between hopes and reality
- Be frustrated
- Feel incompetent and confused
- React negatively toward the initiators of study groups
- Want permission to act
- Desire confirmation that what they are doing is right
- Feel unsure about what will benefit everyone
- Prefer to withdraw from the group
- Believe that the group process is too difficult
- Be impatient with other members
- Compete for attention
- Feel stuck
- Focus their concerns on group management issues
- Perceive that the process is very mechanical

The grumbling stage is not an unproductive stage. It is a growing stage that groups go through on their way to being productive. This is usually when the seeds are sown for creativity and the valuing of differences. Concerns during this stage are processes of group membership. Members struggle with the best use of time, information, and resources. Issues related to efficiency, organization of the work, and roles and responsibilities are foremost in their minds. It is during this stage that members focus on the short-term value of study groups and take little time for reflection. They tend to concentrate more on themselves and the mechanics of the process than on their students (Figures 3.1 and 3.2). The work of the group often seems poorly coordinated and superficial. One might hear a teacher say, "I could get more done in my room by myself."

Study groups require much support and encouragement in this phase to move to the next stage. This is the stage in which external support is most important. The principal and other support persons at the school and district level should respond to each study group's action plan. It is especially critical that the principal lets each group know that he or she is aware of what the group is doing. The principal can be encouraging by making suggestions to the group regarding how student needs have been expressed, actions the group plans to take, and resources that the group has identified. The log that each study group keeps should be carefully responded to for at least the first three or four meetings. This is the point at which the principal will have the greatest influence on the outcome of the study group work. The quicker the principal acknowledges what a group is doing, the faster it will move into a more productive stage. What principals show by their actions to be important, teachers will generally take as important. Teachers should also know that district-level leaders are aware of each group's work and are ready to support it. Study groups in this stage often require a push for them to move to the next stage. When the logs are read, the principal will see a dominance of passive verbs, such as "discussing" and "reviewing." At this point, the principal should ask, "And what action in the classroom will that lead you to?"

Helping study groups move through the forming and grumbling stages of group development requires direct support and encouragement from the principal and district staff. Study groups, for instance, experience both support and pressure from having permission to release students early 1 day a week for study groups to meet, from having a content specialist meet with the group once a month, and from the principal's attentiveness to action plans and study group logs. In this context, support and pressure are positive dynamics. Without high expectations, which is a form of pressure, resources are wasted. Without support, individuals become alienated from the process and from school leaders. Principals need the will and skill to guide and facilitate the movement of study groups into the final two stages.

Stage 3: Willingness

It is during the willingness stage that group members become open to each other and willing to work cooperatively so the group can function successfully. Competition fades, collaboration increases. In this stage, there is a sense of expanding energy as the group pulls itself together to focus more clearly and effectively on intended results of the group's action plans.

During this stage, study group members may experience the following:

- Resolve discrepancies between expectations and reality
- Decrease dissatisfaction
- Develop harmony, trust, support, and respect
- Increase self-esteem and confidence
- Be more open
- Share what is not working in their classrooms
- Visit each other's classrooms
- Give more feedback to each other

- Share responsibility and control
- Use common language
- Feel comfortable with sharing leadership
- Focus concerns on the impact of the group's work on students

During the willingness stage, group members begin to develop new and refined instructional strategies and materials, share interdependently with each other, and introduce new practices that have a positive impact on their students. In Figure 3.1, the concerns being expressed are on the impact of the study group work and the communication between and among groups. Likewise, Figure 3.2 reflects that members are refining the process so that it has more personal meaning to what they do in their classrooms and are integrating the work of WFSGs into other school structures. When reviewing study group logs, the principal will see that there are many overt activities. The section of the study group log titled "Discussions and Activities Focused On" will most likely use active verbs such as "practiced," "demonstrated," "reflected," "monitored," "worked," "experimented," "taught," and "interviewed." Teachers are doing collaborative work, which means that they are taking joint responsibility for efforts in their classrooms and for their students' work. In particular, the "classroom application" section of their log is full, and student work is routinely brought to study group meetings. When study groups are in the willingness stage, there are high levels of synergy in groups and energy throughout the school. A cultural change is evidenced in both formal and informal conversations between principals and teachers, teachers and teachers, students and teachers, students and students, and parents and teachers. Study group members are focused more on the impact (Figures 3.1 and 3.2) their work is having on students than they were in the forming and grumbling stages.

Stage 4: Consequence

In the consequence stage, study group members have a high awareness of the consequences of the group's actions. Their concerns focus on the impact of their work on students. As shown in Figure 3.1, the concerns being expressed are for students. The levels of use (Figure 3.2) indicate that teachers are continually refining the process to meet the specific needs of their students. In the forming stage, initiators of the group process tell teachers that forming study groups is a means to greater student success, whereas in the consequence stage teachers fully understand from their study group experiences that this is indeed true.

During this stage, study group members may experience the following:

- Keep student work as the study group's centerpiece
- Find strength from the group
- Participate fully
- Feel positive about the group's influence on each other and on students
- Be highly motivated to continue
- Seek more collaborative relationships in and out of school
- Focus concerns on coordination and cooperation with others
- Commit to more intellectually rigorous work
- Be dissatisfied with passive action, seeking more purposeful student interventions
- Combine efforts with colleagues to achieve a collective impact on students

- Sense empowerment
- Perceive a strong feeling of personal dignity
- Accept a high degree of commitment to all the students at the school
- Integrate study group work into other forms of professional development
- Have more positive views of students

In the consequence stage, teachers actualize the concept that students are at the center of professional development. Teachers in study groups focus on the impact that the work of the study group is having on students. They use words such as "our students" instead "my students." At this stage, group members require many opportunities to share what their study group is learning and doing that is changing what their students are learning and achieving. Results of increased student learning must be shared! Data that show students doing better on end-of-chapter tests, completing more assignments, reading more books for pleasure, and entering more science fairs, as well as data showing fewer students being referred to the office, should be collected and charted. Teachers should see the data and celebrate their successes. They need to see evidence that the collective power of their study group is making a real difference with students. At the beginning of a new school year, it is also this knowledge and its acknowledgment that will importantly change the question "Will we have study groups this year?" to "What student needs are we going to address this year?"

More Circular Than Linear

When group conditions change, the developmental stages are repeated to some degree, and the stages become more circular than linear. Conditions change, for example, when a teacher takes a leave of absence in the middle of the year and is no longer a member of the group, when a teacher new to the school joins the group, when there is a major change in contextual conditions, when the group decides to rewrite the action plan and to select a new student need, and when new expectations are imposed on the group. Groups that have formed and are working in the willingness stage will find themselves having to reform, if only for a meeting or two. The second time around, grumbling will be at a minimum and will have less impact on the functioning of the group. Members will quickly recommit to each other with a renewed sense of willingness to move ahead and accomplish the goals of the group.

Time in Each Stage

Typically, if study groups begin meeting weekly by the middle of September, it will be November before most of the groups have cleared the grumbling stage. Few will reach the consequence stage by the end of the first year. When the second year begins, groups will return to the forming stage, even those study groups that do not change membership. If a study group does remain intact, the reforming stage will only last a meeting or two. If people are in different study groups than they were the year before, the forming stage may continue into the fourth meeting. The grumbling stage is usually shorter for groups during the second year because individuals have had a year of experience, and they see that the study group initiative did not "go away." More study groups will reach the consequence stage during the second year because all the teachers will be encouraged and motivated by the study groups that reached the consequence stage during the first year. When the third year begins, more groups, even those groups in which membership changed, will move more quickly though the first two stages. During the third year of implementation, most groups will reach the willingness stage by the fourth meeting. The variable that has a major effect on the growth of study groups is other initiatives that teachers are confronting, both new and carryovers.

During a school year, the factor that has the most influence on a study group's movement through the stages is how often it meets. Projections in the foregoing discussion are for study groups that meet weekly or, at the very least, 90 minutes every other week. In schools in which study groups meet only once a month, the groups will most likely remain in the forming and grumbling stages the entire school year because by May the group will have met only seven or eight times. Study groups that meet weekly will have met seven times by November.

From year to year, the factors that have the most influence on the start-up and continuation of study groups are contextual. For example, the number of new initiatives that the school has adopted, changes in personnel, and the level of ongoing district support all have the potential to inhibit or stop the process.

SUMMARY

Schools that authentically apply the 15 procedural guidelines and adhere to the WFSG guiding principles have justification to use the term Whole-Faculty Study Groups to describe their collaborative improvement design. Schools with evidence that the WFSG approach has had positive effects on student achievement and on the culture of the school have followed closely the 15 procedural guidelines presented in this chapter. When faculties ask Murphy if it is acceptable to alter a guideline (e.g., not meet weekly or have more than six in a group), her standard answer is, "That is your choice. If you alter the guidelines, you can't expect to get the results that schools have gotten that followed the guidelines." The guidelines evolved over a period of at least 14 years with real school experiences in all kinds of schools throughout the country and include the results of many revisions and refinements. Since 1993, the authors, after reflecting on the work in progress in very different schools, have reexamined and revised the guidelines at the end of each school year.

7

Identifying Student Needs for Targeted Study

The Seven-Step Decision-Making Cycle

QUESTIONS THAT DRIVE THE WHOLE-FACULTY STUDY GROUP DECISION-MAKING PROCESS

In Chapter 1, we presented the questions that are the foundation of the Whole-Faculty Study Group (WFSG) system. Here, we repeat those questions because in this chapter we describe how we determine the answers to the following fundamental questions:

> • What do students need for teachers to do so that teachers will have a deeper understanding of what they teach?

- What do students need for teachers to do so that teachers will be more skillful in how they teach?
- What do students need for teachers to do so that teachers will challenge students to learn difficult and fundamental concepts?
- What do students need for teachers to do so that teachers will give students skills to be deep thinkers and problem solvers?

THE DECISION-MAKING CYCLE

The decision-making cycle (DMC) (Murphy, 1999) outlines a series of seven steps. This cyclic process is recommended for making decisions regarding what study groups will do, leading to how study groups will be formed and organized. The cycle represents 1 year in the life of a WFSG school, from the beginning of the school year, when data are analyzed to identify student needs, to the end of a school year, when data are analyzed to determine if the identified need areas have improved. Each year, the cycle is repeated, with each yearly cycle spiraling to a higher level of work.

The DMC's seven steps have been successfully followed in schools that are very different with regard to school size, grade level, demographics, location, and leadership styles of the principals. After a decade of trials in many different schools, the DMC evolved into how it is depicted in Figure 7.1. The length of development time means that it has been proven effective and efficient, over time, in leading faculties through a series of steps that will ultimately determine what individuals do when they meet in study groups. Its evolution, including continuous adjustments based on use, should give participants confidence in the DMC. Individuals who lead the whole faculty through the steps of the cycle must carefully follow the instructions provided in this chapter and in Resource D. Although those leading the DMC may have firm opinions as to how study groups should be formed and what study groups should do, they must maintain open minds, keep their opinions to themselves, and be totally free in letting the faculty find its own way. It is critical that the whole faculty participates in Steps 1 through 4 of the cycle. Every faculty member should have a voice in how groups are organized and what groups will be doing. Open participation now will diminish problems after study groups begin their work. Teachers own the process and should feel that ownership. When the whole faculty works together during these early stages of decision making, teachers feel empowered and begin to see that they do have a say in what is going to happen. Teachers begin to feel a part of the effort and, as a result, feel less coerced during the implementation stage. During the initiation stage, when everyone is involved in the decision making, the faculty sees the process for what it is intended to do. Those who may have been skeptical about the process and indicated a minimum level of willingness during the consensus-forming stage often become more willing when their voices are heard in this developmental phase. Some teachers will still continue to believe that the process is contrived collegiality until, in their study groups, they experience total control over what they choose to do to address a set of student needs and how they go about doing it.

Figure 7.1 shows the seven steps. Steps 1 through 4 are completed with the whole faculty in approximately 3 hours. Step 5 is completed during the first two study group meetings. Step 6 is a series of continuous cycles, usually during a school year. Step 7 is continuous and at the end of the school year. The whole faculty

WFSG
Decision-Making Cycle

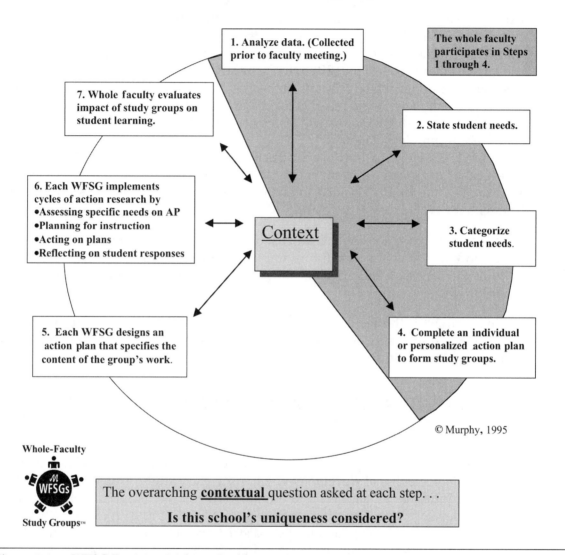

Figure 7.1   WFSG Decision-Making Cycle

- Step 1: Analyzes data
- Step 2: Identifies student needs
- Step 3: Categorizes student needs
- Step 4: Completes individual or personalized action plans

Each study group

- Step 5: Designs a study group action plan
- Step 6: Implements cycles of action research
- Step 7: Assesses the impact of study groups on student learning

THE DECISION-MAKING CYCLE AND SCHOOL IMPROVEMENT PLAN

Most schools have a plan, the school improvement plan (SIP), that the district expects them to implement. Steps 1 through 3 in the DMC should affirm the instructional component of the SIP. Even though there is a SIP, it is strongly recommended that Steps 1 through 4 of the DMC be completed at the beginning of each year. Often, the improvement goals in the SIP are too general to give a study group specific direction. Steps 1 through 4 take only approximately 3 hours, and it is well worth the time for every faculty member to feel that he or she had a direct voice in making the decisions about what study groups will do. Short-circuiting the process will only create more serious problems later.

As WFSGs work to improve instruction, ideas about best practices begin to emerge that all groups will want to use. At Clarke Middle School in Athens, Georgia, for example, the faculty decided to begin "banking" ideas from the study groups. The school's WFSG newsletter states,

> We are beginning to store the suggestions and programs we want to consider as an entire staff for near-future implementation. Starting in February, we will work through and prioritize the list together and add items to our school improvement plan.

In April 2004, the faculty met to consider all the ideas in the study groups' idea banks. Resource C describes how the Clarke Middle School faculty sorted, prioritized, and included the ideas in its 2004–2005 school improvement plan.

AN INDIVIDUAL'S PROFESSIONAL DEVELOPMENT PLAN

The study group's action plan, developed in Step 5 of the DMC, is, in large part, an individual's professional development plan for each study group member. Most districts require that all teachers and administrators have individual plans for professional development. The proposed work of a study group includes what each member must do to help accomplish district expectations. In the Springfield, Missouri, public schools, for instance, where WFSGs are districtwide, the study group action plan is the individual teacher's professional development plan. Figure 7.4 (see p. 135) illustrates how the study groups, the school improvement plan, and individual plans for professional development all work together.

DECISIONS MADE BEFORE BEGINNING THE DECISION-MAKING CYCLE

Prior to experiencing the DMC, the following four important decisions will have already been made:

1. Whether the WFSG approach is to be put in place at the school and whether the principal will actively support WFSGs

2. The time for study groups to meet

3. Who will lead the whole faculty through an inquiry process to decide what groups will do and how groups will be organized (Steps 1–4 in the DMC)

4. What data will be examined to determine student needs when the faculty experiences Steps 1 through 4 in the DMC

The first decision to be made by the whole faculty is whether the WFSG approach will be put in place at the school. This decision is made after all faculty members have had an orientation to and been given information about the WFSG system. Typically, this is done in a general faculty meeting. In some schools, the principal or other school leaders meet with grade-level or department groups. In other schools, printed materials are distributed, and the principal follows up with individuals. In any case, the faculty knows the definition, guiding principles, functions, and procedural guidelines for WFSGs. Regardless of the process used, it is important to let faculty know up front how the decision will be made and the criteria for approval. If the faculty is to vote, everyone needs to understand what percentage of approval will require all faculty to be members of study groups. If approval will be by consensus, everyone needs to understand how consensus will be determined. After the decision is made, however, it is expected that all faculty members will participate in a study group.

Directly related to the decision to begin WFSGs is the commitment of active support (i.e., strong sponsorship) by the principal for the launch, implementation, and institutionalization of the WFSG system. Schools must have the daily, active support of the principal and assistant principals for WFSGs to succeed. In the WFSG system, the principal is expected to support and facilitate the orientation of staff to WFSGs and take part in the launch process (Steps 1–4 of the DMC). The principal is also expected to read study group action plans and logs, provide regular feedback and support to study groups, assist with the identification of resources to support study groups, participate in instructional council meetings, establish mechanisms to share the work of the study groups, and integrate the work of WFSGs within school improvement planning.

The second decision to be made before beginning WFSGs is to determine when study groups will meet or, at least, the options for finding time. It is important to decide this before taking the faculty through Steps 1 through 4 of the DMC because teachers always want to know that time will be provided for study group meetings before they make choices about student needs and forming study groups. Because many teachers are skeptical of new programs and the school's and district's support for implementation, deciding up front when study groups will meet demonstrates commitment to support WFSGs.

Study groups should meet for 1 hour every week or for 2 hours every other week. Study groups that meet less than this will probably not be successful in changing practices and improving student performance. Because all certificated staff in the school participate in study groups, the time for study groups to meet must be built into the school schedule in a way that respects teachers' contractual obligations. Usually, study groups meet during the school day, before school, or after school. A number of options that schools have used for study group time were discussed in Chapter 4. It is not uncommon for schools to use one approach in the first year and then try a different approach in the second year. How this decision about time is made can be just as important as the decision as to when the groups will meet. Ideally, the exploration of options and dialogue and discussion about these options should involve the school's shared decision-making team or focus team or both and the entire faculty to ensure understanding and ownership of the decision. A related time issue to be addressed before launching WFSGs is finding time for the entire faculty to go through Steps 1 through 4 of the DMC.

The third decision is most often made by the principal and includes identifying those individuals who will lead the whole faculty through an inquiry process to determine what groups will do and how groups will be organized (Steps 1–4). Most often, this is done by a team from the school called the focus team. Focus teams attend a 2½-day training session conducted by members of the staff of the WFSG National Center. Focus teams go to the center either in February, when the WFSG national conference is scheduled, or in June and July, when WFSG institutes are scheduled. If several schools in a district are going to implement WFSGs, associates from the national center may come to the district or a regional service agency to train focus teams. When a focus team is trained, members of the team experience the DMC and become knowledgeable of the intricacies of the WFSG system so that they can provide instruction and support to their colleagues, not only in the beginning but also when maintaining high-performing groups becomes a challenge. Rather than having a focus team from the school lead the faculty, a principal may ask an associate from the national center to lead the faculty through the decision-making process. Some schools have had both a focus team and an associate from the center work with a faculty.

The fourth decision is the key to whether the needed student improvement will occur. School leaders must decide what data will be examined to determine student needs when the faculty experiences Steps 1 through 4 in the DMC. Data must be collected and organized for the faculty to use in making decisions about student needs, what study groups will do, and how study groups will be organized. What student data and general information about students the faculty will review is one of the most important decisions that leaders of WFSGs will make. All future decisions will be shaped by what data the faculty analyzes. If the data will not lead to the most serious instructional needs, the whole process will be in danger of failing to accomplish intended results. If, for example, the most serious need of students is in the area of reading and the faculty does not have data to validate that need, the faculty may miss its opportunity to address that critical need.

Guidelines for selecting and organizing data are discussed later. Just as with making decisions about when study groups meet, how decisions are made about what data to bring to the WFSG launch session is important for convincing faculty that the WFSG system is different from traditional top-down interventions. Ideally, a school's shared decision-making team or focus team should lead the discussions about what data to bring to the faculty so that everyone knows before starting Step 1 how and why data decisions were made.

TIME NEEDED

The faculty will require approximately 3 hours to experience Steps 1 through 4 of the DMC. The faculty will meet and be led by the focus team or by a WFSG associate from the WFSG National Center. It is important that time be set aside for this task as soon as the decision is made to implement WFSGs. The best time to be engaged in the DMC process is within the first 4 weeks of the new school year. A faculty with contractual days at school before the students arrive or with a staff development day within the first month of school can use part of one of those days. Some principals pay faculty members to arrive a day early. Some schools take 90 minutes after school on two different days. Schools have used a variety of methods to make the time for Steps 1 through 4. Nonetheless, the first order of business is identifying the time when all teachers will be together to experience Steps 1 through 4.

Considering the seven steps of the DMC in relation to time, it may not be apparent that there are substantial differences in the amount of time it takes to complete each step. Steps 1 through 4 together can be completed in a 3-hour session, but Step 5, design an action plan, requires approximately two study group meetings. Step 6 requires the remainder of the school year (i.e., 7 or 8 months); during this step, the work happens in individual study groups, and it involves meeting after meeting. Step 7 should be occurring formatively during the entire time that a study group meets but summatively at the end of the year. Although they require various amounts of time, all steps in the DMC are crucial to the WFSG process.

LEADING THE FACULTY THROUGH THE DECISION-MAKING CYCLE

Resource B contains a script for how the focus team may want to lead the faculty through the DMC.

Parameters for Identifying Student Needs

During the orientation to WFSGs and before beginning the DMC, it is important that everyone understands the types of student needs that become the focus of the work of WFSGs. Teachers should know that only those data sources that indicate the academic and instructional needs of students will be included in the data to be analyzed. Student needs that do not fall within these parameters would be assigned to a committee, department chairs, grade-level chairs, or any other appropriate organizational structure. Typical student needs that fall outside of the parameters include discipline, absenteeism, and tardiness. Just because a student need is deemed not appropriate for a study group does not mean that the need is not valid. It simply means that there is a more appropriate way within the school than study groups to address the need. No student need should be ignored.

To keep teachers' work focused on instruction, there are three parameters that give faculties direction with regard to student needs to be addressed by WFSGs:

- Student need is evident in work that students produce. Teachers look at student work for evidence of the impact of study group work on student learning.
- Student need can be addressed through how and what teachers teach.
- Student need is an enabling need, one that enables students to be academically successful, such as the need to comprehend what they read, express themselves orally and through their writing, compute, and understand science concepts. An enabling need could also be classified as a "terminal" need, meaning that at some point the need will no longer exist as it did or at the level it

existed because teachers intervened and took corrective action. Teachers have direct control or influence on terminating the need. This is unlike a perennial need—that is, a student need that is always there, such as the need to attend school, feel good about self, cooperate, be respectful, behave, and have parents involved. Perennial needs are best addressed through an enabling need. For example, as study group members address student learning needs in mathematics, they will also be targeting ethical issues. As study group members learn to appropriately use a range of teaching strategies that actively involve students, discipline will improve. Study groups will have primary focus on enabling or terminal student needs. At the same time, study groups could have several perennial student needs that weave in and out of what all groups do. Student needs clarification is important because districts and schools make the decision to use Murphy's WFSGs for one primary reason: to increase student learning. Therefore, study group work must be clearly targeted to student achievement.

Preparing the Setting

The whole faculty convenes in one place to experience Steps 1 through 4 of the DMC. It is best that the faculty remains together for the entire exercise with teachers seated at tables of no more than five per table. This approach explicitly models one of the WFSG guidelines—that study groups are composed of three to five members. If there are more than five at a table (or in a study group), it is likely that participation will be unequal, and that the group will not have enough time to complete its tasks. Also, it is important to ensure that the five people represent different grade levels, middle school teams, or departments.

One technique is to tape a sheet of paper to a table with Pre-K Teacher, Music Teacher, Second-Grade Teacher, Fifth-Grade Teacher, and Special Needs Teacher written on it, giving teachers choices within a contained setting. If there are four first-grade teachers, there will be four tables that have First-Grade Teacher on the list, meaning that such a teacher has four seating choices. This arrangement will facilitate the analysis of the data. For instance, first-grade teachers can explain tests that are administered at the primary levels, and fifth-grade teachers can explain tests that are administered at the upper grade levels. In addition, mathematics teachers can explain mathematics exit exams to language arts teachers and vice versa. In this way, teachers will experience working with teachers with whom they may not have worked, and they are beginning to model the study group experience.

For large faculties, there may be parts of the exercise in which groups can be assigned to classrooms to work. In convening rooms, individuals would sit at tables with not more than five at a table, and facilitators would ensure that table groups represent different grade levels or departments. Prior planning for all such circumstances is the key to managing the logistics well. Ideally, faculty members would be given a loose-leaf binder with information required to begin and continue the process. Each binder should have five sections. Section 1 contains general information about WFSGs, including definition, principles, functions, procedural guidelines with rationales that all study groups will follow, and roles and responsibilities. Most of the information in Section 1 was presented when the faculty was introduced to WFSGs. Section 2 contains the DMC, including worksheets and lists to help them complete WFSG action plans. Section 3 contains blank action plans and logs, checklists, protocols, and other materials that groups may use during the school year. Section 4 is empty and is reserved for the study group's completed action plan and copies of its completed logs. Section 5 is reserved for artifacts from a group's meetings, such as articles, rubric group designs, handouts from trainers, and examples of student work.

In the middle of each table, leaders place a folder. The folder contains five pieces of color-coded data. It is important that there be just one piece of data for each person sitting at the table. One piece of data, for example, may be a stapled set of Iowa Test of Basic Skills (ITBS) scores. Folders on every table contain exactly the same five pieces of data. The color coding will let the leader know at a glance who has the ITBS data at all the tables.

The SIP is not used at this time because these plans are usually too voluminous and contain needs that study groups would not address, such as facility needs. Also, most SIPs include broad improvement goals, such as that at least 80% of students will score "proficient" in reading. The DMC works because everything the faculty is asked to do is clear, concise, and timed. After Step 3, there will be a list of specific student needs that have been grouped and are choices for study group work. With everyone in place and with the required materials, leaders are ready to begin Step 1 in the DMC. Steps 1 through 3 can be accomplished in approximately 90 minutes.

Prior to Step 1: Identify and Organize Data

School leaders identify and organize data that describe the status of student learning for faculty review. The focus team or the principal, with a group of teachers, identifies which data sources are most relevant for identifying specific instructional needs of students. The faculty as a whole will analyze the data. The most important responsibility of the focus team is to make decisions about data that the faculty will review. What study groups will do and how they will be organized will depend on the conclusions drawn from the data that the faculty analyzes. Experience indicates that it is best to limit the pieces of data to five, one piece for each person sitting at a table. For instance, in an elementary school, folders may include (a) a stapled set of ITBS grade summaries for fourth graders for 3 consecutive years, (b) a stapled set of state criterion reference test summaries for second graders, (c) results of checklists developed by the publisher of the reading series used at the school, (d) results of the Early Literacy Test for kindergarten, and (e) a district's Benchmark Test results for fifth graders. High schools should consider data from elementary and middle schools that feed into the high school. Similarly, elementary and middle schools should consider data from the high schools their students will attend. To identify specific student academic and instructional needs, the whole faculty should spend time reviewing the data compiled for the faculty for the purpose of establishing WFSGs. In general, the more specific and disaggregated the data, the more useful the data are for determining student learning needs. Where possible, data should be disaggregated for specific skills, concepts, and understandings within each subject area; types of performance tasks (multiple choice vs. open response); and different student group characteristics (e.g., ethnicity, gender, socioeconomic status, and disability). For example, the faculty should not only see data for "reading" but also see data for reading comprehension, vocabulary, and word attack skills. If the faculty has had little or no experience in examining and discussing data on student performance, the principal or the focus team may want to have a practice session prior to the launch with similar types of data.

At this point in the process, the faculty reviews whole-school student needs, not focusing on any one grade level. After the study groups are formed, one of the first orders of business for all study groups is to examine a variety of data sources that further delineate or clarify the needs of their students in the category they are targeting. Members of study groups will add to what the whole faculty reviewed, including classroom assessments to the standardized data. If, for instance, a study group is targeting vocabulary development, members may look at a collection of student work to verify and identify their students' specific vocabulary needs. We recommend that student work become a data source after the groups are formed because the scope is narrower than when the whole faculty reviewed data. Members may also develop assessments to certify where their students are currently so that in 6 weeks the study group can reassess and determine what growth has occurred.

Table 7.1 gives the types of data that faculties study to identify and track specific student needs. Most of the data sources are more appropriate for tracking student performance during the school year. The table lists 26 data sources and the considerations of each for use in Step 1 of the DMC.

SEVEN STEPS OF THE DECISION-MAKING CYCLE

Step 1: Analyze Data

Those leading the faculty will indicate when the items in the data folder are to be distributed, with each person taking one item. After the leader identifies each data source, the faculty will have 30 minutes to analyze the information. First, individuals focus on the piece of data they received, taking 10 minutes to look for patterns and trends, gaps or anomalies, areas of strength, and areas of weakness. Individuals may mark items, highlight items, and write questions to the side of items. This is individual work with no discussion. Next, each person shares at the table the key points on his or her data. After 20 minutes, the leader calls for everyone's attention. Resource B contains a script for this step.

Step 2: State Student Needs

In the binders teachers were given, there is a section that is actually a "workbook" for the DMC. This workbook is Resource B. To complete Step 2, teachers are asked to use a specific worksheet in their notebooks. The leader asks the teachers to refocus on the piece of data they received and to write on the worksheet specific student needs they see evidenced in the data. When stating student needs, teachers should be reminded of the parameters discussed previously. Can the need be evidenced in student work and addressed through how and what teachers teach? The faculty is instructed to write each need so as to complete the sentence stem "Students need to . . . " by adding an appropriate phrase similar to the following:

1. Improve and enlarge vocabulary in all content areas

2. Meet mathematics measurement standards

3. Use correct grammar, punctuation, and spelling in all areas of the curriculum

4. Communicate their thinking of mathematical processes (oral and written)

Data Source	Considerations for Use in Step 1 of the DMC
Standardized test results over a span of several years	Useful if disaggregated by subgroup and proficiency level and linked to specific content strands or skill clusters.
Performance of students on the district's content standards	Useful if disaggregated by subgroup and proficiency level and linked to specific content strands or skill clusters.
Student work	Useful if already analyzed to identify student learning needs. In the DMC Step 1–4 session, there isn't time to use a looking at student work (LASW) protocol to examine samples of work and reach conclusions about the student learning needs evidenced in the work. This examination could be done before the DMC session.
Pre- and post-teacher-made assessments	Useful if the data from the assessments have been analyzed to identify areas of strength and weakness for different groups of students and linked to standards.
Early Literacy Assessment or other tests in pre-K to second-grade classes	Useful if the data show levels of proficiency on specific skills and, ideally, performance for different subgroups.
Oral reading assessments	Useful if the data show levels of proficiency on specific skills and, ideally, performance for different subgroups.
End-of-unit tests	Useful if the data have been analyzed to show levels of proficiency on specific skills and concepts and, ideally, performance for different subgroups.
End of grading period, e.g., 6 weeks grade (A–F) distribution by subject, grade, and teacher	This data will not generate specific student learning needs. It will identify groups of students, subjects, and classrooms to investigate further to try to figure out WHY some students are failing.
Informal reading inventories	Useful if the data show levels of proficiency on specific skills and, ideally, performance for different subgroups.
Exit exams from high school courses	Useful if the data have been analyzed to show levels of proficiency on specific skills and concepts and, ideally, performance for different subgroups.
Criterion-referenced tests	Useful if the data show levels of proficiency on specific skills and concepts and, ideally, performance for different subgroups.
Student portfolios	Useful if all portfolios or a sample have already been analyzed against a rubric to identify student learning needs. In the DMC Step 1–4 session, there isn't time to examine student portfolios and reach conclusions about the student learning needs evidenced in the work. This examination could be done before the DMC session.
Writing assessments	Useful if the data from writing assessments have already been analyzed to show levels of proficiency on specific skills and concepts and, ideally, performance for different subgroups.

Table 7.1   Student Needs Data Sources

(Continued)

Table 7.1 (Continued)

Data Source	Considerations for Use in Step 1 of the DMC
Journals and authentic writing samples	Useful if all journals or writing samples, or a sample, have already been analyzed against a rubric to identify student learning needs. In the DMC Step 1–4 session there isn't time to examine student journals or writing samples and reach conclusions about the student learning needs evidenced in the work. This examination could be done before the DMC session.
Checklists from textbook companies (e.g., reading series often have end-of-book or unit tests)	Useful if the data from the checklists or end-of-unit tests have already been analyzed to show levels of proficiency on specific skills and concepts and, ideally, performance for different subgroups.
Performance assessments	Useful if the data from performance assessments have already been analyzed to show levels of proficiency on specific skills and concepts and, ideally, performance for different subgroups.
Results of open-ended response questions	Useful if the student work on open-ended response questions has already been analyzed against a rubric to show levels of proficiency on specific skills and concepts and, ideally, performance for different subgroups.
Results of tests given by Title I and other special testing programs	Useful if the data show levels of proficiency on specific skills and concepts and, ideally, performance for different subgroups.
Results of state tests in subject areas (e.g., New York State's Regents Examinations)	Useful if the data show levels of proficiency on specific skills and concepts and, ideally, performance for different subgroups.
Cumulative grade point averages by subject area and grade for a random sample of students	This data will not generate specific student learning needs. It will identify groups of students to investigate further to try to figure out WHY students in certain grades or subjects are having difficulty.
The numbers of students placed in advanced placement courses and in remedial or lower-level courses	This data will not generate specific student learning needs. It will identify groups of students to investigate further to try to figure out WHY they are not taking AP courses.
Promotion and retention rates by grades and subjects	This data will not generate specific student learning needs. It will identify groups of students to investigate further to try to figure out WHY they are failing.
Responses by teachers and/or students to questionnaires and interviews	Useful if the responses have been analyzed.
An analysis of circulation reports from the school library (as a check on independent reading)	This data will not generate specific student learning needs. It will identify groups of students to investigate further to try to figure out WHY they are not reading independently.
An analysis of students enrolled in debate, academic bowls, and other activities that are subject area related	This data will not generate specific student learning needs. It will identify groups of students to investigate further to try to figure out WHY they are not participating.
State Report Card for schools	Useful if the report cards give information about levels of proficiency for subgroups of students on skill or concept clusters.

5. Have the ability to sequence events in a story

6. Know how to solve word problems

7. Know how to locate the main idea in a paragraph

8. Write and speak for an audience or a purpose

9. Use the five-step process in writing persuasive and expository pieces

10. Read for meaning

11. Know how to proofread and edit work

12. Increase syllabication skill

13. Incorporate technology in gathering, understanding, and evaluating information

14. Recognize letters and sounds of the alphabet

After individuals have listed student needs they see evidenced in the data they reviewed, the leader instructs the table groups to compile all the student needs on the individual lists onto chart paper. The leader cautions the groups to list only student needs that they see in documents in the data folders. They are reminded that after the groups are formed, they will have an opportunity to consider additional data. The leader also instructs the table groups to begin each need with a verb (to complete the sentence stem) and to number the student needs. The importance of the numbering will be clear in Step 3. After most of the groups have completed the task, the groups are asked to tape their charts to a wall.

After all the charts are taped on a wall or are displayed in some way, the leader will choose one chart, usually the one with the longest list, and call it the master list. The leader will ask one person from each table to stand beside that table's chart. As the leader reads each student need on the master list, the people representing each table mark off the student needs that appear on the table's chart and on the master list. If the master list has 14 student needs listed, the leader will move to one table's chart and make the first student need not marked off as number 15. If other tables have that student need on their charts, it is marked off the other charts. This process is continued until each table marks through a student need that has been accounted for or that has been numbered. By the time the leader gets to the last table's chart, usually all the listed student needs are marked off because the needs have appeared on other lists. Also, by this time, the master list has as many as 20 to 30 student needs. The leader has moved from chart to chart, marking off duplicate items and numbering sequentially those not crossed off the charts. Duplication is expected because the data folders on every table have the same data. The differences will be in how individuals express the needs. It is up to the individuals at a table whether they want to accept the master list's or previous lists' wording or whether their wording will remain. If a table wants its wording of an item to remain, that table would keep the need on its list and it would be given a number. Duplication in this process is a positive sign; it reinforces that others are seeing the same needs.

While the leader is working with the charts, one person in the audience is entering the student needs into a laptop computer. By the time the leader completes the numbering, the person entering the data will have finished entering the list in the computer. At that point, the leader will give the faculty a 10-minute break or spend approximately 10 minutes debriefing what has occurred to this point. During the break or debriefing, the list will be printed, and each faculty member will be given a copy. The final list has every faculty member's interpretation of the student needs.

Step 3: Categorize Student Needs

Everyone is given the printed list of student needs. This list is numbered sequentially and may contain a sizable number of student needs. At this point, the list is not organized in any way. Several needs may be very similar, which is okay because the wording represents how different teachers interpreted the need. Now the task is to organize the list so that similar needs are grouped together. The teachers have a worksheet for putting the list of student needs into groups.

The leader instructs everyone to review the list, find needs that can be grouped together, and give the group a name; this process is called categorizing student needs. Each person is to work alone on this task, making a determination, for example, of whether a need would fit into a reading category, a writing category, or both. Teachers may form as many categories as they want in a designated amount of time and may place a need in more than one category. For instance, "increase vocabulary" could be in reading, writing, mathematics, and/or science categories. To save time, teachers are told that they may use the numbers in front of the needs to form categories. After the leader sees that everyone has formed at least two categories, he or she calls for everyone's attention.

The leader will go to a chart or to the overhead projector and say, "Raise your hand if you would like to share a category." The person raising his or her hand will call out the name of the category and the numbers for the student needs. After the person has finished, the leader will ask, "Is there someone else who had the same category and wants to put additional needs in that category?" The leader will add the numbers he or she hears. After giving others an opportunity to add numbers to the category, the leader will repeat the process. After a number of categories have been given, the leader will ask everyone to scan the master list of student needs to determine if every need is in one of the categories. If a need is missing, the leader will ask if there is a category already named in which the need could fit or if another category is required for the missing need. When all the needs are covered, the faculty has a list of categories that contain all the student needs the faculty identified in the data.

The key to this exercise is acceptance. Accept whatever someone offers. Do not debate or get into a discussion about whether a need fits in this or that category. It really does not matter. Do not get into a debate about the name of a category. If one teacher says that she has a "communication" category, even though reading and writing are communication, the leader labels the category as communication and lists the numbers the teacher wants to list. This is how a teacher perceives those needs, and we honor the teacher's opinion. The purpose is to organize the needs into workable groups and to have all the needs in at least one group or category. As Murphy often says, "It all comes out in the wash."

The following is an example of categories formed from the list of student needs shown in Step 2:

Reading comprehension: 1, 4, 5, 6, 7, 10, 11, 13

Math: 1, 2, 3, 4, 6, 8, 10, 13

Writing: 1, 3, 4, 5, 8, 9, 11, 13

Project-based learning: 1, 2, 4, 5, 8, 10, 11, 13

Word analysis: 12, 14

We have already noted that after the study groups are formed, groups will review more data to become clearer about their students' needs in their category of choice. For example, teachers who choose word analysis will find additional word analysis needs in data sources not included in the data the faculty analyzed.

Categorizing is simply a way to organize the student needs. The names that a faculty gives to the groups of student needs are unimportant. Two faculties with the same list of student needs will categorize the needs differently and give different names to the categories. For example, the category named *project-based learning* could also be called *critical thinking skills*. The important factor here is that all the student needs on the list are in at least one category. What teachers see in the process of categorizing the needs is that a student need can be addressed through more than one content area or through different lenses. In the previous list of categories, student need No. 1 appears in four categories. The need will simply be approached from different perspectives, which is a very important understanding. In Figure 7.2, we refer to the different approaches or perspectives as "doors," meaning that study groups enter the room of whole-school improvement through different doors or entrances (Joyce, 1991). Groups may enter the room bringing with them the same student need (e.g., increase vocabulary, spell correctly, and comprehend what they read). Looking at the writing, reading comprehension, math, problem solving, listening, and study skills doors, each study group would approach the needs through different content.

We are often asked, "Wouldn't it be better if all the study groups addressed the same student need instead of having five 'topics'?" First, we explain, what we have are five channels through which to address the same student need. Second, study groups do not address topics. Study groups address student needs or categories of student needs. "Topic" is a no-no word because it sounds too elective, like pulling a topic out of the air. Third, it is important for study groups to have choices. Study groups will produce better results if they are working on student needs they care about and if they have choices in the approach (door) they take to address the needs. Finally, the data shared with the faculty in Step 1 will drive the number of needs and the different categories identified. In the DMC, every step has been tested, and the vocabulary we use is very important to the whole process.

Step 4: Complete an Individual or Personalized Plan to Form Study Groups

With full faculty participation, student needs have been identified and put into categories. Now it is time for faculty members to make personal choices, keeping in mind what their students need for them to do. The leader gives everyone a blank study group action plan. In describing what happens next, we use the student needs in the list in Step 2 and categories shown in Step 3.

The leader tells the faculty members that during the next 15 minutes, they are to work as individuals, not sharing their thinking with anyone, and they are to focus on what their students need for them to do. The leader goes on to say that each

WFSG Open Doors To Whole School Improvement

Think of a "category" as a "door" to the Room for Whole School Instructional Improvement. It really doesn't matter which door a study group uses. What is important is that the whole faculty is in the same room.

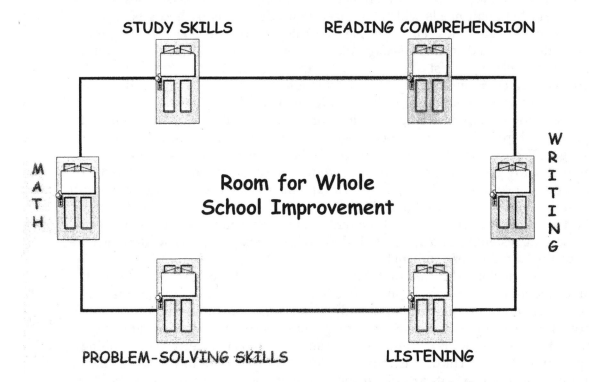

- Study groups may enter through different doors or categories to get into the same room. The room is where data-based student instructional needs are addressed.

- Most often, one or more of the same student needs will be placed in all the categories, i.e: "Students need to expand their vocabularies."

Whole-Faculty

WFSGs

Study Groups™

Figure 7.2   Doors to Whole-School Improvement

individual is to design a study group action plan tailored to meet his or her students' needs and, therefore, personalized to them. Using a blank study group action plan (see Resource A), the faculty follows the following directions:

1. Choose the one category on the school's list of categorized student needs that *your students* need for you to address in a study group because they are not showing adequate progress in this area (e.g., writing and reading comprehension). Write or check the category at the top of your action plan.

2. In the box titled "Students need to:," write out the specific student needs in the category that you should target for your students. Refer back to the categories (Step 3) that were formed out of the list of student needs (Step 2). If there are six student needs in that category, choose the two or three that are most aligned with the students you teach. The student needs you write on your action plan must be from the school's master list and in the category you chose.

3. In the box titled "When our study group meets, we will:," write the actions you want to take when your study group meets. The following are examples of actions:
   - Examine student work routinely using a protocol
   - Practice teach lessons we plan to teach in the classroom
   - Model effective strategies and activities
   - Read and discuss pertinent articles and chapters from selected books
   - Discuss the application of strategies gleaned from books and articles
   - Have a skillful person attend meetings to train and guide study group members (expert voice)
   - Develop lessons for implementing what members have been trained to do
   - Develop rubrics for a consistent grading system
   - Practice and critique teaching strategies used with a specific lesson
   - Reflect on new knowledge and on current classroom practices
   - Identify, discuss, and practice strategies that help develop reading skills, such as vocabulary skills and skills to decode words
   - Identify, discuss, and practice strategies for teaching reading through mathematics, social studies, and science
   - Evaluate assessment techniques used in the classrooms
   - Develop skills and plan for routine use of various forms of technology
   - Identify different types of word problems and strategies for solving them
   - Discuss case studies that have been selected from field-tested cases describing a teaching experience that had an unexpected outcome or ran into difficulty
   - Investigate various diagnostic resources and techniques for testing reading comprehension and strategies for remediation of deficiencies
   - Design a mathematics dictionary or a strategy for students to develop one
   - Examine a variety of sample tests to determine skills necessary for success
   - Examine, develop, and critique the use of rubrics
   - Invite students to attend meetings to gain students' points of view
   - Explore and identify specific instructional strategies for reducing the achievement gaps among different ethnic groups

- Investigate research on differentiated writing curriculums
- Identify proven (best) practices in teaching reading, select at least three to use, and, after use, compare results
- Develop a unit of study to be taught in classes that integrates three major areas of the curriculum and addresses the student needs that are being targeted.

(Note that all the actions listed are what teachers do in their study group meetings, not what they will do in their classrooms with their students.)

4. Write in the space in the middle of the action plan an *essential question* that captures what you want to investigate. This could be considered the problem to be solved. An essential question guides the work of a study group. The question should encompass the specific student needs listed on the individual or personal plan. Members should be able to answer the questions by doing what is listed on the plan as actions the group will take when it meets. The following are examples of essential questions:
   - Reading: How can we teach students to comprehend what they read?
   - Measurement: How can we teach students to develop measurement skills in all content areas?
   - Communication: What should we teach students so that they can communicate effectively?
   - Problem solving: How can we help students effectively use problem-solving skills and strategies? How can we teach students to communicate their reasoning for arriving at a solution to a given problem?
   - Writing: How can we help students become better writers?
   - English language arts: How do we teach so that students' writing is well organized, is thoroughly developed, and reflects use of effective language?

While individuals are working, the leader is moving about the room, as are others from the focus team, making sure that everyone is doing what they have been asked to do. After each direction (1–4), the leader pauses to give individuals an opportunity to ask questions and then follow that direction. After the leader sees that everyone is on task and has done what was asked, he or she moves to the next direction.

When the top half of the study group action plan is complete, the leader states that it is now time to form study groups. For each category formed in Step 3, the leader asks individuals to identify their choices. For example, "If you chose the category *reading comprehension*, please stand." The leader counts those standing. If five or fewer stand, the leader says that they are a study group. If more than five stand, the leader tells those standing to go to a designated classroom and follow the written instructions in their notebooks. Briefly, the written instructions tell them how to divide themselves into groups no larger than five and no smaller than three. The instructions are as follows:

1. Those who chose the same category will go to a designated room or area.

2. Individuals in the same room or area are to orally share their individual plans.

3. Individuals may want to arrange themselves in a circle so as to see each other.

4. Individuals are to take turns reading the following:
   - The essential question he or she wrote
   - Two specific student needs that he or she wrote

5. After all the plans have been shared, individuals will need to subgroup themselves according to the individual plans that are most similar in terms of the essential questions or specific student needs written on the plans or both. Groups should be no smaller than three and no larger than five.

6. One person in each group is to write the names of the members of the study group on a piece of paper, which is to be given to the principal. At the top of the paper, write the category of student needs that will be the focus of the study group.

7. When Items 1 through 6 have been done, everyone reconvenes in the large meeting area or they are dismissed.

In this way, study groups are formed. Everyone saves his or her individual or personalized plans for the first study group meeting. At their first study group meeting, members will again share their individual plans to guide their thinking toward the one study group action plan that will represent all members of the study group.

In some schools, there is an intermediate step between completing the individual plan and forming the study groups. If all the study groups are going to meet at the same time, what has been described will work because it does not matter who is in a group. Study group membership is solely based on what student needs teachers are going to target. If the faculty has decided that study groups will meet during one planning period per week, then teachers who have the same planning period will need to meet to subdivide themselves into study groups. When all the teachers who have the first period of the day for planning meet, they share their individual plans and subdivide accordingly. For instance, one middle school that is using one planning period per week for the study group meetings has approximately 12 teachers scheduled for planning each period of the day; that is, three study groups meet during each period on WFSG day. In elementary schools, teachers on a grade level may determine that they want to address the same student need category. If so, they would go through Steps 1 through 3 with the whole faculty, and after completing the individual action plan, they would meet and subdivide according to the differences in the plans as if there were more than five teachers at that grade level. Even if there are two study groups of fourth-grade teachers, the two groups could meet every third meeting to compare notes and share ideas. It is important for the principal to monitor that study group meetings do not become grade-level meetings in which administrative or managerial concerns take priority. Grade-level groups are also more likely to get into curriculum development work, writing curriculum for the coming school year; this is not study group work. Study group work is designing and practicing what is being taught now, not next year. Also, when study groups have the same membership as existing structures, established habits carry over from one setting (study group) to the other setting (grade-level group). For example, individuals who are late to grade-level meetings will be late to study group meetings because members accept that those individuals have that habit. Sometimes, familiarity is not facilitating of the study group process.

After the whole faculty has completed Step 4 on the DMC, all of the faculty members will be in study groups. This completes the 3-hour session with the whole faculty. Steps 5 through 7 are done as part of the study group meetings.

Step 5: Each Study Group
Designs a Study Group Action Plan That
Specifies the Content of the Group's Work

During their first study group meeting, members begin developing the study group action plan (SGAP). It is expected that all but the bottom section of the plan will be completed by the end of the second meeting. Often, the portion of the plan that requires the group to state how it will assess changes in student performance relative to their specific student learning needs, baseline data on the learning needs for their current students, and performance targets for their students on each student need is not completed within the first two meetings because study groups must analyze student needs and collect data from their students. Frequently, groups require feedback from the principal or other support staff on how to most effectively set and monitor improvement targets.

All study group members completed half of the SGAP when they did an individual plan in Step 4. Study groups use their individual plans to develop the group's plan. Each study group will have one SGAP. Members begin by sharing, consolidating, and reaching consensus on the items that were completed in Step 4. After members have reached consensus and completed the top of their SGAP, they are ready to move to the items that were not discussed at the meeting during which the whole faculty experienced Steps 1 through 4 on the DMC.

After agreeing on the essential question that will guide the work of the study group, the group discusses the resources that it will need to answer the essential question. In the appropriate place on the form, members suggest resources and record them in the plan. Study group members are expected to learn and build their knowledge and expertise by bringing outside resources into the study group and not just by sharing what they already do as individuals. For resources, members should rely heavily on materials that are included with programs and textbooks adopted by the school. For example, if the group chose the reading comprehension category, members should consider the reading materials and programs they are expected to use with their students. Groups give special attention to what and who will provide the expert voice because this is the source of information that will give the group knowledge and skill it does not already possess. The expertise may come from reading books and articles, attending workshops and conferences, having a trainer or other knowledgeable person attend one or more study group meetings, utilizing Web sites on the Internet, using computer software, viewing videotapes or DVDs, and applying other forms of technology. Members will continue to add to the resource section of the SGAP as the group proceeds with its work and uses resources not considered when the plan was originally written.

The next section of the SGAP is where the group writes its study group norms. Often, this section of the plan is completed before any of the other sections.

The last section of the SGAP is where the group specifies how it will assess changes in student performance relative to their specific learning needs, the baseline data on the learning need for their current students, and performance targets for their students on each student need. The bottom of the action plan has five columns in which members indicate what they want the students to be able to do as a result of the study group's work. Members need to go back to the student needs listed in the top left box of the SGAP. Student needs are those on which the study group wants to improve their students' performance. The five columns are completed as follows:

Column 1: List the student needs indicated in the top left box of the SGAP. Only two or three needs may be listed in the beginning, and others may be added when this portion of the plan is revised at 6- to 12-week intervals.

Column 2: Indicate, for each need, the data source(s) or assessments to track students' progress during the school year as the study group addresses the need (e.g., teacher-made tests, teacher observations, 6-week averages, and textbook checklists). Use the same data source or assessment to collect data for determining the baseline starting point for your students, checking progress while you work on this need, and to determine actual progress achieved by your target date. The cumulative impact of the formative assessments should be reflected in state tests; state test results, however, are not reported often enough to track ongoing progress.

Column 3: For each need, write what data indicate is the current (baseline) status of the need.

Column 4: For each need, write what you want data to indicate after 6 to 12 weeks. This is the targeted result.

Column 5: For each need, write what data actually show after 6 to 12 weeks of study group work.

Columns 3 through 5: If percentages are used, they should be the percentages of students in all the members' classes. For example, of a total of 75 students in three teachers' classes, 60% (45 students) demonstrate the need to increase spelling accuracy.

An illustration of the five columns is provided in Table 7.2. Resource A contains a blank SGAP.

Notice that page 2 of the SGAP has additional assessment charts. The first chart at the bottom of the action plan is completed when the plan is first developed as the study group begins its work. A new chart is completed every 6 to 12 weeks. When the second chart is completed, the text in Column 5 (the "actual" results) becomes the "baseline" result, moving everything forward. For example, using the chart in

Specific **Student Needs** listed on Action Plan. *Students need to:*	**Data Sources** that document need <u>and</u> will be evidence of impact of group's work	**Baseline—** what data indicate when work begins on: **DATE** <u>9/10</u>	**Target**—what study group projects will be the results of the work on: **DATE** <u>11/01</u>	**Actual**—what data indicate **now** (complete every 6 to 12 weeks): **DATE** <u>11/01</u>
Demonstrate ability to spell correctly Use correct grammar	Spelling tests Written assignments 6 week average in Lang. Arts Written assignments	40% routinely spell correctly 60% made C or better	60% will routinely spell correctly 80% will make C or better	55% are routinely spelling correctly 85% made C or better

Table 7.2   Action Plan, Data Sources, and Results Chart

Table 7.2, on November 1, when the actual results are recorded, a new chart is completed; the baseline is now 55%, the target may now become 70%, and the actual (in 6–12 weeks) may become 80%.

The SGAP should be in front of the study group at all times. It is put in the WFSG notebook so that every few meetings, members have the plan and can review it to determine if it needs to be revised. The assessment portion of the plan should be revised approximately every 6 to 12 weeks.

The key to a strong, meaningful SGAP is the feedback that the study group receives from the principal and other support staff, not only when the first draft of the plan is completed but also for the duration of the school year. The SGAP is a living document that should change as the study group gains knowledge and skill and students show improvement. Student needs can be adjusted as the group examines additional data. The group may believe that the actions listed originally on the plan are too passive. Additional resources may be identified. Adjustments may be required in the study group norms. Also, as just described, the targets will change.

Step 6: Each WFSG Implements Cycles of Action Research by Assessing Specific Needs, Planning for Instruction, Acting on the Plans, and Reflecting on Student Responses

The action research cycles would look like the following:

1. The group looks at classroom-based data regarding the essential question to establish baseline data for its students.

   Questions to ask: What skills and knowledge must our students understand and apply to be proficient relative to this need? We have to unpack the need. Do we already have data sources or assessments and scoring rubrics we can use to collect baseline data on our students for this need and that will reveal whether they have the necessary skills and knowledge? If not, what do we need to do to create or find an appropriate assessment task? How well did our students do on the baseline assessment (by performance level), and what patterns do we see in these results? When we examine samples of student work from the baseline assessments, what is causing students difficulty in this area? Why? What are the problems students are having with regard to this student need?

   Action to take: Develop a deep understanding of students' challenges with this need.

   Time: This requires one meeting to several meetings, depending on whether the group already has unpacked the need, identified an assessment tool and scoring rubric, and collected baseline data.

2. The study group reviews current research or information describing practices that have shown effectiveness in addressing this need.

   Questions to ask: What do we need to learn to improve our understanding of the skills and knowledge required of students to become proficient in this need? What instructional strategies have proved successful in improving proficiency in this need for students like ours? What expert voices in this

Whole-Faculty

WFSG CYCLE OF TEACHER INQUIRY
Step 6: WFSG Decision-Making Cycle

Study Groups™

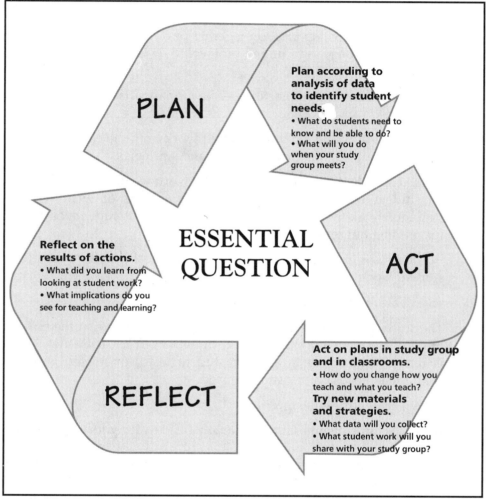

© Murphy, 1995 www.MurphysWFSG.org

Figure 7.3   WFSG Cycle of Teacher Inquiry

school, our district, or elsewhere can we bring in to inform ourselves about this student need?

Possible resources to use: Texts, Internet, experts, and professional articles.

Action to take: Locate and share resources. Examine resources, and identify best practices.

Time: This requires one meeting to several meetings, depending on the group's required learning.

3. The group develops lessons that incorporate what was learned from the examination of effective practices and use the strategies and materials in their classrooms.

Questions to ask: What can we try in our classrooms to meet this student need? How will we use our assessment tool(s) for students to demonstrate what they can do relative to this need? How will we monitor our students' reactions during the lessons?

Action to take: Develop a lesson together or develop lessons separately. Then, in the study group, use a tuning protocol to revise plans before using them in class.

Time: This requires two meetings—one to plan what to do and the second to tune plans.

4. Individuals in the group bring student work from the classroom to assess the effectiveness of the classroom lessons and strategies.

Question to ask: What differences did the work we did in our classrooms have on student learning? What are the implications of what we see in our students' work for the next steps to take with our students on this need and for revising our lesson for future use?

Action to take: Use a Wows and Wonders protocol or other protocol to look at student work.

Time: This requires one meeting.

5. The study group looks at classroom-based data regarding the essential question to determine if (a) the targeted student need has been met, (b) the group is ready to move on to another student need, or (c) the group needs to continue its focus on this student need.

Time: This requires one meeting.

6. Begin the cycle again—either for a new need or for your current need.

One cycle requires five to eight study group meetings to complete, depending on the complexity of the needs and the interventions. For study groups that meet weekly, one cycle will take 1 or 2 months. Because this is a cyclic process, it is very important for groups to meet weekly. If too much time passes between steps within the cycle, the power of the process is diluted.

Step 7: The Whole Faculty Evaluates the Impact of Study Groups on Student Learning

The chart on the bottom of the SGAP and the additional charts that keep track of the status of the student need are the assessment of impact of the study group on student learning. The assessment process was explained in Step 5. In Resource A, the most frequently used forms, Assessment of WFSG Work I through IV, are given.

There are questions about context, process, content, and results that guide the annual evaluation of the WFSG system in a school, both at the individual study group level and for the whole school.

For individual study groups,

1. How has our students' performance improved in the specific student learning needs we addressed?

2. How did our teaching practice improve as a result of our study group work?

3. Does our action plan, with revisions, accurately reflect what we did this year?

4. How well did we work together as a study group and in following the WFSG process guidelines?

5. What should we improve if we continue together next year?

For the school,

1. Has student performance improved as a result of our study group's work?

2. Has teacher practice improved as a result of our study group's work?

3. How well were study groups supported in moving to the consequence stage?

4. How well did we do as a school in following the WFSG process guidelines?

5. How effectively have we shared the work of our study groups among other study groups and with students, parents, and other schools?

6. Have we provided effective contexts (e.g., time and resources) for study groups?

7. What should we improve for next year's study groups?

Although the primary focus of Step 7 is on a summative evaluation at the end of the year, formative evaluation should occur throughout the time that study groups meet. The regular instructional council meetings provide an opportunity to surface issues or concerns and monitor study group work. Resource A contains examples of forms that can be used during the year to do "status checks" on study group progress.

THE DECISION-MAKING CYCLE REPEATS ITSELF EACH YEAR

At the end of a school year, all study groups go to Step 7 on the DMC. At the beginning of a school year, all study groups return to Step 1. It does not matter if study groups are continuing from the year before or if they have reconfigured. All study groups return to the data for guidance as to what they will do.

SUMMARY

Increased student learning is the goal of WFSGs. Thus, use of data regarding the level of students' achievements before, during, and after the study is essential. The

DMC is a quick, exacting, and tested process for making decisions about what study groups will do and how study groups will be organized. It is not the time to teach faculty how to analyze and interpret data. If a faculty is unfamiliar with a school's data or lacks skills in interpreting data, a workshop should be held for the purpose of teaching the faculty how to interpret the school's data. It is a mistake to try to develop data analysis skills at the same time the faculty is using data for organizing study groups. We do not want misplaced frustration and anxiety from not understanding the data to be overlaid on the WFSG decision-making process.

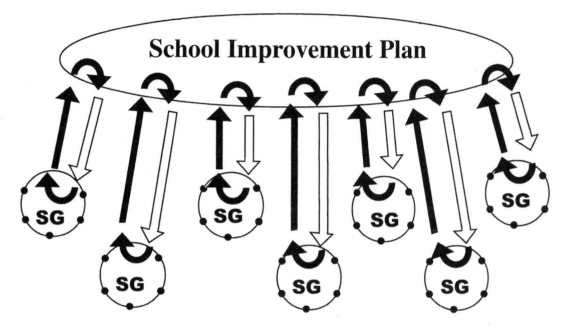

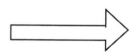
The school improvement plan gives direction to study groups.

Study groups give direction to the school improvement plan. The study group action plans are the instructional improvement component of the school improvement plan.

Individuals in each study group use the study group action plan as the major component of the individual professional development plans.

Figure 7.4   WFSG Support Plans for Improvement

8

Content: Curriculum and Instructional Strategies

ontent refers to the actual skills and knowledge that educators want to possess or acquire through staff development or some other means. The context and process components of Whole-Faculty Study Groups (WFSGs) are often invisible. The context reflects the conditions of the workplace, and the process is how individuals work together. The descriptors of the context and process can be seen, but by virtue of the definitions, they are often without form. This is not true of content. Content can usually be seen, handled, and manipulated. It has form. It is a book, a video, an article, a lesson plan, a packaged program, an activity, or a strategy, and it can even be represented by a person. Content is what study groups do. High-performing study groups perform intellectually rigorous work, meaning that the content is substantive enough to sustain and challenge the members as they strive for a deeper understanding of what they teach.

THE HEART OF WFSGs

The heart of the study group process is what teachers do to develop understanding of what they teach, what teachers do to become more knowledgeable of what they teach, what teachers investigate, and what teachers do to become more skillful in the

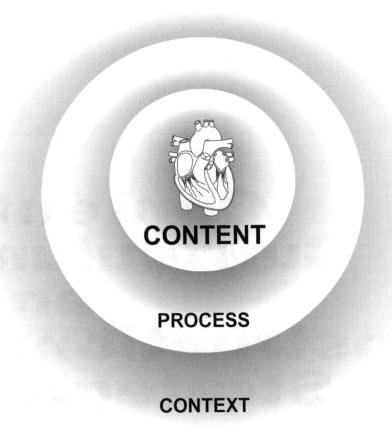

CONTENT

PROCESS

CONTEXT

Figure 8.1 Content: The Heart of the Process

classroom with students (Figure 8.1). That "what" is the content of study groups, and without appropriate content, the process is empty. Without intellectually rigorous work, the process is boring and can be a waste of time. It is substantive teacher work that requires teachers to immerse themselves in searching for deeper understandings of what they teach that creates high-performing, motivated study groups.

> The process, by itself, has little power to change what teachers actually do with students. Change in what students know and do is the end result of WFSGs. If students are to become more knowledgeable and skillful, then teachers must have control of the academic content they teach and have an expansive repertoire of instructional strategies to deliver that content to students. Teachers increase their teaching repertoires so that students will increase their learning repertoires.

The need to continuously examine and expand the tools of teaching is directly aligned with the constancy of change in the work life and workplace of teaching. Each new set of students, each new expansion of knowledge, each new set of circumstances, each new set of curriculum guidelines and materials, and each new set of regulations and expectations create the need for teachers to examine what and how they teach.

NATIONAL STAFF DEVELOPMENT COUNCIL'S STAFF DEVELOPMENT CONTENT STANDARDS

The National Staff Development Council's (NSDC) staff development standards (NSDC, 2003) are grounded in research that documents the connection between staff development and student learning. The standards are organized into context standards, process standards, and content standards. The content standards recognize that staff development that improves student learning for all students provides for the following:

- Equity: Prepares educators to understand and appreciate all students; create safe, orderly, and supportive learning environments; and hold high expectations for their academic achievement
- Quality teaching: Deepens educators' content knowledge, provides them with research-based instructional strategies to assist students in meeting rigorous academic standards, and prepares them to use various types of classroom assessments appropriately
- Family involvement: Provides educators with knowledge and skills to involve families and other stakeholders appropriately

In WFSGs, the search for content begins with identifying student instructional needs. The decision-making cycle (DMC) is a step-by-step set of procedures for establishing the student needs that study groups will address. The student needs lead members to what the study groups will do. The content of WFSGs is what study groups do to become more knowledgeable and skillful. Content is the substance of the WFSG process. One of the primary functions of WFSGs (see Chapter 2) is developing a deeper understanding of academic content. For teachers, it is teaching students how to read and the history, English, science, and mathematics that they teach. Content is also how to teach for understanding and what brain research tells us about how to meet student needs. Learning how to use effective teaching or learning strategies is study group content. What teachers teach and how teachers teach are the content of WFSGs.

THE WFSG RUBRIC: CONTENT

The WFSG rubric has three components: context, process, and content. The eight content descriptors and four stages of implementation are described in Table 8.1.

Selecting Content

As discussed previously, teachers begin with student needs. In Chapter 4, we described how the faculty analyzed data to identify student needs. Each study group develops an action plan. In their action plan, teachers agree on the specific student needs they will address and what they will do in their study group to address those student needs. In this way, students' needs precede what teachers do. Thus, in study groups, teachers do what students need for them to do. Answers to the four

	Not Yet	Beginning Implementation	Developing Implementation	Advanced Implementation
Content	• Members are focused on the needs of the teachers in the group, not students.	• While student needs guide the group's work, considerable time is spent on hearing opinions of group members.	• Members use classroom data to understand student learning needs and research strategies to try. They spend little energy rehashing opinions.	• Members are focused on the learning needs of the students in their classrooms and engage in cycles of action research in their study group meetings.
Content	• Members are trying to figure out what a study group does. The mechanics of the group take a significant amount of time. (Mechanical)	• Members have established a routine for their study group meetings, but mastering the process guidelines gets in the way of the work. Members primarily "share;" this is the most frequent verb used in logs. (Mechanical to Routine)	• Members are focused on their work and comfortably follow the process guidelines. They examine key issues deeply and incorporate expert voices into their work. (Routine to Refinement)	• Members find the work of the group rigorous, stimulating, and directly connected to their students' learning. They assess the impact of their work and make deliberate efforts to coordinate with other groups. (Integration and Renewal)
Content	• Members only address what is in their comfort zone and what is of interest to them.	• Members identify key issues related to student learning needs and their teaching, but only skim the surface.	• Members work together to learn and experiment with best practices, actively engaging their students in work emanating from their study group.	• Members examine key issues deeply and challenge each other's assumptions, evaluating all input for its value and usability.
Content	• Looking at student work (LASW) using a protocol is seldom, if ever, done.	• Members share examples of their best students' work after the lesson is completed.	• Members share examples of a range of student work, discussing how to improve it.	• LASW together using protocols is the heart of group work. It is used routinely, varying levels and content.

Table 8.1   WFSG Rubric: Content

	Not Yet	Beginning Implementation	Developing Implementation	Advanced Implementation
Content	• Members rely on what they already know.	• Members bring some types of literature into the meetings, only discussing material superficially.	• External content "experts" are invited to group meetings but members do not hold each other accountable for using the expert knowledge.	• Members actively seek multiple sources to push themselves to higher levels of understanding of academic content and effective pedagogy.
Content	• Logs indicate that members spend a lot of time on administrative and managerial issues.	• Members focus on designing instructional projects for others to implement.	• Focus is on improving teaching but not on improving student learning.	• Members have internalized: "What do students need for us to do so that we will challenge them to learn difficult and fundamental concepts and develop the skills to be deep thinkers and problem solvers?"
Content	• Members do not focus on any of the school's current instructional initiatives or try to align study group work with school instructional initiatives.	• Members refer to new programs at the school in the study group action plan or logs, but there is no deliberate effort to connect the initiatives to the study group's work.	• Members are committed to using new materials and strategies from the school's current instructional initiatives appropriately in classrooms.	• Members are focusing on the integration of new programs with existing programs for coherence and assimilation.
Content	• Members share lessons they developed in the past and tell stories about their classrooms.	• Members develop lessons separately and sometimes share what they are going to do or have done.	• Members develop lessons separately but with input from the study group. They regularly share classroom results.	• Joint work is the norm, working on the development of all lesson components together, demonstrating, and debriefing results together.

Table 8.1 (Continued)

fundamental questions at the beginning of Chapters 1 and 7 tell leaders of WFSGs what teachers should know and be able to do. Students and their work are the source for determining what teachers need to know and be able to do. Results of various performance assessments tell teachers what they should know and be able to do with skill in the classroom. This is the content of WFSGs.

WARNING

Simply having study groups in place at a school will not increase student achievement. It is what teachers do in those study groups and in their classrooms that will increase student achievement. Study groups are a means through which teachers work together to make academic content more meaningful to students so as to increase students' understanding. Murphy cannot give a simple "yes" answer to the question, "Will study groups increase student achievement?" Her answer would have to begin with, "It depends, in large part, on what study groups do."

WFSG STRATEGIES: INTEGRATING THE HOW WITH THE WHAT

In the classroom, it is difficult to separate what teachers teach from how teachers teach. This is true in WFSGs (Figure 8.2). Study groups use multiple professional development strategies that examine the content of teaching. The following sections describe several strategies that study groups use to become more knowledgeable about what they teach.

The following strategies are discussed in this chapter:

- Examining student work
- Sharing observations of students at work
- Training
- Conducting action research
- Conducting lesson study
- Comentoring
- Listening to students
- Shadowing students
- Videotaping
- Learning from case studies
- Developing curriculum
- Immersing in academic content
- Journaling
- Keeping portfolios
- Using protocols
- Reading books and other professional literature

Examining Student Work

Looking at student work is a basic strategy and an integral part of the study group process. It is the one action that leaders expect to be listed on every study

Whole-Faculty

Study Groups™

Whole-Faculty Study Groups:
A Recipe for Teacher & Student Learning

RECIPE

Before beginning preparations have information about those you are serving.

Equipment needed: processor with large, see-through blender; strong lid; solid base; power cord; 3 to 6 rotor blades

In large blender, put the following ingredients:
- 1 action plan
- Instructional materials
- Instructional strategies
- District/state standards
- Curriculum framework (sequence of learning)
- Academic knowledge.

Mix for 1 hour once a week.

Stir in student work.

Add according to taste:
- Training (on-site or away)
- Discussing books and articles members read
- Sharing observations of students working in members' classes
- Demonstrating to each other strategies that work
- Viewing or discussing videotapes members take of themselves teaching
- Examining the research on best practices
- Interviewing students to hear what they think about current classroom practices
- Digging deeper into academic knowledge

© Murphy, 1995

Figure 8.2 WFSGs: A Recipe for Teacher Learning

group action plan (SGAP). What is so special about teachers looking at student work? Little, Gearhart, Curry, and Kafka (2003) state that teachers examine artifacts by students all the time. They read, review, grade, and celebrate student work every day. They do so most often on their own, however, possibly in conference with a student or parent but almost always in isolation from colleagues.

Kate Nolan writes (http://www.philaedfund.org/slcweb/prolog.htm.),

Habit and tradition cause teachers to spend a lot of time studying what to teach, but curiosity and fascination bring us together to study what we have taught and what students have learned. The teacher who is a learner is eager and hungry for the kind of discussions we can have when student work is the focus. We work together like an artists' colony, considering our craft and our materials, the quality of the process and the product, generating ideas about how to make our work better.

Teachers do not often arrive at the WFSG table eager for discussions about student work. We have found that teachers more often approach looking at student work with some fear and discomfort. Getting teachers to where Nolan suggests takes gentle and firm pressure and support from leaders of WFSGs. Teachers have concerns about their own personal comfort and that of their colleagues. We and others have found that looking at student work is a delicate process that can be "broken and hard to mend" if teachers are not sensitive and affirming with their colleagues.

WFSGs look at student work as part of a data-collection process that documents current conditions relative to a study group's essential question. Student work indicates to what degree a student is or is not meeting one or more student needs that a study group is addressing. Student work that is examined by a WFSG is aligned with the essential question and the specific student needs stated in a group's SGAP.

Teachers look at student work all the time. What they do not do is look at student work in a collaborative setting. Consequently, WFSG leaders introduce the faculty to the importance of collaboratively looking at student work as a routine activity of study groups as soon as possible. Often, it is done in the first WFSG orientation, not for training purposes but so that teachers will understand what is meant by the phrase "looking at student work."

The leader of the orientation may bring a piece of student work for all the teachers to look at and ask them to pretend that they are a group of five teachers. Everyone is given a copy of the same work, and the leader serves as the presenting teacher and has another leader serve as the facilitator. With a protocol in the hands of everyone, the leaders guide the faculty through a brief protocol. This exercise gives teachers a brief glimpse into the process. After the study groups are organized, the first new training piece is on how to look at student work using protocols. This training can be done in several ways. In one way, the whole faculty is introduced to the procedures of a protocol at the same time. Another way is to have a consultant meet with the instructional council, which has a representative from each study group. The study group representative is then responsible for introducing the protocol to his or her study group. If all of the study groups do not meet at the same time, a consultant may meet with each study group.

We agree with Judith Warren Little and colleagues (2003) that one purpose of looking at student work is to transform "long-standing workplace traditions of privacy and noninterference" by asking teachers to put the work of their students on the table for others to consider and discuss. The WFSG system, when implementers maintain the integrity of the design, does transform the workplace of teaching. Looking at student work is one of the basic strategies for building collaboration around the work of teaching and learning, for developing joint responsibility for the students, and for framing precise talk about teaching.

In WFSGs, looking at student work is part of the action research cycle. Study group members identify a best practice, develop a lesson using the practice, teach the lesson, and, as a collaborative group, look at the student work that results from the lesson. On the basis of the discussion, there is another round of development work, teaching, and assessing. Student work constitutes the evidence that it is improving (or not). Student work is one source of data. Study group members also look at the construction of teacher-made tests, developing and using rubrics, paying attention to measures developed by textbook publishers, and keeping track of district and state standards.

From the beginning, when looking at student work is introduced, it is with a protocol. A protocol consists of agreed on guidelines for a conversation, and it is this structure that permits a certain kind of conversation to occur. Protocols are vehicles for building the skills and culture necessary for collaborative work. Thus, using protocols often allows groups to build trust by actually doing substantive work together. A protocol creates a structure that makes it safe to ask challenging questions of each other; it also ensures that there is some equity and parity in terms of consideration of each person's issues. The presenting teacher has the opportunity not only to reflect on and describe an issue or dilemma but also to have interesting questions asked of him or her. (See www.lasw.org/protocols.html.)

Students use a variety of formats to show what they are learning and what they know and understand. Student work can be seen, read, heard, and felt in a number of ways. For study groups to examine the work, it is usually brought to a study group meeting. Therefore, student work should be in a tangible format that members can handle, see, hear, or all three, as follows:

- Written work on 8 ½ × 11-inch paper
- Worksheets
- Video of a class completing an assignment in the classroom
- Recording of an oral reading
- Computations in various oral (e.g., recorded or videotaped) and written formats
- Debates, recorded or videotaped
- Projects (e.g., manipulative science experiments, drafting, and woodworking)
- Models
- Exhibits (e.g., posters, triboards, and cutouts)
- Performances, recorded or videotaped
- Illustrations, diagrams, tables, and graphs
- Visual artwork in all forms
- Skill development (e.g., physical education), videotaped
- Computer-generated work
- Portfolios containing an assortment of work over time

WFSGs include the following procedures for looking at student work:

- A teacher in the study group commits to bring students' work to the next study group meeting. It will be work generated from a lesson targeting one or more of the student needs on the study group's action plan.
- A presenting teacher will select one student's work. It is the teacher's choice as to whether she considers work that is above average, average, or below average. The choice will depend on the type of feedback he or she wants. The work has not been "graded." The presenting teacher makes copies of the work for the other members. If it is a large piece of work that everyone can see (e.g., a poster), it is not necessary to make copies.

- A presenting teacher may choose to bring a different student's work for each teacher in the study group. If so, it should be work from the same assignment in the same class.
- Students' names are not visible on the work. It is preferable that study group members not know the identity of the student because it does not matter who owns the work. Teachers' focus should be on the work and what can be learned about what the student did or did not do. The discussion should relate to what the teachers decide to do next.
- A presenting teacher selects the protocol he or she wants to use for examining the work. The facilitator is the leader of the study group for that meeting, unless he or she is the presenting teacher.

Gene Thompson-Grove, in her instructions to workshop participants at the 2004 National WFSG Conference, asked participants to bring student work that raised a genuine question or puzzled them and related to their practice. Concern examples follow:

- "I'm not sure what to make of these students' work. What would other educators see in it?"
- "There is always a handful of students who never seem to get really engaged in this particular assignment. How could I improve the assignment so that it works for all of the students?"
- "Students all completed this final exam, but their performances were spotty, and now I am not sure their work really tells me what I need to know about their learning. How might I revise this assignment task?"

For more information about specific protocols and more details about looking at student work, see the following:

- Coalition of Essential Schools, www.essentialschools.org
- Annenberg Institute, www.annenberginstitute.org
- Harvard's Project Zero, www.pz.harvard.edu/research/evidence.htm
- Academy for Educational Development, http://scs.aed.org/rsw
- National School Reform Faculty, www.nsrfharmony.org (contact for Gene Thompson-Grove)
- Teachers College, http://www.teacherscollegepress.org
- ATLAS Communities, www.ATLASCommunities.org

Sharing Observations of Students at Work

As you now know, the work of WFSGs is shaped by what students need for the teachers to do. There are several sources for identifying student needs, including looking at student data, listening to students, examining student work, hearing teachers talk about their students, and observing students. The most current and probably the most reliable information is gleaned from looking at students' work and observing them working. Teachers in the same study group can pair themselves in any way at any time and observe each other's students during instruction.

Imagine the following situation. During several study group meetings, members develop concept attainment lessons. In their group meetings, they practice the lessons. They then inform each other as to when they will be teaching the lessons during the following week. The teachers pair up and work out a schedule for observing in each other's classrooms. When observing, teachers focus on how students are responding to the lesson. During the next group meeting, teachers debrief the observed lessons and share how students responded, and the data are used in the next round of lesson development.

It has been Murphy's experience that teachers learn most about what works and what does not work for a new strategy when another teacher observes students' responses and reports on those responses. Conversations and work prior to the observations and those after the observations are all part of the comentoring process explained in a following section. Teachers in the same study group should observe each other's students at least once a month as an ongoing data-collecting strategy. Such observations should be standard procedure among and between study group members. The length of time in each other's classrooms is not important. Because the teachers routinely work together in study groups, they know the context and the pre- and postconditions for the lessons. Ten minutes is long enough to see how students are responding. Usually, study groups establish norms for student observations. Prior to the first student observation, the norms are written in the log. The following are examples of such norms:

- The focus is on student behavior.
- The focus is on the student needs that the study group is addressing.
- Pairs can be any combination of study group members.
- Pairs inform each other of student behaviors on which they want data collected.
- Data are used for the ongoing work of the study group.
- Information from observing students is shared only with study group members.

Teachers observing each other's students in classrooms is a huge break with school traditions and norms. As with looking at student work in a collaborative setting, the norms regarding privacy and isolation are so strong that it takes gentle but firm leadership to "open up" the workplace. Many teachers have had negative experiences regarding observing with other teachers. In many schools, the practice of coaching has swung in the direction of evaluation and has become so structured that the original intent (Joyce & Showers, 1982, 1983, 1988, 1995, 2001; Showers, 1985) of the process has been lost. What is different here for study groups is the circumstances: Members enter each other's rooms to observe students during a lesson that the study group jointly developed. As looking at student work and observing students in classrooms become common practices in schools, schools are transformed. To push teachers to observe in each other's classrooms as part of the study group work, a principal must say, "In the next log, I want to see that you are sharing how students responded to a lesson one of the members observed being taught."

A study group at Hubbard Primary School in Monroe County, Georgia, describes how it combined the looking at student work and the observing student work strategies:

Group 4: The most effective WFSG strategy that we used was a classroom observation followed by using the Tuning protocol with work from the lesson we observed. We had the opportunity to observe a teacher's lesson on "making connections." Teachers were able to view firsthand student's initial thoughts and reactions to the new strategy of "making connections." Members of our group felt it was more beneficial to interact with students as they are learning than to simply view the finished product or work sample. When we used the Turning protocol looking at student work from the lesson we observed, teachers were able to ask specific questions in regards to the lesson as well as giving "warm" and "cool" feedback. This experience gave those of us who observed the lesson and the teacher who was observed significant time to reflect on our individual thoughts about the lesson. We found that pairing the observation and the protocol was very valuable, and we recommend that this become standard practice.

Training

One of the most effective strategies study groups use to hear the expert voice is to have the expert voice attend one or more study group meetings. This could be a teacher on the faculty in another study group, a teacher from another school, a consultant from the district office or regional office, a consultant from a university, or a representative from a publisher or other commercial source.

If the focus of a study group is to learn how to use new skills in the classroom, one or more members will require training. The study group may invite a skilled person to meet with the study group routinely over time, go to a workshop, take a course together, or have a member represent the group in a workshop or course. One study group wanted to become more skillful in using mathematics and science manipulatives. One person in the group enrolled in a course. After each class, that person worked with members using the manipulatives, related materials, and techniques learned in class. Not only did this help other members but also it gave the person enrolled in the class an opportunity to practice the new skills. The teachers had an agreement that they would use the strategy in their classrooms during the week after they had been introduced to the new materials and techniques. This increases the level of use and the impact of the new practices on students.

Conducting Action Research

Action research is a disciplined inquiry. Step 6 of the DMC (Chapter 7) is a series of action research cycles that look similar to the following:

1. The study group looks at classroom-based data related to the essential question to establish baseline data for their students.

2. The study group reviews current research or information about effective practices that have been shown effective in addressing the identified student need.

3. The study group develops lessons that incorporate what was learned from their study of effective practices and uses the strategies and materials in classrooms.

4. Individuals in the study group bring student work from the classroom to assess the effectiveness of the classroom lessons and strategies.

5. The study group looks at classroom-based data related to the essential question to determine if the targeted student need has been met.

6. If there is progress, the group may continue by designing similar lessons or focusing on another need in the action plan.

7. Begin the cycle again, either for the current need or for another student need.

A cycle takes approximately four to six study group meetings for groups that meet weekly for 1 hour.

The process described previously is not as formal as some described or endorsed by individuals who specialize in the field of action research. There are much more complete descriptions of action research conducted by individuals, teams, and whole faculties (Calhoun, 1994). We are presenting, perhaps, an over-simplification of the process. Our intent is to get study groups to think and act more like research teams. Our more casual approach, however, seems to work best for study groups.

Murphy tells of an incident in the mid-1990s at a session in Round Rock, Texas, with representatives from schools implementing WFSGs. Several teachers indicated to her that they would be leaving her session early to attend another workshop. When Murphy inquired as to the name of the workshop, the teachers said, "We are going to learn about action research." Until then, Murphy had not used the term "action research" to describe what the study groups were doing, knowing that names of processes often confuse teachers and get in the way of teachers actually doing what you want them to do. However, as a result of this incident, Murphy started using the term action research with clarifications. One can see the problem with names when teachers are asked to list the initiatives at their schools and they list study groups, action research, data-based decision making, collaborative teaming, looking at student work, and so on. When everything has a name, teachers tend to focus on the name and consider each component of a design as a separate entity rather than a whole process consisting of multiple components. The latter is the healthier perspective from an organizational standpoint.

When action research is practiced by study groups, members track the effects of interventions on students. At the end of the school year, a group has a "track record" if the charts in the action plan (see Chapter 6, Guideline 6) have been completed. Monitoring effects of new teaching practices and materials is a basic function or purpose of study groups.

Conducting Lesson Study

In the February/March 2004 issue of the NSDC's *Tools for Schools*, Joan Richardson reported that "lesson study" is different from "lesson planning" because it focuses on what teachers want students to do rather than on what teachers plan to teach. She stated that in lesson study, a group of teachers develop a lesson together, and ultimately one of them teaches the lesson while the others observe the students learning. The entire group meets to debrief the lesson and often revises and reteaches the lesson to incorporate what has been learned.

WFSG Action Plan Cycle:
Plan - Act - Reflect

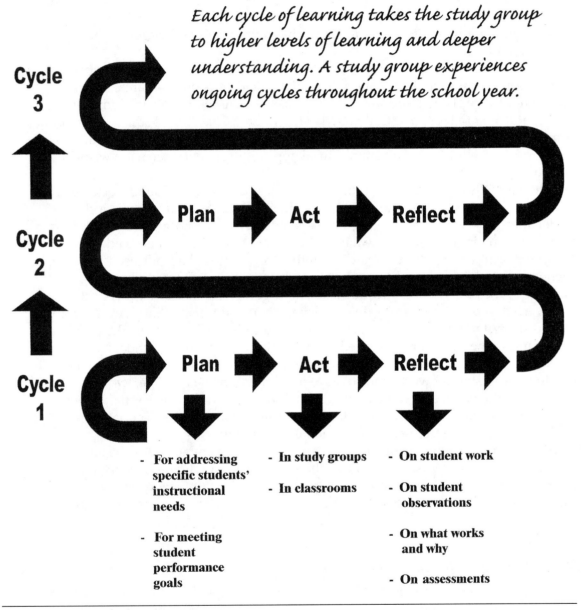

Each cycle of learning takes the study group to higher levels of learning and deeper understanding. A study group experiences ongoing cycles throughout the school year.

Cycle 3

Cycle 2

Plan → Act → Reflect

Cycle 1

Plan → Act → Reflect

- For addressing specific students' instructional needs

- For meeting student performance goals

- In study groups

- In classrooms

- On student work

- On student observations

- On what works and why

- On assessments

Figure 8.3   WFSG Action Plan Cycle

The WFSG structure creates the setting for lesson study. Members of a study group who choose to follow the formal approach of a lesson study, however, will need to be taught the format. It is recommended that a study group identify an expert voice to guide the lesson study. This could be a university professor, a high school teacher, or any other individual who has a high degree of knowledge of the content of the lesson. A study group may engage is a series of lesson studies or do one lesson study cycle following specific guidelines. The steps of a lesson study are as follows:

1. *Focus the lesson study.* The lesson would be within the context of the study group's action plan. If the study group is addressing measurement, the lesson would be on some aspect of measurement.

2. *Plan the lesson study.* If the study group is meeting weekly, this could take 1 month. If the study group is meeting only every other week, planning could take as long as 2 months. Planning includes research, going online with colleagues in other schools, assessing current knowledge, and anticipating student responses.

3. *Prepare for the observation.* One study group member will teach the lesson to his or her students. Other members will be assigned key tasks. Materials should be prepared for the observers, such as worksheets that teachers will use and a seating chart including the names of the students. It is recommended that group members agree on where observers will be stationed in the room as the teacher presents the lesson and how they will circulate to observe students working.

4. *Teach and observe the lesson.* Observers take notes on student responses, look for examples of how students construct their understanding, and document a variety of methods individual students use to solve problems. The study group may develop a form for what they want to make sure they observe.

5. *Debrief the lesson.* Group members share their "learning" from the observation.

6. *Reflect and plan the next steps.* The group may decide to revise and reteach the lesson. It may decide to apply what it has learned to its other ongoing work.

WFSGs do lesson study as part of the routine of the group's work. Often, however, it is not formalized as in Items 1 through 6. For more information about lesson study, see the following:

- Lesson Study Research Group, www.tc.edu/centers/lessonstudy
- Research for Better Schools, www.rbs.org/lesson_study

Comentoring

Comentoring occurs when members of a study group agree to mentor each other. This happens when teachers are in their study group meetings, when they talk one-on-one between meetings, and when they are in each other's classrooms. The 12th WFSG procedural guideline states, "Recognize all study group members as equals."

This means that regardless of years of experience and level of certification, all teachers have information and skills to share. When one teacher in a study group has recently attended training in a particular teaching strategy, that teacher will be the one to demonstrate the strategy to the other study group members either during a study group meeting or in the classroom with students. If another teacher in a study group has had the opportunity to become more immersed, for example, in a new mathematics program, that teacher will demonstrate the new knowledge either in a study group meeting or in a classroom with students. Spending time in each other's classrooms is a natural outgrowth of the WFSG process. In a study group, teachers coach and comentor one another, plan together, and teach lessons and demonstrate effective practices to each other.

"The Coaching of Teaching" (Joyce & Showers, 1982) introduced to the field of staff development the notion that teachers could work with each other much like coaches work with their players. Since then, many coaching systems have been introduced to teachers. Many such systems have been so formalized and structured that the original concept that Joyce and Showers (1982) envisioned has been compromised. In many schools, the word "coaching" is an automatic turn-off for teachers. "Peer observation" is another term that carries baggage from prior experiences. Many evaluation systems have a peer observation component, and the term has a negative ring to teachers. It has been our experience that using these terms creates teacher tension and resistance. In comentoring relationships within groups, members determine when and how to use each other's classrooms as learning laboratories. Chapter 9 provides more details about comentoring.

Listening to Students

Listening to students is another strategy for hearing the student voice and for making student-based decisions. Study groups are encouraged to invite a student to attend a portion of a study group meeting as a data-collection strategy. Study group members decide prior to interviewing a student what the group wants to gain from the interview. One middle school study group addressing mathematics asked a high school student to attend a study group meeting. The members asked the student what experiences he had in middle school that best prepared him for high school mathematics. An elementary school study group addressing student needs in the area of writing invited a first grader to attend a study group meeting and asked her what she most liked about writing. Such information helps a study group shape its work.

Shadowing Students

Teachers can learn from a student's routine. One or more teachers in a study group can shadow middle and high school students to learn from them. If a study group is targeting writing, a teacher would watch for the opportunities students have to write in different disciplines during a school day. A study group in a high school that was addressing higher-order thinking skills decided to have one teacher in the group shadow a student for a day, to have another teacher shadow a second student for a day the next week, and to have a third teacher shadow still another student the subsequent week. Each teacher kept a record of all opportunities students had to use problem-solving skills and how they responded to each opportunity. This data-collection technique gave the study group its most valuable input. The study group compiled and analyzed the information, and during a sharing session, it seriously applied the data. It is this type of real-world data that the faculty should gather, understand, and use. Teachers learn from watching students, not just their own students but students in contexts other than their own classroom. Note that not only do teachers learn from watching students, but also students learn what is perceived to be important from watching the routines and behaviors of teachers (Sizer & Sizer, 1999).

Videotaping

All teachers in a study group have access to blank videotapes. Suppose a study group is addressing a student need in reading, and the group has examined a number of materials and strategies. Over a period of a week, each teacher does the following: videotapes students as he or she is covering a reading lesson in a content area, views the tape in privacy, lists several things he or she liked about what was done and several things that he or she would change, and erases the tape. At the next study group meeting, each shares what he or she wrote about the taped lesson. In 3 or 4 weeks, the group repeats the process, and over time the cycle is repeated several times. At some point, after one of the cycles, teachers may want the study group to view a tape. After the group views the tape, the teacher will share his or her reflections on the lesson and how the students responded. This works especially well if the teacher brings student work that was done during the taping or as a result of the lesson that was taped. For such taping, a tripod is usually placed in the front of the room facing the students. When a teacher is teaching, so much thought is going into the content of the lesson that he or she often misses how the students are responding. Watching the students or particular students at the completion of the lesson and in privacy typically yields surprising results.

Learning From Case Studies

Case-based learning involves using carefully chosen, real-world examples of teaching and learning (Barnett, 1999). A study group focusing on student mathematics needs, for example, can select cases from a source such as the Mathematics Case Methods Project and discuss a common case. The case, selected from a book of field-tested cases and written by teachers, describes a classroom experience that had an unexpected outcome or ran into difficulty. The author of the case uses dialogue and student work to describe how the instruction was planned and what actually happened. Teachers in the study group try the suggested instructional strategy and materials and determine if they have the same or different results.

Developing and Testing Curriculum

A study group identifies a student need, searches for best practices and materials to meet that need, uses those materials and strategies in members' classrooms, and assesses effects. Curriculum committees usually begin with someone at the district level stating, for example, that the science curriculum needs to be updated. What a study group does that is focusing on student needs in science can be fed into a committee that is revamping the science curriculum. In this way, a study group adds a dimension to curriculum development, especially if members of the study group are also members of the curriculum development committee. If this is the situation, after a committee decides what should be included in a new curriculum, members would try the material and strategies in their classrooms if the particular material and strategy are aimed at the student need that the study group is targeting. It is only after trials and reflections on the trials that the outcomes are shared with other science teachers. Note that WFSGs are not curriculum development committees; that is, the purpose of a study group's work is not to recommend what others are to do or to produce a document for others to follow. Curriculum development usually means that teachers are researching and writing what is to be taught at some future time, after a document is produced. WFSG work focuses on what is happening now and what students need for teachers to do and to learn now.

Immersing in Academic Content

Students should be taught by those who have a deep knowledge of what they teach (Chapter 2, first function of WFSGs) (Figure 8.4). Loucks-Horsley (1998a) states that the need for more challenging mathematics for students means that their teachers also must learn more challenging mathematics content and how to teach it.

Immerse means to plunge into, as if into a liquid; to absorb deeply; engross. This is precisely what teachers of mathematics, science, literature, history, art, music, or any content must do to be effective teachers. If students are not performing at higher levels on content area tests, could it be because the teachers do not know and understand their content deeply enough? If teachers do not have a deep understanding of what they teach, they cannot expect students to learn and understand deeply enough. If teachers do not fully understand what they teach, they cannot design thought-provoking learning activities, and their students will be less likely to be successful on assessments that require them to apply their knowledge in new ways.

In WFSGs, teachers select a student need and convert that need into an area of study. In their study groups, teachers talk to one another to build their own and each other's understanding. They share, for example, what they know about reading to deepen their understanding; they search for new ways to apply their knowledge, enabling them to more effectively teach their students. They develop analogies of an idea or concept so they can help students develop analogies. In WFSGs, teachers immerse themselves in the academic content they teach and in the strategies that enable students to be more successful learners.

Journaling

One procedural guideline for WFSGs is that teachers reflect on the work of study groups and the impact of current practice on student performance. It is recommended that teachers keep a personal reflective journal of their study group work. Their journal would not only include actual experiences in the group but also their reflections on the activities and relationships. It would even include what happens in their classrooms as a result of group meetings. In their journals, they would also include other professional development experiences. Journals provide teachers with an opportunity to analyze their own practices, record their perceptions, voice their joys and fears, and reconstruct their experiences. It is a permanent record. Occasionally, teachers may share parts of their journals in their study group. Time should be allocated at designated meetings for this purpose.

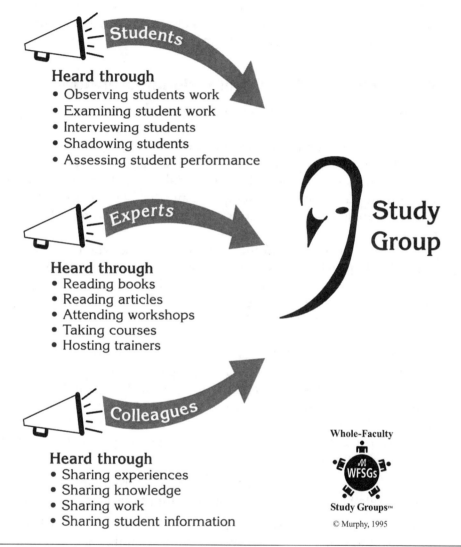

WFSGs
Hear Expert Voices

Heard through
- Observing students work
- Examining student work
- Interviewing students
- Shadowing students
- Assessing student performance

Heard through
- Reading books
- Reading articles
- Attending workshops
- Taking courses
- Hosting trainers

Heard through
- Sharing experiences
- Sharing knowledge
- Sharing work
- Sharing student information

Study Group

Whole-Faculty Study Groups™
© Murphy, 1995

Figure 8.4   WFSGs Hear Expert Voices

Keeping Portfolios

In a study group, teachers may choose to keep individual portfolios or a group portfolio of their work. In one elementary school, teachers in a technology study group constructed a portfolio of their work and displayed it at the end of the school year at a PTA meeting. The following school year, a new technology study group used the portfolio to get ideas about how it might build on the lessons learned from the preceding year's technology study group, contributing to "building a knowledge community."

Using Protocols

Regarding looking at student work, we previously discussed the importance of using protocols to structure and purpose conversation. A protocol is a purposeful and thoughtful way to have conversations in study groups. There are many protocols that have been developed and field-tested for a number of different purposes; for more information on protocols, see the resources listed at the end of the Examining Student Work section in this chapter. These resources also offer suggestions for protocols for examining teacher work as well as analyzing data and having text discussions.

Reading Books and Other Professional Literature

Most study groups use as the group's expert voice some form of professional literature, usually books and articles. Books are seldom read from "cover to cover." The group selects one or more chapters that specifically address the needs the group is addressing. If the group agrees to read a chapter from a book or an article, the group members should debrief the material and determine what the implications are for their classrooms. For example, if an effective practice is described in the material, individuals would agree to try the strategy and to report on its use at the next meeting.

Instead of purchasing a set of the same book for the whole faculty, schools that implement WFSG purchase sets of five copies of the same title, and a set of five books may be used by different study groups at different times.

Strategies, activities, and protocols for debriefing articles, books, and selected chapters from books are as follows:

1. *The final word:* Groups of five or six read the same material. One person begins by directing the others to the page and paragraph that contains the passage that "struck them the most" and tells why he or she selected that passage. After the passage is shared, the other individuals respond to the passage. After everyone has responded, the person who started the round has the final word. The round is repeated until everyone in the group has "the final word." No dialogue is allowed.

2. *Carousel brainstorm:* The purpose is to allow participants to share ideas and build a set of common questions and assumptions before they begin to read.

3. *Plan a 30-second speech:* After participants finish reading an article, invite them to pause and plan a 30-second speech about what they learned from the article.

4. *Jigsaw readings:* The jigsaw enables the group to read a lengthy article quickly by dividing the reading into parts for each member to read and report on.

5. *Become an expert:* Articles are distributed in advance of the workshop, and participants are asked to read them and come prepared to "be the experts."

6. *Magnetic questions:* Participants are given key questions that are thought provoking and provocative. They choose one that either angers or resonates with them and use this question as their "stand" as they discuss the article or video with others in the group.

7. *Text-based discussion:* Participants are given a reading and key questions prior to coming to the workshop. The discussion is focused on the viewpoint of the author, using citations from the text as reference points.

RESOURCES TO SUPPORT THE CONTENT

The following resources may help teachers become more certain about what a study group will do and strategies the group will use to do its work:

1. *Student work:* The work of students is a group's most valuable resource.

2. *Teachers' manuals:* This is one of the most underused resources that teachers have. Manuals that go with textbooks have a wealth of information about how to teach the content. Bringing manuals to study group meetings to explore how basic skills are introduced at each grade level is valid work. Supplementary materials accompanying the text also should be examined.

3. *Student textbooks:* Because developing vocabulary is one student need often addressed, study groups frequently examine textbooks in one content area (e.g., mathematics). This examination usually leads teachers to be more consistent with the vocabulary they use when teaching. Although publishers have produced vocabulary lists, actually manipulating student texts would give teachers a greater feel for what students experience. In heterogeneous study groups, some teachers have not looked at student texts at other grade levels. Some upper-grade teachers who teach one subject area have not reviewed student texts in other subject areas.

4. *People* (real live): People from district offices, other schools within a district, teachers within the school, regional service agencies, universities and colleges, technical schools and centers, state departments, textbook representatives, independent consultants, other school districts, and local businesses and community agencies can be rich sources of information. Once the study group matches itself with a resource person, it is suggested that the individual work with the group on some sort of routine basis, for example, once a month.

5. *Books:* Sources include textbooks from courses previously taken (e.g., reading courses), college bookstores, publishers' lists, and catalogs from professional organizations, such as the Association for Supervision and Curriculum Development and the National Staff Development Council. A book will give a study group more structure. A cycle for using a book could be to read a chapter or section of the book, discuss and reflect on the reading (one meeting), try ideas in classrooms, share results of actions in classrooms and demonstrate lessons taught (one or two meetings), reflect on outcomes and examine student work (one meeting), and go on to another chapter and repeat the process. The cycle (plan, act, and reflect) for one reading could take up to four study group meetings.

6. *Articles:* School libraries usually subscribe to periodicals, such as *The Reading Teacher, The Journal of Reading, The Journal of Educational Research,* and *Educational Leadership.* If an article is to be used to generate ideas for actual classroom trials, it should be copied for everyone in the group. The plan-act-reflect cycle described in Item 5 should be considered. The Final Word protocol is also a good way to debrief readings.

7. *Videotapes and DVDs:* The Video Journal of Education has outstanding videos on a range of curriculum and instructional materials and strategies

(www.TeachStream.com). Also, the National Staff Development Council (www.nsdc.org) and the Association for Supervision and Curriculum Development (www.ascd.org) have catalogs that describe relevant programs.

8. *The Internet:* There is unlimited information from this resource.

9. *Computer software:* Computer programs in all content areas and reference materials that go beyond anything we could have imagined a few years ago are available and abundant.

10. *Public television:* Many state departments of education and universities offer courses and other professional opportunities via television or online.

11. *Workshops and conferences:* One person from the study group may attend workshops and conferences and bring the information to the study group.

12. *Commercial sources:* In many states and communities, businesses and agencies have materials that stress the importance of reading, writing, mathematics, and other content areas. In Georgia, the Georgia Power Company, Pizza Hut, the Atlanta Braves, and Six Flags Over Georgia have materials that teachers can order.

13. *Students:* A student invited to attend the first 5 or 10 minutes of a study group meeting could, in an interview format, give study group members valuable information about instructional practices. The study group would decide what it wants to ask prior to inviting the student. Students at any grade level, including kindergarten, can provide helpful and interesting information to a study group.

14. *Program materials:* Most instructional programs that schools adopt have an array of materials in print, video, and audio formats. These programs also have individuals who are trained in the use of program strategies.

15. *District and state sources:* State departments and school districts have materials specifically developed to help teachers implement frameworks, standards, and curriculums endorsed by local units.

The previous resources will give the content substance. It is what teachers have in their hands when they walk into a study group meeting that gives substance to the work. It is what is on the table around which the teachers sit that gives the meeting substance. All workers need tools. The "stuff" we carry in our hands and put on the table are a study group's tools. A carpenter would not go to work without tools. Neither would a teacher go to a study group meeting without tools—materials with which to work.

Others may help, but no one outside the study group can make the work of the group meaningful. That is a task and challenge for its members. When members state that study group meetings are a waste of time, the person hearing the statement should say, "And who determines what the group will do?" There is so much work to do in schools. The study group is a place to do that work with colleagues, not in isolation, as has been the case in the past for most teachers. The content of the work of study groups is the work teachers have to do to prepare themselves to help their students learn more.

CONTENT IS OFTEN PROBLEMATIC

Murphy has found that of the three components or elements of a professional development design—context, process, and content—for study group members, content is the most problematic. Teachers have no difficulty deciding what students should know. Teachers design curriculum for other teachers to use with students. In curriculum guides that are developed by teachers, they specify objectives, select materials, and design activities for students. When it comes to designing curriculum for themselves, however, it is like hitting a brick wall. When it comes to specifying what they should know, what they need to do to gain new knowledge and skill and the content of their learning, content becomes somewhat of a mystery.

Once the student needs are identified, in relation to the study group process, content includes two considerations: (a) what teachers will study when the group meets to become more knowledgeable and skillful and (b) strategies the group will use to master the new knowledge and skills.

In a conversation with a consultant for WFSGs, the consultant said, "It is so difficult to get teachers to understand the importance of the content of teacher work." This is puzzling because teachers understand the importance of the content of student work. Teachers in study groups should determine what will be the "teacher work" just as they determine what will be the "student work." Teachers teach mathematics content, social studies content, science content, and reading and writing content. Every day, teachers make decisions about what strategies or activities they will use in teaching content. What to learn and how to learn it are the two aspects of study group content. The other puzzling aspect of teachers having difficulty identifying substantive and engaging content stems from what teachers say (Table 8.2).

In the Augusta, Georgia, schools, where the WFSG work began, the content was predetermined. As described in Chapter 1, the content (what study groups do) was part of the school improvement package. The package included being in a study group that focused on implementing in classrooms several models of teaching. Faculties that voted to implement the improvement program were told before they voted that the content would be several models of teaching, and that the process for learning teaching strategies would be to organize the entire faculty into study groups. Once the improvement program began, there were pockets of resistance. Some teachers resisted the process—being in a study group; some resisted the content—the models of teaching; and some resisted both the process and the content. A visitor to the school could hear a teacher say, "I am so frustrated with this new program." The visitor would ask, "Oh, you don't like the models of teaching?" To which the teacher would say, "The models are great! I don't like meeting in those groups every week." The same visitor would see another teacher, and the teacher would say, "This new program is really difficult." The visitor would ask, "Oh, you don't like weekly study group meetings?" To which the teacher would say, "I love meeting with my colleagues each week; the models of teaching are just too hard." The one thing visitors did hear from all teachers was that students were learning more. This acknowledgment confirmed that centralized or district-sponsored initiatives can be effective and beneficial to students.

When Murphy began working in other districts, it was assumed that the content, what teachers do in study groups, would not be the source of teachers' grumbling. If teachers selected the content, Murphy wondered, would the process seem more

Teachers Say	We Say
We have too much to do.	Pool resources and strengths to reduce the time it takes to individually develop lessons.
Too many new programs. Don't have time to figure out how to use these materials.	Select the new writing program and take the time to immerse yourselves in how to use the materials to increase writing scores.
The study group is a waste of time.	Who decided that you would do what you are doing?
There's no time to align new math standards with math curriculum.	Do that in your study group.
No time to prepare to implement what we were trained to do.	In a study group, work with teachers who attended the same training and practice new strategies together.
We don't know enough about what we are trying to do.	Ask the principal to locate a specialist in that area to work with you.
My study group is boring.	How would you respond to a student in your class who said that?

Table 8.2   Responses to What Teachers Say

democratic? Would the study group work seem more relevant? Would there be more buy-in? Would the process not seem so "top down"? Would teachers not feel so coerced? Generally, Murphy has found that initially there is a higher sense of teacher satisfaction when teachers choose the student needs that groups will address. That satisfaction, however, does not continue if teachers do not see changes in student learning. Most often, grumbling persists. The source of the grumbling is the outward frustration of teachers realizing that the content they chose is not having the desired impact or what they chose to do is not useful. Self-selection does not necessarily mean that the end result of the work of study groups will be higher levels of student learning. If the faculty does not have all the data for the choices that students require the faculty to make, and if the faculty does not have leaders who will speak for students, then the faculty may make choices that, over time, will create dissatisfaction and will not result in changes in their behavior or in changes in student behavior. Still, even when teachers are shown evidence that student learning increased in places where district leaders used districtwide data to determine what study groups in schools would do, they are clear that they do not want to be told what they are to do in their study groups.

There are study groups in WFSG schools that have difficulty connecting teacher learning to student learning. Once this is evident in the action plan and in the first few logs from a study group, the principal or other support person must intervene. Chapter 10 describes how leaders should intervene. The intervening person should be one who

- Knows the context
- Has reviewed the study group's action plan and logs

- Knows the status of student learning in the members' classrooms
- Knows the instructional initiatives that are currently operational at the school
- Knows what resources are available, both human and material
- Knows the skill level of teachers in the study group in the specific content areas

The people who usually have this knowledge are the principal and one or more district leaders. That person should meet with the study group, examine the student needs that the group is targeting, and determine what resources are available to get the group moving. Study groups experience the greatest content success if someone in the district has expertise to help the groups as they confront new knowledge and the need for new skills. When someone accessible to the study group can provide resources to the group and can meet with it on a regular basis, the study group is much less likely to go astray. If there is no one in the district who can supply that service, then the school should secure the services of a content specialist. The key to the success in the Augusta schools was the content expertise that consultants brought to study groups.

What some teachers have found helpful when trying to get a handle on the content of their work is to equate the study group work to a college course. Teachers usually select college courses or they are expected to take courses because of the course's content. Here, we draw some parallels. The SGAP is the course syllabus. The study group logs are the notes for each class meeting. The notebook that every study group member keeps has the action plan and logs in it along with the artifacts from each meeting (e.g., articles and lesson plans the group develops). Artifacts would be the same as course handouts. The work between study group meetings would be the homework or the practicum side of the course. In a college course on reading, what would be the content? What would teachers learn in the course? What would materials be that teachers would use and read? What materials would teachers be expected to develop in the course as part of the course work? What instructional strategies would the course instructor use? Answers to these questions tell us about the content of the course. In some districts, if a study group is addressing reading, the study group members can apply for course credit and, on examination of what the group did, receive credit for a reading course equivalent to a college course.

Once student needs are identified and groups are formed, a study group designs its own work just like a college instructor designs a college course, except the study group's design will be more practical. The course that study group members design is tailor-made for the study group. The work that the study group plans for itself is the content of the study group's work. What teachers work on and what strategies the group uses to do that work become the study group's content.

If the study group's general category of student need is mathematics, the content of the group's work could be the district's mathematics standards. If the general category is writing, the content of the group's work could be a new writing program that the district is initiating. Generic content for either of these two areas of work could be the latest brain research or the use of technology. Whatever the study group selects, its content should be aligned with student needs. Teachers must do what will enable their students to become more knowledgeable and skillful. The study group's action plan will indicate student needs and what teachers will do when the group meets to address student needs. Again, what teachers will do and how teachers will go about doing it become the study group's curriculum of study, the content.

CONTENT QUESTIONS TO ASK

When thinking about the appropriateness of study group content, ask, does the content

1. Require the group to examine student work?

2. Require the group to examine teacher work?

3. Require "intellectually rigorous" work?

4. Have promise for positively impacting the identified student needs?

5. Require the group to examine current classroom practice?

6. Limit the rehashing of what individuals already know?

7. Push individuals beyond where they currently are in regard to skill and understanding?

8. Have a research base?

9. Require members to engage in reflective dialogue?

10. Require members to implement new materials and strategies in the classroom?

11. Keep members focused on the learning needs of their students?

12. Cause members to actively seek multiple sources to push themselves to higher levels of understanding of the academic content they teach?

SUMMARY

Without content that will change behaviors of teachers and behaviors of students, the WFSG process has little power to change anything. The power of collaborative relationships is in the following:

- What teachers study
- What teachers investigate
- What teaching strategies teachers add to their repertoires
- What materials teachers add to their resource bank
- What teachers do to become more skillful in their classrooms
- What strategies members use when the study group meets to accomplish its intended results

9

Supporting Synergistic Groups and Learning Teams

TEAM BUILDING

Effective study groups are effective teams! No study group will be effective if it does not have real teamwork. Teamwork is what differentiates an effective study group from a typical committee or other work group. The following is an insightful story of four people named Everybody, Somebody, Anybody, and Nobody, which very nicely helps us understand what teamwork and team building are not:

> There was an important job to be done, and Everybody was sure that Somebody would do it. Anybody could have done it, but Nobody did it. Somebody got angry about that because it was Everybody's job. Everybody thought Anybody could do it, but Nobody realized Everybody wouldn't do it. It ended up that Everybody blamed Somebody when Nobody did what Anybody could have done.

On the positive side, the great automobile industry leader, Henry Ford, gives us a sense of the meaning of teamwork: "Coming together is a beginning; keeping together is progress; and working together is success."

A group of friends went down the Colorado River in an inflatable raft. After two days, as Pat Riley (1994) describes in *The Winner Within*, "the river became a great equalizer. People accustomed to being pampered and indulged had become a team, working together to cope with the unpredictable twists and turns of the river" (pp. 56–57).

The twists and turns that study groups encounter are as real and personally as scary as those in the raging river. Consequently, study groups cannot make it as just a collection of individuals but, instead, can work together cooperatively and have tremendous success as an effective team.

Teamwork is the ability of people to work together in a genuinely cooperative manner (i.e., interdependently) toward a common vision. Teamwork means joint work and joint responsibility. Teamwork is a vehicle that allows common people to attain uncommon results.

Good examples of teamwork are California's giant Sebring trees. Their roots are barely below the surface of the ground. The Sebring grow in groves, and their roots intertwine. When strong winds blow, the intertwining (i.e., interdependent) roots of the Sebring help hold them all up.

Another impressive illustration of teamwork happened in the 1980 Winter Olympic Games at Lake Placid, New York. Rather than just trying to find the top players, the coach of the U.S. ice hockey team selected individuals who could function in a team setting and respond effectively under pressure. The U.S. team began ranked seventh in a field of eight. When the closing seconds ticked away, however, the final score read USA 4 and USSR 3. Maybe the USA team did not have the best players on the ice, but it did have the best team! It was a synergistic team, collectively striving for a common vision, interdependently playing and empowering each other, and functioning as the best Olympic ice hockey team in the world.

True (i.e., authentic) teamwork is called *synergy*; it occurs when the teamwork of a group allows it to get the maximum results from the available resources. Effective study groups are synergistic, self-directed, learning teams.

In the remaining sections of this chapter, we describe and discuss the specifics and details of this type of teamwork, including its prerequisites, the process for attaining it, and its development in study groups.

SYNERGISTIC RELATIONSHIPS

In a group or team, relationships are established that make the group more productive or less so. If a group collectively is less productive than the sum of what the individuals would produce, we say we have a *self-destructive relationship* in the group. This, unfortunately, happens frequently and comes about in a group because of such things as poor communication or miscommunication, lack of trust, blaming, defensiveness, self-centeredness, backbiting, and internal competition.

In a group with self-destructive relationships, the group uses up so much energy in nonproductive ways that it has little additional energy to be creative and to generate new ideas and more effective processes. No doubt you have seen groups composed of bright, capable individuals that could not seem to accomplish much of anything, and it made you wonder, how could such a strong group of individuals be so ineffective? Unfortunately, the individuals were most capable, but the relationship in the group was self-destructive, keeping the group from effectively using the many talents of the group.

Typically, self-destructive groups or teams are self-defeating and negative in a school setting, making it even more difficult to accomplish school goals. These are the groups that generally function at the level of the lowest common denominator of the group and accomplish less than if the members worked alone. Peter Senge (1990), in his book on learning organizations, *The Fifth Discipline*, describes destructive teams in what he calls the "myth of teamwork": "Most teams operate below the level of the lowest IQ in the group. The result is skilled incompetence, in which people in groups grow incredibly efficient at keeping themselves from learning" (pp. 9–10).

Another type of relationship exists in a group or team when the group produces the same as would be produced by the members individually. In this case, we say we have a *static relationship* in the group. Static relationships exist because of some of the same types of negative, nonproductive features described for self-destructive groups. Static relationships produce enough energy to get by but nothing extra for doing new and creative things beyond what the individual group members could have produced. In static relationship situations, hopes are generated for groups and teams, but little is gained by having people working together.

A third type of relationship in a group, the desired one, is the *synergistic relationship*. In a synergistic relationship, the members of a group or team work together to produce a total result that is greater than the sum of the efforts of the individual members. In other words, the synergy of a group or team is the combined cooperative action in the group or team that generates additional energy beyond that consumed by the group and produces a total outcome beyond what could be obtained by the individual members. In a truly synergistic group, people energize and inspire each other, and the diversity of ideas and openness to them provide the basis for new creative ideas and approaches.

The power of synergy or synergistic relationships is well illustrated by the following physical example. If you take a piece of wood 2 inches by 4 inches and 8 feet long and place it on blocks at the ends of the 2-by-4, the 2-by-4 will hold 100 pounds of weight before it breaks. If, however, you take two 8-foot 2-by-4s and glue them together, the pair will hold a staggering 800 pounds! Why? The glue bonds the two boards together, creating a synergistic relationship between them so that when the fibers in one board run in different directions to those of the other, one gives strength at the places where the other might be weak. This significantly enhances the total strength or weight capacity of the combination. The expected or intuitive increase in strength in this situation would have been twofold; instead, the synergy or synergistic relationship in this situation gave an eightfold increase in strength.

In the hockey team example discussed previously, the coach said that he did not necessarily have the best players but he did have the best Olympic hockey team that year. Why? Because the players functioned as a synergistic team. They were striving together for a common vision, playing in an interdependent manner (genuinely cooperative), and significantly empowering each other for the collective best of the team. As a result, they functioned that year as the best Olympic hockey team in the world. Another good real-world example of synergy is that found in a healthy marriage. In a healthy marriage, the spouses develop a caring support system in which they genuinely and openly cooperate with each other, set common goals, and provide creative sharing and assistance toward reaching their common goals. Weaknesses of one are offset by strengths of the other, and they feed off each other's encouragement and creative ideas and challenges.

Communication is an important part of effective, synergistic teams. In *The Seven Habits of Highly Effective People*, Covey (1990) says about communicating synergistically, "You are simply opening your mind and heart and expressions to new possibilities, new alternatives, new options" (p. 264). He adds the following about synergistic groups: "You begin with the belief that the parties involved will gain more insight, and that the excitement of that mutual learning and insight will create a momentum toward more and more insights, learning, and growth" (p. 264).

The characteristics that Covey (1990) described are among the critical factors for turning groups into effective, synergistic groups or teams. What exactly are the vital prerequisites for synergistic groups, and how do we generate them? In the next two sections, we discuss the four prerequisites for synergistic groups and teams and a four-step process for developing them.

SYNERGY PREREQUISITES

Just how important is synergy in our work with study groups? Daryl Conner (1993), one of the world's top experts in change and effectively dealing with change, says that synergy is the "soul of a successful change project" (p. 188). Our efforts with study groups are aimed at change projects that, ultimately, will help enhance student learning and improve our schools. Thus, synergy and synergistic study groups will be critical to our success; they will be key vehicles to increasing both quality and productivity.

In one high school involved in the study group process, the focus team discussed the important nature of synergy in their work as follows (Murphy & Lick, 1998):

> The logistics of how the focus team conducted their work was secondary to the synergy that was created by the joint work of the team. The team felt that they had the power to influence the future of their school and conditions of its students. Five interdependent focus team members became many interdependent individuals in the study groups. The momentum generated by their collaborative efforts made the mountain easier to climb. (p. 91)

In another school, a study group said the following about its synergy (Murphy & Lick, 1998):

> Most important, the rapport that grew from becoming more open about our beliefs and classroom practices increased our willingness to try new methods and to share how those strategies worked for our students. For the first time, we openly shared lessons that were not effective and jointly worked on ways to make the lessons more powerful. (p. 86)

When we talk about the *capacity* of a group to do something, we find that we must take into consideration two factors, the group's *willingness* and its *ability*. To be effective, a group must both be willing and have ability. If either of these factors is missing, then the group has a lesser capacity. The same is true when we consider the potential capacity for synergy. That is, for a group to be synergistic, it must be willing to do what is required to bring about synergy, and it must also have the ability to do so. Most groups fail to be synergistic because they are not willing to do what is required, they do not have the ability or circumstances for them to be synergistic, or both.

In his more than 20 years of research and experience with change, Conner (1993) found that the key fundamentals for the development of synergy in a group were (a) willingness, arising from the sharing of common goals and interdependence (i.e., mutual dependence and genuine cooperation); and (b) ability, growing from member and group empowerment and participative involvement.

Consequently, the four prerequisites for synergistic study groups are as follows:

Willingness	*Ability*
1. Common goals	3. Empowerment
2. Interdependence	4. Participative involvement

As we have seen from the examples in this chapter, synergistic relationships are both powerful and productive. Most groups do not function synergistically, however; they do not understand the fundamentals of synergy or do not apply them very well. Why? Because developing and maintaining synergy in a group, although vitally important, is not an easy task.

One of the key things to remember when working with people and trying to develop synergistic relationships is insightfully expressed in the following quotation by Covey (1990):

> People are very tender, very sensitive inside. I don't believe age or experience makes much difference. Inside, even within the most toughened and calloused exteriors, are the tender feelings and emotions of the heart. That's why in relationships, the little things are the big things. (pp. 192–193)

WILLINGNESS: COMMON GOALS AND INTERDEPENDENCE

The first step in creating a synergistic group is the development of a common goal or common goals for the group. This gives a clear-cut focus for the group and can be an inspiring incentive to keep the group on track. Unfortunately, most groups do not initially take the time and make the effort to clarify or create the common goals that the group is working together to accomplish.

A common goal for a study group, for example, in the context of enhancing student learning and improving the effectiveness of its school, might be to understand a new learning process and successfully implement it in its school or to do research on a new student evaluation system, understand the new system, and successfully integrate it into the learning processes of its school.

Willingness to seek, create, and continue to focus on a common goal or goals for a group is critical to the complete success of the group. The same can be said for the group's willingness to function interdependently—that is, for the members of the group to operate in a genuinely cooperative and mutually dependent fashion.

People in a group do not have to agree on everything to have a synergy. In fact, having differing ideas and bringing diverse information, opinions, and approaches to the group are part of the building blocks for successful synergistic groups. To be synergistic and effective, however, groups must agree on and focus on common goals and must function interdependently.

For example, consider two soldiers in a foxhole in a raging battle. Their common goal is survival. One has the ammunition, and the other has the machine gun. They are genuinely dependent on each other, one to provide the ammunition and the other to fire the gun. It does not matter whether they like each other or care about the same things in the other parts of their lives. What matters now is that they clearly know what their common goal is (survival) and that they work interdependently (feeding the ammunition into the gun and effectively firing the gun). This kind of willingness, a clearly defined common goal and effective interdependence, we refer to as a *foxhole mentality*.

A foxhole mentality is when people who may have different backgrounds and viewpoints accept that they have the same intent and are willing to genuinely cooperate. For study groups to be effective, they must develop a foxhole-type mentality, in which diverse members are willing to set and accept common goals and to work in a genuinely cooperative and mutually dependent manner with each other. They must determine that their differences are less important than their need to work together.

Often, foxhole mentalities, having common goals and functioning interdependently, happen as the consequence of special opportunities that would not be realized without synergistic teamwork. The key for successful study groups is either to exploit naturally formed foxholes (e.g., groups that spontaneously and sincerely come together around a common intent and openly and freely work together as a team) or build new foxholes that have the potential for successful teamwork.

When study group members believe that they are in a foxhole situation with each member working with them and that success depends on working together, synergy can occur. If those in the study group believe that they are the ones "carrying the ammunition" or "firing the gun," it boosts their sense of self-worth and team worth. They believe that the study group "needs me," I "need the study group," and we "must work together" to accomplish our important goals. Such relationships motivate team members to be willing to do what is required for having a synergistic and successful study group.

ABILITY: EMPOWERMENT AND PARTICIPATIVE INVOLVEMENT

Common goals and interdependence motivate and are necessary for people to work together synergistically, but more than these are required for teams to be fully effective and synergistic. For study groups to operate at or near their maximum effectiveness, their members must feel empowered, and they must participate completely in the activities and work of the study group. That is, empowerment and participative involvement are key abilities that study group members must have to function synergistically with other team members and increase team synergy.

Empowerment is not the same as delegation. Someone may give you the authority to take responsibility for or make the final decision in a particular matter. That is not empowerment but delegation. Empowerment is quite different. You have a sense of empowerment or are empowered when you believe that you have something valuable to contribute to the situation, and that what you offer might have a bearing on the final outcome. In other words, the circumstances are such that you feel you have something of value to contribute, and what you contribute may affect the decisions being considered. With empowered study group members, each person is more willing to share his or her part of the diversity of the group, increasing the potential for new and potentially valuable information, knowledge, and ideas to be added to the work of the group.

In a study group, if members are comfortable saying what they believe about each matter under consideration, they are empowered by the group and circumstances and can be important contributors to the success of the study group. Study groups have their best chance for success when their members feel empowered and want to openly and fully express their views and ideas throughout the work of the study group.

Empowering study group members is not always an easy task, however. The circumstances of the study group and how other members of the study group behave are critical. For members to feel empowered, they must be willing to overcome their inhibitions and feel a sense of personal security that others will respect what they say, not judge them, and consider their input seriously.

Feeling a sense of empowerment is necessary for an ability to function synergistically, but it is not enough by itself. You must not only be empowered but also have the opportunity to share your knowledge and ideas. Members of a study group have *participative involvement* when they are encouraged and free to openly and fully share their skills, knowledge, and ideas in the study group.

Participative involvement is both a philosophy and a method of operating study groups. Philosophically, participative involvement focuses on the belief that all study group members have a genuine interest in the success of the study group, and each member has something valuable to contribute. Participative involvement is also a method for managing human resources, whereby circumstances are created so that study group members are respected and their contributions are encouraged, valued, and used. Like empowerment, participative involvement does not occur easily. It requires conscious concern and deliberate action for how the study group will operate. The leader and the members of the study group must understand the concept and importance of participative involvement and then together, collectively and individually, work toward its becoming a reality for the operation of their study group. To do so will mean that strong egos and aggressive personalities must be kept in check, and that the normal competitive interplay among study group members gives way to an open and balanced approach in the discussion and consideration of matters before the study group. Everyone must have and feel comfortable with their opportunity for full participation in the business of the study group.

The ability of a study group to operate synergistically requires both member empowerment and participative involvement. This approach offers potential for substantially increasing the effectiveness of the study group and involves members freely and fully sharing knowledge and ideas and functioning as an entity, a team, to learn together, plan initiatives, make decisions, solve problems, and evaluate results. When study groups operate synergistically in this manner, the productivity and quality of their efforts are increased significantly.

SYNERGY PROCESS

As we have said, the prerequisites for synergistic study groups are the willingness of members to establish common goals for the group's initiative and develop a genuine interdependence among its members and their ability to create circumstances that provide empowerment for members of the group. This can give them a sense of importance and free them to participate and offer participative involvement so that they interact openly and fully in the work of the study group.

Now that we know and understand the fundamental prerequisites for synergistic groups, what is the process for creating these prerequisites and synergistic study groups? To answer this question, we turn once again to the master of change dynamics, Daryl Conner (1993). His research and writings give us an effective four-step process for building synergy in study groups:

1. Interaction

2. Appreciative understanding

3. Integration

4. Implementation

Interaction

The dictionary (*Webster's New World Dictionary*, 1986) defines *interaction* as "action on one another or reciprocal action or effect." The first step in the process states that if study groups are to be synergistic, they must be interacting—that is, they must have members acting on one another or reciprocating.

Most of us have been in groups in which some of the members do not say anything. Clearly, in this situation, those individuals are not interacting. As a result, the group will have a difficult time being as effective as it might have been because those noninteracting individuals are not helping to enrich the group's mix of knowledge and ideas. In fact, they are often a deficit to the group because they are filling positions that more contributing, interacting people might have taken. By the same token, those who interact too much (e.g., members monopolizing the discussions) also have the potential for diminishing the study group's effectiveness.

The three elements of interaction that reduce related group problems (e.g., misunderstandings, alienation, and confusion) and enhance group potential are (a) effective communication, (b) active listening, and (c) creating trust and credibility.

In the development and operation of synergistic study groups, effective communication among members is essential. Effective communication means direct communication in a well-understood language, covering relevant and thoughtful material, and reflecting an undistorted sense of what the communicator believes.

In most groups, the typical approach of members is the competitive one, in which each person is an advocate for certain ideas, makes that case at each opportunity, and listens with an ear attuned to information for countering contrary ideas rather than trying to see the merits in others' ideas. Such approaches are usually destructive and seriously hamper the prospects for study group synergy.

Instead, study group members must become active listeners. Active listening means that a study group member will eliminate, as much as possible, his or her competitive aggressiveness and listen intently to understand, appreciate, and search for value, meaning, and application in the communications of others.

To be synergistic, study group members do not have to be friends or even like each other, but they must generate relationships among themselves that create trust and credibility. Trust is fundamental to the development of synergy in a study group. If the members of a study group communicate effectively with one another and listen actively to their colleagues, over time, the relationship that develops has the potential to be one of trust and credibility. People begin to let down their guard with each other and allow themselves to become vulnerable within the group. When this level of trust occurs, the group has an opportunity for genuine sharing and use of the valuable diversity that each person in the group brings to the discussions.

Appreciative Understanding

As we work to develop synergy in our study group, we find that meaningful interaction (i.e., effective communication, active listening, and trust and credibility) is a necessary element of synergy but is not sufficient to guarantee it. Something more is generally required. In the previous section on synergistic prerequisites, we presented a Covey (1990) quotation that reminded us that "people are very tender, very sensitive inside. . . . That's why in relationships, the little things are the big things" (pp. 192–193). A key for dealing with these sensitivities is the operational concept of appreciative understanding. Appreciative understanding is the capacity to value and use diversity. For the members of a study group to achieve appreciative understanding, each member must understand why others see things differently than he or she does and work to appreciate the differences.

Covey (1990) reminds us that we cannot achieve win-win ends with win-lose or lose-win means. If we want to have the team success of synergy, win-win ends, in our study group, then we must have genuinely effective means, win-win means, in our group relationships.

The four methods for building appreciative understanding (i.e., win-win means and relationships) are to (a) create an open climate, (b) delay negative judgment, (c) empathize with others, and (d) value diversity.

The effective communication, active listening, and trust generated by genuine interaction by members of a study group lay a foundation for appreciative understanding to develop. In particular, even with the inevitable differences of opinion and perspectives of members, conflicts, and possible misunderstandings, members realize that all of this is fundamental to surfacing important issues, understanding different frames of reference, seeing things in a new light, and generating the basic building blocks for new and potentially better solutions.

An *open climate* in an environment is where study group members allow and encourage constructive discussion, conflict, and differences to take place, fostering win-win relationships and helping members understand relevant issues and gain new insights. By creating an open climate, study group members learn to appreciate conflict and differences and use them to broaden their basis of understanding toward the development of potentially more valuable answers and solutions.

Have you ever been in a group discussion in which someone offers a thought that seems silly or out-and-out stupid, and yet from that idea comes a cascade of ideas that leads to new insight and a better solution for the original problem? If someone had intervened earlier in that sequence of ideas and said "That's a dumb idea," then that discussion would have no doubt been cut short, the innovative cascade of new ideas would not have taken place, and the better solution might very well never have been discovered. Events comparable to this latter situation happen all the time, creating win-lose relationships and effectively inhibiting real synergy in the group. Most new and creative ideas or perspectives come from sensitive people and are extremely vulnerable to attacks by others. At the same time, they frequently are the very ideas and perspectives that have the highest potential for leading to innovative solutions and productive synergy. Consequently, study groups function best and have the greatest potential for synergy when team members have the discipline to delay forming negative judgments about the ideas and perspectives of other members.

The dictionary (*Webster's New World Dictionary*, 1986) defines *empathy* as "the projection of one's own personality into the personality of another in order to understand him better" or the "ability to share in another's emotions or feelings." When we empathize with other study group members, we are allowing ourselves the opportunity of knowing what the others are experiencing and feeling and being emotionally sensitive to these.

Although showing empathy to other team members' ideas and perspectives does not necessarily mean agreeing with them, it does provide a good position from which to understand others' ideas and perspectives, why they feel about them as they do, and how their ideas might fit into the overall discussion and possibly become part of the desired solution. When members empathize with others on their team, they increase the group's chances of generating greater team synergy and building meaningful solutions.

Whether we want to admit it or not, we are all sensitive about our ideas and perspectives, especially those that are personal to us. As a result, we tend to hold them back and only slowly let them come out as we test the water to see how others will respond to them. Yet these ideas and perspectives in a study group are the very diversity that gives the group its unique strength.

By genuinely valuing diversity in a study group, members are showing their respect for each other and their ideas and perspectives, increasing trust, enhancing cohesiveness, and searching for the most appropriate input and building blocks. In such situations, study group members are committed to finding positive aspects in the input of others, each member is motivated to freely and fully share his or her diversity, and the team and each member have an improved basis for generating synergy and the best solutions.

Integration

Synergistic interaction (i.e., effective communication, active listening, and creating trust) and appreciative understanding (i.e., having an open climate, being nonjudgmental, showing empathy, and valuing diversity) provide a strong foundation for effective study group teams. With these effective relationships and mechanisms in place, a study group is in an excellent position to take on the difficult task of integration: considering all input from the group, evaluating its value and usability, and collaboratively pulling together the appropriate ideas and perspectives to generate the best available solutions or outcomes. Experience has shown that the effectiveness of the integration process is enhanced by tolerating the ambiguity of the discussions and being persistent, flexible, creative, and selective as you work toward the best solutions or outcomes (Conner, 1993).

Many of the problems facing study groups will be complex and will lead to ambiguous information, ideas, perspectives, and circumstances. Like most people, study group members have a tendency to seek quick, easy solutions. Frequently, this approach proves to be nonproductive or leads down a path to a less valuable result.

Consequently, study groups must shift from the more typical quick-fix approaches to problem solving and be more persistent with the ambiguity of the input and circumstances as they bring them together and flexibly, creatively, and selectively integrate their relevant ideas and perspectives into the best available solutions.

Implementation

The first three steps of the process to generate synergy—interaction, appreciative understanding, and integration—provide the study group with its desired outcome. Thus, the remaining step in the synergy process is to implement the solution and introduce the various parts of the desired outcome effectively in the school. The four key elements of successful implementation are to (a) strategize, (b) monitor and reinforce, (c) remain team focused, and (d) update.

To increase the likelihood that the study group outcomes will be implemented and managed effectively, the group must strategize, creating a plan for the implementation that sets its direction, manages the resources, determines priorities, and ensures that the various implementation steps are compatible. Once a strategy and plan have been developed and the implementation process has begun, it is critical that the process be monitored and reinforced to ensure that appropriate behavior and progress are sustained.

In the implementation process, there will be potential for some members of the study group and others involved in the implementation to move ahead more rapidly than their colleagues. Doing this has the potential for getting people out of step with each other and reducing the synergy of the total effort. Consequently, it is important and valuable to remain team focused, respecting the team's common goals and interdependence and continuing to function as a unified, integrated work team. Just as the best solutions were created using a team focus, the best approach to implementation and any refinements to it should likewise be team focused.

Circumstances and environments may very well change during the implementation process. When this happens, there should be an updating of the study group's implementation and action plan. Teams have a tendency to fall in love with their plans and become resistant to changing them. The implementation process is most effective, however, when an action plan is continuously and appropriately updated through a team-focused approach.

SYNERGY DEVELOPMENT

Creating strong, effective study groups means doing those things necessary to build synergistic teams. Developing synergistic teams requires a substantial commitment and effort, but the cost for not operating in this manner is high, and the potential for producing meaningful results is reduced dramatically. The synergistic process is a powerful approach for increasing the effectiveness, productivity, and quality of the work of study group teams.

As you attempt to apply the concepts, principles, and approaches discussed in this chapter to create synergistic study groups, it will be beneficial to occasionally stop and monitor how your efforts are going. The synergy checklist or audit that follows should be helpful in identifying which elements of the synergy development process are working well and which require improving.

SYNERGY CHECKLIST

The following question sets provide a practical checklist or audit for assessing the effectiveness of a group and identifying how to make it more synergistic:

1. *Common goals:* Has your study group discussed, agreed on, and written a clearly and precisely stated goal or goals for its work?

2. *Interdependence:* Has the discussion, interaction, and sharing in your study group been interdependent (i.e., mutually dependent and genuinely cooperative)?

3. *Empowerment:* Do members of your study group feel a sense of empowerment? That is, does each member feel that what he or she has to offer is important and valuable and may have an effect on the outcome of decisions?

4. *Participative involvement:* Do the members of your study group feel that they can and do openly and freely participate in group discussions and activities?

5. *Interaction:* Do the members of your study group, individually and collectively, interact effectively? That is, do they communicate effectively and actively listen to each other, and has a sense of trust and credibility been created in the group?

6. *Appreciative understanding:* Do the members of your study group show appreciative understanding for each other and each other's ideas? That is, does the group have an open climate and value diversity, and does each member delay negative judgment and empathize with the ideas of others in the study group?

7. *Integration:* As those in your study group work to consider all input, evaluate its value and usability, and pull it together to generate the best solutions or outcomes, do they show persistence in their deliberations and tolerate its ambiguity, and are they flexible and open, creative, and selective as they consider the issues and transition toward their final results?

8. *Implementation:* Once your study group arrives at the desired outcomes to be completed, are the members effectively initiating and managing the implementation process for a successful conclusion? That is, did your study group create a plan for the implementation that sets its direction, manages the resources, determines priorities, and guarantees that the various steps are completed; that ensures that appropriate behavior and progress are sustained; that provides for team, not individual, focus; and that continuously and appropriately updates the action plan for the implementation?

SYNERGISTIC GROUP DEVELOPMENT

Creating a strong, effective synergistic study group means taking steps to build intentional and proactive commitment and effort of members into the group. The cost for not operating in this manner is high and even wasteful of human potential. The following is a process for the development of synergistic relationships in a study group:

1. At an initial meeting, introduce the general concept of synergy, and discuss how it can help the study group become an effective synergistic group.

2. After the study group is introduced to the critical notion of synergy, the group and its members should take time to learn about synergy and its implementation. An early understanding and application of synergy can pay handsome dividends later.

3. Once an understanding of synergy has been established, develop an agreement to the effect that the study group and its members will strive to function as a synergistic team and together fulfill the synergy guidelines.

4. If a member exhibits nonsynergistic behavior, this should be diplomatically dealt with by the leader and members of the group, either during the meeting or immediately following the meeting.

5. Periodically, the group and its members should apply the synergy checklist to assure themselves that the group is continuing to function synergistically or determine which areas of synergy require additional attention.

COMENTORING GROUPS

The concept of a comentoring group and its application were discussed in detail in Chapters 7 and 8. Additional and valuable depth in this important topic is provided in this section.

A comentoring group is one in which members of the group all agree to mentor each other. In effective comentoring groups, each member acts as a sponsor, advocate, or guide and teaches, advises, trusts, critiques, and supports others to express, pursue, and finalize goals (Vanzant, 1980), as well as, in general, being competent, supportive, sharing, unexploitive, positive, and involved (Cronan-Hillix, Gensheimer, Cronan-Hillix, Cronan-Hillix, & Davidson, 1986). Ideally, in a comentoring situation, "each member of a group offers support and encouragement to everyone else which expands individual and group understanding, improving the group's effectiveness and productivity" (Mullen & Lick, 1999, p. 209). A comentoring group, for example, might be a study group that explores a learning area together and whose members assist one another in increasing each other's capacity for understanding.

Synergy and comentoring can be meaningfully combined in study groups, as synergistic comentoring, to generate unusually effective and productive teamwork. This is illustrated in a study group of six high school science teachers, in which one member, a physics teacher, wrote the following (Murphy & Lick, 1998):

> Our group's foremost benefit was that I got to know the teachers in my department much better than I had in 7 previous years. We grew to understand each other's priorities and view of science and education, invented new labs, researched and designed a new curriculum in marine science, worked together to calibrate old equipment, learned of treasure we could borrow from each other's hoards, and laughed a lot at ourselves, each other, and our big city high school. The meetings were our responsibility—ours to make productive or frustrating, enlightening or confounding. It left us with the lingering, seductive taste of "freedom." (pp. 87–88)

Multiple Levels of Synergistic Comentoring

In the Whole-Faculty Study Group (WFSG) process, a synergistic comentoring group functions on several significant levels to enhance its total effectiveness and productivity, as described in detail in the article, "Whole-Faculty Study Groups: Facilitating Mentoring for School-Wide Change" (Lick, 2000).

When those in a school decide to approve the study group process, that establishes a collective sponsorship base, a serious buy-in, for leaders and teachers to become potential synergistic comentoring support groups for the process. This in turn gives the school and its leadership overt commitment for their faculty's total involvement in such efforts. When the faculty accepts the study group process, this commits every teacher to the process, to faculty-led, fundamental change in the school and being an active member of a study group. This in turn creates a powerful "whole-faculty-change" sponsorship for the change process. This then provides the basis of support for the faculty becoming a synergistic comentoring team of the whole, agreeing to share overarching common goals for their school, function interdependently, empower each other, and actively participate in the change activities of the process. This creates a driving force toward progressive, schoolwide change.

As we have outlined, early in the process, the principal typically appoints a leadership group of teachers, a focus team, that along with the principal initiates the study group process, generates a step-by-step plan for the faculty to implement the process, and coordinates and monitors the overall effort. The focus team also meets regularly with study group representatives to assist them with their expectations, activities, concerns, resources, and results. This initial approach alone gives three potential levels for synergistic comentoring: the focus team and the principal, the focus team itself, and the focus team and representatives of individual study groups. In particular, these opportunities provide for the creation of synergistic comentoring to increase communication, interdependence, and empowerment for those involved and, indirectly, the study groups. In addition, they cultivate circumstances for sustaining sponsorship of the study group process and for promoting transitioning change agent activities.

Furthermore, key synergistic comentoring opportunities occur in the study groups. The unique strength of study groups derives from their functioning as self-directed, synergistic comentoring teams, setting common goals, working interdependently, empowering one another, and, in a balanced fashion, openly sharing their ideas and perspectives. In these colearning, action research, synergistic, comentoring groups, the basis for meaningful learning and change can be naturally built in, and the intellectual and emotional commitment for progressive classroom and school transformation can be generated.

Additional levels of involvement come from students, parents, and the community. Students desire to help and are receptive to new approaches and materials from their teachers. Students can also be active participants in the synergistic comentoring processes with teachers, classmates, and others. The same kinds of synergistic comentoring possibilities exist for parents and the community with respect to school activities and improvement.

Moreover, a vertically structured synergistic and comentoring arrangement, involving the community, parents, students, and study groups through the top leadership, seems to accompany growing synergistic comentoring relationships among these various levels. This parallel advancement further strengthens team building, sponsorship, advocacy, support, and commitment to significant change in the school culture, programs, and materials, leading to enhanced student learning and school improvement.

LEARNING TEAMS

When study groups reach the relationship level of being synergistic comentoring groups, they have the required basic prerequisites (i.e., synergy and comentoring) to become powerful learning teams. As learning teams, study groups have the capacity to accomplish the following:

- Re-create themselves
- Do things that they were never able to do before
- Reperceive the school, its programs, and their students and their relationships to these
- Extend their capacity to create and be part of a major generative process in the lives and activities of their students and school

From his research on group dynamics and change and learning theory, Lick (2003) developed a learning team model for the development of learning teams. The group characteristics of his learning team model are as follows:

1. Group synergy

2. Comentoring group

3. Learning resources: The group utilizes a wide variety of potential learning resources, including research, literature, internal and external expertise, related experience, and relevant learning models.

4. Integration and creation: The group pulls together all the information and knowledge available to the group and integrates it creatively into one or more potential solutions or learning models.

5. Application and shared practice: The group members apply the new solutions or learning models in their workplace and share their findings with other members of their group.

6. Evaluation and assessment: The group evaluates and assesses the results and findings of the applications of the new solutions and learning models and modifies them accordingly, as well as repeats Items 3 through 6 until the group is satisfied with the final outcomes.

LEARNING TEAMS AS DRIVING FORCES

The driving force in the coordinated, schoolwide WFSG system is its self-directed, synergistic comentoring learning teams (Lick, 2003). When study groups reach the level of a learning team, as described and characterized previously, they creatively have the capacity to do the following:

- Produce learning communities and set common goals, support member interdependence, empower participants, and foster active participation

- Plan and learn together
- Engage broad principles of education that modify perspectives, policies, and practices
- Construct subject-matter knowledge
- Immerse members in sustained work with ideas, materials, and colleagues
- Cultivate action researchers who produce, evaluate, and apply relevant research
- Struggle with fundamental questions of what teachers and students must learn, know, and apply (Murphy & Lick, 1998, p. 2)

As discussed in Chapter 1 and throughout the book, the focusing question for study groups is the following:

> *What is happening differently in the classroom as a result of what you are doing and learning in study groups?*

With that vision, "study groups, as learning teams, are motivated, work harder, and take responsibility for the successful implementation of required processes and procedures" (Murphy & Lick, 1998, p. 18) to increase the learning of their students and improve the quality of their schools.

SUCCESS FACTORS

The study group process, centered on multilevel synergistic comentoring, is, in fact, a massive change leadership and change management process. It is one of the most practical and effective approaches we have seen in our research and studies. In particular, the WFSG system dramatically and effectively focuses on and enhances the following key transformational factors relating to increased student learning and school improvement:

1. *Focus on imperative changes,* as determined by school personnel

2. *Change sponsorship effectiveness,* both in projects and schoolwide

3. *Preparation of change agents,* including the principal, faculty, and others

4. *Commitment of targets and the reduction of resistance*

5. *Positive advocacy,* including that of the school board, superintendent, principal, faculty, students, parents, and others from the general community

6. *Increased individual, group, and school resilience,* making stakeholders more change adaptable

7. *Knowledge of change and change principles* for stakeholders

8. *Organized processes for transition,* including integrated, cocreative learning experiences that are teacher and student centered, experimental and research oriented, reflective, supportive, and inspiring

9. *Group synergy, comentoring, and learning team development*, setting new school operational and relationship norms for action research and improving faculty, study group, and school learning

10. *School and educational culture modification*, allowing a critical reexamination of basic assumptions, beliefs, and behaviors and required learning systems and practices (Lick, 2000; Mullen & Lick, 1999)

The WFSG process, through the listed 10 transformational concepts for modifying schools and their practices, methods, and systems, generates collective and inspiring vision and creates a high level of synergy and comentoring, allowing substantive learning, change, and continuous improvement to become the norm in the school workplace, operations, and culture for increased student achievement and more effective schools.

10

Sustaining School Improvement Efforts

t is well-known in the field of professional development that more is understood about initiating and implementing change than about maintaining or continuing the change. As educators, we are good at initiating and becoming better at implementing new initiatives. Often, however, maintaining what we start is problematic. Administrative and support personnel in schools and school districts spend most of their time, energy, and budgets initiating new programs, obtaining new materials, and training teachers to implement such programs and materials. The missing link is the institutionalization of innovative programs, materials, and behaviors and the transformed culture to sustain them. It takes not only vigorous initial support, encouragement, strong sponsorship, and success but also comparable ongoing supports, over time, for creative strategies and behaviors to become routine and sustained long term—institutionalization. This chapter focuses on providing support for study groups during the implementation phase and into the maintenance and institutionalization phases of the Whole-Faculty Study Group (WFSG) process.

REVIEWING THE PHASES OF CHANGE

The Initiation Phase

The initiation phase for WFSGs is usually started the year prior to seriously beginning the WFSG process. As previously mentioned, this phase includes gathering information, contacting and contracting with consultants, purchasing materials, meeting with teachers, getting approval from district leaders, budgeting funds, gathering pertinent data, articulating intended results, and deciding to begin. The primary source of support during this time is the principal and an expert source within or outside of the school. The initiation phase extends into getting a focus team trained to take the lead in starting the process. The team or a consultant will lead the whole faculty through the decision-making cycle (DMC). When all faculty are in study groups, the implementation phase begins.

The Implementation Phase

The implementation phase begins when study groups are formed. Once groups are formed, the work of addressing specific student needs with colleagues gets under way. Groups develop study group action plans (SGAPs) and follow them. During the first year, members are adjusting to working in a small group of colleagues, following established norms, serving as leader, completing logs, using data to make decisions, adjusting to the time requirements, making how they teach more public, and getting accustomed to regular feedback from the principal. All these procedural requirements consume much energy and receive most of the attention. Most remarks that teachers make about study groups concern procedural expectations. During the second year, the procedures become more the norm, and attention is focused more on the content of the group's work. Also, looking at student work becomes more routine, and observing students in each other's classrooms begins to occur. If, at the end of the second year, there are fewer questions about whether "we are going to have study groups next year" and continuation is assumed, we are headed toward WFSGs becoming an established routine of the school workplace.

The Institutionalization Phase

Institutionalization occurs when practices that were once new become integrated into and an important part of the fabric of school and teacher structures and routines. This phase is also called maintenance, continuation, incorporation, or routinization and relates to whether the change gets built in as an ongoing part of the system or whether it disappears by way of a decision to discard it or through attrition (e.g., either it is killed or it dies from neglect). Successful institutionalization requires continued support, encouragement, strong sponsorship, and recognition. How long institutionalization takes is unclear. Contextual factors are most often what determine whether a practice is continued and maintained. With WFSGs, you can usually see the signs of institutionalization in the third year when time is being built into schedules and calendars, funds are being allocated, and personnel assignments are being made. Also, when new personnel are being hired, the district will clarify to potential principals that WFSGs are in place at the schools and are expected to continue; principals will clarify for new teachers that WFSGs are in place at the schools and participation is expected.

A 3-YEAR INITIATION, IMPLEMENTATION, AND INSTITUTIONALIZATION PLAN

A 3-year plan for initiating and implementing WFSGs so that institutionalization will be more likely can be obtained from CarleneMurphy@BellSouth.net. The plan was developed by the WFSG National Center. Without assistance from external consultants, it is strongly recommended that leaders follow the program of activities. The WFSG National Center is unaware of any schools that have institutionalized WFSGs without some form of external consultation.

MAINTENANCE

Maintenance means the support, encouragement, and recognition given to an initiative to keep it going. Maintenance tasks should start at the beginning, during the initiation phase, and continue. Maintenance tasks never end. If leaders of a school or district want a structure and practice to continue, then they must continue to provide pressure, support, and strong sponsorship for continuation. This is truer for a process or structural change, such as WFSGs, than for instructional materials and strategies. An individual teacher may continue to use a specific book or strategy when visible support for it is no longer obvious. One reason is that using the book or strategy is an individual task that can be done as an individual action. Changes that are more procedural and structural and require the involvement of others, however, cannot be continued alone and in isolation.

One important aspect of maintenance leadership is to put in place conditions, processes, and techniques that keep individuals implementing new procedures and materials and programs energized. Study group members are more likely to feel bored or dissatisfied with the study group process if the group is engaged in passive work and does not change what it does. If group members spend meeting after meeting discussing concerns, gathering information, researching materials, and only telling stories about what is happening in their classrooms, they will eventually lose interest. Such groups experience information overload and burnout. For such struggling groups, leaders must gently push them out of the collecting and discussing routine toward more active strategies. Keeping the action research cycle in front of everyone is one way of generating more active work. Typically, the more varied, supported, and progressive the strategies, the less likely the group will become dissatisfied with its work. Chapter 8 included a discussion of effective strategies that any study group can use to give it an increased sense of movement and enthusiasm.

WFSGs: A BUNDLE OF INNOVATIONS

What makes maintenance issues so complex is that WFSGs reflect a bundle of innovations. An innovation in this context is anything that is new to an individual. In the WFSG system, teachers confront many innovations, such as the following:

- New relationships with individuals with whom they may not have worked
- New circumstances—work in small groups in which individuals are more vulnerable
- New roles, where each serves as leader and individual responsibility is paramount
- New expectations as the principal and colleagues are more observant and involved in all aspects of what groups and individuals are doing

- New visibility as work of the group and individual participation are more public
- New ways of looking at student work
- New materials to plan for using
- New teaching strategies to demonstrate and describe
- New time schedules and requirements

STAGES OF CONCERN AND LEVELS OF USE

In Chapter 3, we presented the concerns-based adoption model (CBAM) when we reviewed the research on the change process. Figure 3.1 illustrated the stages of concern about an innovation. With each of the innovations in the above section, each individual in a study group may be at a different stage of concern. For example, an individual may feel personal concern about new time requirements and looking at student work and management concerns about new teaching strategies. Figure 3.2 illustrated levels of use of the innovation. For each of the previously mentioned innovations, each study group may be at a different level of use of practices that make up the WFSG system and are given in the WFSG rubric.

This material is reviewed here because these understandings are what make maintaining the WFSG system so complex. Murphy often comments that on the surface, WFSGs appear to be a simple, straightforward collaborative structure. Once into the system, individuals begin to understand that the system and maintenance issues are very complex. Diagnosis of problems in the system is difficult and complex. Often, there are no simple answers. The amount of resistance principals encounter from individuals is directly correlated with where an individual is relative to the stages of concern with a particular aspect of WFSGs. A principal can often determine the stage an individual has reached by listening to what the individual says (Hord, Rutherford, Huling-Austin, & Hall, 1987). If an individual uses "I" and "me" in relation to his or her concern, we know that the individual is in the personal stage of concern. To help the individual move on, we have to address those concerns. If an individual is constantly expressing concern about doing the logs, we have to address those management concerns by clarifying why the logs are important, or if the logs are being handwritten, determining whether there is a way to do them electronically. We know that WFSG work is not going to impact students until we can get individuals and groups beyond the lower stages of concern.

USING THE WFSG RUBRIC

The primary purpose of the WFSG rubric, shown in Tables 4.1, 6.1, and 8.1, is for study groups to use it to determine the degree to which the groups are meeting expectations. The rubric tells everyone what the system looks like in action, when fully implemented. The WFSG rubric is divided into the three components of the WFSG system: context, process, and content. The rubric describes what each of the components looks like in practice. A rubric is similar to an innovation configuration (Hall & Hord, 2001; Hall & Loucks, 1981). Both identify and describe, in operation, the major components and the practices within each component of the innovation. Both represent the patterns of innovation use, usually on a scale using specific descriptors of behavior, and are ways to precisely define quality and measure fidelity. The National Staff Development Council (NSDC) has developed innovation configuration maps for NSDC's staff development standards (Roy & Hord, 2003) and is an excellent source for learning more about innovation configurations. Rubrics are often associated more with classrooms, measuring the performance level of students; therefore, they are seemingly more evaluative. The WFSG rubric is not an evaluation instrument. Even so, we use the term "rubric" because teachers more commonly use the word, and it does not require an explanation. The WFSG rubric measures the fidelity of study group members to the desired behaviors. The ideal description of an implementation behavior is to the far right on the rubric. Advanced implementation, with less desirable behaviors, is along the continuum to the left. For example, one desirable WFSG practice is for members of a study group to rotate leadership every week or every 2 weeks. The least desirable indicator of that practice is for the same person to lead the study group all the time. The scale of implementation is "not yet," "beginning implementation," "developing implementation," and "advanced implementation." The WFSG rubric will determine to what degree study groups are using the proven practices that, when authentically applied, have resulted in higher student achievement.

The Springfield, Missouri, schools used the WFSG rubric for the first time during the 2002–2003 school year. One school enlarged each component of the rubric to poster size, and each study group was given a set of dots of a certain color. With all the study groups in one room and after each study group had reached consensus on where to place a dot on each continuum, a representative went to the poster boards and placed a dot on the continuum for each practice that best described the group's behaviors. After all the groups had placed their dots on all the continuums of best WFSG practices, everyone could see where groups needed support and assistance. Most important, each group knew what it had to do to reach the desired behaviors or level of implementation.

Several schools in Cherokee County, Georgia, used the WFSG rubric for an exercise to demonstrate the status or level of implementation of the desired practices. With all the teachers in the cafeteria, signs were posted on four walls. A sign on one wall read "Not Yet," that on the second read "Beginning," that on the third read "Developing," and that on the fourth read "Advanced." The leader asked one person from each study group to stand. The leader read a best practice or level of implementation, telling the representatives to stand beside the sign that best described the behaviors of their study group. After all the representatives were standing by a sign, the leader asked the representatives questions. For example, to one of the representatives standing by "Beginning," the leader asked, "What will facilitate the group's movement to 'Developing?'" The activity reinforced expectations. In the weeks after the activity, the principal commented on the number of groups that seemed more focused on doing the right things to get the desired results—higher levels of student learning. When using the rubric, faculties have to be told repeatedly that the desired practices on all three components of the rubric—context, process, and content—are proven practices. The WFSG rubric was developed in 2002 after years of experimentation with what works best. The desired outcomes on the rubric have been proven in practice in many schools with very different demographics and at all levels.

PRINCIPALS PROVIDE FEEDBACK TO WFSGs

The person most central to maintenance issues is the principal. He or she is the primary sponsor and provider of support, encouragement, and pressure. One primary role and responsibility of the principal is to give feedback to study groups on the action plans and logs. If groups are not productive and are not functioning as envisioned, the first questions to ask concern "feedback." If a group feels separated from the whole and that no one truly cares about its work, motivation to continue will spiral downward.

Principals Give Feedback on Study Group Action Plans

The SGAP is the single most important document that groups will produce. SGAPs identify the student needs a group will target and indicate what the group will do when it meets. If the plan is off target, the group will be off target. Study groups need to know immediately if there are concerns or questions about their SGAPs. There should be clear, written procedures for submitting the SGAP to the principal. The following procedures are most often used:

- SGAPs are completed by the end of the second study group meeting.
- SGAPs are given to the principal at the end of the second study group meeting.
- SGAPs are reviewed by the principal or his or her designee, and written feedback is given before the group meets again. The written feedback is provided to the leader of the next meeting.
- SGAPs are finalized by the third study group meeting, copied and given to each member of the group, and put in a public place or posted electronically.
- SGAPs are reviewed at the first instructional council meeting. Each study group representative is given a set of action plans. At the next round of study group meetings, the individuals representing the groups will share what the other study groups are doing.
- Feedback may be written directly on the action plan; on a Post-it note and "stuck" on the plan; in memo form; in an e-mail message, using Outlook Express for communication with a group; or in a computer dialog box if a plan is transmitted via the computer.

Principals may also meet with study groups to give feedback. The following are examples of such feedback:

- Have you thought about . . .
- It is not clear what you mean by . . .
- You have listed what you are going to do with students. This plan should be about what you will do with your colleagues. Please redo the top right quadrant.
- You may want to call ____ for information about resources.
- The plan is not complete.
- I think what you are doing will be very helpful to your students.

- This looks like a good start.
- I can't seem to figure out what the student work will be if you go in this direction.
- Do you need ____ (a support person) to meet with the group?
- You seem to be focusing on what you think teachers outside of your group need, such as "compile list of all software". What do you need to do to make changes in how you teach and what you teach?
- This would not be the work of a study group. A committee may need to be formed to address the need as you have defined it. Could we talk about how this could possibly be refocused into substantive work?
- Data sources listed for tracking the status of student needs will not give the group feedback within a 6- to 12-week period. Use more immediate measures.

Principals Give Feedback on Study Group Logs

Principals use study group logs (SGLs) to give support, guidance, encouragement, and suggestions and to communicate expectations to study groups. There should be clear, written procedures for the SGLs. The following procedures are most often used:

- SGLs describe what a group does at a group meeting, and the SGL should be consistent or aligned with the group's SGAP. The log may be handwritten or computerized.
- SGLs are completed at the end of every study group meeting and copies are made for the principal, the clipboard, and all study group members. If the log is computerized, it would be e-mailed to the principal and to others as appropriate.
- SGLs are given to the principal or put in a designated place for the principal within 24 hours after a study group meets.
- SGLs are reviewed and responded to by the principal before the next study group meeting or on a rotating schedule. This task may be assigned to an assistant principal or another person who has schoolwide leadership responsibilities. If this is done, it should be done publicly, such as at the first faculty meeting. Giving this assignment to another individual does not relieve the principal of the responsibility of knowing what all groups are doing at all times.
- SGLs have a box at the bottom for questions or concerns from the study group that must be promptly responded to if the SGLs are to have any credibility!
- Feedback may be written on a Post-it note and stuck to the log; on a separate paper; in an e-mail message to all members of the study group; directly on the log; or in a dialog box on a computerized log form.

Feedback may be as follows:

- Questions:

  Where is this leading?

  Have you thought about . . . ?

  What other types of student work can you bring?

Do you feel comfortable using the collaborative assessment protocol? It would have been a good choice for the student work you examined this week.

Did you know the staff development center has materials on this topic?

- General comments:

As I look back over the last several logs, I do not see evidence of an action research cycle. I see that you identified strategies, but I don't see where you have looked at student work from the lessons using the strategies. Nor do I see signs of replanning and reteaching.

I have highlighted all the verbs in the logs. All seem to be very passive: shared, discussed, and explained. I'd like to see more modeling, demonstrating, constructing, and practicing.

- Specific suggestions:

As you know, there are two other study groups focusing on listening skills. The three groups might want to meet together for their next study group meetings. I will suggest the same to those groups.

- Specific offer:

I can contact Paul Benson for you.

In Resource C, there are excellent examples of feedback that the principal of Clarke Middle School gave to eight study groups after one round of study group meetings.

As stated previously, the principal may share the responsibility of providing feedback to study groups. At Paul Robeson High School in Brooklyn, New York, the principal and four assistant principals serve as "readers" of the action plans and logs, giving feedback to study groups. Each takes responsibility for four study groups. The readers meet once a week to discuss the work of study groups and to share the types of feedback they are providing to their assigned groups. Resource E gives an example of how a principal of a middle school provided feedback to study groups.

Principal Study Groups

We have previously discussed principal study groups. For principals to fulfill expectations, they need a support group. It is very difficult for principals to maintain their energy and increase their confidence and expertise without a strong support system. Just as maintenance is an issue for the study groups, maintaining a constant level of high-quality support to study groups is an even larger issue for the principals. In districts in which only one school is implementing WFSGs, the principal study group may consist of the principal, the assistant principal, and one or two district-level leaders. In districts in which several schools are implementing WFSGs, the study groups are composed of those principals and some district-level leaders. Generally, the principal study groups share and discuss logs, getting ideas and suggestions for how best to respond to situations. In addition, the groups may have a new learning strand for themselves. In Chapter 4, we discussed the work that the principal study groups are doing in Springfield, Missouri.

UNPACKING THE WFSG BUNDLE: CONTEXT, PROCESS, AND CONTENT

To determine what types of assistance a study group needs to be more productive, we need to unpack the bundle of innovations into the three major components discussed in earlier chapters: context, process, and content. To diagnose why a study group is not being productive, we examine each of these components. If our car stops running, the mechanic does not stand back and look at the whole car in hopes of spotting the problem. Instead, the mechanic looks at the major parts of the car, such as the engine. To sustain WFSGs, to diagnose why a group is not moving, and to provide technical assistance, we begin by asking three questions that focus on the major elements of WFSGs:

- Is it the context?
- Is it the process?
- Is it the content?

Returning to the car analogy: Is it the engine? The transmission? The electrical system? Just as the engine has individual parts, so does the context of schools. Just like the transmission, the process has parts—those that we call guidelines. The electrical system of a car runs throughout all the systems and can cause disconnections at many points, much as study group content can cause members to become disconnected from the process. Support people and individual study group members need to understand that often the answer to why a study group is not productive is not obvious. We have to dig deeper, take apart the engine, unpack the WFSG bundle.

In the following sections, we consider each component of WFSGs and discuss what study group members and support people need to consider.

CONTEXT-PROCESS-CONTENT QUESTIONS

For the purpose of attaining the highest levels of implementation of the WFSG system and the WFSG rubric, leaders need to ask the right questions.

Context Questions

Conditions at a school that may be hindering WFSGs suggest the following questions for school leaders:

- What norms of the workplace are interfering with a group's work (e.g., isolation vs. collaboration and risk taking vs. staying with what is safe)?
- Do teachers perceive the principal as a strong sponsor for the study groups, the "cheerleader," and one who will go the extra mile with the district administration to get what the faculty requires to be successful?
- Do teachers feel administrative interference (e.g., taking time from study groups and assigning them unrelated tasks)?
- Is the principal knowledgeable about what groups are doing?
- Did the whole faculty participate in Steps 1 through 4 of the DMC?

- Has the instructional council (IC) met so that representatives from each study group can share study groups' work and identify common problems?
- Is there clarity among the faculty in terms of people's roles?
- Are those roles respected (e.g., a grade chairperson who just wants to be an equal participant in a study group)?
- In a large school, has the principal delegated the day-to-day, routine school-wide leadership role of the study group process to another staff member (e.g., the assistant principal)?
- With delegation, has authority to act been given?
- Has delegation been done in some public way with the faculty?
- Are group meeting times interfering with the productiveness of study groups?
- What is the understanding with the faculty regarding people outside the school reviewing and making comments on action plans and logs?
- Are study group action plans and logs posted in a public place?
- Do teachers feel comfortable responding to logs from other study groups?
- Is the work of the study groups considered private work or public work?
- For teachers not attending group meetings, how is this problem being addressed?
- Have faculty sharing times been held and scheduled for the remainder of the year?
- Is there a schedule for IC meetings?
- Is there visible support from the district office for WFSGs?
- Has the superintendent recognized in some way what the study groups are doing?

Process Questions

Understanding about how group members are interacting can be gained from reading study groups' logs and observing a study group. To get a study group moving toward its intended goals, a question may prompt what the principal should do:

- Is the group too small or too large?
- Do individuals have a common commitment to student needs in their action plan?
- What strategies is the group using to do its work?
- Has the study group established group norms?
- Are norms being revisited and revised as needed?
- Are norms that cause conflict in the group being recognized and addressed?
- Is leadership being rotated?
- Do group members understand the role of the leader?
- Do members accept the notion of shared responsibility and equality of members?
- Does the study group have an agreed-on procedure for keeping its members focused on the meeting's agenda?
- Do logs note things that members should do for or bring to the next meeting?
- Does a study group take the last few minutes of a meeting to establish what the agenda will be at the next meeting?
- Do group members receive a copy of the log within 24 hours of the meeting?

Content Questions

Understanding whether the content is substantive enough to hold the group together can be gained from reading the group's action plan and logs and observing in study groups, classrooms, and IC meetings. Most schools have access to content area specialists through the school district, departments of education, universities and textbook companies, and independent consultants. The most common reasons study groups feel "stuck" are content related. The value of the study group process depends on the relevance and substance of what the group is studying, investigating, and becoming more skillful at doing and what is happening differently in classrooms. The content is the glue that pulls and holds the group together. To get a study group moving toward its intended results, it may only take a question to prompt the principal on what to do, such as follows:

- Once the study group was formed, did it go deeper into student data to discover and be clear on the student needs that the group should address?
- What specific actions did the study group agree to take in its action plan?
- What actions have been taken?
- Is student work giving the group its direction?
- What materials do members bring to the study group meeting?
- Are resources (human and material) substantive enough to give the study rigor?
- What evidence of impact is the study group collecting?
- What strategies is the study group using to get its work done (e.g., action research, visiting each other's classrooms, and using protocols)?
- Does the content require that members be trained in specific techniques or strategies to increase the level of appropriate use of these in their classrooms?
- If the focus of a group's work is teaching practices, models, or strategies, are members practicing and demonstrating these behaviors in their group meetings?
- If the focus of a group's work is the academic content that teachers teach, are content specialists being used? Could the study group benefit from using a book (e.g., reading in the content areas) to organize and guide its work? Some groups need the concreteness of a book to guide the study.
- Are members actually doing joint work—that is, working together to produce products (e.g., integrated units) or materials for which all will take responsibility?

EIGHT-STEP TECHNICAL ASSISTANCE PLAN

When a study group loses momentum, we often refer to the study group as being stuck. Just as Rosenholtz (1989) described "moving," "moderately stuck," and "stuck" groups in her work on organizational groups, we also have moving, moderately stuck, and stuck study groups. When study groups get stuck or seem to be at an impasse, it may be due to context, process, or content issues. Study groups can lose their momentum in any stage of development. A study group may be in the consequence stage and for some reason lose its focus. The following discussion covers in detail both the reasons why study groups may get stuck in the various stages and what leaders can do.

The eight-step technical assistance plan outlined here is more detailed and overly specific than such plans need to be. It is presented in this way, however, so that individuals may pick and choose what is relevant in different situations. We cannot imagine a situation in which a technical-assistance provider would go through every step and every question. Most likely, it will take only one question or suggestion within a step to give the support person the direction needed. Intervention strategies should be followed as soon as there is evidence that a study group is floundering.

A study group that seems to have lost its momentum, regardless of the stage of development, requires some type of facilitation or assistance. The assistance may be as simple as asking study group members clarifying questions, such as "How do you plan to test the instructional strategies you are identifying as effective?" People available to provide such assistance are the principal, an assistant principal, a district-level support person, an external consultant, and anyone within or outside the school who is familiar with the process and content of study groups. Most technical-assistance suggestions given here are framed as if the principal is the chief giver of support and pressure. Technical-assistance suggestions are also presented as if there is a logical sequence of events. Every suggestion, however, has to be judged for appropriateness in terms of its context and circumstances. Steps may take a shortcut at any point. The principal and other support people may skip any step or begin the support process at any point, again depending on the circumstances. Often, one question will prompt the support giver as to what he or she should do. It is recommended that the principal and other appropriate people read all suggestions early in the initiation stage. Simply becoming aware of behaviors that may cause study groups to lose momentum will prevent some problems from happening. When problems do occur, the principal can pick and choose suggestions that fit the situation. Sometimes, asking the simple question, "What is your problem?" is all a principal needs to do. To ask that question, a principal should know what the study group has been and is doing. The following steps and questions within the steps cover the bulk of the problems a study group might have.

Step 1

Study group members recognize when they are not being productive. Individuals feel frustrated and confused. Members are saying to each other and colleagues not in the group that study group meetings are a waste of time and nothing is being accomplished. Study group members may even be using the word "stuck." If this is not being said directly to the principal, it will surely get to him or her secondhand. In most situations, at least one group member will ask for help from someone. What we do not want to happen is for a group to remain in a nonproductive stage for as long as two or three meetings. An intervention should occur as soon as there are indicators that help is required.

To reduce chances that study groups will get stuck early in the process, the IC should meet before the third round of study group meetings. The representative from each study group will learn from other representatives' sharing. All groups will feel a little shaky, so just seeing that this is a normal state of affairs for this stage of the process will build confidence. A helpful piece of content for this first IC meeting is information about developmental stages of groups. At the IC meeting, what the representative from each group shares will have meaning for every other group.

When one representative says that the group is struggling with how to keep its focus, others will say they, too, are having similar problems. Also, they will begin to give each other advice. A person will often see someone else's problem more clearly than his or her own. As a result, as people give suggestions to others, they will see the need for their groups to do something similar.

Step 2

The principal will recognize that a study group is a stuck or low-performing group. This will most likely happen through the following:

- Comments from a member of the study group
- Comments from a visitor (e.g., content specialist to the study group)
- Reviewing action plans and study group logs
- Personal observation
- Comments made at the IC meeting
- Observations or comments from a focus team member

It would be helpful at this point for the principal to review the descriptors of study groups at the forming and grumbling stages. In the grumbling stage, a study group will express levels of dissatisfaction. Often, to move on to the next stage, members require only additional assurance of support and confirmation that the group is on the right track. The following steps are suggestions for study groups that require more direction; it will not be necessary to do all of them.

Step 3

The principal reflects on his or her role and observations to this point. Talking with an internal or external support person often helps. Thinking about answers to the following questions will bring some clarity to what should be done next. Sometimes, all it takes to get a group moving is for the principal or another person to see what has not been done and to make the group aware of the oversight.

- What indicators does the principal have that the group is struggling?
- Is the study group addressing a need that can be evidenced in student work?
- Are student needs being addressed too ambiguously?
- What has the principal done to provide support?
- What type of feedback did the principal give the study group when its action plan was completed and reviewed?
- What type of feedback has the principal given the study group through its logs?
- What does the principal think the group should be doing or have done by now?
- When the principal observes in classrooms, can behaviors be noted that directly relate to what the study group is doing?
- Has the study group requested resources?
- Has anyone external to the school been invited to attend a study group meeting?
- Is there a group member who the principal feels is the root of the problem?
- Is the problem process related (e.g., how the group is interacting)?
- Are process guidelines being followed?

Step 4

The most appropriate person should intervene. Appropriateness depends on the perceived reason why the study group is stuck. Is the problem contextual, process related, or content specific? The person who intervenes may be the principal, another internal support person, or a support person external to the school. The following lists contain conditions to help determine whether it should be the principal or another person.

The principal intervenes if

- The principal has not given the study group feedback on the group's action plan

  Intervention: Do it now.

- The IC has not met

  Intervention: Call a meeting.

- The principal has not responded to concerns or recommendations in logs

  Intervention: Do it now.

- The principal has questions about the level of work reflected in logs and has not yet communicated those questions to the group

  Intervention: Do it now.

- The logs reflect that the study group does not have adequate resources

  Intervention: Ask questions now.

- There is a person in the group who is obviously disrupting the group's work

  Intervention: Talk to that person, or observe the study group.

- One or more people are routinely absent or late

  Intervention: Talk to the individuals to determine the root of the problem and make expectations clear.

- Leadership is not being rotated

  Intervention: Remind the group that shared leadership is nonnegotiable.

- The study group is not revisiting or following its norms

  Intervention: Remind the group.

- The study group could use a process observer

  Intervention: Serve in that capacity, or invite a person who has that skill.

- The group does not see how what it is doing will affect the whole

  Intervention: Review with the group its action plan relative to total school effort.

The principal invites a content specialist or a district-level support person to intervene if

- The stuck condition is primarily due to the content in the study
- There are questions about the scope and sequence of a part of the curriculum, or there are new materials that group members have not mastered
- The group lacks expertise for members to help each other with required skills
- There are questions about how to get access to available resources
- Teachers want to know about or visit teachers in other schools that are using strategies and materials with success in areas that the study group is investigating
- The teachers in a study group require specialized training

If the person who is to intervene is external to the school, that person should be well informed about the study group process.

Step 5

An external intervener should do the following:

- Review the study group's action plan for the answers to the concerns.
- Note on the action plan and make a copy of what is to be seen in observations.
- Look to see how specific student needs are stated.
- Look to see how specific group actions are for when the group meets, such as

Do actions have promise for affecting stated student needs?

Is looking at student work a routine activity of the group?

How is the study group getting its work done (e.g., action research, using protocols, or demonstrating teaching practices)?

What would you expect members to bring to the study group meeting?

What additional resources are available to the group?

- Try imagery. With your eyes closed, try to imagine a group doing what the group has stated that it wants to do. Compare it with what the group is doing.
- Review all the study group's logs for answers to the following questions:

Is the work consistent with your imagery? If not, what is the inconsistency?

Has the group established group norms?

Does the group revisit its norms?

From the group's log, can you tell what the group will do at its next meeting?

Does the work appear to be more passive than active?

What materials are members bringing to study group meetings?

When you review the logs, does one name appear more often than the others?

Is leadership being rotated?

Are members often absent or tardy?

The external support person shares his or her observations with the principal or a focus team member. The appropriateness of someone observing the study group is determined. The observations would be to note interactions among members and the substance of the work. As appropriate, the principal tells study group members the following:

- Who will observe
- When the visit will occur
- Why the visit will occur
- That the observer will visit the study group twice, if possible
- That the first visit is only to observe the group work
- That the second visit is to share with group members what was observed and have them reflect on the observations
- Not to expect to engage the observer in a dialogue during the first observation

It is preferable for the observer to attend two consecutive study group meetings. If this is not possible, the person should establish a day and time when he or she will meet with the study group. The second meeting may be later on the same day as the first observation. The study group should be given feedback as soon as possible.

Step 6

After the study group knows what to expect when the principal or other support person observes a study group meeting, the observer attends the designated meeting. The observer reminds the group that it should continue its work as planned and do exactly what it would do if he or she were not there. The observer sits with the group, not outside the group. Body language and facial expression should indicate a willingness to learn from the group, as opposed to a stance that indicates that this is a critique or evaluation. In other words, the person is to observe as if present as a learner, not someone looking for something wrong. If the observer is asked a direct question, a response might be "That's a point that we might consider when I share my observations with you." The observer should not get drawn into the discussion! The observer should not noticeably be writing or looking down at a tablet. He or she should keep his or her eyes on the group. Instead of writing complete sentences, the observer should have a code of short words or symbols that can be interpreted later. It may also be helpful to have a seating plan for members. Arrows can then be used to indicate the flow of the discussion. The observer should watch for the following:

- The times when members arrived
- What individuals bring with them to the meeting
- How the meeting begins
- How focused each member is
- What strategies the group uses during its work
- How this meeting is connected to the last meeting
- Interactions among group members (e.g., synergy)
- What part of the action plan members appear to be doing
- How students are brought into conversations

At the end of the meeting, the observer might ask each member to write on a piece of paper (no name) a list of adjectives that would describe the study group's meeting. The observer could ask any other type of reflective question that would give insight into the functioning of the group. Collecting the papers, the observer confirms with the group when he or she will meet with it to share his or her observations.

After the meeting, the observer should go to a quiet place in the school where there is privacy to complete notes, writing impressions in more detail and preparing recommendations. To sharpen the observer's thinking, it may be helpful to write five verbs that describe the group's actions and five adjectives that describe the group. The observer's final conclusions should indicate whether the root of the dysfunction is more context, process, or content related. If the observer is not the principal, the observer shares his or her observations and conclusions with the principal.

Step 7

The observer meets with the study group to share his or her observations. The observer describes what he or she saw in the observation, action plan, and logs, stating what "I saw" or "I did not see." Staying away from judgmental statements, appropriate statements might be similar to the following:

- I saw that at 3:00, only one person was present, at 3:05 four members were present, and at 3:10 all members were present.
- I did not see in the log of the meeting that preceded the one I observed what you would do at the meeting I observed; and I did not see in your other logs that you routinely indicate what is to happen next.
- In your action plan, I saw that you stated that you intend to (read actions). I could not tell which of these actions you were implementing when I observed you.
- I did not see any evidence that you routinely look at student work.
- I saw that only one member brought anything to the meeting.
- I did not see in your logs that you had revisited the group's norms.
- I saw that two members did not say anything during the meeting.
- I did not see student work discussed or shared.
- In your action plan, I saw a list of resources. In your logs, I do not see evidence that those resources were being used.
- I saw that one person did most of the talking when I observed.

The observer reads responses to the reflective questions that he or she raised. The observer invites members to respond to the observations. Integrating responses from members, recommendations might be similar to the following:

- Revise the action plan to make it consistent with what you currently feel you should do to meet the student needs you have identified.
- Review roles: leader's role and individual member's role.
- Revisit group norms.
- Agree to only those norms that you are willing to support.
- I recommend that (name) meet with you and share a protocol for looking at student work.
- I recommend that (name) provide you with several books that will give your work direction and will describe strategies to try with your students.
- I will share with you information about several workshops and conferences that you may want to consider attending.

Step 8

If the observer was not the principal, he or she should share the outcome of the meeting with the principal. If the recommendations require contacting a person to be used as a resource, it should be decided who will make the contact. If recommendations require obtaining a book or other material for the study group, decide who will do that. The study group should know what is expected to happen next. Whatever should be done, confirm who will do what, and communicate the results of actions with the group.

As previously mentioned, it will be a rare occurrence for all eight of the steps to be carried out. These steps are offered to provide principals and support people with a technical-assistance plan from which they can choose appropriate actions. It is the principal's judgment as to the appropriateness of each step and subset of a step. Appropriateness is contextual and circumstantial.

SUMMARY

Maintenance is much more complex than initiators might appreciate when a new innovation or new system is put in place. Diagnosing implementation glitches takes a skilled leader knowledgeable of the change process. In this chapter, we reviewed the stages of change, the concerns individuals feel about a change, the levels of use of the practices that make up a system of changes, and the questions that leaders need to answer to help groups move to the highest levels of use of the practices. Is there any wonder why major changes do not get imbedded into the routine of schools? Often, people give up long before they get to where they want to go. It is just too difficult. Frequently, the extent of concerns about the innovation or a bundle of innovations makes initiators wish they had never started.

Teachers often complain because leaders keep introducing new programs, materials, and practices. Leaders will hear teachers say, "Why do we keep changing things? Let's just stay with what we have." When you stick with an initiative, you will hear, "How much longer do we have to do this?" Trying to stick with an initiative that works will often bring with it "stick-with-it-ness" problems of another sort, such as boredom and anxiety with the realization that what everyone thought would go away is actually here to stay. Maintenance work is often not fun work for leaders because they get bored, too. They get bored with saying the same things repeatedly and with fighting the same battles. Initiating change has a certain level of excitement to it, like going to a place you have never been. Sometimes, however, getting somewhere is more fun than being there. Many leaders are more competent at initiating and implementing change than at maintaining and institutionalizing changes that they have started. As this happens, leaders who initiated the changes must identify someone to help maintain them.

Creating commitment and maintaining it are two different things; each requires different approaches. At the beginning of an initiative, you can generate commitment by vocalizing obvious needs. To maintain that commitment, do not let people forget why you started the program in the first place: Do not let them let go. We know that people who are well informed about effects of an initiative hold it in higher esteem than those who either do not have the information or do not pay attention to it. In school districts, it is often people outside the school who are the greatest threats to a school's ability to continue. Budget ramifications and political factors, which have nothing to do with the merits of an initiative, often "do in" highly effective programs, materials, and practices.

One of the best pieces of advice that Bruce Joyce gave Carlene Murphy during her work in Augusta, Georgia, was, "Smile. Be kind. Don't stop." That pretty much sums up what maintenance is all about. It is the most difficult work for staff developers and leaders but among the most critical!

11

Success: Learning From National, State, District, and Local School Experiences

For effective staff development, meaningful school reform, and real school transformations, schools must not only determine what changes and reforms are required but also implement an intentional, well-designed transition process to deal with societal, organizational, cultural, and interpersonal barriers affecting schools. Schools must find ways to transition individuals and groups from old to new paradigms and related processes and circumstances from the previous to the required ones. Furthermore, teachers, administrators, and other key stakeholders must be broadly and intimately involved in the process.

Where properly implemented, the Whole-Faculty Study Group (WFSG) system has been unusually successful in facilitating schoolwide change and enhancing student learning (Joyce, Murphy, Showers, & Murphy, 1989; Murphy, 1991b, 1992, 1995). The driving force in the WFSG process is its self-directed, synergistic comentoring learning teams (Lick, 1998, 2000). Such teams creatively (a) produce learning communities and set common goals, support member interdependence, empower participants, and foster active participation; (b) plan and learn together; (c) engage broad principles of education that modify perspectives, policies, and practices; (d) construct subject matter knowledge; (e) immerse everyone in sustained work with ideas, materials, and colleagues; (f) cultivate action researchers, producing, evaluating, and applying relevant research; and (g) struggle with fundamental questions of what teachers and students must learn, know, and apply (Murphy & Lick, 1998, p. 2).

Once again, the focusing question for WFSGs is the following:

> What are students learning and achieving as a result of what teachers are learning and doing in study groups?

With that vision, "study groups are motivated, work harder, and take responsibility for the successful implementation of required processes and procedures" (Murphy & Lick, 1998, p. 18).

In this chapter, we discuss a sample of major "learning experiences" relating to the WFSG system and organize those experiences as follows:

- A national experience: ATLAS Communities
- A state experience: State of Louisiana Department of Education's LINCS program
- A district experience: Springfield, Missouri, public schools
- A local school experience: Elder Middle School, Sandersville, Georgia

In addition, Resources C and D contain descriptions of student achievement goals that study groups have targeted. These considerations are not meant to be a comprehensive review of WFSG efforts but only a glimpse of a few major WFSG involvements. We close this chapter with a brief discussion of how the study group process has the potential to move schools toward becoming more like learning organizations (see Chapter 11; Senge, 1990).

A NATIONAL EXPERIENCE: ATLAS COMMUNITIES

ATLAS Communities is a national comprehensive school reform design; it began its formal relationship with the WFSG system in 1997. The WFSG system is the centerpiece of professional development in all ATLAS Communities' schools, requiring all the ATLAS schools to implement WFSGs as part of its commitment to improving teaching, learning, and assessment. More than 100 schools nationwide have implemented the ATLAS design since its inception. We use two schools to illustrate increases in student achievement that we are seeing in schools that have implemented WFSGs through ATLAS Communities: a high school in Brooklyn, New York, and an elementary school in Albany, New York.

Paul Robeson High School has experienced a steady upward gain in student achievement during the past 4 years. Robeson launched WFSG in January 2000. The school which contains Grades 9 through 12, has 1,470 students (90% Black, 8% Hispanic, 2% Asian, and 2% White), and 91% of its students are eligible for free lunch. The faculty is among the nation's most dedicated, determined to make this inner-city school in the heart of Brooklyn one of New York City's finest high schools. The fact that most of Robeson's students live in low-income public housing only adds to the faculty's commitment to see that every student who enters Robeson in the ninth grade graduates in 4 or 5 years. This dream is quickly becoming a reality. Insideschools.org placed Robeson on a list of 30 New York City high schools with good graduation rates when compared with the "level" of their entering students. This is remarkable considering that there are 335 high schools in the five boroughs that make up New York City. In an article titled "Against All Odds: Graduating Kids on Time," Insideschools.org (insideschools.org/nv/NV_quiet_success_nov03) reported,

> Insideschools.org has compiled a list of 30 high schools that have an unusually good graduation rate when taking into account the level of skills of their entering ninth grade. We did this in an attempt to recognize the achievements of schools that help kids complete high school within 4 years, even if these students enter ninth grade reading below grade level. We believe schools should be judged by how far their students travel—not by where their students begin. Using a statistical method called regression analysis, we looked at the 2002 graduation rates and compared them to the proportion of those students who entered ninth grade reading at grade level, as determined by the standard eighth-grade English Language Arts exam. Schools whose students traveled the farthest from ninth grade to graduation made our list.

Robeson's graduation rate was 65% (class of 2003), and it was 85% after 5 years. Compare this with a recent study by the Civil Rights Project at Harvard and the Urban Institute that states only 35% of black and Latino students finish high school in 4 years in New York State—slightly more than 50% is the national average (insideschools.org). The study was commissioned by Advocates for Children and can be found at www.advocatesforchildren.org/pubs/LosingOurFutureMainReport.

Another indication of Robeson's climb to the top is its steady rise in the percentage of students who met graduation standard on Regents exams as shown in Table 11.1. Principal Ira Weston states that although the statistical numbers are not where the school wants them to be, there is evidence that continual improvement is taking place. Resource D contains an action plan and set of study group logs from one of the WFSGs at Robeson.

Arbor Hill Community Elementary School is in Albany, New York. Arbor Hill began implementing the ATLAS design, including WFSGs, in September 2001. The school has 519 students in Grades prekindergarten through 6, and 96% of the students are eligible for free lunch. Principal Robert White leads with a steady hand and high expectations, demonstrating confidence and pride in the staff at Arbor Hill. He does not hesitate to make clear to everyone that the progress the school is making is due to the dedicated, hard-working professionals at the school. Table 11.2 illustrates the achievement of Arbor Hill's fourth graders during a 5-year period.

Marcia Whitney, the ATLAS site developer for Arbor Hill, wrote the following note to Carlene Murphy on April 28, 2003:

Area Tested	Percentage of Students Who Met Graduation Standards on Regent's Exam		
	2000–2001	2001–2002	2002–2003
Biology	14%	59%	64%
English Lang. Arts	19%	57%	70%
Global Studies	41%	56%	75%
US History	41%	56%	75%
Math A	4%	25%	33%
Foreign Language	65%	98%	98%
Chemistry	22%	59%	60%

Table 11.1   Percentage of Students Meeting Graduation Standards

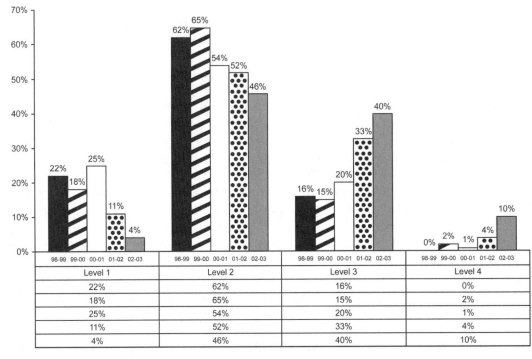

Arbor Hill Community Elementary School
Albany, NY
New York State Assessment of English Language Arts
Year by Year ELA Comparison
Grade 4

	Level 1	Level 2	Level 3	Level 4
	22%	62%	16%	0%
	18%	65%	15%	2%
	25%	54%	20%	1%
	11%	52%	33%	4%
	4%	46%	40%	10%

Level 1 These students have serious academic deficiencies
Level 2 These students need extra help to meet the standards and pass the Regents examination
Level 3 These students meet the standards and, with continued steady growth, should pass the Regents examination
Level 4 These students exceed the standards and are moving toward high performance on the Regents examination

Table 11.2   Grade 4 Student Assessment Percentages by Level

The WFSGs at Arbor Hill Elementary School and Doyle Middle School have come such a long way this year. Ten of the 19 study groups are routinely looking at student work with a protocol. At Arbor Hill, we formed cross-grade groups (different from their regular grade-based ones that we had last year). The groups have been designing performances of understanding and assessments and looking at Level 4 work across the grades to identify strengths and gaps. It was not perfect but a great start, and teachers wish to continue the discussions generated. They just received news that their students performed very well on this spring's grade 4 English Language Arts New York State test. They missed the New York State cutoff point for "passing" by one point . . . an incredible jump from last year! Their AYP was 119 last year, and they scored 149 this year. They are very excited to say the least, and the momentum there is strong. Thank you from all of us here—kids, teachers, parents—as you have really impacted us.

ATLAS Communities commissioned Social Policy Research Associates (SPRA) in Oakland, California, to do an independent research study on the perceptions of its organization and processes (ATLAS Communities, 2003). One of the processes on which data were collected was (whole-faculty) study groups. The study included schools in four districts—one in upstate New York, two in Washington, and one in Georgia. In the four districts, 19 schools and 715 teachers were included. All of the teachers and principals completed a questionnaire. A sample of teachers and all the principals were interviewed. Data were collected in the spring of 2002 and the spring of 2003. Of particular interest to WFSGs and this book are the Key Findings in the Professional Development Outcomes section of SPRA's report involving (whole-faculty) study groups:

- Study groups fostered both greater collaboration and reflection on practice.
- Study groups have improved camaraderie and increased opportunities for collaboration, sharing of student work, reflection on teaching techniques, and development of useful teaching and assessment strategies.
- The quality of the study group experiences appears to be highly dependent on study group composition, structure, teacher training in study group design, and teachers' enthusiasm for collaboration.
- Communication and sharing of student work through study groups give teachers a better understanding of student needs, allowing them to pinpoint how to improve their instruction and address those needs.
- Teacher collaboration enhances coordination of lesson planning across subject areas and, in some cases, among teachers across grade levels.
- Study groups have been effective in part because they create a safe space for teachers to share their concerns, struggles, and questions in an environment designed to provide mutual support.
- Study groups have influenced many teachers' instructional practice. Study groups not only led individual teachers to examine their practice but also led to a schoolwide examination and inquiry about curriculum and pedagogy.
- Many teachers find it difficult to apply what they discuss in study groups to their classroom practice. Some teachers noted that study group activities such as examining student work do not necessarily lead teachers to engage in meaningful reflection about how they teach.

- Many teachers find that they lack sufficient time to implement new strategies. When study groups do lead to changes in classroom practice, those impacts appear to be highly individualized and dependent not only on study group composition but also on the ability or willingness of individual teachers to reflect on and alter their practice.

For more information about ATLAS Communities and its documented results, see its Web site, www.atlascommunities.org.

A STATE EXPERIENCE: STATE OF LOUISIANA DEPARTMENT OF EDUCATION

The State of Louisiana Department of Education began its formal relationship with the WFSG system in 2000. This relationship was established through the Learning Intensive Networking Communities for Success (LINCS), a program to elevate and sustain teacher and student content knowledge and performance in 172 low-performing schools throughout the state through high-quality professional development.

LINCS serves as a catalyst for the institutionalization of systemic, standards-based reform in schools, districts, and universities. The LINCS program requires a 5-year commitment. Aligned with the requirements of the No Child Left Behind Act and the staff development standards of the National Staff Development Council, the WFSG system is one of the most integral components of the LINCS process and is an ongoing part of the structure that continues throughout all phases of implementation.

The LINCS process establishes professional learning communities in which classroom teachers build content knowledge and strengthen their ability to design and implement content-rich, technology-enhanced lessons into their daily instruction to improve student achievement as demonstrated by increased performance on the Louisiana Educational Assessment Program (LEAP 21) and the Iowa tests.

Results from an evaluation study of student performance in LINCS schools during the past 2 years show that the growth on the Iowa Test of Basic Skills and fourth-grade LEAP for mathematics has been striking.

The "2004–2005 Request for LINCS School Applications" document of the Louisiana Department of Education, dated December 2003, stated, "Major change in our schools requires active and effective scholarship—support, encourage, pressure, and accountability—from leadership. If genuine reform is to come from within our schools, then teachers and school personnel must be meaningfully and intensely involved." The document continues,

> One of the most effective research-proven approaches to reform and change in education is involving the whole faculty in professional study groups. The Whole-Faculty Study Group process is a step-by-step practical methodology for the development of study groups in schools to facilitate schoolwide change and enhance learning processes and outcomes. The power in the WFSG process rests in the promise that teachers will become more knowledgeable and skillful at doing what will result in higher levels of student learning.

The document highlights the following statement: "A major strength of this process [the WFSG process] is that the structure ensures that study groups become a routine for the school culture and that faculties of participating schools develop into professional learning communities."

LINCS is content driven, and the content specialties of English language arts, science, mathematics, and social studies are the drivers. The WFSG process is the vehicle that connects training in the content areas to the classroom.

A DISTRICT EXPERIENCE: SPRINGFIELD, MISSOURI, PUBLIC SCHOOLS

The Springfield public schools (SPS) began their formal relationship with the WFSG system in 2001. As of September 2003, 45 of their 51 schools were using WFSGs as the vehicle for implementing school improvement plans. Anita Kissinger, director of staff development, reported the following findings for her schools at the 2004 WFSG National Conference:

- When interviewed, a large majority of principals indicated that WFSGs had positively impacted student performance.
- The percentage of schools implementing WFSGs had increased from approximately 60% in year 1 to 90% in years 2 and 3—that is, 45 of its 51 schools began implementing WFSG in September 2003.
- For 2000–2001, the SPS were 1 point above being "provisionally accredited"; for 2002–2003, they received all the possible points and were "accredited with distinction."

Among the specific test data reported for SPS were the following:

	Reading Index Scores, Missouri School Improvement Program		
	2001	*2002*	*2003*
Third grade	205.1	222.4	215.8
Seventh grade	204.0	218.5	217.3

	Communication Art, Missouri Assessment Program Performance Index		
	2001	*2002*	*2003*
Eleventh grade	191.0	188.7	194.7

	Mathematics, Missouri Assessment Program Performance Index		
	2001	*2002*	*2003*
Fourth grade	217.5	221.7	222.5
Eighth grade	175.6	177.6	185.7
Tenth grade	168.5	163.8	167.2

As Kissinger describes the involvement of SPS with WFSGs, she offers her insight through a disclaimer:

- Our implementation of WFSGs is not perfect.
- What SPS did is working for us.
- Others need to analyze what will and will not work for them.

Finally, Kissinger discussed SPS perspectives on their rationale for employing "collaborative teams" (study groups) from the WFSG system:

- They work!
- They have the greatest chance of changing the culture.
- They provide a vehicle for dealing with change, now and in the future!
- They can be accomplished with a limited budget.
- Professional development became site specific, which creates buy-in.

A LOCAL EXPERIENCE: ELDER MIDDLE SCHOOL

In Chapter 9 in the 2001 edition of this book, we featured Elder Middle School in Sandersville, Georgia. The school implemented WFSG in the fall of 1992. For an update on the school's use of WFSGs, we asked the principal, Bern Anderson, to write a summary. The following is his response:

Elder Middle School is remaining steadfast in its commitment to WFSGs. We are totally focused on instruction, and we use study groups as a means to significantly improve the quality of teaching. During the school year of 2001–2002, we implemented the Writers' Workshop format into our language arts classes, and the entire faculty took an in-depth look at national standards and at assessing student work through study groups. From that we began using our monthly faculty meetings (staff seminars) to conduct "show and tell" to share the results of our study group sessions. Each teaching team makes a presentation of their student work to the faculty. They state the standard met and the rubrics used for grading. Specific commentary on work is also provided. In addition, each leadership team meeting has a time allocated for grade chairpersons to present student work that is linked to the study group topic for that time.

In September 2003, we began studying the use of exemplary practices. We studied the works of Max Thompson and Robert Marzano. Teachers studied these scientifically based strategies in their study groups, put them to use in their classrooms, and shared results in the study group meetings and in monthly staff seminars. Also, we are incorporating the work of Ruby Payne and how to utilize best practices for children in poverty. Teachers continue to meet weekly during the school day to develop lesson plans, examine student work, monitor student progress, and assess the effectiveness of instruction. In addition to providing teachers the structure to examine exemplary practices, WFSGs provide teachers the opportunity to share successes and receive suggestions from other study group members regarding lessons that might have been less than successful. We will continue to use the staff seminar as an avenue for sharing exemplary student work.

We realized significant increases in our CRCT reading and math scores for sixth and eighth grades. We attribute this to the conscious effort our teachers made to use content presented in study groups (essential questions, acceleration, cooperative learning, and activities to tap into prior knowledge and to increase knowledge base) to drive instruction.

Writing remains a top priority for study groups. We have had the services of a literacy coach since SY 2001–2002. Our writing scores have continued to improve. The first year for Writers' Workshop resulted in 92% of our students meeting or exceeding the state standards. Our scale score was 1 point below the state, but we had 12% more students meeting standards from the year before. Last year, we exceeded the state's scale score, and 94% of our students either met or exceeded the standards for the Middle Grades Writing Assessment. In addition, we had 16% more students exceeding the standards for the 2003 administration than from the 2002 testing.

Resources C and D provide additional examples of what local schools are doing in WFSGs to target student instructional needs.

THE WFSG QUESTION MOST OFTEN ASKED

Will WFSGs increase student achievement? This is the question asked most often of us. The answer is this: It depends on what the study groups do, the types of support study groups receive, and the amount of time the groups have to work together.

This question becomes Murphy's dilemma as she works in schools and is asked, "What research do you have that indicates that study groups increase student achievement?" In the Augusta, Georgia, schools in which she was a district-level leader, she had joint control over the design for training (the process), the content of the study groups, and the data collection procedures. As a longtime member of the staff of the district, she understood the contextual conditions that affected the work of the schools. As an external consultant in the WFSG process, she has had no control over what study groups do (the content), what data collection instruments and procedures will be used in the districts and schools in which she works, or the contextual elements that affect success. She is now an independent consultant without a research unit. Therefore, Murphy can only report what she sees in the schools, what she reads in the reports from the schools, and what she is told by teachers and other school and district leaders.

What has been stated in other sections of this book needs to be repeated here. Simply having study groups in place at a school will not increase student achievement. It is what teachers do in the study groups and in their classrooms that will increase student achievement. Study groups are a means through which teachers work together on how to make academic content more meaningful to students so as to increase the students' understanding of what they are taught. There is no simple "yes" answer that Murphy can give to the question, "Will study groups increase student achievement?" Her answer would have to begin with, "It depends on . . . "

CREDIT FOR IMPROVEMENT

Who or what gets the credit for improvement in student achievement? The possibilities are endless. The reality is complex, although simple. The credit goes to the individual school: to its students; the parents, who love and care for their children; its teachers, who day after day teach with skill, knowledge, and heart; and its principal, who leads all efforts. We do not believe that the "credit" finger can be pointed to anyone outside of the school. District-level support staff and consultants facilitate, support, provide resources, and encourage change. New instruction programs, materials, and textbook series, new and improved instructional strategies, and other resources give substance and expertise to school improvement efforts. Comprehensive school reform designs and models make available to schools authoritative and scientifically researched ideas and support for implementing those ideas. All these initiatives and innovations give schools at least one very important and necessary ingredient to whole-school improvement—hope. Many teachers have lost hope, and when the school environment becomes saturated with new resources, ideas, and individuals with influence, everyone perks up. Still, what makes improvement actually happen is what each individual teacher decides to do when he or she closes the classroom door. It is what the teacher does when he or she is with students that transforms expert advice and materials into student achievement. Regardless of external forces, including WFSGs, it is what the individual teacher decides to do with his or her students that will cause students to learn more.

We emphasize this truth because in this chapter we describe what we have seen and heard that causes us to believe that WFSGs will have a positive impact on student achievement. In sharing the examples, we are not pointing the credit finger at WFSGs, although it may seem that way. We are merely sharing what teachers who have been members of WFSGs have done and the influence we believe the work has had on improving the whole school.

Increases in student achievement can rarely be attributed to one factor. In schools, there are so many factors or variables constantly interacting and changing moment by moment. In any one school year, teachers are using new and refined materials, adhering to new standards, using new teaching strategies, talking more to each other, involving parents to a greater degree, attending district-level training sessions, benefiting from more resources and allocations of money, using more technology, having an increase in personnel, being given more technical assistance through the adoption of national comprehensive school reform designs, benefiting from repairs to the physical facilities, being led by new school or district leaders, and so on. How can any one of these factors be singled out as the reason test scores went up or went down? WFSGs, however, pull many of these key factors together so that the environment is more cohesive and initiatives are made more seamless.

The schools are reliable sources of information, and reports from testing and state agencies indicate what students are accomplishing in terms of state and local standards. The WFSG schools described in this chapter used a variety of data sources to determine whether school and student needs were being met.

SCHOOLS BECOMING LEARNING ORGANIZATIONS

As discussed in earlier chapters and in the previous examples, the WFSG process has the potential for transforming schools and bringing about major change efforts for enhancing student achievement and school improvement. The soul (i.e., vital and essential part; Guralnik, 1986) of this massive, structured, schoolwide, faculty-directed change process is multilevel synergistic comentoring (see Chapter 9). Through this innovative approach, learning becomes an investment; the norm, common goals, and expectations are set; compelling sponsorship for change is communicated and accepted; and creative synergy is enacted, enriching and enhancing everyone's efforts. Centering on synergy and comentoring approaches, the study group process becomes a meaningful and effective change process. It examines school and learning needs and underlying assumptions, beliefs, and behaviors (the culture) and helps transition them to new sets of school and learning patterns and approaches and a fundamentally modified culture. In the final analysis, through the study group process, a school and its stakeholders are change catalysts for their school becoming more like a learning organization (Lick, 2000).

Among the many definitions of learning organizations, that by Graff (1996) seems most appropriate here for schools:

> A *learning organization* is one in which the organization itself is committed to individual growth, learning, and creativity as a path to institutional growth. In such an organization, systems are in place to capture, share, and institutionalize the insights of individuals and teams. The institution, as a whole, [builds off of past failures and successes and] gets smarter [and more effective] as a result of the shared learning of its members. (p. 5)

Learning organizations leader Senge (1990) reminds us that "the organizations that will truly excel in the future will be the organizations that discover how to tap people's commitment and capacity to learn at all levels of the organization" (p. 4).

The WFSG system provides a process for a school to become more like a learning organization in which people continually expand their capacity to create the results they desire, new and expansive patterns of thinking are nurtured, collective aspiration is set free, and people are continually learning how to learn together (Lick, 2000).

In summary, the WFSG system, through its study groups and general processes, has the potential to move schools toward becoming more like learning organizations. As this happens, not only will student achievement increase but also schools will make a transition to a new class of schools—ones that "will truly excel in the future," becoming more meaningful and more effective.

12

Fourteen Key Lessons

Since 1986, when the work began in Augusta, Georgia, many lessons have been learned about the initiation, implementation, and institutionalization of Whole-Faculty Study Groups (WFSGs). Today, there is a national thrust for leaders of change to focus on whole-school change. Increasingly more funding sources are requiring whole faculties to be involved in whatever is the improvement design. Also, it is difficult to read an educational journal that does not have an article or feature on professional learning communities. After so many years of work with whole faculties in professional learning communities, it is like a dream come true to find that all the doors are opening to the concepts on which the early WFSG work was based. Such futuristic thinking is credited to visionary people such as Bruce Joyce, author of *The Models of Teaching, Student Achievement Through Staff Development*, and other groundbreaking books and articles.

For those who are involved in or considering a whole-school change model, Murphy's (1991b) article, "Lessons From a Journey Into Change," may be helpful. The lessons shared in that 1991 article have been reinforced with experiences since the article was written, and new insights into the change process have been learned. The lessons shared here are reflective of earlier and recent experiences. Certainly, there are more lessons we have learned; the ones discussed here, however, are those we judge most relevant to the content of this book. The order in which we list the findings is not an indication of the degree of importance of each finding. Lesson 14 is just as important as Lesson 1.

Lesson 1: Everyone at a school has to be involved

The whole school must focus on the goal of the school: That all students should have equal opportunities to learn to the best of their abilities, in the best environment, and under the best conditions.

This is not an option for the whole school. Every teacher and administrator in the school must get better at meeting student needs. The school has a choice of what design or model to use for whole-school improvement. Once the choice is made, everyone participates.

Volunteerism most often supports individual development, not organizational development. It has not been Murphy's experience that a school can start with volunteers and have one, two, three, or four study groups while teachers not in study group are sitting back and watching. In such a "volunteerism" case, it is assumed that, over time, everyone will want to be in a study group. That assumption has not been validated. The distance between the "we" and the "them" just gets wider. The division grows. It is a cultural bomb. The nonvolunteers get more entrenched, even in the face of documented improvement in the classrooms of the teachers who are in study groups. It will actually be more difficult to get whole-school involvement when study group membership is at first optional. Once resisters are in a study group, there is a better than average chance that they will become committed. Left out, they will remain onlookers and, most likely, become saboteurs to the whole change effort.

This reality of whole-school participation raises many issues. One is the issue of voting whether to have a collaborative model in place at a school. Should that be a choice? Do teachers have a choice as to whether they will collaborate with colleagues on a regular basis? When we started the work in Augusta in 1986, our staff development colleagues were astounded, and some were horrified, that we would expect teachers to be in study groups that were not part of the voting majority. What we believed and acted on in 1986 has become the main stream of thought, which is that school improvement is too important for it to be an option not to participate.

We agree with Leonard and Leonard (2003) when they say that it is time for district-level administrators, policymakers, and principals to unequivocally communicate expectations that administrators and teachers value professional learning communities.

Lesson 2: The credit for school improvement goes to the school and its teachers

When there is evidence of increased student achievement, the credit goes to the teachers, students, principal, and parents at the local school level. One of the major mistakes consultants and others external to the school make is to seem to take credit for what has happened at the school. If the teachers perceive that individuals, groups, agencies, organizations not part of the individual school community, or all these are taking credit for a school's improvement, a permanent barrier is created between the credit claimers and the school.

Lesson 3: Often, school leaders do not understand that the content of what study groups do is the point of WFSGs

Yes, a short definition of WFSGs is teachers working together in small collaborative groups. That is not the point, however. The point is that teachers are working together on content that has promise for increasing student achievement. So many school leaders and individual study groups miss this point. They mistakenly think that the purpose is just to get together and collaborate. We would ask, "On what?" Just having professional learning communities will not increase student achievement. Again, we would ask, "Learning what?" Murphy is often asked, "Do you teach groups how to be a group?" Murphy says "No." Substantive, meaningful, student-impacting work will hold a group together while the group is learning to be a group. The truth of this lesson was clear when the first work with study groups was done in Augusta in 1987. The work was the point in getting a group together. The work was that every teacher in a school would appropriately and routinely use several models of teaching with students. The task was difficult, and the work was demanding. Through the work, however, the groups functioned at high levels, and student achievement increased.

Lesson 4: Many teachers do not value collaboration with their colleagues

This is a difficult lesson to report and to acknowledge. Many fine and dedicated teachers believe they can learn nothing new from their colleagues and time spent in collaborative work would be time better spent working alone. This belief seems to stem from the heavy work load and the pressure of increasing work demands. When observing some study groups, one can almost hear the unspoken voices saying, "Let's hurry, I've got work to do in my classroom."
Murphy (1992) reported,

> An insight that came early on was contradictory to my assumption that teachers would eagerly jump at the opportunity to meet regularly with colleagues to focus on their own new learnings and that of their students. I was not prepared for the resistance. Teachers accustomed to following instructional materials closely and letting the textbook do the planning sometimes found that thinking through lessons was onerous work. Some felt that asking for help was a sign of weakness. A few wondered whether colleagues were a legitimate source of help and were not sure that their colleagues knew enough. (p. 74)

Today, the resistance is less overt, and there is more willingness on the part of a majority of teachers to begin. There is still that lingering attitude, "we'll give it a try," signaling a lack of confidence that "it" will actually be beneficial.
Leonard and Leonard (2003) report that teachers continue to lament persisting negative mind-sets about the actual desirability of shared work and the resistance to moving beyond the traditional models of teacher relationships. We see teachers who say they want to collaborate with colleagues and complain about the lack of opportunities, but when the means to collaborate become a reality, their actions do not match their words. This reality is a constant source of tension for the teachers and for school leaders. Leaders think they are giving teachers what they want—more collaborative time; when the leaders find ways to create the structures and the time for collaboration, the teachers want to use the time in other ways. We have found that leaders in schools that release students for the express purpose of study group meetings have to "fight" some teachers who want to work alone on what the teachers refer to as "their work." We find ourselves having to repeat again and again that the time is for collaborating on student work. Lest we sound too skeptical about

these attitudes, we are hopeful that a clear expectation from school and district administrators that collaboration for improved instruction is "the way we do things here" will continue to create a positive shift in teacher attitudes.

Lesson 5: Looking collaboratively at student work and observing students working in other teachers' classrooms are practices that are not yet common in most schools

Even with increased attention given to looking collaboratively at student work, it is a difficult practice to initiate. Within the past few years, most professional journals have included articles on the practice, and there have been sessions at national professional conferences on conference programs. The lack of interest or desire to routinely look at student work in a collaborative setting seems to be for the following reasons:

1. There are not many individuals skilled enough in the practice to teach teachers how to effectively look at student work. One skill that teachers need is the ability to use protocols to structure the conversation around the work. The protocols can seem difficult and too lengthy, structured, and formal. Without a skillful, knowledgeable, experienced trainer in appropriate use of protocols, the value of their use is often lost. Just looking at student work is not going to reap the benefits that could be gained by using the appropriate protocol. Knowledgeable consultants can be reached through the Web site www.nsrf harmony.org.

2. Teachers fear that they will be criticized or faulted by their colleagues. Most teachers know other teachers by reputation. Teachers who have been on the faculty for a number of years are known by the "stories" students, parents, and other teachers tell. When teachers look at other teachers through the work of their students, what they see may be inconsistent with reputations and impressions. Teachers are fearful that the work of their students will reflect negatively on them. This is one reason why teachers initially are hesitant to bring student work from low-achieving students to the study group meetings.

3. Looking at student work (LASW) using a protocol will take 1 or 2 hours, and time is not built into schedules for teachers to routinely meet for this purpose. For schools that do not have WFSGs or some other collaborative structure in place, grade-level and department meetings could be used for LASW; because these groups usually have long business agendas, however, time is not available.

Teachers are also hesitant to make arrangements to go into each other's classrooms to observe student work. Peer teacher evaluation systems and peer coaching systems that put teachers on the defensive have made it difficult for teachers to trust the intent of colleagues coming into their classrooms. Much of the distrust is due to what one teacher tells another teacher or a principal of what he or she sees in classrooms that may cast a negative light on a teacher. In WFSGs, we tell teachers to look at the students, to look at the work the students are doing, and not to focus on the teacher. Even so, many teachers are generally mistrustful of adults in their classrooms.

Lesson 6: The principal is the most important factor in the successful initiation, implementation, and continuation of WFSGs

This lesson was learned early in the work of major school improvement efforts and is reflected in the research on leadership in Chapter 3. Even so, it is clearer to us now. The lesson was made especially apparent through the actions of principals in schools implementing the WFSG were system. We learned from many. Here, we share how five principals deepened our understanding of the role of the principal.

For us, Barry Shelofsky, principal of Winograd Elementary School in Greeley, Colorado, reinforced that the principal can be the initiator. He initiated the WFSG approach at Jackson Elementary School after attending a national institute in the spring of 1994 during which WFSGs were presented. Shelofsky worked with a team of teachers from his school in designing a WFSG implementation plan and was key in getting 100% teacher agreement to begin.

Kenneth Sherman, principal of Clarke Middle School in Athens, Georgia, provided more proof that a principal can appeal to a superintendent for special considerations and be successful. He met with the superintendent numerous times to present his case for early release of students to make study group time for his teachers. He communicated with parents about the possibilities of early release for teacher learning. The superintendent approved the release time schedule proposed by Sherman, and parents were receptive to the schedule. This was quite remarkable considering that Clarke Middle School was the only school in a 21-school district releasing students 2 hours early 12 times during the school year for teacher collaboration.

In Ira Weston, principal of Paul Robeson High School in Brooklyn, New York, we saw another example of how a highly visible, enthusiastic principal with clear expectations and knowledge of the instructional program can keep a faculty focused on student achievement. Weston can be seen in the halls and in the classrooms cheering the students and teachers on to do their best. He held the highest standards before the teachers as he examined the action plans and logs, asking them questions if he had any doubts about how the study group work would benefit students. Looking at student work, using different protocols, and observing in each other's classrooms became routine. There were no questions at the end of a school year about whether study groups would be in place next year. In particular, the budget, personnel, and schedule supported continuation.

Lynne Miller, principal of Williams Elementary School in Springfield, Missouri, underscored for us how important it is for principals to lead through example. Miller is a member of a study group of principals and shares what she learns with the teachers. She tries new instructional strategies with students, spending time in classrooms, and demonstrates her use of data in making decisions.

Fay Philips, principal at Mangham Elementary School in Mangham, Louisiana, makes it clear that principals must follow up and let teachers know that what they are doing is important. Philips contacts every study group, even after reading the logs, to personally ask questions about how members are connecting the study group work to what they are doing with students in the classrooms.

These principals have many things in common, but the one common factor most outstanding is their moral purpose (Fullan, 2001b). It is absolutely clear that the betterment of students drove every decision these principals made. It is also abundantly clear to teachers that it is not a choice as to whether they will collaborate with colleagues on how to improve student learning. It is an expectation of the workplace.

Lesson 7: Support and encouragement from district-level leaders are absolutely essential and play a key role in facilitating school change

The superintendent and other top district leaders establish the climate, direction, and sponsorship required to enable WFSGs or any whole-school change program to become successful and sustained. Institutionalization or continuation is directly attributable to the support and technical assistance provided by and through district leaders. Expectations for change must be clear and supported, and structural changes must be made to provide time for study groups to meet and effectively function. The district usually determines what new initiatives will be seriously considered and implemented each year. The district also controls most budget considerations and determines what time schools begin and end each day, as well as other scheduling concerns that affect the school year calendar. In most districts, schools are asked for input and can make requests and recommendations; the superintendent and board of education, however, make final decisions about issues raised and supported. All these issues affect what schools can do. A school may have the resources to begin an initiative without district involvement, but it is unlikely that, over time, the school can maintain and continue the work without district involvement and support.

For understanding the role of district leaders, Springfield public schools are a model lesson. The director of staff development attended a national institute on WFSGs, returned to the district and informed district leaders, provided orientations to the principals, and made provisions for district support staff to be trained in the WFSG system. Within 3 years, 45 of the 51 schools in Springfield were using the system as the major vehicle for implementing school improvement plans. Furthermore, in April 2004, when principals wrote what they wanted included in the postings for teacher vacancies at their schools, most included WFSGs in the description, as seen in the following:

> Elementary certification required through grade 5. Prefer a diverse experience in teaching a variety of grade levels. Knowledge and/or experience in using Kagan Cooperative Learning, Whole Faculty Study Groups (best practices), Love & Logic, Big 6, Reading/Writing workshop, and 6+1 Traits Writing are required. Willingness to be involved in site committees, duties, and programs is required.

Postings of available positions at schools unequivocally communicate expectations.

Lesson 8: Creating agreement to begin and maintaining commitment to continue are two different things that require two different approaches

Initially, the principal is working for agreement from the faculty to just get started, to begin. The principal must verbally or through written materials describe the initiative with clarity and give examples of where the initiative has been successful.

Schlechty (1993) states that in the beginning, faculties may need the following:

- A concept development lesson: What is it?
- A demonstration lesson: Can it be done?
- A values clarification lesson: Should we do it?
- A skill development lesson: How do we do it?

In the beginning, it is important that the principal take responsibility for framing the work in such a way that the faculty members are confident the principal knows what the change is and how it will affect them.

With WFSGs, there is a clear, comprehensive, straightforward implementation plan. Chapters 6 and 7 tell initiators exactly what to do. WFSGs have a well-defined structure, a step-by-step implementation strategy. Giving examples of successful WFSG sites is one way to demonstrate that it can be done.

It is during the early implementation stage when teachers are in study groups that they develop their own personal clarity as to the meaning of study groups. As the meaning becomes clearer, the commitment grows. We cannot ask teachers to be committed to something in the beginning before they understand the meaning and implications of the change. We can only ask for their agreement to begin. With more knowledge and competency comes commitment. The sooner teachers start working in a small group, and the more they see positive changes in their classrooms, the more committed they become.

To continue the WFSG approach over time takes an equal mixture of support and pressure that can enhance continuation or disrupt it. The initiation and first year of implementation are most often energizing. Continuing into the second and subsequent years is more difficult because as study groups are being continued, other initiatives are being introduced. When new curriculums and instructional initiatives are introduced, it is essential that leaders use the study group structure for training in the content of the initiatives and for supporting high levels of use of the new initiatives. If not, the teachers will not see the benefits of continuing the study groups. For initiatives to continue, teachers need to see that the information they received in the beginning is consistent with the way things are now. For example, when WFSGs have been initiated, teachers are told that a study group is a vehicle for doing what teachers have to do. If principals and other school leaders do not use study groups as the place to work on new initiatives, such as a new math series, continuation becomes increasingly difficult. Teachers will see that school and district leaders are not using the study group structure for the declared purposes (see Chapter 2). Teachers will have been told one thing and will see that reality is another thing.

Continuation takes great persistence. It takes constant tending. If the principal cannot do it for whatever reason, then he or she should make sure that someone is publicly assigned that task. Some leaders are better at initiating and encouraging during the early stages of implementation. Those same leaders may find it difficult to keep providing support and pressure over time. With other principals, it is just the reverse. They have difficulty getting faculties to agree on an initiative, but once the decision is made, they are excellent at sustaining it.

Lesson 9: Continuation, incorporation, and institutionalization of change systems, such as WFSGs, are much more difficult than we thought when we started, and we do not see that they are becoming any easier

Whether what was once considered an innovation gets built in as an ongoing part of the system or whether it disappears because it gets killed or dies of neglect is difficult to predict. The question can more easily be answered if we know the type of innovation. New materials most often become incorporated into a teacher's personal resource file. We know teachers who continue to use materials that were new to them 30 or more years ago. Teaching strategies often become part of a teacher's repertoire, permanent additions to be recalled when needed and appropriate. Teachers who learned new models of teaching in the mid-1980s when Murphy's work in Augusta was new tell her that they still use the strategies. Change systems are not so easily maintained. They permeate all aspects of the context, creating instability for a time. Change systems also permeate all processes that are in place for how the work gets done, creating a lack of clarity. They change roles and relationships in ways that alter status and power. The WFSG system is a cultural change and a structural change system, compounding the complexity of institutionalization. Change systems impact what individuals actually do and often cause teachers to say, "Am I not a good teacher? Is what I have been doing all wrong?" The turmoil can be so great that no one individual or team of individuals can overcome it until the dust clears.

Adding humor to the gravity of the issues raised, when leaders speak to teachers about institutionalization, we wonder if teachers do not think that it is the leaders who need to be institutionalized.

Lesson 10: Even if continuation is not assured, we have to begin

We have no choice except to begin, if the work is embedded in moral purpose: what is best for students. Initiators of change should be joyful in the work of the day and be encouraged by its benefits. While working toward institutionalization, we should not lose sight of the present. Someone once said, "Today is all we have." Therefore, sponsors of change, whether it is whole-school change or individual change, have to do what is in the best interests of students today and build for tomorrow. What may or may not happen tomorrow cannot keep us from doing the work and progressing today. We hope that once WFSGs are initiated and implemented, the structure and practices will become and remain centerpieces for future professional development at the school. In some schools in which we work today, the reality is that after our direct involvement ends, the faculty may revert to former practices. What may or may not happen tomorrow cannot diminish the importance of the work for today's students and teachers and the importance of its impact on their later lives.

Lesson 11: Using data to make instructional decisions is not a routine practice in most schools

In many schools, teachers and principals are unaccustomed to collecting data about student learning; analyzing data they collect or data from district and state assessments; and using the data to make decisions about what to teach, how to teach, or what supports children need to improve. Frequently, someone else collects and analyzes the data and tells principals and teachers what they should do. The situation is often made worse by using data analysis as an opportunity to blame one group or another for poor performance. The WFSG process is built around the assumption that data about student learning is essential to the work of study groups. Data about student learning are used in the decision-making cycle (DMC) to identify student learning needs and form study groups. Data about student learning are used in each study group to determine what each group's targets are for improvement, to assess the effectiveness of new instructional strategies, and to monitor progress in reaching the targets. One challenge for schools initiating WFSGs is how to help teachers and principals build comfort in, and proficiency with, using data.

For many years, we have used different types of standardized measures for grouping students. What we have not done as well as we should is to use daily work to measure and monitor the result of what we do today to determine the impact of a strategy or new material on student learning and to use data to modify what we do tomorrow. When we ask teachers to indicate how they will know that what they are doing will cause a student, for example, to increase his or her vocabulary, almost always they respond by writing the name of a standardized test or some other measure administered by the state or district. At least 75% of all action plans from WFSG schools list such measures. Schools routinely have 6- or 9-week grading periods; teachers, however, are less likely to use the measures they routinely use to determine averages to decide the status of student needs they are addressing in a study group. It is a deliberate strategy, in working with faculties, to get teachers to look at immediate measures and to stress that it is the cumulative effect of those measures that will be reflected in annual state and district tests.

Another repetitive lesson we learn relates to the vertical analysis of student data. When the whole faculty comes together to complete Steps 1 through 4 in the DMC, we include data from the whole school and, often, from a school within the school's feeder pattern. For example, if it is an elementary school, we may include the middle school writing test scores. Often, elementary teachers in the same school will not have reviewed the results of primary tests, and primary teachers will not have seen upper elementary test results. As we described in Chapter 7, to deal with this, when we analyze data in Step 1, we mix teachers from different grade levels at tables. Comments indicate that the cross-grade data are both new and of great interest. Opportunities to examine information in mixed groups of teachers are important to whole-school improvement.

Lesson 12: The importance of scheduling time within the workday for professional development and teacher collaboration is not an accepted practice in schools in the United States

For WFSGs to be successful, all certificated staff must participate in study groups, and the study groups must meet the equivalent of 1 hour per week. In addition, schools implementing WFSGs need time for instructional council meetings, whole-faculty meetings for the DMC or to celebrate and share study group work, and for ongoing professional development related to their students' learning needs.

This is not volunteer or optional time but required time for work that is an integral part of being a professional. This means finding time within the contractual time allocations specified in district policies and teacher agreements. Unfortunately, most school systems operate on a "factory" model of schooling in which teachers report to school soon before students arrive, spend the majority of their time in class with students, and leave soon after the students. This pattern has been exacerbated in recent years by budget constraints and rising state and federal standards that have tended to lengthen school days for students and reduce release time for professional development. Although many WFSG schools have found creative ways around this standard pattern, they have been finding time despite, rather than because of, the system. For WFSGs to flourish, districts will need to rethink how they provide time for professional development and teacher collaboration.

The first National Staff Development Council staff development standard is "Meets regularly with colleagues during the school day to plan instruction." The highest indicator on a 6-point scale of meeting the standard is "Meets regularly with learning team during scheduled time within the school day to develop lesson plans, examine student work, monitor student progress, assess the effectiveness of instruction, and identify needs for professional learning." In the WFSG rubric, the highest indicator of meeting the guideline related to time is "Meets at least 1 hour a week or 2 hours every 2 weeks within the school day." Amazingly, many schools are figuring out how to do this; sadly, not nearly as many as should be are doing so.

It is not just parents and the general public who are hesitant to find creative ways for teachers to have time during the school day to learn more about their craft; many educators do not see the need or do not seem to think that the struggle to find such ways is worth the effort. Superintendents have to be convinced, as do boards of education. Principals are often hesitant to go to their supervisors and ask for special considerations for their teachers. We do know that for WFSGs to have the desired effects and to become a routine practice, time must be allocated within the school day for the study groups to meet. The amount of time that study groups have to work together is directly correlated with the impact groups have on increasing student achievement.

Lesson 13: People fail to appreciate the magnifying power of synergistic group efforts

When we go to a symphony concert, we enjoy the beauty of the harmonious music being played. How amazing it is to our senses when all the sounds completely blend together in something beyond the ability of any one of the instruments. If just one player misses his or her part, however, everyone's ears let the listeners know immediately, and the quality of the music is diminished noticeably. It is that harmonious collaboration of all the instruments, the "synergy of the symphony," that makes the music sound so wonderful.

Synergy in groups is the same. People working together, as a team, toward common goals, interdependently, empowered, and fully participating in the collaborative effort, provide potential outcomes far beyond anything that any single member could have accomplished. When people perform together in this way, synergistically, they become a powerful team and have the potential to be able do things that no one could have possibly expected.

If study groups, for example, function to become synergistic teams, their potential is magnified manyfold. By comentoring each other in their synergistic group and deliberately adding resources and working to learn together, they have the foundation in place for becoming a learning team. As a learning team, the group members gain the potential to re-create themselves; do things that they were never able to do before; reperceive the school, its programs, and their students and their relationships to these; and dramatically expand their capacity to create and be part of a major generative process in the life and activities of their students and school. With a school completely made up of learning teams, the school now has the potential to move toward becoming a learning organization, with creative powers for increasing student learning and advancing the school far beyond our wildest imagination. Of course, the same potential is possible for any group, in almost any environment, that chooses to become a synergistic group, a genuine team.

Lesson 14: Public school teachers are magnificent and real heroes

Murphy says that she has known since childhood the impact a teacher can have on a child. It was not until, during a 10-year period (1993–2003), she traveled more than 1 million miles on Delta Airlines visiting hundreds of schools in different places, however, that she witnessed the true heroics of teachers. The genuine greatness of the average teacher in this country is sadly unknown. Most of us only know the teachers in the schools our children attend or where we work. Teachers in the same school know each other and may know other teachers in the district that teach the same grade or subject; most teachers do not fully appreciate each other, however. Teachers are part of the fabric of all communities. Even so, the average citizen does not fully appreciate the range of talent in U.S. schools. The teacher-of-the-year awards do not even scratch the surface of these truly remarkable human beings that fill K–12 classrooms and buildings in school districts throughout the nation. The lesson is that we cannot allow a small minority of teachers who make loud noises of dissent to overshadow the stellar teachers in a majority of classrooms who will do anything, anytime, if it will serve the best interests of the students they teach.

Murphy's work in public schools for more than 45 years has brought her in contact with teachers in just about every circumstance—teachers teaching on Indian reservations in Arizona and South Dakota; in schools with few supplies and crumbling buildings; in large inner-city schools with security guards at every entrance and the ends of all hallways; in rural, isolated communities with few, if any, resources; in affluent suburbs with more resources than they can use; with students who do not understand the languages the teachers speak; in makeshift classrooms; with children with severe mental, emotional, and physical handicaps; in temporary facilities due to being displaced from their schools on September 11, 2001; in fortified schools, locked inside for their protection and the students' protection; in well-equipped, safe, and beautifully designed schools with more than ample resources; and, in general, in conditions for which teacher education programs could not have prepared them.

Whatever the circumstances, teachers teach. Teachers want the best for their students. Teachers work long hours, expending every ounce of energy they have. Teachers often work when they are sick rather than leave the important work of teaching to a substitute. Teachers neglect their own children for other people's children. The miracle is that most of these teachers love what they do, and they do what they do with knowledge, skill, and dedication. We have to remind ourselves of this truth, lest we let the other 10% keep us from doing the really important work of helping schools better meet the needs of all students.

SUMMARY

There are more lessons to be learned, many more. Everyone working in schools to improve student learning continues to learn. After all, learning is why we do what we do. There is still so much to learn.

Resource A

Forms

- Study Group Action Plan

- Study Group Log

- Study Group Log

- Study Group Meeting Report for Looking at Student Work

- Checklist for First Three Meetings

- Checklist for How to Write Student Needs

- Checklist for Writing "Actions" on the Action Plan

- Checklist for WFSG Procedural Guidelines

- Checklist for Content

- What Is Changing

- Study Group Status Check

- Reflection on the Process and Examination of the Inquiry

- Assessment of WFSG Work–I

- Assessment of WFSG Work–II

- Assessment of WFSG Work–III

- Assessment of WFSG Work–IV

Whole-Faculty Study Group Action Plan

School _____ Study Group # _____ Date _____

Group Members _____

What is the general category of student needs the group will address?

____ Reading ____ Writing ____ Math ____ Science ____ Assessment Other: _____

Data indicate that students need to: (be very specific)	**When our study group meets, we will:**

The **ESSENTIAL QUESTION** that will guide the group's work is:

_____

Our resources are:	**Our norms are:**

Specific Student Needs from above—*Students need to:*	**Data Sources** that document need and will be evidence of impact of group's work	**Baseline**—what data indicate when work begins on: **DATE ____**	**Target**—what study group projects will be the results of the work on: **DATE ____**	**Actual**—what data indicate now (complete at end of 6 to 12 weeks) **DATE ____**

Specific Student Needs Listed on Action Plan *Students need to:*	Data Sources that document need and will be evidence of impact of group's work	Baseline—what data indicate when work begins on: DATE _____	Target—what study group projects will be the results of the work on: DATE _____	Actual—what data indicate **now** (complete at end of 6 to 12 weeks): DATE _____

Specific Student Needs Listed on Action Plan *Students need to:*	Data Sources that document need and will be evidence of impact of group's work	Baseline—what data indicate when work begins on: DATE _____	Target—what study group projects will be the results of the work on: DATE _____	Actual—what data indicate now (complete at end of 6 to 12 weeks): DATE _____

Complete a chart every 6 to 12 weeks to track progress of study group work.
Column 1: List two or three of the SPECIFIC student needs on the SGAP.
Column 2: Use data sources that track current progress (i.e., teacher-made tests, teacher observations, 6-week averages, and textbook checklists). The cumulative impact of the formative assessments should be reflected in state tests; however, state tests are not given and results reported frequently enough to track ongoing progress during the school year.
Columns 4 and 5: The dates should be the same.
Columns 3, 4, and 5: If percentages are used, it would be the percentage of students in all the members' classes. For example, if there are 75 students in three teachers' classes, 60% demonstrating the need to increase spelling accuracy would be 45 students.

Examples for completing top quadrants of the study group action plan:

Category of student needs: Writing

Data indicate that students need to: (be very specific)	**When our study group meets, we will:**
– *Write a story or draw a picture story with a beginning, middle, and end* – *Improve and enlarge vocabulary* – *Use the five-step writing process effectively: prewriting, drafting, proofreading, editing, and publishing* – *Use correct spelling and punctuation* – *Know how to organize what they want to write*	– *Share strategies that will improve students' writing skills* – *Examine student work using protocols* – *Have someone with expertise in our areas of focus meet with us* – *Model effective strategies we use in classroom* – *Develop writing topics to be used at different grade levels* – *Examine assessment tools, including rubrics*

Category of student needs: Math

Data indicate that students need to: (be very specific)	**When our study group meets, we will:**
– *Know basic math facts (S, A, M, & D)* – *Use manipulatives to solve problems* – *Create original word problems* – *Learn steps to solving problems* – *Apply mental math strategies*	– *Share strategies for working with whole class and with students who are not making progress* – *Develop center activities using manipulatives* – *Develop plans for using journal writing in math* – *Investigate technological strategies for teaching problem-solving skills* – *Develop plans for observing in each other's classrooms and how we will follow up the observations*

Category of student needs: Reading Comprehension

Data indicate that students need to: (be very specific) 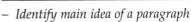	**When our study group meets, we will:**
– *Identify main idea of a paragraph* – *Sequence main events in a story* – *Use context clues* – *Construct mental images representing the ideas in text* – *Increase word recognition* – *Know how to summarize* – *Analyze characters/setting*	– *Demonstrate strategies that work for us* – *Examine the scope and sequence of introducing comprehension skills in our textbook series* – *Look at student work (comprehension)* – *Research best practices and develop model lessons for each practice* – *Develop plans for observing in each other's classrooms and how we will follow up the observations*

Whole-Faculty Study Group Log

School _____ Log # _____ Date _____

Group Name or # _____ Leader _____

Members Present _____

What happened today? Brief summary of discussion and activities. Keep artifacts in notebook.

Classroom application: What are students learning and doing as a result of what the study group is learning and doing?

Did you examine student work today?		Who brought?	
General comments, such as: What you are ready to share, IC/Reps meeting.		What concerns or questions do you have for leaders or what do you want them to know?	

Next Meeting (agenda items, work to prepare) _____

_____

Date: Time: Leader: Location:

Whole-Faculty Study Group Log

School _____ Log# _____ Date _____

Group # _____ Today's Leader _____

Members Present _____

What did we do in our classrooms that relates to the work we did in our last meeting?

Teacher	Classroom Application

Which action on our action plan did we take today?

Which student need did we address today?

What did we discuss, examine, research, and/or create around our essential question?
(Attach artifacts used; i.e., article, teacher work, student work, protocol, and Web sites used)

What did we discover about:

our students' learning?	our instructional strategies/materials?

What is the strategy/lesson that we are all going to try before our next meeting?

Next meeting agenda (i.e., work to prepare):

What questions do we have?

Study Group Meeting Report
for
Looking at Student Work

When looking at student work, using this form (in addition to log) is optional.

Date _____ Study Group Name or # _____

Members present:

Describe the assignment(s):

What we learned about student LEARNING:

What we learned about INSTRUCTION:

What will we do to IMPROVE LEARNING?

If practical, please attach copy of the student work.

Checklist for the
First Three Whole-Faculty
Study Group Meetings

First Meeting

1. **Attend to logistics:**

   ☐ Choose a group leader for this meeting.

   ☐ Choose a group member to record today's decisions and activities on the log.

   ☐ List the projected dates for each study group meeting.

   ☐ Decide on the beginning and ending times for each meeting.

   ☐ Count the approximate number of hours the group will be meeting until the end of the school year.

   ☐ Decide where the group will meet.

   ☐ Decide on the schedule for the leadership rotation.

   ☐ Decide on the schedule for the rotation of recorder.

   ☐ Decide on the rotation for attending the meetings.

2. **Decide on group norms:**

   ☐ Decide on operating procedures, standards of behavior, or **norms** for the group. Consider including norms for
   - Consensus
   - No-fault
   - Collaboration
   - Responsibility for the work

   ☐ Confirm that the norms are written on the log, that the group understands the norms will be routinely revisited, and that the norms may be revised at any time to accommodate the needs of all the members.

3. **Begin developing a study group action plan:**

   ☐ Review together the action plan form, making sure that everyone understands what is to be written at the top of the plan and in each of the quadrants.

   ☐ If in the whole-faculty decision-making meeting each individual wrote a personalized action plan, share highlights.

☐ Confirm the general category of student needs the group will address.

☐ Share everyone's essential question and reach consensus on the one that will be written on the group's action plan.

☐ Share everyone's specific student needs and reach consensus on the student needs that will be written on the group's action plan. Confirm that all the needs are on the master list that the faculty identified in the general category the group is addressing.

☐ Decide if there are other specific needs in this category that the faculty did not identify that group members have evidence (data) are needs.

☐ Decide if data the faculty reviewed should be revisited and if the group should review additional data, and if so, what data.

☐ Put the norms on the action plan.

4. **Decide what needs to be done at the next meeting:**

☐ Establish what needs to be done to finish the action plan at the next meeting, such as
- Bring data to review
- Bring a list of ideas for what the group will do when it meets
- Bring ideas for resources

☐ Confirm the leader, the recorder, the date, the time, and the location of the next meeting.

☐ Confirm that the leader of today's meeting will make copies of the log for all members, the principal, and the clipboard or will post the log on the school's electronic mail system.

Second Meeting

1. **Attend to logistics:**

☐ Acknowledge the leader and the recorder.

☐ Confirm that the norms will facilitate the work of the group.

☐ Acknowledge and discuss any feedback on the log from the first meeting.

☐ Share reflections and thoughts about the first meeting.

2. **Continue developing the study group action plan:**

☐ Discuss and review student needs, looking at any data members brought.

☐ Confirm the specific student needs that the group will address in its work.

☐ Share actions that members feel would be appropriate for the group to do when the study group meets that will address the student needs.

☐ Decide on the actions to list on the plan.

☐ Share the resources that members feel would benefit the group's work.

☐ Decide on which resources to list on the plan.

☐ Discuss how the group will track the status of the student needs, including the data sources the group will use. The group will need to decide how it will pre- and post test each student need, using classroom measures. The sources might be teacher-made tests, end of 6-week averages, and textbook checklists. At the end of each 6- to 12-week period, the group will complete a chart (bottom of action plan and page 2 of action plan) to check the status of improvement.

☐ Confirm that the leader will give the study group action plan to the principal, even if it is not complete.

3. **Take action:**

☐ Decide which of the actions listed on the plan will be the first action the group will take.

☐ Decide what each member will need to bring to the next meeting and what each member will need to do prior to the meeting to ensure a productive third meeting, remembering that each member is responsible for the work of the group and the level of productivity.

4. **Bring closure to the meeting:**

☐ Confirm the leader, the recorder, the date, the time, and the location of the next meeting.

☐ Confirm that today's leader will make copies of the action plan and the log for each member, the principal, and the clipboard or post the plan and log on the school's electronic mail system.

Third Meeting

1. **Attend to logistics:**

☐ Acknowledge any feedback from the principal on the log from the last meeting.

☐ Acknowledge any feedback from the principal on the action plan.

☐ Share reflections about the last meeting.

2. **Revisit the study group action plan:**

    ☐ Discuss any new thoughts, perspectives, and suggestions.

    ☐ Discuss any adjustments needed as a result of feedback from the principal.

    ☐ Complete the assessment portion of the plan if it is not complete.

3. **Take action:**

    ☐ Do what the group decided to do at the last meeting.

4. **Bring closure to the meeting:**

    ☐ Have at least one member respond to the question on the log, "What major implication does what we did today have on our classroom practice?"

    ☐ Confirm what actions will be taken at the next meeting.

    ☐ Confirm what members need to bring and be prepared to do at the next meeting.

    ☐ Confirm the leader, the recorder, the date, the time, and the location of the next meeting.

    ☐ Confirm that copies of today's log will be made and distributed or posted.

Continuation of Meetings

One action research cycle will take approximately four study group meetings to complete for study groups that meet weekly for 1 hour or every other week for approximately 2 hours. The action research cycles will consist of the following:

1. The group looks at classroom-based data around the essential question to establish baseline data for **THEIR** students.

    Question to ask: What is causing students difficulty in this area? Why? What are the problems students are having around this student need?

    Action to take: Focus on this need.

    Time: Parts of several meetings.

2. The group reviews current research or information about the need and describes practices that have been shown to be effective in addressing this need.

    Question to ask: What expert voices can we bring in to inform ourselves around this student need?

Possible resources to use: Texts, Internet, experts, professional articles, etc.

Action to take: Examine resources and identify best practices.

Time: One meeting.

3. The group develops lessons that incorporate what was learned from the examination of effective practices and uses the strategies and materials in classrooms.

   Question to ask: What can we try in our classes to meet this student need?

   Action to take: Develop a lesson together or develop lessons separately; then, in the study group use a tuning protocol to revise plans before using them in class.

   Time: One meeting.

4. Individuals in the group bring student work from the classroom to assess the effectiveness of the classroom lessons/strategies.

   Question to ask: What differences did the work we did in our classes have on student learning?

   Action to take: Use a Wows and Wonders protocol to look at student work.

   Time: One meeting.

5. The group looks at classroom-based data around the essential question to determine: (1) if the targeted student need has been met; (2) if you are ready to move on to another student need; or (3) if you need to continue your focus on this student need.

   Time: Part of a meeting.

6. Begin the cycle again—either for a new need or for your current need.

Whole-Faculty

WFSGs

Study Groups™

Checklist for
How to Write Student Needs

Do the student needs listed on the <u>study group action plan</u> meet the following criteria?

If you can say "Yes" to a descriptor, put a ✓ in the blank.

_____ The student needs are the result of the data analysis.

_____ The student needs are on the master list.

_____ The student needs are in the category the study group chose.

_____ The student needs can be evidenced in student work, meaning that members can routinely bring student work to the study group meetings and examine the work to determine if students are improving.

_____ The student needs can be addressed through **what** teachers are currently teaching.

_____ The student needs can be addressed through **how** teachers teach.

_____ The student needs are needs over which teachers have direct control or influence.

Whole-Faculty

WFSGs

Study Groups™

Checklist for Writing "Actions" on the WFSG Action Plan

Do the actions listed on the <u>study group action plan</u> tell what the study group members will do when the study group meets?

If you can say "Yes" to a descriptor, put a ✓ in the blank.

The actions

_____ begin with an action word that tells what the teachers will do when the study group meets. For example,

– examine	– develop	– design	– create	– use
– construct	– model	– make	– practice	– demonstrate

_____ give the reader a visual image of what study group members will be doing when they sit around a table to work together.

_____ do **not** describe what the teachers will do in their classrooms with their students.

_____ do **not** describe what the students will do.

_____ are aligned with the student needs, meaning that all the actions the study group will take will address the stated student needs.

Whole-Faculty

Study Groups™

Checklist for
WFSG Procedural Guidelines

Directions: As a group, rate your study group using the following symbols:

    * = We're there!
    > = We're developing!
    < = We're struggling!

_____ The size of our group provides for participation from all group members.

_____ We have established a regular meeting time, which is:

_____ We have established group norms, which are:

_____ We adhere to our established norms.

_____ We have established a rotation of leadership schedule.

_____ We have an action plan.

_____ Our study group action plan has been posted in a public place.

_____ We complete a log after each meeting and follow procedures for posting it.

_____ We maintain an instructional focus during meetings.

_____ Our work is impacting our instructional practices in the classroom.

_____ We routinely examine student work when we meet.

_____ Our group works well together and shares responsibilities.

_____ We are sharing our work with other study groups.

Whole-Faculty

WFSGs

Study Groups™

Checklist:
Clarifying the CONTENT

The heart of the study group process is **what** teachers study, **what** teachers investigate, and **what** teachers do to become more skillful in the classroom with students. The process, by itself, has little power to change what teachers actually do in their classrooms.

In the questions below, "the content" is <u>what</u> the teachers are learning to do. "The content" is the study group's curriculum (the actions it will take and the "stuff" it will work with).

---

1. Does "the content" require the group to examine student work?

2. Would "intellectually rigorous" describe the work of the study group?

3. Is "the content" aligned with the student needs that the study group is addressing?

4. Does "the content" require you to carefully examine classroom practice?

5. Will "the content" deepen your own understanding of the content you teach?

6. Is "the content" a review or a rehashing of what individuals already know?

7. Will "the content" push individuals beyond where they currently are in regard to skill and understanding?

8. What research supports "the content"?

9. What resources will be required to effectively implement "the content" in the classroom?

Whole-Faculty

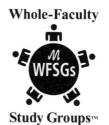

Study Groups™

What Is Changing as a Result of Your WFSG Work?

1. Do you have more knowledge and a deeper understanding of subject matter content (e.g., math, science, writing, reading, language development, history)? ____ Y ____ N

2. Do you use materials and resources in new and different ways? ____ Y ____ N

3. Are you modifying and using teaching strategies in your repertoire in new and different ways? ____ Y ____ N

4. Are you now using teaching strategies and practices that you have not used in the classroom? ____ Y ____ N

5. Have you modified how you plan and organize for instruction? ____ Y ____ N

6. Have you modified how you assess student learning, or are you using new assessment practices? ____ Y ____ N

7. Do student needs guide what you do? ____ Y ____ N

8. Are teachers more willing to collaborate and to accept joint responsibility for all students? ____ Y ____ N

9. What changes have you made that have had the greatest impact on students?

Whole-Faculty

Study Groups™

WFSG Status Check

Going around the table, one member completes the first sentence (orally). Without discussion, the second member completes the same sentence. Repeat until each member has shared his or her ending of the first sentence. Was there consensus? Discuss. Follow the same pattern with all or any four of the following items.

1. In our study group, we started

2. The hardest thing for us to do seems to be

3. As far as student changes, I see

4. Our group seems to be making the most progress in

5. Our greatest challenge is

6. One of my disappointments is

7. It's encouraging to see

8. To go deeper into the content of our work, we need to

9. Bringing student work is

10. To observe students in each other's classrooms, we need to

Whole-Faculty Study Groups:
Reflection on the Process and Examination of the Inquiry

School _____ Study Group # _____

Each study group or the focus team, which includes the principal, discusses the following questions. In the spaces provided, one member records the responses. This form is either given to the principal or taken to the last instructional council meeting.

Reflection on the Process	*Examination of the Inquiry*
How do you feel the following facilitated or impeded the work? Time of the meetings Group size Composition of groups Rotation of leadership Group norms Sense of equality Focus of work Communication among groups Level of participation of all members	What is the evidence that teaching strategies, attitudes, assessment practices, and materials are changing as a result of the study group's work?
What evidence is there that the school exemplifies a professional learning community with commitment to continuous learning for the benefit of students (e.g., focus on a shared vision, level of trust, norms of decisions making, sense of oneness, and norms of collaboration)?	What is the evidence that the student needs listed on the action plan have improved?

Whole-Faculty

Study Groups™

Assessment of WFSG Work–I

Name _____ Study Group _____

This page is completed by individual study group members.

To respond to the questions on this page, individuals will need to refer to their study group action plan and logs for indicators of frequency.

During your study group time, how often does your group engage in the following?

Activity Engaged In	Almost Every Time	Most of the Time	Sometimes	Rarely
Addressing issues of curriculum				
Focusing on instructional strategies				
Designing and/or redesigning lessons and units to develop deeper understanding				
Looking at student work to improve teacher practice				
Looking at student work to deepen student understanding				
Looking at teacher work to improve teacher practice				
Looking at teacher work to deepen student understanding				
Bringing in references to research regarding teaching practices				
Focusing on reaching students with learning differences				
Engaging in reflective dialogue				
Working on authentic assessments				

Whole-Faculty

Study Groups™

Assessment of WFSG Work–II

Name _____ Study Group _____

This page is completed by individual study group members.

In what ways have you personally benefited from being in a study group?

Benefits to Me	Definitely Yes	Somewhat	Little or None
Greater sense of collegiality with other teachers			
I use more varied instructional practices			
I feel more effective in my teaching			
I have fewer classroom management problems			
I am able to reach my students better			

In what ways have your students benefited from your participation in a study group?

Benefits to Students	Almost Every Time	Most of the Time	Sometimes	Rarely
More actively engaged in their work				
Demonstrating better performance in the learning needs you have been working on				
Demonstrating deeper understanding of key concepts and ideas				
Taking more responsibility for their learning				
More reflective on their own learning				
Other:				

The items on this assessment are from a survey prepared by Rosenblum Brigham Associates for ATLAS Communities.

Whole-Faculty

Study Groups™

Assessment of WFSG Work–III

Study Group _____ Date _____

As a study group:

Examine the artifacts from the work the study group did this year.

In the following spaces, share what evidence you have that teaching practices have changed as a result of the work of the study group. For example, what were common teaching strategies, assessment tools, types of teaching materials, or lesson formats that have now been changed, revised, or discarded?

BEFORE the study group began its work:	AT THE END of the study group's work:

Whole-Faculty

Study Groups™

Assessment of WFSG Work–IV

Study Group _____

What evidence does the group have that student performance changed in each of the student needs listed on your action plan?

Specific Student Needs listed on action plan. *Students need to:*	Data Sources that document need and are evidence of impact of group's work	Baseline— what data indicate when work began in: **Aug./Sept.**	Target—what study group projected would be the results of the work in: **May**	Actual—what data indicate **now:** **May** _____

Column 1: List two or three of the SPECIFIC student needs on the SGAP.
Column 2: List data sources you used to track progress (i.e., teacher-made tests, teacher observations, 6-week averages, textbook checklists, and benchmark tests).
Column 3: What the data indicated when you began meeting (Aug.–Oct.).
Column 4: What you wanted the data to indicate at the end of the year.
Column 5: What the data indicate at the end of the year.
Columns 3, 4, and 5: If percentages are used, it would be the percentage of students in all the members' classes. For example, if there are 75 students in three teachers' classes, 60% demonstrating the need to increase spelling accuracy would be 45 students.

Resource B

Workbook for the Decision-Making Cycle

The Faculty Workbook is for faculty members to use as they are led through Steps 1–4 on the Decision-Making Cycle (DMC).

After the faculty completes Steps 1–4, the Workbook is to be used by the individual study groups to guide their understanding and completion of Steps 5–7 on the Decision-Making Cycle.

The Decision-Making Cycle represents one school year. At the beginning of each year the whole faculty returns to Step 1.

Time spent on the DMC Steps:

- Step 1–4: Approximately 2½ hours with the whole faculty together
- Step 5: One or two study group meetings
- Step 6: From the third study group meeting to the end of the school year
- Step 7: Continuous with a summative report at the end of the school year

WFSG
Decision-Making Cycle

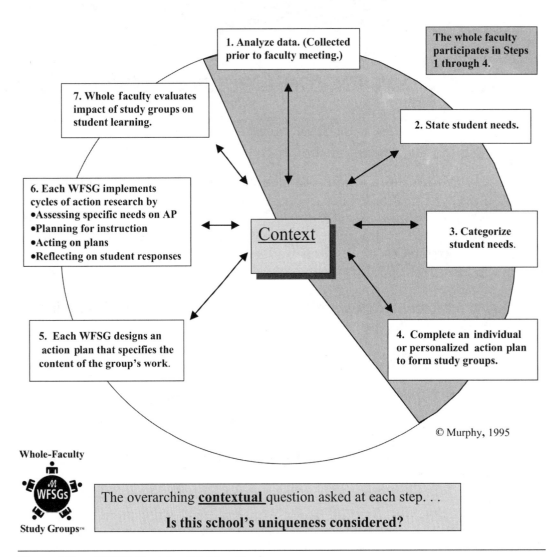

1. Analyze data. (Collected prior to faculty meeting.)

The whole faculty participates in Steps 1 through 4.

7. Whole faculty evaluates impact of study groups on student learning.

2. State student needs.

6. Each WFSG implements cycles of action research by
•**Assessing specific needs on AP**
•**Planning for instruction**
•**Acting on plans**
•**Reflecting on student responses**

Context

3. Categorize student needs.

5. Each WFSG designs an action plan that specifies the content of the group's work.

4. Complete an individual or personalized action plan to form study groups.

© Murphy, 1995

Whole-Faculty

WFSGs

Study Groups™

The overarching **contextual** question asked at each step. . .

Is this school's uniqueness considered?

Figure 7.1   WFSG Decision-Making Cycle

Whole-Faculty

Study Groups™

WFSG Target Instructional Student Needs

<u>Before getting started</u>, let's confirm that WFSGs address instructional or academic needs of students. Data faculty reviews are to reflect academic/instructional needs.

Before writing a student need for WFSGs to address, the need should fit within the following.

The student need

- Is evident in the work that the student produces; therefore, examining student work will be an activity of the study group.
- Can be addressed through how and what teachers teach.
- Is an "enabling" need, meaning it is a need that enables the student to be academically successful, such as reading and writing; or, you could say it is a "terminal" need, meaning at some point the need will no longer exist or will end. This is unlike a "perennial" need, meaning a need that is always there, such as the need to attend school, to feel good about self, and to cooperate. <u>IN OTHER WORDS</u>, teachers can do something about the need; the need is within their realm of influence; the teacher has some control over eliminating the need.

<u>**Noninstructional student needs**</u> are important and should be addressed. Needs not appropriate for study groups may be assigned to the administrative team, a task force, a committee, grade-level meetings, department meetings, team meetings, committees, student council, advisory councils, or any other group that oversees general student and school needs.

Whole-Faculty

Study Groups™

WFSG
Decision-Making Cycle

Prior to Step 1:
Collect Data

Prior to today, data were collected for the whole faculty to review.

TODAY, the whole faculty will briefly review the most pertinent data for the purpose of determining the major foci for the work of study groups. Once the study groups are formed, each study group <u>should revisit the data most relevant to the student needs each group is addressing.</u> **Data analysis is an ongoing function of all study groups!** Within the framework of the DMC, only approximately 30 minutes is allocated to data analysis for the purpose of pinpointing the specific student needs appropriate for study groups to address.

The school improvement plan (SIP) usually includes student improvement goals that are too broad (i.e., increase the number of students proficient in reading) to give study groups specific direction. For that reason, the SIP will not be a part of today's data review. However, the results of today's work should affirm what is in the SIP.

Whole-Faculty

Study Groups™

WFSG
Decision-Making Cycle
Step 1

Analyze Data

A. There is a folder on each table.

B. As directed by a leader, give each person at the table one piece of data in the folder.

C. A leader will identify each piece. **5 minutes**

D. Each person is to study the piece he/she has. Individuals may mark or highlight items or write questions. Look for patterns and trends, gaps or anomalies, areas of strength and areas of weakness. **10 minutes**

E. Individuals at each table are to have a general discussion about the different pieces of data. **15 minutes**

Total time: 30 minutes

REMEMBER:

Individual study groups will return to this data after the study groups are formed. At this time, we are focusing on schoolwide needs that are reflective in state and district assessments. Additional data sources will be reviewed by individual study groups in the area of needs being targeted by a study group.

Whole-Faculty

Study Groups™

WFSG
Decision-Making Cycle
Step 2

State Student Needs

The table groups have discussed the data in the folders. Individuals are focused on one or two pieces of data assigned to them. Now:

1. **Each person is to use the space at the bottom of this page as a work sheet and write** the specific student needs evidenced in the data he or she has. In the left column, write the specific needs; in the right column, write the data that document the needs. Be as **specific** as you can; do not state broad, general needs. The first word in the need statement should be a VERB. **10 minutes**

   For how to write student needs, see examples on the next page!

2. **When told by a leader, compile the student needs on a piece of chart paper.** You may write student needs that were not on any one's individual list. However, the needs must have been reflected in the data the group reviewed. **On the chart paper, be sure to number each need. 15 minutes**

3. When each table has listed all the student needs on chart paper, the charts from all the tables are taped to walls or other structures so all the charts can be viewed by everyone.

4. The leader selects one chart to be the **Master List of student needs** and goes through a process of compiling all the student needs on all the charts onto the **Master List.**

5. The **Master List of student needs** is entered into a laptop computer then printed and copied for everyone.

6. Everyone is to keep the **Master List of student needs** in the WFSG binder/notebook because the list will be needed.

REMEMBER: Additional student needs may be identified after the study groups start meeting. Study groups will review additional data!

Whole-Faculty

Study Groups™

Examples of Specific Student Needs

Students need to

1. Demonstrate the ability to use context clues.

2. Demonstrate the ability to locate the main idea in a paragraph.

3. Be able to sequence events in a reading passage.

4. Read for locating and recalling information.

5. Construct complete sentences.

6. Improve and enlarge vocabulary.

7. Demonstrate the ability to distinguish between significant and insignificant oral and written information.

8. Use correct grammar and punctuation in all areas of the curriculum.

9. Use higher-order thinking skills to solve problems.

10. Spell correctly.

11. Reflect on own and others' work to improve depth and quality.

12. Demonstrate the ability to gather and synthesize information.

13. Communicate their thinking of mathematical processes (oral and written).

14. Plan and complete projects that demonstrate content-specific skills and understandings.

15. Develop listening skills to promote understanding for what is presented orally.

16. Solve word problems to standard.

17. Demonstrate understanding of probability and statistics.

18. Demonstrate understanding of the language of mathematics.

19. Demonstrate how to interpret and graph data for a purpose.

20. Demonstrate how to apply and explain mathematical problems.

21. Know how to proofread and edit work.

22. Incorporate technology in gathering, understanding, and evaluating information.

23. Increase computation skills.

24. Understand figurative language.

25. Integrate and apply math and science knowledge and understanding in real-life experiences.

26. Draw diagrams and tables to aid in solving problems and visualizing solutions.

27. Write and speak with clarity for audience/purpose.

28. Evaluate their work using a rubric.

29. Write a nonfiction summary with a topic, main idea, and supporting details.

30. Improve phonetic analysis skills.

Whole-Faculty

Study Groups™

WFSG
Decision-Making Cycle
Step 3

Categorize Student Needs

Using the master list of student needs that the faculty identified in Step 2,

1. We are going to organize the Master List of student needs that the faculty identified.

2. Working alone, categorize the student needs by sorting the needs that are similar or 'go together' into groups, putting needs together that could be addressed as a group. [Instead of writing the needs again, indicate which student needs are in the same category by writing the number that is in front of the need on the Master List.]

3. Give each category (group) a name, i.e., Critical Thinking Skills, Study Skills, Word Attack Skills, Reading Comprehension, Problem Solving, Writing.

4. A student need may fit in more than one category.

5. EXAMPLE, using the list of student needs on the preceding page:

Reading Comprehension:	1, 2, 3, 4, 6, 7, 12
Problem Solving:	4, 6, 7, 9, 13, 16, 26
Writing:	1, 3, 4, 5, 7, 8, 9, 17, 18, 23, 25

(Note: Student need #7 fits in all three of the above categories and would fit in most any category, meaning that teachers addressing different categories will still be addressing many of the same student needs. Needs that fit in more than one category would be addressed from different perspectives or through different lenses. In this way, every study group could be addressing the <u>same student needs</u> but one study group may be doing so through the reading lens and another through the math lens or writing lens).

A leader will ask for volunteers to share their categories, with the corresponding numbers for student needs on the Master List. The responses will be recorded. When the faculty is satisfied that all the student needs are represented in at least one category, STOP. The listed categories become the basis for forming study groups.

Whole-Faculty

Study Groups™

WFSG
Decision-Making Cycle
Step 4–Part 1

Write an Action Plan for "Yourself"

Everyone is to think about an "individual" or "personalized" study group action plan for themselves. This is to be a plan that the **individual knows will target his or her students' needs.**

On a blank <u>study group action plan</u>:

1. Choose the one category on the school's list of categorized student needs that <u>YOU</u> want to address in a study group. Write or check the category at the top of the action plan.

2. In the box titled *"Students need to,"* write out the **specific student instructional needs** that you want to address in the category you chose. Remember: You have a list of the student needs that came from the data you reviewed; those were the needs put into categories. The student needs that you write on "your" action plan **must** be from the school's master list and in the category you chose.

3. In the box titled *"When our study group meets, we will,"* write the **actions** you want to take when your study group meets. **Examples:**
   • Examine student work routinely using a protocol.
   • Design lessons that integrate different curriculums.
   • Practice teach lessons to be taught in the classroom.
   • Model effective strategies and activities.
   • Read and discuss pertinent articles and chapters from selected books.
   • Discuss application of strategies gleaned from books or articles.
   • Have a skillful person attend meetings to train/guide study group members (expert voice).
   • Develop lessons for implementing what members have been trained to do.
   • Develop rubrics for a consistent grading system.
   • Practice and critique teaching strategies used with a specific lesson.
   • Reflect on new knowledge and on current classroom practices.
   • Identify, discuss, and practice strategies that help develop reading skills, such as vocabulary skills and skills to decode words.
   • Identify, discuss, and practice strategies for teaching reading through mathematics, social studies, and science.

- Evaluate assessment techniques used in the classrooms.
- Develop skill and plan for routine use of various forms of technology.
- Identify different types of word problems and strategies for solving each type.
- Discuss case studies that have been selected from field-tested cases describing a teaching experience that had an unexpected outcome or ran into difficulty.
- Investigate various diagnostic resources and techniques for testing reading comprehension and strategies for remediating deficiencies.
- Design a math dictionary or develop a strategy for students to design one.
- Examine a variety of sample tests to determine skills necessary for success.
- Examine, develop, and critique use of rubrics.
- Invite students to attend meetings occasionally to listen to students' points of view.
- Explore and identify specific instructional strategies for reducing the achievement gap among different ethnic (race) groups.
- Investigate the research on differentiated writing curriculums.
- Identify proven (best) practices in teaching reading, select at least three we will use, and, after use, compare results.
- Develop a unit of study to be taught in our classes that integrates three major areas of the curriculum and addresses the student needs we are targeting.

Example for completing top quadrants of study group action plan:

Category of student needs: Reading Comprehension

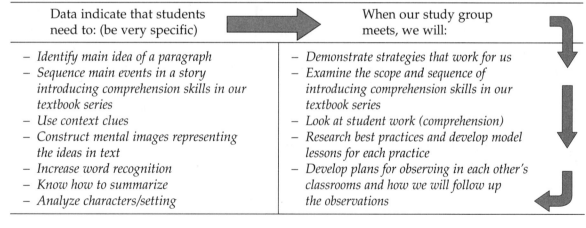

Data indicate that students need to: (be very specific)	When our study group meets, we will:
– *Identify main idea of a paragraph* – *Sequence main events in a story introducing comprehension skills in our textbook series* – *Use context clues* – *Construct mental images representing the ideas in text* – *Increase word recognition* – *Know how to summarize* – *Analyze characters/setting*	– *Demonstrate strategies that work for us* – *Examine the scope and sequence of introducing comprehension skills in our textbook series* – *Look at student work (comprehension)* – *Research best practices and develop model lessons for each practice* – *Develop plans for observing in each other's classrooms and how we will follow up the observations*

4. Write in the space in the middle of the action plan an **<u>essential question</u>** that captures what you want to investigate. This could be considered the problem to be solved. An essential question guides the work of a study group. The question should encompass the specific student needs listed on the plan. Members should be able to answer the questions by doing what is listed on the plan as actions the group will take when it meets. Examples of essential questions are

   - **Reading:** How can we teach students to comprehend what they read?
   - **Measurement:** How can we teach students to develop measurement skills in all content areas?
   - **Communication:** What do students need to know to communicate effectively?
   - **Problem solving:** How can we help students effectively use problem-solving skills and strategies? Or, how can we teach students to communicate their reasoning for arriving at a solution to a given problem?
   - **Writing:** How can we help students become better writers?
   - **English language arts:** How do we teach so that students' writing is well organized and thoroughly developed and reflects use of effective language?

The essential question is what gives the study group its focus. It is the problem that is to be solved. The study group will collect information to help answer the question. That information may come from books, articles, sharing among members, and guests/trainers invited to attend the meetings. Members will, over time, identify what they already know about the "problem," what they still need to know about it, and their understanding of the variables affecting the problem. The members will plan interventions, such as using new materials or existing materials in different ways and using new teaching strategies or modifying what they have been doing. Continuous assessments will tell the members whether the question has been answered.

5. Stop. You are now ready to form study groups!

Whole-Faculty

Study Groups™

WFSG
Decision-Making Cycle
Step 4–Part 2

Form Study Groups

The leader will ask for all of the individuals that chose a specific category (i.e., writing) to stand. Those standing will be asked to go to a designated room or to a designated area. The leader will do this for each of the categories the faculty formed. Once all the teachers who chose the same category are together, the following suggestions will facilitate the process of group organization.

1. Individuals in the same room or area are to share the individual plans that each developed.

2. Individuals may want to arrange themselves in a circle or in such an arrangement that everyone can see each other.

3. Individuals are to take turns reading
   - The essential question he/she wrote, and
   - Two specific student needs that he/she wrote

4. After all the plans have been shared, individuals will need to sub-group themselves according to the INDIVIDUAL plans that are most similar in terms of the essential questions and/or specific student needs written on the plans. Groups should be no smaller than three (3) and no larger than five (5).

5. One person in each group is to write the names of the members of the study group on a piece of paper that is to be given to the principal. At the top of the paper, write the CATEGORY of student needs that will be the focus of the study group.

6. When 1–5 have been done, everyone will reconvene in the large meeting area <u>to be dismissed or may</u> <u>be dismissed from the 'break-out' rooms.</u>

END of session with whole faculty.
Next event: 1st study group meetings

[Note: Using the 'Individual or Personalized Action Plan', each study group will develop <u>one</u> Study Group Action Plan which will be reflective of the individual plans of the members. This will be the first opportunity for the individuals in a group to reach consensus around a common task.]

Whole-Faculty

Study Groups™

WFSG
Decision-Making Cycle
Step 5

Developing Study Group Action Plans

This will be each study group's first meeting, usually a week or two after the whole faculty meeting when the whole faculty went through Steps 1 through 4 on the DMC.

Refer to "Checklist for First Three Study Group Meetings."

Members of the study group will have their individual or personalized action plans. Members will share the information on the plans and consolidate the information onto one study group action plan. This will be a consensus process, the first cooperative experience in the context of a WFSG.

If individuals did not complete the Resources section on the action plan, the group will need to discuss what the group will use for its work and for its "expert voice."

The last section (assessment) of the SGAP is where the group specifies how it will assess its work. The bottom of the action plan has five columns. Here is where members indicate what they want the students to be able to do <u>as a result of the study group's work.</u> Members need to go back to the student needs listed in the top left box of the SGAP. The student needs listed are the improvement targets. The five columns are completed as follows:

- **Column 1:** List the student needs listed in the top left box of the SGAP. Only two or three needs may be listed in the beginning, adding others when this portion of the plan is revised at 6-week intervals.
- **Column 2:** Use data sources that track current progress (i.e., teacher-made tests, teacher observations, 6-week averages, and textbook checklists). The cumulative impact of the formative assessments should be reflected in state tests; however, state tests are not given and results are not reported frequently enough to track ongoing progress.
- **Column 3:** For each need, write what data indicate is the current (baseline) status of the need.
- **Column 4:** For each need, write what you want data to indicate at the end of the study group's work. This is the targeted result. The date will be the same date as in column 5.

- **Column 5:** For each need, write what data actually show after 6 to 12 weeks of study group work. The date will be the same date as in column 4.
- **Columns 3, 4, and 5:** If percentages are used, it would be the percentage of students in all the members' classes. For example, if there are 75 students in three teachers' classes, 60% demonstrating the need to increase spelling accuracy would be 45 students.

EXAMPLE:

Specific Student Needs listed on action plan. *Students need to:*	Data Sources that document need <u>and</u> will be evidence of impact of group's work	Baseline— what data indicate when work begins on: DATE <u>9/10</u>	Target—what study group projects will be the results of the work on: DATE <u>11/01</u>	Actual— what data indicate **now** (complete every 6 to 12 weeks): DATE <u>11/01</u>
>Demonstrate ability to spell correctly	Spelling tests Written assignments	40% routinely spell correctly	60% will routinely spell correctly	55% are routinely spelling correctly
>Use correct grammar	6-week average Written assignments	60% made C or better	80% will make C or better	85% made C or better

WFSG
Decision-Making Cycle
Step 6

Implement Cycles of Action Research

By

- *Assessing specific needs listed on action plan*
- *Planning for instruction*
- *Acting on the plans*
- *Reflecting on student responses*

The action research cycles will consist of the following:

1. The group looks at classroom-based data around the essential question to establish baseline data for **THEIR** students.

   Question to ask: What is causing students difficulty in this area? Why? What are the problems students are having around this student need?

   Action to take: Focus on this need.

   Time: Part of a study group meeting.

2. The group reviews current research or information and describes practices that have been shown effective in addressing this need.

   Question to ask: What expert voices can we bring in to inform ourselves around this student need?

   Possible resources to use: Texts, Internet, experts, professional articles, etc.

   Action to take: Examine resources and identify best practices.

   Time: One meeting.

3. The group develops lessons that incorporate what was learned from the examination of effective practices and uses the strategies and materials in classrooms.

   Question to ask: What can we try in our classes to meet this student need?

   Action to take: Develop a lesson together or develop lessons separately; then, in the study group use a tuning protocol to revise plans before using them in class.

   Time: One meeting.

4. Individuals in the group bring student work from the classroom to assess the effectiveness of the classroom lessons/strategies.

   Question to ask: What effects did the work we did in our classes have on student learning?

   Action to take: Use a Wows and Wonders protocol to look at student work.

   Time: One meeting.

5. The group looks at classroom-based data around the essential question to determine (1) if the targeted student need has been met; (2) if you are ready to move on to another student need; or (3) if you need to continue your focus on this student need.

   Time: Part of a meeting.

6. Begin the cycle again—either for a new need or for your current need.

One cycle would take approximately four study group meetings to complete, or approximately 1 month for study groups that meet weekly for 1 hour or every other week for approximately 2 hours.

Whole-Faculty

Study Groups™

WFSG
Decision-Making Cycle
Step 7

Assessment of WFSG Work

The assessment of the work of WFSGs is **Step 7 of the Decision-Making Cycle:** *Whole faculty assesses the impact of study groups on student learning.* To do this, the study group returns to what members indicated on the chart at the bottom of the SGAP and the duplicate charts completed during the year. One form used is titled "Assessment of WFSG Work."

<u>Specific</u> **Student Needs** listed on action plan. *Students need to:*	**Data Sources** that document need <u>and</u> are evidence of impact of group's work	**Baseline—** what data indicate when work began in **Aug./Sept.**	**Target—**what study group projected would be the results of the work in **May**	**Actual—** what data indicate **now May** _____

Column 1: List two or three of the SPECIFIC student needs on the SGAP.
Column 2: List data sources you used to track progress (i.e., teacher-made tests, teacher observations, 6-week averages, textbook checklists, and benchmark tests).
Column 3: What the data indicated when you began meeting (Aug.–Oct.)
Column 4: What you wanted the data to indicate at the end of the year.
Column 5: What the data indicate at the end of the year.
Columns 3, 4, and 5: If percentages are used, it would be the percentage of students in all the members' classes. For example, if there are 75 students in three teachers' classes, 60% demonstrating the need to increase spelling accuracy would be 45 students.

Other assessment forms are in Resource A.

Resource C

WSFG Rubric

Resource C: WSFG RUBRIC

Not Yet	Beginning Implementation	Developing Implementation	Advanced Implementation
• Members disregard, resent, or do not receive feedback from the principal.	• Members review principal's feedback with no action.	• Members discuss and follow up on principal's suggestions.	• Members often refer to principal's helpfulness and invite him or her to meetings.
• Members do not use feedback given to the group by the principal and/or instructional council.	• Members pose few questions for feedback and are unsure what to do with the feedback received.	• Members appreciate the feedback the group receives, sometimes acting on it, sometimes not.	• Members engage in a rich dialogue with those giving the group feedback.
• SGAPs and logs are not posted or have a number of logs missing.	• SGAPs and logs are posted but not immediately upon completion; members often have to be reminded.	• SGAPs and all of the group's logs are posted in a timely manner.	• Items are promptly posted; members show evidence of reviewing and using the feedback from other groups.
• Members show no awareness of and no interest in what other study groups are doing.	• Members indicate some interest in learning about what others are doing.	• There is evidence in logs that the study group is discussing the workt of other groups.	• Members frequently seek out and use work from other study groups at the school.
• Members do not show evidence of their willingness to be vulnerable within the group.	• Members are hesitant but will share what is not working.	• Members accept suggestions and share the results of the revisions.	• Members are genuinely open with one another about their strengths and weaknesses.
• Members rarely, if ever, buy in and commit to decisions.	• Members feign agreement during meetings.	• Members are cautious but show willingness to confront and be confronted on expected behaviors and actions.	• Members openly call each other on behaviors and actions that are not consistent with agreed on behaviors and actions.

(Continued)

Not Yet	Beginning Implementation	Developing Implementation	Advanced Implementation
• Individuals do not connect their work to others in the group.	• Members connect to each other but not to whole school improvement.	• Members talk about whole school improvement but show no evidence of tying their work to SIP.	• Members continually refer to SIP and their role in meeting schoolwide goals.
• Members are not focused on improving student performance in specific learning needs for their current students.	• Members are easily distracted and express doubt that results are possible.	• Members refer to data and express concern and desire to attain results.	• Data are always on the table in some form, and members hold themselves accountable for attaining results.
• Members have no interest in observing in each other's classrooms.	• Members have invited other members to observe in their classrooms but no action.	• Members are observing in each other's classrooms but not debriefing within the group.	• Members routinely observe in each other's classrooms and pre- and postconference within the group.
• Members are focused on teacher needs, not on student needs.	• Although student needs guide the group's work, considerable time is spent on hearing opinions of group members.	• Members use classroom data to understand student learning needs and research strategies to try. They spend little energy rehashing opinions.	• Members are focused on the learning needs of the students in their classrooms and engage in cycles of action research in their group.
• Members are trying to figure out what a study group does. The mechanics of the group take a significant amount of time.	• Members have established a routine for their meetings, but mastering the process guidelines gets in the way of the work. Members primarily "share"; this is the most frequently used verb in logs.	• Members are focused on their work and comfortably follow the process guidelines. They examine key issues deeply and incorporate expert voices into their work.	• Members find the work of the group rigorous, stimulating, and directly connected to their students' learning. Members assess the impact of their work and make deliberate efforts to coordinate with other groups.

(Continued)

Not Yet	Beginning Implementation	Developing Implementation	Advanced Implementation
• Members only address what is in their comfort zone and what is of interest to them.	• Members identify key issues related to student learning needs and their teaching but only skim the surface.	• Members work together to learn and experiment with best practices, actively engaging their students in work emanating from their study group.	• Members examine key issues deeply and challenge each other's assumptions, evaluating all input for its value and usability.
• Looking at student work (LASW) using a protocol is seldom, if ever, done.	• Members share examples of their best students' work after the lesson is completed.	• Members share examples of a range of student work, discussing how to improve it.	• LASW together with using protocols is the heart of group work. It is used routinely on varying levels and content.
• Members rely on what they already know.	• Members bring some types of literature into the meetings, only discussing material superficially.	• External content "experts" are invited to group meetings, but members do not hold each other accountable for using the expert knowledge.	• Members actively seek multiple sources to push themselves to higher levels of understanding of academic content and effective pedagogy.
• Logs indicate that members spend a lot of time on administrative and managerial issues.	• Members focus on designing instructional projects for others to implement.	• The focus is on improving teaching but not on improving student learning.	• Members have internalized: "What do students need for us to do?"
• Members do not focus on any of the school's current instructional initiatives.	• Members refer to new programs at the school in the study group action plan or logs, but there is no deliberate effort to connect the initiatives to the study group's work.	• Members are committed to using new materials and strategies from the school's current instructional initiatives appropriately in classrooms.	• Members are focusing on the integration of new programs with existing programs for coherence and assimilation.

(Continued)

Not Yet	Beginning Implementation	Developing Implementation	Advanced Implementation
• Members share lessons they developed in the past and tell about their classrooms.	• Members develop lessons separately and sometimes share what they are going to do or have done.	• Members develop lessons separately but with input from the group and share classroom results.	• Joint work is the norm, working on the development of all lesson components together, demonstrating, and debriefing results together.
• The same person leads the group each time it meets.	• Leadership is rotated.	• Leadership is rotated, and group members feel comfortable with this.	• Each member willingly takes his/her turn leading the group.
• The group has not agreed on a set of norms.	• Norms are written but not honored.	• Group norms are written and mostly honored.	• All feel responsible for the success of the group and hold each accountable to the group's norms.
• The action plan is not complete and/or recommended revisions have not been made.	• The action plan is complete. Occasionally, the group reviews it and makes minor revisions.	• The action plan is complete and is revised, adding and deleting as work progresses.	• The action plan is complete and often referred to during meetings, is a living document, and is kept in front of the group at all times.
• Logs are not turned in, not complete, or do not accurately describe what the group did.	• Logs are turned in, but group members do not use them as a point of reference for future work.	• Logs are helpful reminders of the work of the group.	• Logs tell a rich story of dialogue and action around student learning.

(Continued)

Not Yet	Beginning Implementation	Developing Implementation	Advanced Implementation
• The group does not LASW or reflect on their own learning and teaching.	• LASW is occasional. Reflection on learning and teaching is practiced as debriefing.	• LASW is routine but does not generate reflection on practice.	• LASW is the basis of reflection on learning and teaching and guides actions.
• There is no instructional council (IC) for members to attend.	• The same member of the study group attends every meeting of the IC.	• Members rotate attending IC, but little, if any, time is spent sharing what took place.	• Members rotate attending the IC, discuss and use information from the IC, and tie what the IC is doing to what other groups are doing.
• Group size is not within the guidelines.	• Group size is five or fewer, but one member dominates.	• Group size is five or fewer, but several members are not fully engaged.	• Group size is five or fewer, and all members are fully engaged.
• The group meets once a month.	• The group meets every other week for 1 hour.	• The group meets three times a month for 1 hour.	• The group meets weekly for at least 1 hour.
• There is a hierarchy within the group.	• Some members have more influence than others.	• Equality is on the surface but not always evident.	• Equality is evident in all behaviors and actions.
• The group uses annual district and state assessments to measure changes in student performance on their student learning needs.	• Some members use a classroom assessment to assess student results at the end of the year on the study group's chosen student learning needs.	• The group uses a common classroom assessment to collect baseline data and assess student results at the end of the year on the group's chosen student learning needs.	• The study group uses a common classroom assessment to collect baseline data, monitor student progress every 6 to 12 weeks, and assess results at the end of the year on the study group's chosen student learning needs.

Resource D

Clarke Middle School

Documents and Artifacts From

Clarke Middle School
Athens, GA
Clarke County (GA) School District

Lewis Holloway, Superintendent
Jose Boza, Assistant Superintendent for Instruction
Kenneth Sherman, Principal
Kim Reynolds-Manglitz, Instructional Lead Teacher

The documents included in this section have been modified and revised to fit the purpose of this section. Some of the logs have been reduced, meaning some sections were deleted, so that the material fits on one page.

Clarke Middle School
Athens, GA
Whole-Faculty Study Groups
Schedule for Early Release
2003–2004

1. There will be 12 early release days. (See schedule below.) We will bank 24 hours during 168 regular days. This works out to 24 hours × 60 minutes = 1,440 minutes to recoup divided by 168 days = approximately 8 minutes per day to add to the regular schedule. On our regular days, therefore, our core classes need to total 308 minutes.

2. We are combining the CNN-TV/current events and silent reading time back into the core classes.

3. Periods are now 55 minutes each × 5 core periods = 275 minutes, + 33 minutes reading/study/homework/tutoring during lunch = 308 minutes.

On early release days, the students will be dismissed at 1:30. WFSG will begin at 2:00 and end at 4:00, the end of a regular teacher day. The early release days are 9/9, 9/23, 10/28, 11/11, 11/18, 12/9, 1/13, 1/27, 2/10, 2/24, 3/16, and 4/13.

The districtwide teacher planning dates are 10/13, 12/19, 1/5, 2/17, and 4/26. WFSG will meet for 2 hours on each of these dates.

This schedule will allow study groups to meet for a total of 34 hours for the school year.

Daily schedule:

Homeroom (nonacademic)	8:15–8:25
Period 1	8:25–9:20
Period 2	9:20–10:15
Period 3	10:15–11:10
Period 4	11:10–12:05 (22 minutes 6th grade lunch, 33 minutes academic)
Period 5	12:05–1:00 (22 minutes 7th grade lunch, 33 minutes academic)
Period 6	1:00–1:55 (22 minutes 8th grade lunch, 33 minutes academic)
Period 7	1:55–2:50
Period 8	2:50–3:45

Schedule on early release days:

Homeroom (nonacademic)	8:15–8:25
Period 1	8:25–9:03
Period 2	9:03–9:41
Period 3	9:41–10:19
Period 4	10:19–10:57
Period 5	10:57–11:35 (6th grade lunch, 23 minutes lunch, 15 minutes academic)
Period 6	11:35–12:13 (7th grade lunch, 23 minutes lunch, 15 minutes academic)
Period 7	12:13–12:51 (8th grade lunch, 23 minutes lunch, 15 minutes academic)
Period 8	12:51–1:30

WFSG   2:00–4:00

Dr. Ken Sherman, Principal
Clarke Middle School
shermank@clarke.k12.ga.us
(706) 543-6547

Clarke
Middle
School

Study Group Action Plan
Date: 9/23/03 (reflects revisions on 12/19/03) Group Members: Peggy (8th Sc.), Ann (6–8 Tech), Laura Lee (6–8 Art), Amber (6–8 Orchestra), Jeff Hale (7th SST), Jennifer (6th Reading/LGA)

What is the general category of student needs the group will address? (mark appropriate area below)
__Reading __Writing __Math __Assessment __Science __Social Studies Other: **Higher Order Thinking Skills**

Data indicate that students need to:	When our study group meets we will:

1. Demonstrate problem-solving skills, including
  – compare/contrast
  – synthesizing
  – applying knowledge to new situations
  – listening for details
  – hypothesizing
  – using vocabulary prompts
	• Research problem-solving strategies
	• Examine resources within the school
	• Interview students about how strategies and rubric helped or did not help to improve problem solving.
	• Collect problem-solving strategies used in all disciplines.
	• Examine student work using protocols
	• Develop model lessons
	• Demonstrate/practice strategies

Essential Question: How can we help students to effectively use problem-solving skills and strategies and clearly communicate their reasoning with others?

Our resources are:	Our norms are:
Bloom's Taxonomy www.coun.uvic.ca/ Future Problem Solving materials www.glc.k12.ga.us Rubistar Various Web sites for higher-order thinking skills related to art, music, and other disciplines	1. Be punctual 2. Be prepared 3. Be productive 4. Be respectful

We ASSESS to determine what evidence there is that the targeted student needs have improved.

Students need to: (from above list)	Current (baseline) status of need at beginning of study group's work	Targeted results—what we want data to indicate at the end of the study group's work	What data sources will provide evidence of improvement?
Compare and contrast Vocabulary prompts Hypothesizing Apply knowledge to new situations	50% or less of our students use effective problem-solving skills in all disciplines	At least 80% of our students will demonstrate they use effective strategies	Classwork, projects, student and teacher interviews, surveys, problem-solving rubrics, classroom observations

Clarke Middle School

Whole-Faculty Study Group Log

Date: 9/23/03 (2:00–4:00)   Log: #1
Group Name: Higher-Order Thinking Skills
Today's Leader:
Members Present: Peggy, Jennifer, Laura Lee, Jeff, Amber, Ann

What happened today? Brief summary of discussion and activities. Keep artifacts in notebook.
We established our norms: Be punctual, Be prepared, Be productive, Be respectful.   We established leadership rotation: Ann, Laura Lee, Amber, Jennifer, Jeff, Peggy   Representation at IC meetings: Laura Lee—December   Amber—February   Jennifer—March   Ann—April   Laura Lee—May   We shared our "individual" action plans and started working on the group's action plan.
What major implication does what you did today have for your classroom practice?
Did you examine student work today?   Who brought work to share?

General comments, such as: what you are ready to share; IC meeting, etc.	What concerns or questions do you have for leaders or what do you want them to know?

Next Meeting (agenda items, work to prepare):
Continue to discuss action plan and assessments we will use to assess students.

Next Meeting Date: Time/Location: 2:00–4:00   Room 28—Jeff's   Leader: Ann

Clarke Middle School

Whole-Faculty Study Group Log
Date: October 13, 2003 (2:00–4:00)   Log: #2
Group Name: Higher-Order Thinking Skills
Today's Leader: Ann
Members Present: Ann, Amber, Laura Lee, Jennifer, Jeff, Peggy

What happened today? Brief summary of discussion and activities. Keep artifacts in notebook.
Discussion of action plan: Ken's feedback was discussed. Three suggestions: pare down the student needs we have identified to two or three. (We've done that.) Consider how HOTS applies to all academic levels.
How will we assess progress in this less well-defined form? Kim has told us that we don't have to tie in *directly* to CRCT, but find a way to assess, then plan on this effecting CRCT scores indirectly.
Assessment: Ann suggested we use the computer and find a Bloom's Taxonomy concept map.
Laura Lee: Do a simple assessment. Start with a "Compare and Contrast" lesson for example. Make sure kids master that before moving on to other higher-order thinking skills.
Laura Lee has a critique worksheet that she showed the group relating to artwork.
Ann will e-mail each group member a concept map.
Discussion of Student Needs:
Peggy Bailey shared data from the last WFSG leader meeting.
Create baseline of scores for students on higher-order thinking skills. Do a compare/contrast activity through science and social studies as a schoolwide warm-up. We could score it and use it as a baseline. We're going to do this through our science/social studies classes per grade to begin with. We will start with a pretest on compare and contrast and run it.
What major implication does what you did today have for your classroom practice?
We will create a baseline of scores for students on higher-order thinking skills through science and social studies classes per grade.
Did you examine student work today? No   Who brought work to share?

General comments, such as: what you are ready to share; IC meeting, etc.	What concerns or questions do you have for leaders or what do you want them to know?

Next Meeting (agenda items, work to prepare):
Write the pretest and organize how it will be used. Jeff and Peggy will do this.
Others: Look for rubrics for higher-order thinking skills. Amber, Jennifer, Ann, and Laura Lee
Next Meeting Date: 10/28/03   Time/Location: 2:00–4:00   Room 34   Leader: Laura Lee

Clarke Middle School

Whole-Faculty Study Group Log
Date: 10/28 (2:00–4:00) Log: #3
Group Name: Higher-Order Thinking Skills
Today's Leader:
Members Present: Ann, Amber, Laura Lee, Jennifer, Jeff

What happened today? Brief summary of discussion and activities. Keep artifacts in notebook.
Today all of the study groups met together in the media center. We had two WFSG consultants who demonstrated how to use protocols to look at student work. Study groups sat together so our group had an opportunity to discuss the protocols as we used them. First, the whole faculty practiced the Wows and Wonders using the same piece of student work that the consultants provided. One of the consultants was the presenting teacher, and the other was the facilitator. We did the same thing with the Descriptive Consultancy Protocol.

Laura Lee and Peggy will bring student work to our next meeting.

Also, we are going to meet early one day next week to look at the pretests that Jeff and Peggy have developed. Ann, Amber, Jennifer, and Laura Lee are still looking for rubrics for higher-order thinking skills. |
| What major implication does what you did today have for your classroom practice? |
| As we learn how to use the protocols effectively, we expect to get ideas for how to make our lessons better. |
| Did you examine student work today? Yes
Who brought work to share? The consultants |

General comments, such as: what you are ready to share; IC meeting, etc.	What concerns or questions do you have for leaders or what do you want them to know?

Next Meeting (agenda items, work to prepare):
Laura Lee and Peggy will bring student work.
Next Meeting Date: 11/11   Time/Location: 2:00–4:00   Room 28—Jeff's   Leader: Laura Lee

Clarke
Middle
School

Whole-Faculty Study Group Log
Date: 11/11/03 (2:00–4:00) Log: #4
Group Name: Higher-Order Thinking Skills
Today's Leader: Laura Lee
Members Present: Jennifer, Jeff, Amber, Ann, Laura Lee, Peggy

What happened today? Brief summary of discussion and activities. Keep artifacts in notebook.

1. Will the student work protocols apply to the student work that Peggy brought? Dilemma: Students' inability to respond to questions that require them to apply previous knowledge and synthesize information. Yes, Descriptive Consultancy Protocol.

2. Examined student's still life artwork brought by Laura Lee, Wows and Wonders Protocol. Student demonstrates lack of motivation as well as an inability to understand the concepts inherent in still life drawing. Student is very low and his work is far below expectations and the norm. This worked extremely well as we were able to give positive feedback and workable solutions to LL. Scaffolding techniques, smaller assignments up front, and other suggestions were offered.

3. Examined Peggy's issue/dilemma using Descriptive Consultancy Protocol. Students presented on interplanetary life that they created through answers to a series of questions. The teacher then asked questions about their created life-forms. The students were "frozen in the headlights" and unable to construct logical, coherent responses when asked new questions for which they were not specifically prepared. Dilemma: how to teach the skill of synthesizing information/knowledge and apply it to a new situation on the spot.

   Good solutions included: prep in pairs with questions on note cards; videotaping good answers to show how the process works for next time; if frozen, let them sit down for 1 minute while the pair and the class come up with an answer; have them extend by adding three of their own questions. . . . Also, the next time, students will know what to expect and how to prepare (i.e., it'll go better!).

   It is clear that HOTS is genuinely trying to make the protocols work and solved problems today. Cool feedback is extremely constructive, and the group is developing a comfort level with the process of examining student work. We like how we can be open and honest—and respectful of each other.

What major implication does what you did today have for your classroom practice?

Laura Lee: "I will now use the input given to go on to the next step with my student, using the viewfinder (teacher's) to provide another opportunity to improve."

Peggy: "I've recorded all of the very helpful suggestions and will use them next time I do this. I will also regularly practice giving students 'out of the box' questions."

Did you examine student work today? Yes
Who brought work to share? Laura Lee, Peggy

Next Meeting (agenda items, work to prepare): Bring Future Problem Solving model to discuss ways to use it in classrooms. One person who has not presented student work will do so.
Please forward other agenda items to Amber for 11/18.
Next Meeting Date: 11/25   Time/Location: 2:00–4:00   Peggy's room   Leader: Amber

Clarke Middle School

Whole-Faculty Study Group Log
Date: 11/25/03 (2:00-4:00) Log: #5
Group Name: Higher-Order Thinking Skills
Today's Leader: Amber
Members Present: Peggy, Jennifer, Laura Lee, Jeff, Amber, Ann

What happened today? Brief summary of discussion and activities. Keep artifacts in notebook.

1. Both Amber and Jeff brought student work to share. Laura Lee brought information and hand-outs about Future Problem Solving.
2. The group decided to examine one piece of student work (Amber's) to have time to also look at the FPS information that Laura Lee brought.
3. We used the Wows and Wonders protocol to examine the student work. Amber explained how the lesson connected to her GTEP goals. In this lesson, students were to listen to musical selections from two composers (twice each) in order to compare and contrast them. After listening to the two pieces the first time, students were to jot down similarities and differences between the two selections. They had 5 minutes to do this. Then, they were provided with suggestions about specifically what to listen for. They listened again to the two selections. Then they were given an opportunity to embellish what they had written down the first time. Again, they had 5 minutes to do this. One requirement for their work was that the end product had to be written in complete sentences.

   Positive feedback as well as suggestions were provided. Example: "Using compare/contrast is a great way to have students use HOTS." "The format of this activity (students listen, then write; then listen again for specifics, and then write again) provides a wonderful way to actively engage students."
4. After examining Amber's student's work, a question arose: Is this what we, as a group, are supposed to be doing from now on? We decided that we need to continue to look at student work.
5. We briefly looked at the two Future Problem Solving handouts that Laura Lee brought. She suggested that we think about how we can use it in each of our disciplines.
6. Concern: How can we introduce HOTS to the faculty so that they will regularly incorporate HOTS into their teaching. Some teachers feel that with so many students that need basic skills, there is no time to do HOTS.
7. Concern: Again, what data sources will provide evidence of improvement in HOTS?

Classroom Application: What evidence do you have that students are learning more and have a deeper understanding of the content?

The student work that we examined showed that this student was able to compare and contrast the two musical selections. Compare/contrast activities provide students with the opportunity to use HOTS. The activity that Amber used in her class is easily adaptable to other disciplines. (In fact, Amber credited Laura Lee with this adaptation based on what Laura Lee shared the last time we met.)

Laura Lee will attend the next instructional committee meeting.	1. Laura Lee said that she would speak directly with Dr. Sherman in order to determine what he actually wants from us regarding revisiting our action plan (based on most recent e-mail feedback).

Next meeting (agenda items, work to prepare):

Review action plan and Dr. Sherman's feedback.

Read over the Future Problem Solving handout that Laura Lee provided.

Next Meeting Date: 12/9   Time/Location: 2:00–4:00   Peggy's room   Leader: Jennifer

Clarke
Middle
School

Whole-Faculty Study Group Log
Date: 12/9/03 (2:00–4:00)   Log: #6
Group Name: Higher-Order Thinking Skills
Today's Leader: Jennifer
Members Present: Ann, Amber, Laura Lee, Jennifer, Jeff, Peggy

What happened today? Brief summary of discussion and activities. Keep artifacts in notebook.

Our agenda today was to revisit our action plan and to talk about our midyear report.

We looked at Ken's and Kim's feedback and reflected over what we have done and the direction we are headed. We refined our purpose, as suggested by Ken. We also came up with more ideas about how to share higher-order thinking skills with the faculty. We are going to ask fellow teachers in the building if they are willing to collaborate in developing and using a higher-order thinking lesson plan they could use in their classroom. We will identify a strategy, use the strategy ourselves, and then share what works with a colleague not in our study group. This will be a one-on-one sharing rather than sharing with the whole faculty in a presentation.

Did you examine student work today? No
Who brought work to share?

General comments, such as: what you are ready to share; IC meeting, etc.	What concerns or questions do you have for leaders or what do you want them to know?
We will share our idea for one-on-one sharing—purpose: to facilitate HOTS into daily teaching at Clarke Middle School so more students will benefit from what we discover.	We have made some changes on our action plan—we'll look forward to Ken's feedback.

Next Meeting (agenda items, work to prepare):

By next meeting, we will all approach another teacher (preferably a newer teacher who might need some support in this area) for our HOTS lesson collaboration project. We will bring our lesson plans and share what is working. We'll also research and discuss lesson plans.

Next Meeting Date: 12/19   Time/Location: 2:00–4:00   Room 28   Leader: Jeff

Clarke Middle School
Date: 12/19   Log: #7
WFSG Midyear Status Check (e-mail to CMS All)
Going around the table, each member completes (orally) a sentence stem.

1. **In our study group, we started**
   - becoming more comfortable within our group in sharing ideas.
   - using various protocols to look at student work.
   - looking for ways to help other teachers incorporate HOTS within their lesson plans.
   - building a professional relationship with each other within the group.
   - reevaluating our action plan and became more focused.

2. **The greatest challenge we face is**
   - motivating other teachers to use what we offer.
   - figuring out ways to interact with teachers in ways that will be engaging and helpful.
   - facing the challenge of finding a way to incorporate HOTS into lesson plans that will be used with slower learners.
   - finding strategies that work.
   - finding concrete ways to measure student improvement in problem solving.

3. **As far as student changes, we see** increased opportunities for all students to be involved in HOTS.

4. **It's encouraging to**
   - see other teachers actually want to help us out.
   - see the school working together so well to improve student learning.
   - see the administration and support staff providing feedback.
   - be in a room with other teachers, sharing and learning in a professional manner.

5. **Our group seems to be making the most progress in**
   a. Effectively evaluating student work.
   b. Accepting positive feedback from one another.
   c. Being able to communicate ideas with one another.

Use your responses to these questions to write a paragraph or so describing the overall impact of study groups on teaching (lesson planning, instructional practices, classroom management) and learning in our school.

Our group started with many broad ideas on incorporating higher-order thinking skills into the classroom. We will continue focusing on HOTS for our students but have an idea for how we can also help other teachers incorporate creative, open-ended lessons into their regular lesson plans. Facing the challenge of finding teachers who would be willing to try our ideas, **we set a goal to each ask another teacher outside of our group to work with us.** We would provide a HOTS lesson for those teachers to use in the classroom that would relate to their QCCs. We predicted that new teachers would be the most in need of new ideas. We've had at least four teachers immediately respond. This is so exciting! Our next challenge will be to provide a specific lesson plan for these four teachers and to find a way to evaluate the end result as concretely as possible. Our goal is to provide these four teachers a lesson plan to use by February 2004. The sessions with each of the four teachers will be **in addition to our study group meetings** because these teachers have their own study groups and can't miss those meetings. We are going to call these sessions **EXTREME MAKEOVERS**; actually, Extreme "HOTS" Makeovers. <u>How we will do this is on a separate page.</u>

We find that the professionalism and positive attitude of our group, combined with the support and input of Ken Sherman and Kim Reynolds-Manglitz, have encouraged us continuously in this new process. We like our group, we like what we are doing, and we feel that we genuinely have a chance to make a difference in our students' work using this program. Finally, we've also set a more subtle goal—to be positive leaders and advocates of this WFSG program.

Clarke Middle School, Athens, GA
Attachment to WFSG Log #7
Extreme "HOTS" Makeovers

Imagine a beginning cook trying to decide whether to fix instant macaroni and cheese versus homemade lasagna. One plan is much easier, and a beginner feels that he or she has the best chance of success by keeping it simple. The other takes far more time and effort, but the results are well worth it. But what if you could have the best of both . . . have the dinner catered (at no cost) <u>and</u> receive help from the experts on how to cook? That's the idea behind HOTS makeovers.

Lesson plans that include the higher-level thinking skills are sometimes harder to find and implement, particularly for teachers who have taught less than 3 years. These lessons, though oftentimes the most meaningful, fun, and rewarding, can be overwhelming to plan. We are offering lesson plans using higher-order thinking skills for other teachers at CMS. Here's how it works: We will

- Put out an "all call" inviting any teacher to respond if they would be interested in having HOTS lesson plans that cater to an upcoming lesson based on Georgia's QCCs.
- Visit personally with a few teachers and ask if they might be interested. Our goal is to provide lessons to six teachers during this school year.
- Explain that the HOTS study group will provide lesson plans for at least 7 days that will support the teacher's chosen objective/topic. In return, we ask that the makeover teacher give a pre- and postevaluation to students on that lesson and then share the results with us. Teachers contact us if interested.
- Select and notify the teachers.
- Conduct research. Lesson plans can come from a variety of sources, including within our own group and from other teachers. The Internet is our most effective tool. We will read through, sort, and select the best lesson plans we can find that emphasize higher-level thinking skills. We will e-mail or make copies of the best ideas, sending them to the teachers to review before we meet with them.
- Become very familiar with the lesson plan each of us will present.
- Establish dates for the makeover days and notify "winners" of their appointments.
- Prepare the room for the makeover. (Just as an aside, we provide a tablecloth, flowers, cookies, and soft drinks. Our goal is also to make our teachers feel appreciated.)
- During a session, each HOTS study group member presents a lesson plan to the teacher, along with suggestions and ideas from the group on how to best implement it. This may take more than one meeting.
- Send to all CMS teachers via e-mail the lessons for the selected teachers.
- Check in with the selected teacher prior to the time the lesson is to be taught to see if assistance is needed.
- Review the results of pretests and posttests from the lessons we share.
- Evaluate overall results.

Clarke Middle School

Whole-Faculty Study Group Log
Date: 1/13/04 (2:00–4:00) Log: #9 Group Name: Higher-Order Thinking Skills Today's Leader: Jeff Members Present: Jeff, Laura Lee, Amber, Peggy, Jennifer

What happened today? Brief summary of discussion and activities. Keep artifacts in notebook.

We worked on researching HOTS lessons. We found eight or nine lesson plans on the Web—all higher-level thinking skills lessons that tie in to recycling and are in alignment with GA QCCs. This took most of our time, but we found some really good material. We will all use one or more of the ideas over the next 2 weeks.

What major implication does what you did today have for your classroom practice?

We will make the lesson plans collected available for any teacher doing lessons on recycling who wants some higher-level thinking skill activities.

Did you examine student work today? No
Who brought work to share?

General comments, such as: what you are ready to share; IC meeting, etc.	What concerns or questions do you have for leaders or what do you want them to know?
Amber will attend the Feb. 3 meeting.	

Next Meeting (agenda items, work to prepare):

Each of us will have paperwork and summary of a lesson and be ready to suggest helpful hints in implementing it.

Next Meeting Date: 1/27/04   Time/Location: 2:00–4:00   Room 28—Jeff's   Leader: Peggy

Clarke
Middle
School

Whole-Faculty Study Group Log

Date: 1/27/04 (2:00–4:00) Log: # 10
Group Name: Higher-Order Thinking Skills
Today's Leader: Peggy
Members Present: Jeff, Laura Lee, Jennifer, Amber, Ann

What happened today? Brief summary of discussion and activities. Keep artifacts in notebook.

We shared higher-level thinking skill lesson plans on recycling and demonstrated activities:

Jeff: Waste Disposal—incorporates many disciplines into the lesson, including mathematics and family and consumer sciences. Using cooperative thinking skills, students work together to figure out the word problems based on waste disposal. Jeff brought us back to the low CRCT scores related to math and problem solving. This lesson encourages students to learn from each other. This is a flexible lesson that could last an entire class period or less. Easy to relate to the real world and kids' lives.

Ann: "Attitudes Affect Waste"—students have to gather information by conducting a poll about what kind of products people buy, reusable or not. Students have to come up with a hypothesis and, after conducting research, see if they are correct or not. The class is developing a survey.

Peggy: "Garbage Galore"—fun lesson covering the QCC for 8th grade specifically. **Meets math, Georgia studies, and science QCCs.** Point of lesson is to get students to think about trash and recycling. Used Dr. Seuss's book, *The Cat in the Hat Comes Back.* The book provokes critical thinking about solid waste. Also incorporates guessing game about solid waste. The lesson pushes higher-level thinking skills by asking hypothesis-like questions. Students will also participate in collecting trash and exploring what we waste or throw away each day (weigh waste).

Laura Lee: "Make Your Own Paper"—recycling using paper materials—gives students hands-on experience and gets them excited. She will be working on this throughout the semester. Students are excited and motivated. They will begin collecting paper and T-shirts. Focus will be on introducing new knowledge and comprehension skills and then move to make the paper. Students use higher-order thinking skills as students compare and contrast the paper that they make.

Jennifer: "How Long Does Trash Last"—students work in cooperative learning groups to figure out how long certain trash items last. She brought in items such as a banana, wool sock, Styrofoam cup, etc. Students discussed together how long they believe the items last in a landfill. For example, students will learn that a tin can will last 80 to 100 years.

Amber: "Why Packaging?"—students are becoming aware of packaging and considerations necessary in packaging design. What role does music "play" in packaging? What tunes make you remember a product? How do tunes attract you to a product? Is packaging always recyclable?

What major implication does what you did today have for your classroom practice?

We have demonstrated that regardless of the content area we teach, all of us can identify a generic topic (recycling) and incorporate higher-order thinking skills related to that topic into our content areas: science, social studies, math, art, music, technology. The questions students are asking indicate that they are concerned about the environment and the issue raised by waste materials.

Next Meeting (agenda items, work to prepare):

As a group, we will be researching HOTS lesson plans for Jeff.

Next Meeting Date: 2/10/04 Time/Location: 2:00–4:00 Peggy's cozy trailer Leader: Ann

Clarke Middle School

	Whole-Faculty Study Group Log Date: 2/17/04 (2:00–4:00) Log: #12 Group Name: Higher-Order Thinking Skills Today's Leader: Laura Lee Members Present: Jeff, Peggy, Jennifer, Amber, Ann

What happened today? Brief summary of discussion and activities. Keep artifacts in notebook.

We looked at the student work that Jeff brought. He had asked students to write a few sentences defining "transatlantic." Then, they were to get with one other student, compare and contrast definitions, and rewrite one definition representing the two students. After 10 minutes, they were to form triads and repeat the process. Students could not have anyone in the triad who had been in the same duos. We looked at a sample from one student, from a duo, and from a triad. We did not use a protocol.

During the second hour of our meeting, we discussed the WFSG rubric. Each member had previously read over the rubric and had made decisions about our group's progress. We shared and compared ideas and came up with a consensus about what we believed about our group and **what we could do to improve.** We looked at the "not yet" column to determine this. We agreed to show more interest in other groups by reading their logs and to discuss them in our meetings. Ann suggested that because of time constraints, we each look at one other log and each discuss those logs at the beginning of each meeting.

We were not aware that we were supposed to be observing each other's classrooms, and we will make an effort to begin doing this in the future, possibly when our HOTS lesson plans are being implemented.

Our greatest success to date: Jeff said that we have developed a good rapport within our group and a good relationship among group members. We all feel comfortable sharing and discussing issues of concern.

Specific initiatives for school improvement: We looked at the "emerging ideas and issues bank" to see what other groups are doing to see how each idea pertained to our group. We discussed providing a vocabulary template from the "Bloom's Taxonomy" as another way to incorporate HOTS into the classrooms at CMS. We also discussed how our lesson plan consultation will seek to improve upon differentiation by ensuring that the higher-order thinking activity is appropriate for all students.

Did you examine student work today? Yes
Who brought work to share? Jeff

General comments, such as: what you are ready to share; IC meeting, etc.	What concerns or questions do you have for leaders or what do you want them to know?
We don't want to burden anyone further, nor do we want the burden ourselves, but think that maybe people would read other groups' logs if everything was condensed to one e-mail with a summary of the high points in all logs instead of trying to read everyone else's logs with everything else teachers have to do.	Will we keep our same groups next year? We still have a lot to do.

Next Meeting (agenda items, work to prepare):
Amber will bring student work.

Next Meeting Date: 3/16/04   Time/Location: 2:00–4:00   Wherever there is heat   Leader: Amber

Clarke Middle School

Whole-Faculty Study Group Log
Date: 03/16/04 (2:00–4:00)   Log: #13 Group Name: Higher-Order Thinking Skills Today's Leader: Amber Members Present: Jennifer, Jeff, Ann, Laura Lee, Peggy

What happened today? Brief summary of discussion and activities. Keep artifacts in notebook.

1. Discussion of the last IC meeting and our idea of providing HOTS words to each teacher that might appear on an exam. This vocabulary template (e.g., compare and contrast, etc.) could be posted and might help students with tests and prompt teachers to use these concepts in their practice.

2. Group presentation of other slavery lessons/resources for Jeff. Assistance provided in extending lessons using HOTS.

3. Ideas bank suggestions: We will research terms for the HOTS vocabulary template. We will create a document on 4/26 to be posted in classrooms and ask the office to copy on colored paper and distribute. We will include an explanation of this template for teachers.

4. Down the road, we might assemble a "Teacher Reflection Template" that would serve to record ideas about what worked and what didn't, changes for lessons. It would also provide a laundry list of HOTS and ask the teacher to assess whether the lesson could incorporate any of these skills the next time.

What major implication does what you did today have for your classroom practice?

We agree that because we are so focused on HOTS (i.e., the vocabulary we use), students are also more focused.

Did you examine student work today? No
Who brought work to share?

Next Meeting (agenda items, work to prepare):
Bring ideas for vocabulary template.

Next Meeting Date: 3/26/04   Time/Location: 2:00–4:00   Peggy's room   Leader: Ann

A Principal's Feedback to Study Group Logs

Clarke Middle School in Athens, Georgia, has eight WFSGs. On **February 10, 2004**, all of the groups met for the **12th time**. Kenneth Sherman, principal, e-mailed each study group his feedback on February 13. This is a standard practice after every round of study group meetings. The e-mail messages only go to the members of a particular study group. The 2/10/04 messages (his feedback) are as follows:

Dear CMS WFSG *Writing 1*:

You've gotten a good head start on your ideas bank.[1] Regarding the implications for classroom practice, you've hit on the exact issue that has been debated for many years. Our goal needs to be to find a way to address issues of mechanics, usage, and diction while not "squashing" the voice of those who do speak the King's English. The writing process is designed to begin with voice and a sense of audience and to build in a reason for students to want to correct the writing in order to reach as wide an audience as possible. Two good polar opposites on this issue can be found in Lisa Delpit's "Other People's Children" and Nancy Atwell's "In the Middle." Julie and Kim have ordered some of these books, and they would be worth having your WFSG look at them. Help us price out some dictionaries, and let's work together to see if funds might be available through the district, partners, grants, etc. to provide. Maybe some of the "bicycle" funds[2] could be used for this, too.

Dear CMS WFSG *Writing 2*:

It is great that you are looking at differentiation. Continue to explore this issue and to look at the work of Carol Ann Tomlinson. The school district will also be putting together professional development sessions in that area. You are also wrestling with the difficult task of defining elements of teacher-made tests. This may be something we want to add to our initiatives bank, as a way of improving and making more valid our homegrown assessments.

If you haven't yet looked at the WFSG rubric, you will have a chance to discuss it and respond to it in great detail how your group is doing. As you do this, look back at your action plan. If you are not clear about your "end product," it may be that you need to revisit and refocus your goals, especially with just a few months left for the year. The ultimate goal in this ongoing process, of course, is significant student achievement growth. As you consider this, pay particular attention to question #4 in the directions which were e-mailed to all of you yesterday: "Given where we are in the school year, what specific initiatives for school improvement does our group intend to focus on for its remaining sessions?" Include the answers to all four questions in the log you do after Tuesday's meeting. That will help us focus our efforts as we start to bring our year to a close.

Dear CMS WFSG *Higher-Order Thinking Skills*:

You guys are really gettin' into it! We love it! You are sharing your ideas, creativity, and enthusiasm. Thanks for going the extra mile and sending not only your log but also lessons,

---

[1]The school has an idea "bank." Ideas and suggestions coming from the WFSGs are put in the bank to be stored for consideration by the entire staff. Near the end of the school year, the faculty will work through and prioritize the list. At that time, the approved suggestions will go into the 2004–2005 school improvement plan.

[2]The school is raising funds for special projects through a Bicycle Ride-A-Thon. The principal and some members of the faculty and parents are riding bicycles from Athens to Savannah, Georgia, a distance of approximately 240 miles, on the weekend of May 1.

slave dialogue, and other samples. Keep the HOTS makeovers going, too. We bragged about that innovative approach at last week's WFSG conference. And, yes, this means that we will definitely be continuing the WFSG process. The process is like weight loss. As Dr. Phil explains, weight loss is managed, not cured. So it is with our improvement efforts: They will take continued nurturing attention as long as we work together. The WFSG process will certainly be refined over time, but the basic principles and approach will not change. We will likely keep our groups intact for next year, but exactly how we do that (e.g., with some changes in faculty) is still to be discussed.

Dear CMS WFSG *MOiD* (Moderately Intellectually Delayed):

Taking pictures of activities—great idea. Please share this idea with other folks when we gather on Tuesday. We are going to do the same thing for the entire WFSG process; we are going to start documenting and celebrating with a digital photo bulletin board that will include pictures of meetings and activities, artifacts, and more. Your "banks"—goals bank, job bank, curriculum bank—are a great result of your WFSG work—very synergistic, very productive. You may want to bring some of these items, especially the goals bank, to our next meeting on Tuesday or to an upcoming faculty meeting. It sounds like your group is really working well together, and that would be great to share with other staff.

Dear CMS WFSG *Reading Group 2:*

Please tell us much more about your response to the review of the rubric. In fact, at Tuesday's meeting, you will have a chance to discuss and respond in much greater detail how your group is doing, relative to the areas in the WFSG rubric. When you discuss these items, pay particular attention to question #4, which was e-mailed to all of you yesterday: "Given where we are in the school year, what specific initiatives for school improvement does our group intend to focus on for its remaining sessions?" Include the answers to all four questions in the log you do after Tuesday's meeting. That will help us focus our efforts as we start to bring our year to a close. We think it is great that you are ready to visit each other's classes. You should be able to work out something with your varied planning times. You can probably do most or all of what you want to do without having to bring in outside subs. It would be very helpful to use your sessions to report back on insights gained during these visits. Thank you, we are excited that you sent out the research "buzz word" list to other faculty. This is a great example of the kind of group-to-group communication that is starting to grow. Please let all of us know what kind of response you are getting.

Dear CMS WFSG *Social Studies:*

Your idea of reviewing your action plan at the start of each meeting, to help you focus, is wonderful. Liz's point is also right on the mark—the WFSG process is about what **we** do, how **we** change, what strategies **we** use, to help kids. You'll hear more about this on Tuesday. It would be a great idea to observe other teachers' vocabulary lessons. You should be able to work out something with your varied planning times. It would be very helpful to use your sessions to report back on insights gained during these visits. Tell all of us more about the "4-Square" technique. Is this something more of us should be trying?

Dear CMS WFSG *Science Group:*

Continue to look at specific examples of student work. Also, you may want to start looking at outside research on teaching strategies designed to enhance students' science process skills. Please explain how you are using tiered activities in your classroom. Any good ideas or strategies that you can share with everyone?

Dear CMS WFSG *Reading 1*:

It is exciting that you were "inspired" by the work of the other reading group to look into vocabulary issues. This kind of group-to-group communication and cross-pollination is starting to happen more and more, and that is a great development. The improvement in your students' scores on the recent vocabulary tests is great news. To what do you attribute the improvement? Any strategies and ideas we can all be looking at?

Dear CMS WFSG *Math Group*:

Good work, good thinking. You are giving serious consideration to many aspects of the WFSG process and to math teaching issues. You are absolutely right that you need to hear more from other groups; you will have a great opportunity to do this on Tuesday of next week. Also, we want to encourage more and more group-to-group communication; that's starting to happen, and it is very exciting. We are very much looking forward to your report on the benchmark results, and also to the impact of the benchmark achievement party which is being held today for 7th grade. Clever idea, one we may want to adopt on a wider basis, money permitting. You should have received copies of the new Georgia Performance Learning Standards. See Kim if you need another copy, or go to www.doe.k12.ga.us, and you can print them out.

Clarke Middle School
2004 – 2005 School Improvement Planning Process

April 12, 2004

Dear Faculty,

The first formal step in the School Improvement Planning Process is for each WFSG to make recommendations for actions to be included in CMS's 2004–2005 School Improvement Plan. At the January meeting of the Instructional Council, we agreed on a process for receiving recommendations from WFSG that are ideas to consider for the SIP. In the WFSG January newsletter, we announced: *"With this newsletter we are officially starting our ideas 'bank.' We are beginning to store the suggestions and programs we want to consider as an entire staff for near-future implementation. Later this spring, we will work through and prioritize the list together and add items to our School Improvement Plan."* It is now that time.

On Wednesday, April 21, we will look at recommendations from each study group that are to be considered for inclusion in the SIP. Carlene Murphy will join us at this meeting and we will summarize and prioritize our WFSG-generated list of school improvement ideas for next year.

Whole-Faculty Study Groups only impact the "whole faculty" when best practices from each group are shared with the whole school. The whole school benefits when recommendations from a study group are included in the School Improvement Plan.

If you have not already, please use your next meeting to generate a list of ideas/strategies/ initiatives that your group will be contributing as possibilities for the 2004–2005 School Improvement Plan.

Give some description of each idea you submit, not just a "name," so we will all understand what is being proposed. Indicate whether or not you have already begun implementation of any of these proposed ideas, and share with us the successes you may have had. Please give the list to me by April 19. It is important that you have tried the ideas you recommend and you have seen results from the trials.

Use a version of this chart:

"Name" of Idea	Brief Description	Already Implemented/ Tried Out?	If Implemented, How Successful/ Effective?

Thank you.

Dr. Ken Sherman, Principal
Clarke Middle School

Clark Middle School
WFSG Idea Bank
April 21, 2004

Planning Process for 2003–2004 School Improvement Plan

Recommendations (ideas) from WFSG indicate that at CMS, we need to

- Implement strategies for integrating higher-order thinking skills across curriculum areas.
- Have consistent, schoolwide, content-area vocabulary so that students are getting the same information from grade to grade in each area. This should be done in conjunction with districtwide efforts to standardize terms and required vocabulary. Efforts such as standardizing the "scientific method" and "writing process" are included in this effort.
- Implement vocabulary-acquisition strategies. (This has been a need identified by every WFSG.) In addition to standardized vocabulary lists, we are looking at the use of vocabulary "walls" in each classroom to highlight emerging vocabulary (i.e., words that come up in classroom discussions, readings, videos, and the like). We did this a few years ago and it was a very effective way to "immerse" students in content-related terms and get them excited about the content they are learning. The Functional Curriculum group's "job bank"—with vocabulary words and a picture—is an example of this in action.
- Standardize writing formats across grade levels. We are looking at creating a consistent "Clarke Middle School" approach to writing paragraphs and essays. Again, this should be done together with similar efforts at the district level (Red Clay Project and the TSARS Scoring the MGWA training).
- Have a consistent grade-by-grade literature reading list. We will work with the district to ensure that we eliminate gaps or redundancy in this area.
- Work more on differentiating instruction to ensure that all students have access to all aspects of the curriculum. Of particular concern is the large number of students with poor reading skills. We want to build those skills while simultaneously providing ways for everyone to "get" the information.
- Incorporate more CRCT-style questions in our instructional program—using daily starters/class openers, quizzes/tests, 9-week assessments, and/or the CRCT Item Bank Online.
- Investigate/research and implement a CRCT incentive program schoolwide (pep rally, perfect attendance during testing, etc.).
- Use a variety of evaluation measures more effectively to measure student performance on a daily/weekly/monthly basis.
- Evaluate ourselves more effectively (e.g., the HOTS group's "Teacher Reflection Template"). We need to continue to work on aligning individual/GTEP, WFSG, and SIP goals.
- Continue to improve our communication efforts (i.e., install a WFSG folder on the server, use digital photos to record our work).
- Secure more technology in content areas; more effective use of district technology staff.
- Have dictionaries in every classroom.
- Consider a schoolwide incentive program.
- Secure funding through grantwriting.
- Incorporate reading skills into all content areas.
- Extend learning time for math.
- Have more writing schoolwide.

- Increase silent reading/writing time (structure academic time).
- Establish Web site bank for all content areas and teacher resources by subject area.
- Establish forums/procedures for addressing issues that fall outside the scope of our WFSG work—issues such as discipline, attendance, alternative scheduling, parental involvement, etc.
- Provide relevant field trips to support curriculum/content areas.
- Continue to refine our Whole-Faculty Study Group process by
  - ☐ Continuing to develop our skills at using data to plan, set goals, and assess progress.
  - ☐ Working on taking the ideas emerging from the WFSGs and turning them into specific initiatives for improvement.
  - ☐ Looking closely and honestly at student work, and learning what that work is "saying" to us. Try out a wide array of protocols that will help us focus on the truths that can be revealed by the work our students do.
  - ☐ Celebrating the way the WFSG process has brought us together as a faculty, and continue to hone our skills in group process and sharing.
  - ☐ Making sure that we are using research-based practices.

Clarke Middle School
April 21, 2004

Whole-Faculty Study Group—School Improvement Recommendations:
Planning for School Improvement 2004–2005

<u>Handouts:</u>
1) Agenda
2) Summary of recommendations from WFSG (compiled from lists previously given to Dr. Sherman)
3) Specific recommendations from each study group (8 pages, 1 per study group)

4:00   Everyone reports to media center, seating will be as indicated by signs on tables (mixed by study groups).

4:00   Overview, purpose: link WFSGs to CMS School Improvement Plan

4:05   1) Individuals silently read the summary of recommendations and review the recommendations from "your" study group.
        2) Determine whether or not your group's recommendations are represented in one of the recommendations on the summary list.
        3) If all the recommendations from your study group are not included in the general recommendations, add the recommendation to the list.
        4) Going around the table, each person reports on whether or not all the recommendations from his/her study group are represented on the list; if not, recommendations added to everyone's list at a table.

4:30   Reporter from each table reports to whole group the recommendations that should be added to the summary list.

4:45   Table groups give each recommendation a score:
        1 = a must do
        2 = we should seriously consider doing this
        3 = a good idea
        4 = not necessary, but might work
        5 = not needed or appropriate at this time

5:00   All of the recommendations given a #1 are acknowledged.

5:15   Next steps clarified: Focus Team will compile complete list of recommendations and indicate the priorities. At another faculty meeting, the faculty will determine time lines, costs, responsible persons, etc. This information will become the heart of the School Improvement Plan for 2004–2005.

5:30   Adjourn

Clarke Middle School

School Improvement Planning for 2004–2005

On April 21, the faculty assigned a priority rating to each of the recommendations or ideas from all of the WFSGs. We now need to determine **HOW** the priorities will be accomplished. For each recommendation that was deemed a priority for inclusion in CMS's 2004–2005 School Improvement Plan, study groups are to discuss how each can best be accomplished.

For each priority recommendation:

1. Name the individual/group that should be responsible for leading/completing the recommended action:
   - Individual: _____
   - WFSG: _____
   - Committee: _____
   - Grade: _____
   - Team: _____
   - Department: _____
   - Other: _____

2. Give target date for full implementation, such as:
   - Beginning of school year (Sept. 2004)
   - By midterm (Jan. 2005)
   - By April 2005

3. Indicate resources needed to accomplish the recommendation:
   - Personnel: _____
   - Materials: _____
   - Time: _____
   - Approximate amount of funds to be allocated: _____
   - Other: _____

Recommendation	Responsibility	Time Line	Resources

Resource E

More Action Plans and Logs

<u>*From*</u>

Paul Robeson High School
Ira Weston, Principal
Brooklyn, NY

Hubbard Primary School
Angie Dillon, Principal
Monroe County Schools
Forsyth, GA

Mangham Elementary School
Fay Philips, Principal
Mangham, LA
Region VIII–NE Louisiana (Teri Roberts, LINCS Coordinator)

Crooked River Elementary School
Sheila Sapp, Principal
Camden County Schools
St. Mary's, GA

Summary of Assessment of WFSG Work
St. Mary's Elementary School
Beverly Strickland, Principal
Camden County Schools
St. Mary's, GA

Whole-Faculty Study Group Action Plan

School <u>Robeson High School</u> **Group Name or #** <u>Writing (#5)</u> **Date** <u>9/7/02</u>

Group Members: <u>Cynthia (Business), Janene (Sci), Derek (Business), Stefanie (English), Grace (Sci), Kettie (SpEd)</u>

What is the general category of student needs the group will address? Writing fluency

Data indicate that students need to: (be very specific)	When our study group meets, we will:
Feel comfortable with writing so that they are able to respond with fluency in a variety of subject areas	• Develop learning log prompts and strategies that will help students see writing as a tool for assessing their own learning • Develop strategies for opening up the writing process for students • Develop portfolio projects that will assess students comfortable levels by midterm • Examine student work to assess our work

The **ESSENTIAL QUESTION** that will guide the group's work is: *How can we help students feel comfortable using writing as an essential tool for analyzing, synthesizing, communicating, pleasure, and self-reflection?*

Our resources are:	Our norms are:
<u>Learning to Write—Writing to Learn</u> Research on learning loop and portfolio assignments TFU books	Start and end on time; extend time if needed Always set an agenda for each meeting Give log to reader within 48 hours Be flexible and open-minded Everyone bring student work once a month No cancellation of meeting if someone can't attend Decisions made by consensus Take turn leading when your time

Specific Student Needs from above— *Students need to:*	Data Sources that document need and will be evidence of impact of group's work	Baseline—what data indicate when work begins in: Aug./Sept.	Target—what study group projects will be the results of the work in: DATE: Nov _____	Actual—what data indicate now (complete at end of 6 to 12 weeks) DATE _____

– Write with fluency – Understand the writing process	– Learning logs – Portfolios – Daily writing assignments – Student reflections	Since we do not have baseline data in all our classes, we are going to assume none of our students are doing these things at an acceptable level now.	– 80% increase in participation, length, and depth of learning log entries – 80% increase in student understanding of writing process – All students complete midterm portfolios	

Addendum to Action Plan:

We have received feedback from our reader,[1] Tamika, that she has questions about our student need: "Students need to feel comfortable with writing." The feedback is that the student need is "borderline perennial" and not fully "terminal" or a need that we can satisfy. We acknowledge this is true but support the importance of focusing on this need first because we feel that there are levels of comfortability with writing that can be clearly discerned in an individual student. Stefanie talked with Karl following our full faculty meeting on action plans and student needs. He agreed that sometimes a need can be both perennial and terminal. (This is supported by Murphy in the excerpt shared by Tamika.) Certainly the need to be comfortable with writing is "enabling" in that the teacher focuses on each individual student and through ongoing assessments (for example, changes in learning log entries from a few words or statements that merely copy what was stated in class to more thoughtful and reflective comments) for evidence of growing comfort with writing. We do feel that this need has levels and that all of us as we grow and learn reach another edge of comfort. The growth comes when we can shake ourselves off and stretch once again beyond that edge. Well, this is true about life and this is true about writing. So, we do see obvious ways that we can "check in" and assess our students' comfort through products they produce. We aim to create classroom environments that force them to stretch.

For the purpose of seeing examples of what study groups do, only the top portions of the following study group logs are given.

---

[1]For anyone reading this addendum that is not part of the work at Robeson High School, there are five readers of the logs. These individuals are the principal and four assistant principals. Each has four study groups to support, which includes reading and giving feedback to the weekly logs. Study groups meet on Fridays from 1:40 to 3:00, when students are released early at 1:30. The action plan on the preceding page is the final plan after revisions occurred over several weeks. In the first four or five logs, the group is continuing to refine its plan. The first plan was submitted after the third meeting (the first meeting was actually a time to get organized and was not a full meeting). Revisions to the plan were based on the feedback and subsequent discussions.

Karl is the ATLAS site developer who works with our school, supporting WFSGs and providing technical assistance.

Whole-Faculty Study Group Log

School <u>Robeson High School</u>   Log # <u>1</u>   Date <u>9/5 (Wed.)</u>

Group Name or # <u>Writing</u>   Leader _____

Members Present: <u>Everyone</u>

What happened today? Brief summary of discussion and activities. Keep artifacts in notebook.

The whole faculty met initially to clarify how to write an action plan and the procedures for submitting logs and receiving feedback.
 	
 We discussed and reached consensus on the following:
     – Rotate leadership of group by the month: Cynthia, Stefanie, Janene, Grace, Derek, Kettie
     – Norms (see action plan)
 	
 All of our meetings will be in Room 228 and will begin at 1:40 and end at 3:00, unless we agree we can stay longer when we feel we have not finished our work.
 	
 Next week we will each come in with at least one statement on what we would like to see happen in the classroom pertaining to writing.

Next Meeting (agenda items, work to prepare)   Work on essential question and action plan.

Date: <u>9/7</u>   Time: <u>1:40</u>   Leader: <u>Cynthia</u>   Location: <u>Room 228</u>

Whole-Faculty Study Group Log

School <u>Robeson High School</u>   Log # <u>2</u>   Date <u>9/7</u>

Group Name or # <u>Writing</u>   Leader <u>Cynthia</u>

Members Present: <u>All but Grace</u>

What happened today? Brief summary of discussion and activities. Keep artifacts in notebook.
We worked on forming our essential question and focusing on the student needs—specific to writing—that we will address. We agreed on the question and the needs. We shared Karl's and Tamika's feedback to the work we did on Wednesday. We reviewed the norms and agreed those will work for us. We also used the WFSG book to look at completed action plans.
We also decided to read *Learning to Write—Writing to Learn*. Stefanie will order copies.
Next week we will each come in with at least one action we will take when our group meets.

Next Meeting (agenda items, work to prepare)   Work on essential question and action plan.

Date: <u>9/14</u>   Time: <u>1:40</u>   Leader: <u>Cynthia</u>   Location: <u>Room 228</u>

Whole-Faculty Study Group Log

School <u>Robeson High School</u>   Log # <u>3</u>   Date <u>9/14</u>

Group Name or # <u>WIRED</u>   Leader <u>Cynthia</u>

Members Present: <u>All</u>

What happened today? Brief summary of discussion and activities. Keep artifacts in notebook.
We completed the "actions we will take" on the action plan and listed the resources we will use. We decided to turn in the plan with the assessment portion undone until we think more about how to gather current data.
We discussed or philosophies/theories/understandings about teaching writing and what we want to see in student work (we represent four different areas). Looked through the book *Learning to Write—Writing to Learn*. Assigned Chapters 1 and 2 and will do an activity on page 35 at next meeting.
We decided to call ourselves the **WIRED group**: **W**riting **I**s **R**eal and **E**verywhere **D**esired!!!!!
Derek shared his frustration with 9th-grade English teachers—would like to be working with them more directly. Cynthia will speak to Tamika and Roberta about this.

Next Meeting (agenda items,   Discuss Kettie's student work; also,
work to prepare)   relationship of reading to writing.

Date: 9/21   **Time: 1:40**   **Leader: Cynthia**   **Location: Room 228**

Whole-Faculty Study Group Log

School <u>Robeson High School</u>   Log # <u>4</u>   Date <u>9/21</u>

Group Name or # <u>WIRED</u>   Leader <u>Cynthia</u>

Members Present: <u>All</u>

What happened today? Brief summary of discussion and activities. Keep artifacts in notebook.
We acknowledged feedback to the last log: – Great group name – Will we assess students' reading levels? If so, what tool will we use? – Will the group research the correlation between reading levels and writing ability?
We want Tamika to meet with us on Oct. 5—We have questions about comments and words used (e.g., issues, tools, modeled). We briefly discussed the two questions raised. We will all give more thought to how we will assess the impact of our work. Stefanie will talk to Tamika and see what suggestions she has. On Oct. 28 several members will be attending retreat.
We looked at the student work Kettie brought from one of her Sp. Ed. students.
WOWS: Student connection between veterinary profession and animal rights; relaxed; comfortable; worldview of student expressed.
WONDERS: If student had the opportunity to review; if there will be an opportunity for the student to make deeper connections with this topic.
Kettie's question: What should I do next? (initial assessment piece). Discussion revealed limits to doing things outside of the lock-step curriculum of Sp. Ed. Student's essay developed out of class notes and discussion—Is this really his perspective or just the one Kettie modeled that appealed to him?

Next Meeting (agenda items, work to prepare)   Writing in science

Date: 9/28   **Time: 1:40**   **Leader: Kettie**   **Location: Room 228**

Whole-Faculty Study Group Log

School <u>Robeson High School</u>   **Log #** <u>5</u>   **Date** <u>9/28</u>

Group Name or # <u>WIRED</u>   **Leader** <u>Kettie</u>

Members Present: <u>Kettie and Grace</u>

What happened today? Brief summary of discussion and activities. Keep artifacts in notebook.			
The other group members were away at a retreat. Grace and I (Kettie) discussed writing in science and looked at several example of Grace's students' work.			
Did you examine student work Today?	Yes	**Who Brought?**	Grace

Next Meeting (agenda items, work to prepare)

Date: <u>10/05</u>   **Time:** <u>1:40</u>   **Leader:** <u>Cynthia</u>   **Location:** <u>Room 228</u>

Whole-Faculty Study Group Log

School <u>Robeson High School</u>   **Log #** <u>6</u>   **Date** <u>10/5</u>

Group Name or # <u>WIRED</u>   **Leader** <u>Cynthia</u>

Members Present: <u>All</u>

What happened today? Brief summary of discussion and activities. Keep artifacts in notebook.
Shared Karl's note to us about how we will measure our student need—besides those assessments we listed on the action plan. We need to shape prompts to bring out different skills. The need to become comfortable with writing and using it for self-reflection and pleasure: We see self-reflection now as an activity that might lead to feeling more comfortable with writing. All of us will try a learning log and see what happens.
We rewrote the student need on the action plan.
We discussed what a learning log is: 2 or 3 sentences explaining what you learned.
Tamika visited our group and we clarified issues around how we would assess students "feeling comfortable." She shared the idea of the "whip" as a means to assess quickly where students are with their learning logs so that the teacher does not have to read them all every time.
All of our students are keeping learning logs.

Next Meeting (agenda items, work to prepare)

Share learning logs; look at Grace's student work.

Date: <u>10/12</u>   **Time:** <u>1:40</u>   **Leader:** <u>Stefanie</u>   **Location:** <u>Room 228</u>

Whole-Faculty Study Group Log

School <u>Robeson High School</u>   Log # <u> 7 </u>   Date <u>10/12</u>

Group Name or # <u>WIRED</u>   Leader <u>Stefanie</u>

Members Present: <u>All</u>

What happened today? Brief summary of discussion and activities. Keep artifacts in notebook.			
We like our action plan and it will remain as revised. We looked at the work Grace brought. The assignment was in environmental science. Assignment: Write two paragraphs about a journey you take to the Solar System, going from the school to Pluto where you can see every planet. WOWS: Student's relaxed response to the assignment did reveal factual knowledge as well as imagination. WONDERS: If there was a rubric or set of criteria for this "journal of a journey"; if students were familiar with the genre of scientific journal entries while traveling. Grace wanted to know if the wording of the assignment was explicit enough to generate the results she wanted.			
Did you examine student work Today?	Yes	**Who Brought?**	Grace

Next Meeting (agenda items, work to prepare)   Everyone bring student work and we'll decide whose to use.

Date: <u>10/17</u>   Time: <u>1:40</u>   Leader: <u>Stefanie</u>   Location: <u>Room 228</u>

Whole-Faculty Study Group Log

School <u>Robeson High School</u>   Log # <u> 8 </u>   Date <u>10/17</u>

Group Name or # <u>WIRED</u>   Leader <u>Grace</u>

Members Present: <u>Kettie, Grace, Cynthia, Janene (Stefanie and Derek are at IC meeting)</u>

What happened today? Brief summary of discussion and activities. Keep artifacts in notebook.			
We focused on how to get students involved in writing for different subject areas and feel confident and comfortable with expressing their ideas. We all brought student work—decided to focus on Janene's. We looked at student work that Janene brought which was an example of worksheet she used for comparing and contrasting. We made suggestions about the directions for the activity. Students are keeping learning logs. We are focusing on getting students to use their imaginations in writing.			
Did you examine student work Today?	Yes	**Who Brought?**	Janene

Next Meeting (agenda items, work to prepare)   Writing essays

Date: <u>10/26</u>   Time: <u>1:40</u>   Leader: <u>Stefanie</u>   Location: <u>Room 228</u>

Study Group Meeting Report
for
Looking at Student Work

When looking at student work, using this form (in addition to log) is optional.

Date <u>10/26</u>   **Study Group Name or #** <u>WIRED</u>

Members present: Cynthia, Grace, Janene, Stefanie, Derek, Kettie

Describe the assignment(s):

Derek brought a computer assignment. Students had to open up two documents at the same time. One was article on "cashless society" and the other was a blank document. The students wrote how this would affect life—advantages and disadvantages.

We also looked at an essay on rebuilding the World Trade Center by Kettie's students.

Similar issues revealed in both.

What we learned about student LEARNING:

- Students enjoy grappling with large, complicated ideas just as much as adults.
- To be comfortable as writers they need to be challenged in their assumptions about what writing is for.

What we learned about INSTRUCTION:

- It is often not connected to a larger context—a context of meaning making and understanding. We think this contributes to mediocre work.
- The essay is not a place to begin exploring a topic—too much pressure, expectation, and fear.
- Students need a variety of experiences in order to write meaningful papers.

What will we do to IMPROVE LEARNING?

- We are focusing on developing strategies that will broaden students' understanding of a topic before they write "the essay."
- Through a broader understanding, comfort will develop as will fluency.

If practical, please attach copy of the student work.

Whole-Faculty Study Group Log

School <u>Robeson High School</u>   Log # <u>9</u>   Date <u>11/2</u>

Group Name or # <u>WIRED</u>   Leader <u>Janene</u>

Members Present: <u>Kettie, Grace, Cynthia, Stefanie and Derek</u>

What happened today? Brief summary of discussion and activities. Keep artifacts in notebook.

Tamika visited our group. She is going to read the book we are reading. We discussed how we will evaluate our need. We then discussed the need for students to do a variety of writing, reading, thinking, and discussing activities before asking them to write "the Essay" so that they can develop their thinking on topics that are complicated and encompass many perspectives. Janene shared the difficulty she is having introducing the topic her team is addressing—biological and chemical warfare. Suggestions:
 	
   – Begin with where you are (what you know).
   – What you need to find out.
   – How you are going to find it out.
   – What performances of understanding will you use
      to show you learned?

Classroom Application: What are students learning and achieving as a result of what you are learning and doing?
Our conversation led to the difficulty of some topics for teachers. Janene shared that several of the teachers on her team don't want to talk about biological and chemical warfare. The issue was raised about the need for teachers to be responsible and open up the dialogue without engaging fear or panic building. This is true of many difficult or troubling topics and it is important for the teachers to understand for themselves how they feel. We all agreed that it is possible to examine these types of topics but the teacher needs to feel comfortable with the prospect of discomfort and how to handle it. We agreed that if the teacher is uncomfortable, that discomfort will transfer to the students.

Did you examine student work Today?	No	Who Brought?
General comments: Meeting went overtime but no one was anxious to leave.		Question/Concerns:

Next Meeting (agenda items, work to prepare)   All bring activities that help students delve deeper into topics from a variety of entry points.

Date: <u>11/9</u>   Time: <u>1:40</u>   Leader: <u>Janene</u>   Location: <u>Room 228</u>

[The WIRED group met weekly through 5/17, its 26th meeting.]

Whole-Faculty Study Group Action Plan

School Hubbard Primary   **Study Group** #7 Phonics   **Date** 11/10 & 11/17

Group Members: Bert, Becky, Betty, Marcelle (all are kindergarten teachers)

What is the general Category of student needs the group will address? Phonics

Data indicate that students need to: (be very specific)		When our study group meets, we will:	
– Recognize letters and sounds of the alphabet – Demonstrate understanding of long and short vowels – Develop strategies for applying phoenemic skills learned to decode words to include nonsense words		– Look at student work using protocols – Model effective strategies and activities – Develop lesson plans for implementing what group members have been trained to do (i.e., learning focused strategies) – Have a skillful person attend our meetings (TBD) to train/guide members in the use of effective strategies for teaching phonics	

Using what the data indicate are student needs, the **ESSENTIAL QUESTION** that will guide the group's work is: *How can we help students to become more proficient in phoenemic awareness?*

Our resources are:	Our norms are:
– Scott Foresman Reading – Shannen Harvill— Literacy Coach – Open Count Phonics – Teacher-made phonics activities – Guided Reading books – Manipulative magnetic letters and dry erase board	– Share leadership role – Share responsibilities for doing research and identifying resources – Be on time – Stay on task

Specific **Student Needs** from above—*Students need to:*	**Data Sources** that document need and will be evidence of impact of group's work	**Baseline**—what data indicate when work begins in **September**	**Target**—what study group projects will be the results of the work in **January**	**Actual**—what data indicate *now* in **January**
– Recog. letters and sounds of alphabet – Demonstrate understanding of long and short vowels – Develop ways to apply phoenemic skills learned to decode words to include nonsense words	– Benchmark (BLT) tests – Teacher-made checklists – Textbook check-lists – ABC checklists for letter ID and sounds	On BLT: – 12% (of students) recog. letters – 2% recog. sounds – 0% understand vowels – 0% can decode words – 2% understand CVC pattern words and non-sense words	– 90% (of students) will reach mastery of recog. letters – 60% mastery of con-sonant sounds – 25% mastery of vowel sounds – 10% mastery of decoding words on teacher checklist	– 95% (of students) mastered ABC checklist of letters – 55% mastery of sounds – 30% mastery of long and short vowels – 10% mastery of decoding words on teacher checklist

For the purpose of seeing examples of what study groups do, only the top portions of the following study group logs are given.

Whole-Faculty Study Group Log

School <u>Hubbard Primary</u>   Log # <u>3</u>   Date <u>11/17</u>

Group Name or # <u>#7 Phonics</u>   Leader <u>Becky</u>

Members Present: <u>Marcelle, Betty, Becky, Bert</u>

What happened today? Brief summary of discussion and activities. Keep artifacts in notebook.
<ul><li>We all brought student work to determine the percentage of our students that can recognize letters and sounds. We think we need to focus on teaching sounds earlier. We have good data showing EIP students are on target with kindergarten grade level in recognizing letters.</li><li>We decided to make a change on our action plan. We raised our expectations of recognizing letters to 90% (we originally said 80%). We lowered the percentage for consonant sounds from 80% to 60% because in looking at all our classes, we found 80% to be unrealistic. We began to see gaps that each of us had, and we saw where to strengthen our focus.</li><li>We discussed the need for input from a speech teacher to give ideas and research regarding teaching consonants and vowel sounds.</li><li>We will all bring data (student assessments) to next meeting. For next 2 weeks we are going to concentrate on teaching letter sounds.</li></ul>

Whole-Faculty Study Group Log

School <u>Hubbard Primary</u>   Log # <u>4</u>   Date <u>12/1</u>

Group Name or # <u>#7 Phonics</u>   Leader <u>Marcelle</u>

Members Present: <u>Betty, Becky, Marcelle, Bert</u>

What happened today? Brief summary of discussion and activities. Keep artifacts in notebook.
<ul><li>Becky shared what was discussed at the IC meeting. Betty will attend the next one.</li><li>We reviewed a random sample of student assessments on letter and sound recognition.</li><li>Mrs. Samms (speech teacher) met with us. We learned several new strategies for teaching sounds. We are going to use these strategies and will bring student work to show results. We are also going to use selected strategies in the book *Sounds in Action* that we received today (Thanks to Angie for ordering the books for us!). Betty demonstrated how to use gross motor activities to teach sounds.</li><li>We learned that there are certain sounds that are easier and harder for kindergarten children to make. The easiest: p, m, h, n, w, b. We also found out about a book that gives the hierarchy of sounds for children.</li></ul>

Whole-Faculty Study Group Log

School <u>Hubbard Primary</u>   Log # <u>5</u>   Date <u>12/10</u>   Leader <u>Bert</u>

What happened today? Brief summary of discussion and activities. Keep artifacts in notebook.

- On our last log, Angie suggested we look at Group 5's data on letters. Next meeting we are going to bring our data and compare it to Group 5's. We are going to compile our data to make a graph that shows letters known and number of sounds known. We are going to look at our data to see if our students are having trouble with the same upper- and lowercase letters as Group 5.
- Becky shared how she uses pictures to associate sounds.
- We are going to try using mirrors to show the students how to position their mouth when they make the sounds.
- We are using (1) Feldman and (2) the *Sounds in Action* book as resources for our classroom activities. We are using some of the things Mrs. Samms shared with us, especially working with our children on parts of their mouths that make sounds and using pictures to associate sounds with letters. We are looking for inexpensive hand mirrors.
- We want to put our graph on the bulletin board.

Whole-Faculty Study Group Log

School <u>Hubbard Primary</u>   Log # <u>6</u>   Date <u>1/5</u>   Leader <u>Betty</u>

What happened today? Brief summary of discussion and activities. Keep artifacts in notebook.

- We discussed Angie's comments to our last log.
- All members brought student work to determine which letters our students find difficult to recognize and learn. The capital letters that Group 5's children are having trouble with correlate with ours. The same is true for lowercase letters.
- We worked on compiling data that we brought from our individual classrooms regarding upper- and lowercase letters. We compiled data on 111 kindergarten students (82 are EIP students; we have twice as many EIP students as Group 5). We will work on transferring this information to a large graph and display it in the general meeting room.
- We discovered that (1) overall the students knew more of the capital letters than the lowercase letters and (2) the scores for letters that look very similar were much lower than the scores for letters that do not look similar. [Could this discovery lead to a new way to teach letters that look similar?]
- We saw that the results were very similar to Group 5's results both with capital and lowercase letters.
- We are going to focus on the letters children did not recognize—mostly reversals (d, b).

Whole-Faculty Study Group Log

School <u>Hubbard Primary</u>   **Log #** <u>7</u>   **Date** <u>1/17</u>   **Leader** <u>Becky</u>

What happened today? Brief summary of discussion and activities. Keep artifacts in notebook.

- We considered the making of homework bags. Will think more about this.
- Bert and Becky attended a workshop on Learning Focused Schools. The workshop was on how to write good essential questions—most of ours are too wordy or too hard. We spent a lot of time discussing the materials that Bert and Becky shared and we practiced writing essential questions for our current work.
- We all modeled a strategy we are using to correct common reversals: sorting the letters, writing the letters, etc. We feel the confusion some students are experiencing is linked to their individual development levels.

Whole-Faculty Study Group Log

School <u>Hubbard Primary</u>   **Log #** <u>8</u>   **Date** <u>2/3</u>

Group Name or # <u>#7 Phonics</u>   **Leader** <u>Marcelle</u>

Members Present: <u>Everyone present</u>

What happened today? Brief summary of discussion and activities. Keep artifacts in notebook.

- Marcelle attended the IC meeting last week. She gave us copies of the WFSG rubric. We will each score the rubric and at our next meeting we will have a general discussion and reach consensus on the scoring of it.
- We reviewed the graph we made in December and January. After focusing on letter sounds for the past month, we compiled and tabulated current data on letter recognition and sounds. We added this information to the graph. We all agreed that charting the data has given us a better picture of our students' strengths and weaknesses. It is driving our instruction on sounds. We can see growth based on the instructional changes we have made.
- We all shared activities we have tried with students to teach the sounds students didn't know.
- We are making our students more aware of what they know and what they need to know. Some of us are making classroom graphs with the children. They are excited about getting the graph bars closer and closer to the top. They help each other more readily in order to get the group to the top.
- We will put our February graph on the bulletin board.
- Bert will attend the national WFSG conference in Augusta and will also attend a full-day preconference workshop on looking at student work.

Whole-Faculty Study Group Log

School Hubbard Primary   **Log #** 9   **Date** 2/15

Group Name or # #7 Phonics   **Leader** Bert

Members Present: Everyone present

What happened today? Brief summary of discussion and activities. Keep artifacts in notebook.
• Bert shared with us the protocols received at the Augusta conference for looking at student work. She brought student work on letter recognition and we practiced the Wows and Wonders or tuning protocol.   • We examined the graph, added more results, and shared comments from other teachers who have studied the graph on the bulletin board.   • We are all very pleased with the tremendous growth from the totals earlier in the year. We know that the sharing we are doing has helped.   • The students are excited, too. They can see their growth on the graphs and cheer for each other as they get closer to the top. They have more self-esteem.

The study group continued to meet through mid-May.

Hubbard Primary School

In April 2004, Angie Dillon, the principal, asked study groups to write a paragraph about their WFSG work. Several are given here.

Group 7 (Phonics): Our group's focus has been on phonics (letter recognition and letter sounds), since most of us are kindergarten teachers. We began tracking our students' progress in letter recognition in December. We found, as a group, that our students had many common weaknesses. We shared ideas that targeted the weak areas and implemented these strategies with our students. We saw considerable improvement when we assessed students again in February. We created computer-generated graphs for our own personal use and for classroom activities using the data we collected. Graphing our results enabled us to focus on specific needs. Graphing the results with students allowed them to see their progress as a class. As a result of this, our students became more aware of areas in which they needed help. We followed this same procedure on consonant sound recognition a little later in the year.

Group 5 (Phonics): A great strategy used this year in our WFSG was the use of graphs to record data on student achievement. Targeted skills included letter recognition, consonant sound recognition, and vowel sound recognition. The use of these graphs provided instant data that we used in our meetings to come up with instructional strategies. These strategies helped each of us to better meet the needs of our students. Data proved that end of the year student progress in these areas was dramatically improved.

Group 12: Our group has spent much time looking at student work and analyzing data derived from our examinations of the work. We came to the conclusion that there are "common" errors made by our students. Research shows, after analyzing test results, that students of the same age make similar mistakes from year to year and also from county to county. Therefore, an effective teaching strategy to use is to model the process for students and help them become critical thinkers. Also, giving students more opportunities to practice the skills and to verbalize errors and apply corrective strategies is an excellent way to promote critical thinking and improve student learning.

Group 4: The most effective WFSG strategy that we used was a classroom observation followed by using the tuning protocol with work from the lesson we observed. We had the opportunity to observe a teacher's lesson on "making connections." Teachers were able to view firsthand student's initial thoughts and reactions to the new strategy of making connections. Members of our group felt it was more beneficial to interact with students as they are learning than to simply view the finished product or work sample. When we used the tuning protocol looking at student work from the lesson we observed, teachers were able to ask specific questions in regard to the lesson as well as give "warm" and "cool" feedback. This experience gave those of us who observed the lesson and the teacher who was observed significant time to reflect on our individual thoughts about the lesson. We found that pairing the observation and the protocol was very valuable and we recommend that this become standard practice.

Group 10 (Comprehension): In our study group, we identified a great strategy we all used to help our students comprehend better. The strategy we used was a graphic organizer called the story worm. The story worm had students recall the name of the story or book, the setting, main characters, two events or problems, and the conclusion of the story. This organizer was presented during a whole group reading time and then used during small group guided reading time. After several presentations together as a class and in small groups, students were able to complete an individual story worm by themselves. Students have used the graphic organizer on their own during their supplemental reading time to improve their comprehension. As a result of using this graphic organizer, students' comprehension has improved on their ACR tests as well as comprehension quizzes and practice CRCT tests in both first and second grade.

Whole-Faculty Study Group Action Plan

School Mangham Elem   **Study Group** Problem Solving   **Date** 9/10

Group Members: Nacole (K), Kim (PE), Carol (1st), Brenda (4th), Louise (2nd)

What is the general category of student needs the group will address? Solving problems

Data indicate that students need to: (be very specific) 	When our study group meets, we will:
Have the skills to demonstrate what they know and can do through responding correctly to constructed-response items in all the content areas on the LEAP.* These skills include (1) solving multiple-step problems, (2) writing out their thought processes for how they solve problems, (3) organizing their thoughts on paper, and (4) ordering and classifying information *Louisiana Education Assessment Program	– Research and identify problem-solving skills and best practices for addressing the skills – Look at student work – Explore techniques for teaching students to write what they are thinking to solve problems – Develop and model lessons and strategies to teach and reinforce problem-solving skills in all subject areas and grade levels – Use rubrics to assess constructed-response items

Using what the data indicate are student needs, the **ESSENTIAL QUESTION** that will guide the group's work is: *How can we teach students the skills needed to effectively respond to constructed-response items on the LEAP in all content areas?*

Our resources are:	Our norms are:
LEAP practice materials Web sites Saxon math materials Masterpiece Sentence Theme 4–Square Writing Method Rubrics; reference materials Teri Roberts, LINCS Regional Coordinator	Stay focused Do what we agree to do Bring something to share at every meeting

Specific **Student Needs** from above—*Students need to:*	**Data Sources** that document need and will be evidence of impact of group's work	**Baseline**—what data indicate when work begins in **September**	**Target**—what study group projects will be the results of the work in **November**	**Actual**—what data indicate *now* in **November**
Respond appropriately to constructed-response items by writing what they are thinking to solving problems	– Teacher-made assessments – LEAP rubric – Student work	(We will collect baseline data in our classes during Sept.)	20% increase in baseline data	

For the purpose of seeing examples of what study groups do, only the top portions of the following study group logs are given. The school had a sailing theme. This group called itself the Dinghies.

Whole-Faculty Study Group Log

School <u>Mangham Elementary (LA)</u>   Log # <u>3</u>   Date <u>10/22 1:00–3:00</u>

Group Name or # <u>Dinghies</u>

Members Present: <u>All</u>

What happened today? Brief summary of discussion and activities. Keep artifacts in notebook.

- Patricia, LINCS content leader, gave us a reference to use in evaluating teacher-made tests.
- Kim demonstrated how 4-square writing is used and could be used for all grade levels.
- We looked at some of her students' work. This is a great way to organize writing for constructed response items.
- Each step is written in paragraph form with at least four sentences in each paragraph.

2	3
1	
4	5

Paragraphs 2, 3, 4: Organized categories
Paragraph 1: Topic sentence
Paragraph 5: Conclusion

- Next week bring examples of student work showing multistep problems in math or science.

Whole-Faculty Study Group Log

School <u>Mangham Elementary (LA)</u>   Log # <u>4</u>   Date _____

Group Name or # <u>Dinghies</u>

Members Present: <u>All</u>

What happened today? Brief summary of discussion and activities. Keep artifacts in notebook.

We practiced scoring constructed-response math items using the Louisiana Education Assessment Program (LEAP) rubric. Each member brought student work and we scored the work using the rubric. We recognized that most of our students have trouble completing a multistep question correctly. They do not want to show their work, which they must in order to make a satisfactory score. We need to design lots of opportunities for students to practice showing their work and writing their thoughts mathematically.

Whole-Faculty Study Group Log

School Mangham Elem.   **Log #** 5   **Date** _____

Group Name or # Dinghies

Members Present: Everyone present _____

What happened today? Brief summary of discussion and activities. Keep artifacts in notebook.

We looked at several Web sites (Making Connections and Exemplars) that have constructed-response items we can use with our students. We worked several and used a rubric to score our responses. We looked at work from preschoolers who are learning to order and classify objects. Carol shared that grade one and two students are using C-R items every day with Saxon Math and are doing quite well.

Next week: Brenda is going to meet with us. Bring student work that requires students to use resource or reference materials. We will use a protocol that was presented at the last IC meeting.

Whole-Faculty Study Group Log

School Mangham Elem.   **Log #** 6   **Date** _____

Group Name or # Dinghies

Members Present: Everyone present _____

What happened today? Brief summary of discussion and activities. Keep artifacts in notebook.

Brenda demonstrated a PowerPoint that is a great tool for teaching writing. It can be used with students to illustrate how to use a thesaurus and a dictionary. It also "talked" about good subjects and predicates in writing better sentences. This would prepare students for writing better paragraphs and essays. Also, expanding word usage by using more adverbs and adjectives was presented.

We practiced using the Wows and Wonders protocol with the work that Louise brought.

Next meeting: Bring items you use as reference or resource materials and be ready to share how you use the items.

Whole-Faculty Study Group Log

School Mangham Elem.   **Log #** _7_   **Date** _____

Group Name or # Dinghies

Members Present: Everyone present _____

What happened today? Brief summary of discussion and activities. Keep artifacts in notebook.
Resource and reference materials brought were: Web page Weather page from newspaper Encyclopedia Map of Louisiana Phone book Table of contents from a book Index from a book Dictionary and thesaurus Each member shared how the items were used in classroom activities.

Whole-Faculty Study Group Log

School Mangham Elem.   **Log #** _8_   **Date** _____

Group Name or # Dinghies

Members Present: Everyone present _____

What happened today? Brief summary of discussion and activities. Keep artifacts in notebook.
Kim showed us how to use United Streaming on the Internet in our classrooms. There are subjects related to every grade. We practiced writing constructed-response sentences in story writing and math. Kim brought student work using the 4-square writing method. We confirmed that our students are learning to use 4-Square writing and Masterpiece sentences.

Whole-Faculty Study Group Log

School Mangham Elem.   **Log #** _9_   **Date** _____

Group Name or # Dinghies

Members Present: Everyone present _____

What happened today? Brief summary of discussion and activities. Keep artifacts in notebook.
Louise brought "Sketch and Scribe" booklets that she uses as journals. She shared how these provide a way for her 2nd graders to critique their own handwriting and improve their creative writing. She showed how the students draw and illustrate their stories. She brought student journals with her and we looked at several. She invited us to come into her room to see the literacy centers.

The study group continued to meet through mid-May.

Whole-Faculty Study Group Action Plan

School <u>Crooked River El.</u>   **Study Group** <u>Math Facts</u>   **Date** <u>11/10 & 11/17</u>

Group Members: <u>Janet (3,4,5 Math), Margaret (1st), Cheryl (Para), Wilhelmina (K-2 Math), Paula (3,4,5 Math)</u>

What is the general Category of student needs the group will address? Math

Data indicate that students need to: (be very specific)	**When our study group meets, we will:**
 – Demonstrate understanding of basic numbers – Recall basic math facts in addition, subtraction, multiplication, and division	– Look at student work to determine how effective the lesson or activity was and how to refine lesson – Share resources – Model effective strategies and activities – Share strategies for working with whole class and one-on-one with students having difficulty – Practice using the math materials and programs

Using what the data indicate are student needs, the **ESSENTIAL QUESTION** that will guide the group's work is: *How can we teach students to recall basic math facts?*

Our resources are:	**Our norms are:**
– Touch Math kits – Math Lab (Internet) – PowerPoint presentations – Saxon Math – Web sites – Schoolwide tutorial – Every Day Counts	– Begin and end on time – Do what we say we'll do – Stay focused

Specific **Student Needs** from above —*Students need to:*	**Data Sources** that document need and will be evidence of impact of group's work	**Baseline**—what data indicate when work begins in **September**	**Target**—what study group projects will be the results of the work in **January**	**Actual**—what data indicate *now* in **January**
– Know addition facts – Know subtraction facts – Know multiplication facts – Know division facts	– Benchmark tests – Speed drills – Teacher-made tests – PowerPoint activities	– 26% of 2002–2003 3rd graders on SAT-9 scored below average – 20% of 2002–2003 4th graders on CRCT scored Cat. 1 in math – 35% of our students indicate mastery of grade-level expectation (summer regression)	– 90% of our students will know the math facts they are expected to know	

For the purpose of seeing examples of what study groups do, only the portions of the logs are given that describe what the group did. Logs from some meetings are skipped to conserve space.

Whole-Faculty Study Group Log

School <u>Crooked River Elem.</u>   Log # <u>3</u>   Date <u>9/16/03</u>

What happened today? Brief summary of discussion and activities. Keep artifacts in notebook.
• We decided to focus on the 1st need on our action plan: demonstrate understanding of basic numbers. • Janet brought a Touch Math kit. • We viewed the video for Touch Math and responded to the lessons demonstrated in the video. • We went over the items in the kit and shared how we might use the items. • We are focusing on addition. • We all see evidence that our students are learning how to do Touch Math in addition.

Whole-Faculty Study Group Log

School <u>Crooked River Elem.</u>   Log # <u>4</u>   Date <u>10/1</u>

What happened today? Brief summary of discussion and activities. Keep artifacts in notebook.
• We spent a lot of time discussing the feedback on our action plan from Carlene and have made our student needs more specific. We originally had five general math needs on our action plan and we have reduced that to two specific needs—both focusing on basic math facts. Later, we may add more student needs. • Margaret shared the IC meeting that she attended when Carlene was here. We think we have a better grasp on our work now. • We discussed basic numbers and tried to break down basic numbers into more specific objectives for our work in this group.

Whole-Faculty Study Group Log

School <u>Crooked River Elem.</u>   Log # <u>6</u>   Date <u>10/21</u>

What happened today? Brief summary of discussion and activities. Keep artifacts in notebook.
• We brought our Benchmark results and spent time looking at scores. We think the Benchmark testing may be too broad for us to use. We looked at the SAT-9 results. • Paula demonstrated several strategies for mastering multiplication facts and self-checking multiplication games; we listened to a tape on multiplication that she brought; and she shared her success with Racetrack Speed Drill. • Janet showed the multiplication section in the Touch Math video. • Margaret volunteered to create a PowerPoint presentation to help drill students on multiplication facts and will bring it to our next meeting.

Whole-Faculty Study Group Log

School <u>Crooked River Elem.</u>   Log # <u> 7 </u>   Date <u>10/28</u>

What happened today? Brief summary of discussion and activities. Keep artifacts in notebook.
<ul><li>Margaret showed the PowerPoint presentation on multiplication facts. We spent most of our time practicing the activities and experienced the excitement that children must feel when using this strategy. She said the children are very engaged in the learning and do not want to stop when using the Word Wall PowerPoint presentation in her classroom. We discussed how she puts different skills on different discs. We talked about using this on a smart board. Margaret said she would provide discs for us.</li><li>We celebrated with Janet when she shared that her class is getting the multiplication tables through the use of Touch Math. We need more Touch Math materials!!</li></ul>

Whole-Faculty Study Group Log

School <u>Crooked River Elem.</u>   Log # <u> 10 </u>   Date <u>12/12</u>

What happened today? Brief summary of discussion and activities. Keep artifacts in notebook.
<ul><li>We talked about how we can use the Touch Math materials without making copies for all students (i.e., laminating sheets for reuse, using sheet protectors).</li><li>We shared strategies we are using from Every Day Counts and Saxon—It is important that we use a mix of both programs.</li><li>We see results from using the multiplication songs in Grades 3 through 5.</li><li>Margaret demonstrated the PowerPoint on the 2s and 3s—and brought student work that resulted from an addition PowerPoint activity.</li><li>First graders love the PowerPoint on addition!</li><li>Shared Web sites our students enjoy using.</li><li>At next meeting, we need to examine data to see if we need to revise action plan.</li></ul>

Whole-Faculty Study Group Log

School <u>Crooked River Elem.</u>   Log # <u> 11 </u>   Date <u>1/13</u>

What happened today? Brief summary of discussion and activities. Keep artifacts in notebook.
<ul><li>The PowerPoint presentations on all the tables are complete. Janet and Paula were given a multiplication PowerPoint disc to review and test with students. Will share results.</li><li>Paula expressed a desire for a PowerPoint on subtraction. We will work on that for her.</li><li>We looked at data on how our students are doing with A, S, and M facts. We all see improvement on drill scores!!!!!!</li><li>Janet shared what was discussed at IC meeting.</li><li>This question was asked: When will we be ready to share the PowerPoint presentations to teachers not in our group? After we have all used the presentations and revise according to use.</li></ul>

Whole-Faculty Study Group Log

School Crooked River Elem.   **Log #** 12   **Date** 1/27

What happened today? Brief summary of discussion and activities. Keep artifacts in notebook.

- Janet presented a Touch Math folder from one of her students and showed what the process is for learning each fact. The use of music/song is included for each fact. A multiple fact-finding color sheet is used in this folder for visual learning.
- Paula presented student work samples utilizing Margaret's PowerPoint presentation of multiplication. The majority of the students have improved since the last speed drill.
- Wilhelmina shared student fact assessment samples of using Saxon math techniques.
- Today really reinforced the importance of using multiple sources for teaching and learning. In doing so, we have learned that we have to seamlessly integrate the materials so students don't feel a lack of coherence as we move from one system to the next.
- We all agree that we see that the facts are being mastered and that students show transfer of knowledge from one activity to the next.
- Paula will represent us at the next IC meeting.

Whole-Faculty Study Group Log

School Crooked River Elem.   **Log #** 13   **Date** 2/10

What happened today? Brief summary of discussion and activities. Keep artifacts in notebook.

- Margaret showed us how to develop our own PowerPoint presentations so each of us can include what our students need to know. Cheryl had ideas about adding images of objects to put with the numbers to help the students understand what the numbers represent. Margaret added Stars to the numbers and reduced the amount of speed in which the problem appeared. We discussed how this would be beneficial for PreK and K. We discussed using the space bar feature as a way for younger students to check their answers.
- Janet reported that students in her room are doing well with subtraction with regrouping by using the Touch Math system. Multiplication facts are improving as well. She brought samples of student work but we did not have time to look at the work.
- Students in Wilhelmina's room are working on speed and accuracy.

Whole-Faculty Study Group Log

School Crooked River Elem.   **Log #** 14   **Date** 2/20

What happened today? Brief summary of discussion and activities. Keep artifacts in notebook.

- Gail met with us today. She attended the national WFSG conference in Augusta, where she spent a full day with a national consultant on how to look at student work using protocols. Gail brought work with her and we used the tuning protocol. She gave us copies of materials she received at the workshop and articles to read. We are anxious to use the protocol with our own students' work. Margaret will bring student work to our next meeting.

Whole-Faculty Study Group Log

School Crooked River Elem.   **Log #** 15   **Date** 3/2

What happened today? Brief summary of discussion and activities. Keep artifacts in notebook.

- Margaret brought student work and we followed the tuning protocol.
- Beverly (in another study group) also went to the looking at student work workshop in Augusta and she has done a video with her study group looking at student work using the tuning protocol. We did not have time to view the tape. We may do so at our grade-level meetings.
- Based on what we learned at the last meeting about protocols, Margaret shared a PowerPoint she designed that demonstrates how to use the protocol. Suggestions were given as to how we can examine student work using the PowerPoint protocol.
- Wilhelmina distributed an article from Dr. Sapp entitled "Web Wonders" on integrating reading and writing in all content areas.
- Janet will represent us at the IC meeting next week. We have heard that Carlene will be at the meeting.
- Janet wants us to brainstorm ideas for concept development on fractions at our next meeting.

Whole-Faculty Study Group Log

School Crooked River Elem.   **Log #** 16   **Date** 3/16

What happened today? Brief summary of discussion and activities. Keep artifacts in notebook.

- Carlene was present at the IC meeting. She reviewed a lot of information and Janet shared with us. Carlene stressed the importance of us going into each other's classrooms to observe students working. We have not done this—but, the way Carlene explained it, we will definitely begin to plan to do so. She presented several ideas for assessing our study group work.
- Wilhelmina brought an Insta Learn Teachers Guide from the Media Center to share. We discussed the contents of all the different skills that are offered in the guide. She also brought the Clever Catch Math balls to show. She commented that her students have enjoyed using them.
- Third graders and afterschool tutoring have benefited from the multiplication tape that Paula shared earlier.
- Janet thinks that it would be helpful for second graders toward the end of the year (now). Basic addition and subtraction facts are a struggle for beginning 3rd graders.
- Margaret is ready to share the PowerPoint at an upcoming whole faculty meeting.
- We all received a copy of the WFSG rubric and will review it for next week. Also, we will have choices about the formats we will use to assess our study group's work. All that is coming up!

The study group continued to meet through mid-May.

Whole-Faculty

Study Groups™

Assessment of WFSG Work–III

SUMMARY
St. Mary's Elementary School

BEFORE the study group began its work:	AT THE END of the study group's work:
Group 1 • Rarely used center-focused teaching. • Didn't use research to plan effectively.	• Regularly use center-focused teaching, where children are intrinsically motivated to complete self-selected projects. • Use research to reflect best practices in teaching.
Group 2 • We rarely used available software.	• We always use the Graph Club! The students love it.
Group 3 • We used manipulatives primarily in math. • We rarely used research to improve our teaching practices.	• As a result of our collaboration, we have made a more concerted effort. • We are more cognizant of the importance of utilizing explicit research to improve our teaching strategies specifically in developing higher-order thinking.
Group 4 • I didn't make a special effort to focus on rereading and setting a purpose for reading. • Students read AR books occasionally and many did not test on them. • I didn't look as closely at BM scores and grouping.	• I am very aware of the need to let students read or listen to stories many times and to set a purpose for reading. • Most students read 1 or more AR books and score 80–100% on tests. After reading short stories, students share answers to questions and listening seems to have improved. • I have grouped students according to weaknesses on the test.
Group 5 • We had not all tried the same writing techniques with our classes.	• We have all used with our classes: Power Writing Hamburger method www.creativewriting.com

BEFORE the study group began its work:	AT THE END of the study group's work:
Group 6 • Never used direct listening activities. • Used technology during centers only. • Didn't address vocabulary in-depth.	• Use direct listening activities. • Frequently use technology for centers, word processing, and research. • Weekly vocabulary activity.
Group 7 • We had little knowledge of the Web sites and software that are available to increase listening skills, vocabulary, and higher-order thinking skills.	• Less group work before—more group work for HOTS. • Enthusiasm up with cooperative groups. Improved attitude toward math. • Web sites to increase HOTS. • Software—listening skills.
Group 8 • We did not know how to look at student work collaboratively.	• We are looking at student work from all of our classes and using protocols.
Group 9 • We were not regularly using the Internet as a resource for science/math activity ideas/whole group and individual instruction. • Kindergarten was not completely aware of certain science/math skills that would be assessed in 1st grade. • Children were not given enough "hands on" application of skills. • Kindergarten and 1st grade were not given time to share ideas and brainstorm together. • Our proven ideas were not always validated.	• We have been exposed to and are using many more resources, including Internet resources. These resources and brainstorming allowed more enjoyable activities. • Weak areas that showed up in 1st grade were shared with kindergarten (BM). • More time is being spent to allow students to apply skills. • We enjoyed our sharing time and a bridge was built. • We validated what we knew worked.
Group 10 • All of us did not know about "whole body listening."	• We all review "whole body listening" components before beginning lessons.
Group 11 • The majority of teaching was whole group. • The majority of computer instruction is done in centers and unassessed.	• Substantial increase in small group instruction. • The majority of computer instruction is remediation, direct instruction (involving more logical/reasoning type of games correlating to concepts being taught), and assessed. • The effectiveness of this teaching technique has been critiqued through student input with teacher-made rubrics on researched sites.

Each study group completed the Assessment of WFSG Work–III, and the responses were compiled or summarized onto one form.

Whole-Faculty

Study Groups™

Assessment of WFSG Work–IV

SUMMARY
St. Mary's Elementary School

Specific student needs listed on action plan. *Students need to:*	Data sources that document need *and* are evidence of impact of group's work	Baseline—what data indicate when work began in September	Target—what study group projected would be the results of the work in: May	Actual—what data indicate now May
Group 1 – Demonstrate critical analysis – Demonstrate reading comp. – Increase vocabulary through use of context clues	3rd grade SAT-9 2nd grade BM* 5th grade SAT-9	Below 29% Below 63% Below 29%	>10% gain or above average >10% increase Moody's score >10% gain or above average	
Group 2 – Use higher-order thinking skills	Benchmark I	Test scores indicated students scored low in this area	To increase Benchmark scores	
Group 3 – Apply text factors in reading strategies – Apply problem-solving strategies – Apply problem-solving strategy: draw pictures. – Solve two-step word problems	BM I BM I BM I	15% 5% 20%	Gain of 50% Gain of 50% Gain of 60%	
Group 4 – Use higher-order thinking skills – Listen – Identify extraneous information	BM BM GKAP BM	1st–5% 3rd–15% 1st–11% 3rd–0% K LT	3% increase 3% increase K–80% mastery 3% increase	

Specific student needs listed on action plan. *Students need to:*	Data sources that document need and are evidence of impact of group's work	Baseline—what data indicate when work began in September	Target—what study group projected would be the results of the work in May	Actual—what data indicate now May
Group 5 – Improve writing skills	BM I	Low scores between 31% and 58%	To make a gain of 5% to 10%	
Group 6 – Improve: Listening Vocabulary Reading comp.	BM I and II		Improved BM scores by 3% to 5%	
Group 7 – Improve: Listening Vocabulary HOTS	SAT-9 BM Comp. BM	3rd–51 5th–57 Vocab. 2nd–67 4th–70 Increase 25%	Increase 3% Increase to 70% Increase to 75% Increase to 25%	
Group 8				
Group 9 – Apply and understand estimation and measurement in math-science	GKAP and BM	50%	65%	
– Apply math and science to real life	GKAP and BM	88%	95%	
– Use higher-order thinking skills to solve problems	GKAP and BM	12%	40%	
Group 10 – Develop listening skills – Improve vocab. – Improve listening for information	Stanford 9 (3rd and 5th)		10% increase in each area (3rd and 5th)	
Group 11 59MO304 59MO504	BM II	3rd–25% 5th—65%	3rd–5% (30) 5th–5% (70)	

The locally sponsored Benchmark tests are given in October, January, and March. The content descriptors are matched to the SAT-9 objectives. The tests are given in Grades 1 through 8 in language arts, science, and math. Teachers use the tests to "benchmark" where students are and to plan to meet student needs. The tests are excellent formative measures to guide the work of study groups.

Resource F

The Instructional Council

- Procedures and Agendas

- The First IC Meeting

- Example Agenda for the First IC Meeting

- Reflections Form

- Baseline Data Form

- WFSG Strategies and Resources Form

- WFSG Status Report Form

- WFSG Progress Report Form

- Minutes From IC Meetings

Whole-Faculty

Study Groups™

Instructional Council

Procedures

- Dates are posted on the school calendar for the school year.
- The meetings are usually scheduled 4 to 6 weeks apart.
- At the first study group meeting, members select the IC meeting(s) each will attend. Names with meeting dates are given to the principal.
- Persons who attend the meeting are called "representatives."
- Representatives represent the study group of which they are a member and report what is discussed at an IC meeting.
- If representatives are to bring information to an IC meeting, the information should be collected at a study group meeting immediately preceding the IC meeting.
- The principal or a member of the focus team facilitates IC meetings.
- Meetings can be expected to last from 60 to 90 minutes, depending on the number of representatives present.
- The principal establishes the agenda, with input from others.
- Norms are established for IC meetings.
- Minutes are taken of IC meetings.
- Minutes are distributed to the faculty.
- Guests may be invited to attend IC meetings (e.g., district staff).
- The IC meeting may be a training session when one person from each study group is trained or informed of a strategy or skill to facilitate study group work. The representative is expected to train or inform the members of his or her study group. For example, a protocol may be introduced to representatives.
- End meeting with Reflections, see form.

Agendas

Agendas should match a purpose. When dates are established for the IC meetings, the principal and focus team could also establish the main focus for each meeting. Agendas could include

- Sharing of study group action plans (usually the first meeting)
- Looking at data using Baseline Data Worksheet, see form in this section.
- Reinforcing effective strategies using WFSG Strategies and Resources Report, see form in this section.
- Hearing status reports using WFSG Status Report, see form and WFSG Progress Report, see forms in this section.

The First Instructional Council Meeting

Primary purpose: For one representative from each study group to become familiar with the study group action plans from all the study groups at the school so that the representative can discuss the plans with his or her study group at its next meeting.

It is recommended that the representatives receive a copy of the study group action plans prior to the IC meeting.

The IC meeting is scheduled for no more than 90 minutes, preferably 60 minutes. Therefore, time spent on each plan will be limited.

Regardless of which of the following strategies are used to review the action plans, each representative is given an index card for each study group. If there are 12 study groups, each representative is given 12 index cards. Each representative is to give written feedback to each of the other representatives via the index card. At the end of the meeting, the index cards are given to the appropriate representative. If there are 15 people at the IC meeting, a representative will leave the meeting with 15 index cards. No anonymous feedback! An alternative to this is to have feedback written directly onto the plans and council members return the plans with the comments to the appropriate representatives at the end of the meeting.

Strategies for reviewing the study group action plans:

1. Prior to the meeting, ask each representative to come to the meeting with one aspect of the plan on which he or she would like to receive feedback or one aspect of the plan that really excites his or her study group. Also, inform the representatives that they will have 2 minutes for the presentation. The council will have 2 minutes to respond to the presenter.

2. If it is a large group, form triads. In the triads, each will have 3 minutes to present, and the respondents will have 3 minutes. After 20 minutes, the whole council reconvenes, and one person from each triad takes 1 minute per plan presented in the triad to report to the whole council.

3. If the representatives have been given the action plans ahead of time, the council would focus on one plan at a time. A representative would simply acknowledge his or her study group's plan (with no presentation) and ask for comments/questions. Three minutes per plan.

Agenda for the First
IC Meeting (Suggested)

- Opening

- Establish norms for IC meetings

  ☐ Each representative shares one norm from his or her study group.

- Review the role of the IC (handout)

- Presentation/discussion of the current status of WFSGs by having each representative

  ☐ Share the group's essential question
  ☐ Share the action on the plan that is the current focus of the group

  [For this activity, everyone will need to have a copy of all the action plans.]

- Stages of groups (handout: pages 35-39 in WFSG textbook)

  ☐ Forming (most groups here)
  ☐ Grumbling (some are here; what are strategies for moving through this state? It is a comfortable stage.)
  ☐ Willingness
  ☐ Consequence

- Current challenges: Each representative shares one challenge that is currently impeding the work of the group.

- Announcements

- Adjourn

Whole-Faculty

Study Groups™

Instructional Council

Reflections

At end of meeting, please complete and give to the principal.

Representative _____ Study Group _____

As a result of today's meeting, one recommendation that I will make to my study group is

In listening to other study group reports, I think we should consider the following as follow-up with all study groups:

Based on the reports from study groups, the following actions should be considered for whole-faculty adoption, going into the school's next school improvement plan:

A concern my study group has that has not been resolved is

Other comments and suggestions:

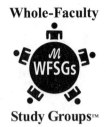

Whole-Faculty

Study Groups™

Instructional Council

Baseline Data Worksheet

Study Group _____ **Representative** _____

The decision-making cycle (DMC), through an analysis of district and state tests, led the faculty to the identification of student needs. Each study group is addressing one group or category of those needs. When a study group begins its work, it must collect more data on the specific student needs the group is addressing through such items as teacher-made tests (pre and post), teacher observation, textbook tests, questionnaires, and student work. This worksheet is seeking more information about how a study group collected more information than was given at the DMC session about the student needs a group is targeting.

1. In reviewing the group's action plan, our study group chose to
   ___ focus on one student need to begin.
   ___ focus on more than one student need to begin.

2. The student need that we researched and on which we collected more data is

3. List or attach the assessment instruments or data sources (e.g., rubric, survey, and writing sample) used:

4. The number of students sampled: ___

5. Range of sample (check one):
   ___ all members' classrooms
   ___ some of the members' classrooms (but not all)
   ___ one member's classroom

6. Data results. Use any meaningful way to present this information (e.g., narrative, charts, tables, and lists). Attach or describe below.

7. Reflections. How will the baseline data guide the work of the study group?

Whole-Faculty

Study Groups™

Instructional Council

WFSG Strategies and Resources Report

Study Group _____ **Representative** _____

This form will assist representatives in presenting at the next IC meeting. The focus at the upcoming meeting will be on strategies and resources the groups are using. The purpose of the form is to make sure that everyone uses the same presentation format, keeping the meeting within its time limits. Each presenter will have 5 minutes to present and 3 minutes to respond to questions from IC representatives. Representatives are expected to inform members of their study groups what other study groups are doing and using that are effective. **Bring 15 copies of the completed form to the next IC meeting.**

Best Practices: Strategies the study group uses when the group meets that are effective in facilitating the work of the group; for example, looking at student work, sharing classroom observations, watching a video, hearing from a consultant, and discussing an assigned reading.

Strategy	How Used	Effectiveness on a 1 to 5 Scale

Expert Voices (Resources and Materials): Titles of books, articles, videos, and other materials the group has used; names of individuals that have met with the group; and workshops and conferences members have attended.

Name/Title	How Used	Effectiveness on a 1 to 5 Scale

What is the next action your study group will take?

What does the study group need to begin or complete this action?

Whole-Faculty

Study Groups™

Instructional Council

WFSG Status Report

Study Group _____ Representative _____

Complete and bring 15 copies of this form to the next IC meeting.

What is the group's essential question?

What specific student need is the group currently addressing?

Share an idea the group has for involving parents in targeting this student need.

Within the next 3 months, have study group members commit to trying at least one of the following strategies. Check the one(s) the group will try.

___ At least one pair of study group members observe in each other's classrooms to watch students work on an assignment that targets a student need the group is addressing. Student work from the lessons is brought to the study group meeting.

___ A member of the study group videotapes himself or herself teaching a lesson the group has codeveloped addressing a student need on the group's action plan and shares the video with the group. Student work from the lesson is brought to the study group meeting.

Give three examples of student work the group has examined, and tell how each example is reflective of the student need(s) the group is targeting.

Whole-Faculty

Study Groups™

Instructional Council

WFSG Progress Report

Study Group _____ **Representative** _____

Study group members should discuss and record the following information before an IC meeting. The representative is to bring 15 copies of the completed form to the IC meeting.

Describe an instructional strategy being used in classrooms as a result of study group work.

_____

Describe the improvement in student learning as a result of using the strategy listed above.

_____

Describe another instructional strategy being used in classrooms as a result of study group work.

_____

Describe the improvement in student learning as a result of using the strategy.

_____

Content of one piece of student work examined:

Protocol used: _____

How did this work assist members in understanding the students' academic needs?

_____

Content of another piece of student work examined:

Protocol used: _____

How did this work assist members in understanding the students' academic needs?

_____

Whole-Faculty

WFSGs

Study Groups™

Example:

Minutes From IC Meetings

Ball Ground Elementary School
Cherokee County (GA) School District
INSTRUCTIONAL COUNCIL MEETING
WHOLE-FACULTY STUDY GROUPS
Thursday, Sept. 16, 2003

MEDIA CENTER: 2:35 PM

Groups:

1. Writing Mechanics

2. Reading Comprehension

3. Vocabulary and Spelling

4. Writing

5. Math Comprehension and Problem Solving

6. Study Skills and Listening Skills

Agenda:

Introduction and establishment of norms: We reviewed the norms set by each study group and adopted norms for the IC. They were: Be prompt, be prepared, stay focused, and follow leadership schedule.

Review purpose of IC: We reviewed the purpose by going over the handout (page 56 in the WFSG workbook). We also reviewed the ATLAS Community principles in a handout.

Look at action plans and last log from each group (received copies). We will report in the order listed above. Discuss issues, concerns, and good things that are happening in our groups.

1. Writing Mechanics: Nancy stated that at its first meeting her study group worked on establishing its action plan. The group kept the same essential question it used last year. Members are excited about using the Shurley method, which will supplement the reading series. They

had a difficult time setting performance goals because the school is lacking current test data in so many grades.

2. Reading Comprehension: Glenda reported that her group had also completed its action plan. She stated that her group is also using multiple strategies to help students improve reading comprehension across the curriculum.

3. Vocabulary and Spelling: Kelly said that her group had completed its action plan. The group's essential question states that it wants to increase vocabulary and spelling in all content areas. Members are also excited about using the Shurley method. At their next meeting, they want to use their new teacher editions in Reading and brainstorm strategies to enhance vocabulary and spelling.

4. Writing: Connie stated that they had worked on their action plan. They changed their essential question so that it asks, "Will the Shurley method improve our students' writing so that it is well organized, thoroughly developed, and reflects use of effective language?" They also changed the student performance goals for 3rd and 5th grade.

5. Math Comprehension and Problem Solving: Patricia stated that they had completed their action plan. She said that they increased their student performance goals to say that 95% of students participate on ADD daily in K–6. Also, her group is thrilled that SuccessMaker is up and running. This is a computer program that reinforces our Math series.

6. Study Skills and Listening Skills: Garry stated that they had also completed their action plan. Each member of the group will be targeting certain groups of students to work on listening skills. The school has adopted a listening program for each grade level, but this program is not being used uniformly across the grade levels. Garry stated that the group had developed a plan so that the listening program would be used more. Hopefully, this will help each grade level.

In the general sharing, everyone agreed that the bottom portion of the action plan (assessing progress) was difficult to do. We also agreed that it is a major improvement and will give us real targets at short intervals—it is more realistic and more meaningful. However, scarier!

Everyone commented on how much we appreciate having all the WFSG events on the school calendar. Also, we like getting the feedback from Mr. Cronic so promptly. The e-mail system for feedback works great!

Next meeting: Dec. 4, 2003, at 2:35 in media center. We will share any problems, dilemmas, or successes with one another at that time.

**Ball Ground Elementary School
Cherokee County (GA) School District
INSTRUCTIONAL COUNCIL MEETING
WHOLE-FACULTY STUDY GROUPS
Thursday, December 4, 2003**

MEDIA CENTER: 2:35 PM

Groups:

1. Writing Mechanics

2. Reading Comprehension

3. Vocabulary and Spelling

4. Writing

5. Math Comprehension and Problem Solving

6. Study Skills and Listening Skills

Agenda:

Introduction and establishment of norms: We reviewed the norms set at the last IC meeting: Be prompt, be prepared, stay focused, and follow leadership schedule.

Review purpose of instructional council.

Reports from each group:

1. Writing Mechanics: This group visited www.learningconcepts.org (Learning Focused Schools—Max Thompson). Concerned about transferring skills across the curriculum. Some ideas are adding writing sections to tests and implementing creative writing assignments. Mr. Cronic, principal, commented that we need to find a good way for teachers to learn about integrating TFU. Max Thompson's model has a lot of possibilities. The step-by-step procedure is worth investigating. Mr. Cronic is attending a meeting next week about Max Thompson. He will share with WFSGs after the meeting and let the groups decide.

2. Reading Comprehension: Sarena reported that her group is using strategies that work. They are wondering how the rest of the faculty would feel about curriculum mapping for each grade level. Mr. Cronic said that he would check with Buffington and how well it was working for them.

3. Vocabulary and Spelling: Jodie said that her group had been gathering information on the Shurley method. It is really helping students use a variety of vocabulary and instilling higher-level thinking skills. Class would change words and use synonyms, etc., in sentences.

4. Writing: Tabitha stated that her group has been focusing on the Shurley method, similar to the Vocabulary and Spelling group. Her group is in favor of curriculum mapping and would like to see it implemented throughout the school. This group and the Writing Mechanics group met together to coordinate their work and will meet together again.

5. Math Comprehension and Problem Solving: Jennie stated that her group really likes SuccessMaker, and it is easy to assess the students' strengths and determine their weaknesses. Using the reports allows the teachers to reteach skills that are weak and see the students' problem areas. Use of the program helps students retain information.

6. Study Skills and Listening Skills: Chassidy stated that her group is in favor of developing a schoolwide listening signal so that all students would know when to really stop and pay attention. "Give Me Five" method will be used. Grade levels will come up with the five things they would like to use for the Give Me Five answers.

We are going to have a special meeting to discuss the status of the assessment of progress (bottom of action plans). We feel we need to see if we are on target. Mr. Cronic will let us know about a date and time.

Next IC meeting: March 2, 2004, at 2:35 in the media center. We will share any problems, dilemmas, or successes with one another at that time.

Ball Ground Elementary School
Cherokee County (GA) School District
INSTRUCTIONAL COUNCIL MEETING
WHOLE-FACULTY STUDY GROUPS
March 2, 2004

MEDIA CENTER: 9:30 AM

Groups:

1. Writing Mechanics
2. Reading Comprehension
3. Vocabulary and Spelling
4. Writing
5. Math Comprehension and Problem Solving
6. Study Skills and Listening Skills

Agenda:

I. Review norms for our instructional council: Be prompt, be prepared, stay focused, and follow leadership schedule.

II. Look at action plans and last log according to numerical order listed above and discuss issues, concerns, and good things going on: Discussion about Carlene Murphy's assistance, Eulouise William's TFU information and documentation, end-of-year WFSG evaluation, and learning-focused schools.

III. Set date and agenda for next IC meeting: May 12, 2004, will be our last date for IC this school year. Look at action plans, discuss issues and concerns, and discuss strategies that might be helpful in the classroom. Make sure that we can document TFU strategies.

1. Writing Mechanics: This group is focusing on students learning how to learn. Using "Essential Questions" was a particularly good activity for teaching art appreciation. For example, "Why was Picasso so influential in the world of art?" The students would also identify a piece of art and describe it in detail and then follow up with a drawing of that same piece using the description they just gave in an "Idea Illustration" activity. The "Understanding Nouns" and "Understanding Big Ideas" rubrics were also found to be helpful in this group.

2. Reading Comprehension: This group utilized a number of things Eulouise gave them. They have been analyzing reading strategies and looking at student work. They have found that *Strategies That Work* by Harvey has been a good source of ideas and information. The use of "word bridges" and "character charts" has been especially helpful. Again, the emphasis is on teaching the child how to learn.

3. Vocabulary and Spelling: This group thought that the ideas Eulouise shared with them were very insightful and beneficial. One particular goal of the group is to communicate with parents more effectively about the new techniques being employed by the faculty. They have been focusing on using "high-level questions" and the list of Bloom's taxonomy verbs. Self-designed rubrics are being used to produce a more comprehensive assessment. Letters were sent home to parents to make them aware of what their children are doing and to explain the different methods of assessment.

4. Writing: They also were very pleased with the visit from Eulouise and what she shared with the group. Teachers from this group have been focused on writing correct sentences. They have also designed their own rubrics for this assessment. Particular attention was paid to primary-level sentences and the use of capital letters, correct spacing, etc. An especially successful technique was to do group work in which the students would take words and cooperatively make sentences and then use rubrics to grade their sentences. Mary said she was pleased that the activity went so well and that the children were very honest and fair in their assessment. An example of that rubric was shared with the other members of the council.

5. Math Comprehension and Problem Solving: Amanda expressed her enthusiasm with the strategies shared by Eulouise at the last WFSG meeting. They have been using several of those ideas in math. Their group members were actively using the "here is the answer" activity along with "math riddles," "word splash," and the "KWL" chart, exploring what the children know about addition, and using the "Venn diagram" on the topic of communities. The Venn diagram was especially effective with the students.

6. Study Skills and Listening Skills: This group is in transition now from listening skills to study skills. The posttest for listening skills revealed an improvement in test scores in both 6th-grade classes. "The listening test" was the test administered on story comprehension, and the results were encouraging. Kelly has sent home literacy family bags with reading material and activities for the parents to do with their Pre-K child, which hopefully will be a head start on developing good study skills. Garry asked the group what study skills seem to the weakest in their classes so he can get an idea of what to focus on when teaching study skills in the future, and Kelly replied that she thought it was in the area of organization.

Next IC meeting: May 12. We will plan our end-of-year WFSG celebration.

Recommended Reading

Branson, R. (1987). Why the schools can't improve: The upper limit hypothesis. *Journal of Instructional Development, 10*(1), 7–12.

Calhoun, E. (1993). Action research: Three approaches. *Educational Leadership, 5*(2), 62–65.

Charles, L., Clark, R., Roudebush, J., Budnick, S., Brown, M., & Turner, P. (1995). Study groups in practice. *Journal of Staff Development, 16*(3), 49–53.

Joyce, B. (1991). The doors to school improvement. *Educational Leadership, 48*(8), 59–62.

Joyce, B. (1992). Cooperative learning and staff development: Teaching the method with the method. *Cooperative Learning, 12*(2), 10–13.

Joyce, B., & Murphy, C. (1990). Epilogue. In B. R. Joyce (Ed.), *ASCD yearbook: Changing school culture through staff development.* Alexandria, VA: Association for Supervision and Curriculum Development.

Joyce, B., Wolf, J., & Calhoun, E. (1993). *The self-renewing school.* Alexandria, VA: Association for Supervision and Curriculum Development.

LaBonte, K., Leighty, C., Mills, S., & True, M. (1993). Whole faculty study groups: Building the capacity of change through interagency collaboration. *Journal of Staff Development, 16*(3), 45–47.

Lewis, C. (2002). *Lesson study: A handbook for teacher-led instructional change.* Philadelphia: Research for Better Schools.

Little, J. (1981). *School success and staff development in urban desegregated schools: A summary of recently published research.* Boulder, CO: Center for Action Research.

Little, J. (1990). The persistence of privacy: Autonomy and initiative in teachers' professional relations. *Teachers College Record, 9*(4), 509–536.

Louis, K. S., & Miles, M. (1990). *Improving the urban high school: What works and why.* New York: Teachers College Press.

Lucas, B. (2000). *Whole-faculty study groups' impact on the professional community of schools.* Unpublished doctoral dissertation, University of Minnesota, Minneapolis.

Miles, M., & Huberman, M. (1981). *Innovation up close: A field study.* Andover, MA: The Network.

Murphy, C. (1990, October 16). *The role of the central office staff in restructuring.* Keynote address at the International Society for Educational Planning, Atlanta, GA.

Murphy, C. (1991). The development of a training cadre. *Journal of Staff Development, 12*(3), 21–24.

Murphy, C. (1993). Long-range planning for individual and organizational development. *Journal of Staff Development, 14*(2), 2–4.

Murphy, C. (1997). Finding time for faculties to study together. *Journal of Staff Development, 18*(3), 29–32.

Murphy, J., Murphy, C., Joyce, B., & Showers, B. (1988). The Richmond County school improvement program: Preparation and initial phase. *Journal of Staff Development, 9*(2), 36–41.

National Staff Development Council. (1994). Powerful designs. *Journal of Staff Development, 20*(3), 22–55.

Raywid, M. (1993). Finding time for collaboration. *Education Leadership, 51*(1), 30–34.

Showers, B., Murphy, C., & Joyce, B. (1996). The River City program: Staff development becomes school improvement. In B. R. Joyce & E. Calhoun (Eds.), *Learning experiences in school renewal: An exploration of five successful programs.* Eugene: University of Oregon Press. (ERIC Document Reproduction Service No. EA026696)

Wieman, H. (1990). *Man's ultimate commitment.* Denton, TX: Foundation for the Philosophy of Creativity.

References

Allen, R. (2003). Building school culture in an age of accountability: Principals lead through sharing task. *Education Update*. ASCD. Nov. 2003.

ATLAS Communities. (2000). *Charting the course: Building ATLAS Communities.* Newton, MA: Education Development Center, Inc.

ATLAS Communities. (2003). *Social Policy Research Associates' Report and Findings.* Cambridge, MA: ATLAS Communities.

Barnett, C. (1999). Cases. *The Journal of Staff Development, 20*(30), 26–27.

Birmbaum, R. (1988). *How colleges work: The cybernetics of academic organization and leadership.* San Francisco: Jossey-Bass.

Blanchard, K., Carew, D., & Parisi-Carew, E. (2000). *The one minute manager builds high performing teams.* Escondido, CA: Blanchard Training and Development.

Blythe, T. (1998). *The teaching for understanding handbook.* San Francisco: Jossey-Bass.

Bodilly, S. J. (1998). *Lessons from new American schools' scale-up phase: Prospects for bringing designs to multiple schools.* Santa Monica, CA: RAND Corporation.

Bradley, A. (1993, March 31). By asking teachers about "context" of work, center moves to the cutting edge of research. *Education Week, 12*(27), 6.

Bryk, A., Rollow, S., & Pinnell, G. (1996). Urban school development: Literacy as a lever for change. *Educational Policy, 10*(2), 172–201.

Bryk, A. S., & Driscoll, M. E. (1985). *An empirical investigation of the school as community.* Chicago: University of Chicago, School of Education.

Calhoun, E. (1994). *How to use action research in the self-renewing school.* ASCD: Alexandria, VA.

Conner, D. (1993). *Managing at the speed of change.* New York: Villard.

Corcoran, T., Fuhrman, S., & Belcher, C. (2001). The district role in instructional improvement. *Phi Delta Kappan*, September 2001.

Covey, S. (1990). *The seven habits of highly effective people.* New York: Fireside.

Cronan-Hillix, T., Gensheimer, L., Cronan-Hillix, W. A., Cronan-Hillix, W. S., & Davidson, W. S. (1986). Students' views of mentoring in psychology graduate training. *Teaching of Psychology, 13,* 123–127.

Darling-Hammond, L., & McLaughlin, M. (1995, April). Policies that support professional development in an era of reform. *Phi Delta Kappan, 76,* 597–604.

Deal, T., & Peterson, K. (1999). *Shaping school culture.* San Francisco: Jossey-Bass.

DuFour, R. (2002). The learning-centered principal. *Educational Leadership,* May 2002 (Vol. 59, No. 8).

DuFour, R., & Eaker, R. (1998). *Professional learning communities at work: Best practices for enhancing student achievement.* Alexandria, VA: Association for Supervision and Curriculum Development.

Elmore, R. F., & Burney, D. (1997). *Investing in teacher learning: Staff development and instructional improvement in Community School District 2, New York City.* New York: National Commission on Teaching and America's Future and the Consortium for Policy Research in Education.

Fullan, M. (2001a). *Leading in a culture of change.* San Francisco: Jossey-Bass.

Fullan, M. (2001b). *The new meaning of educational change.* New York: Teachers College Press.

Glasglow, N. (1997). *New curriculum for new times: A guide to student-centered, problem-based learning.* Thousand Oaks, CA: Corwin.

Graff, L. (1996). Committed to growth through a learning organization. *On the Horizon,* 4(2), 5–6.

Guralnik, D. B. (Ed.). (1986). *Webster's new world dictionary* (2nd ed.). New York: Prentice Hall.

Guskey, T. (1990). Integrating innovations. *Educational Leadership,* 47(5), 11–15.

Hall, G. E., S. F. Loucks, W. L. Rutherford, and B. Newlove (1975). Levels of use of the innovation: A framework for analyzing innovation adoption. *Journal of Teacher Education* 24: 52–56.

Hall, G. E., George, A. A., & W. L. Rutherford (1979). *Measuring the Stages of Concern about the innovation.* Austin: Research and Development Center for Teacher Education, University of Texas at Austin.

Hall, G. E., & S. F. Loucks, (1981). Program definition and adaptation: Implications for inservice. *Journal of Research and Devleopment in Education* 14, 2: 46–58.

Hall, G. E., & Hord, S. M. (1987). *Change in schools: Facilitating the process.* Albany: State University of New York Press.

Hall, G. E., & Hord, S. M. (2001). *Implementing change: Patterns, principles, and potholes.* Boston: Allyn & Bacon.

Hord, S., Rutherford, W., Huling-Austin, L., & Hall, G. (1987). *Taking charge of change.* Alexandria, VA: Association for Supervision and Curriculum Development.

Huberman, A. M., & Miles, M. (1984). *Innovation up close: How school improvement works.* New York: Plenum Press.

Joyce, B. (1991). The doors to school improvement. *Education Leadership,* May 1991.

Joyce, B., & Calhoun, E. (1996). *Learning experiences in school renewal: An exploration of five successful programs.* Eugene: University of Oregon Press. (ERIC Document Reproduction Service No. EA026696)

Joyce, B., Murphy, C., Showers, B., & Murphy, J. (1989). School renewal as cultural change. *Educational Leadership,* 47(3), 70–77.

Joyce, B., & Showers, B. (1982). The coaching of teaching. *Educational Leadership,* 40(1), 4–16.

Joyce, B., & Showers, B. (1983). *Power in staff development through research on training.* Washington: Association for Supervision and Curriculum Development.

Joyce, B., & Showers, B. (1988). *Student achievement through staff development* (1st Ed.). New York: Longman.

Joyce, B., & Showers, B. (1995). *Student achievement through staff development.* (2nd Ed.). New York: Longman.

Joyce, B. & Showers, B. (2001). *Student achievement through staff development.* (3rd Ed.). New York. Longman.

Joyce, B., & Weil, M. (2003). *Models of teaching.* Boston: Allyn & Bacon.

Joyce, B., Weil, M., & Showers, B. (1992). *Models of teaching.* Boston: Allyn & Bacon.

Kaufman, R., Herman, J., & Watters, K. (1996). *Educational planning: Strategic, tactical and operational.* Lancaster, PA: Technomic.

Killion, J. (1999). Journaling. *Journal of Staff Development, 20*(3), 36–37.

Leithwood, K. (1997). *Changing leadership for changing times.* Buckingham, UK: Open University Press.

Leonard, J. F. (1996). *The new philosophy for K-12 education: A Deming framework for transforming America's schools.* Milwaukee, WI: ASQ Quality Press.

Leonard, L. and Leonard, P. (2003). "The continuing trouble with collaboration: Teachers talk." *Current Issues in Education* [On-line], Sept. 17, 2003. Available: hhtp://cie.ed.asu.edu/volume6/number15/

Levine, D., & Eubanks, E. (1989). *Site-based management: Engine for reform or pipe dream?* Manuscript submitted for publication.

Lewis, A. (1997, May/June). A new consensus emerges on the characteristics of good professional development. *The Harvard Letter, 13*(3), 3.

Liberman, A., Falk, B., & Alexander, L. (1994). *A culture in the making: Leadership in learner-centered schools.* New York: National Center for Restructuring Education, Schools, and Teaching, Teachers College.

Lick, D. W. (1998). Proactive comentoring relationships: Enhancing effectiveness through synergy. In C. A. Mullen & D. W. Lick (Eds.), *New directions in mentoring: Creating a culture of synergy.* London: Falmer.

Lick, D. W. (Winter 2000). Whole-faculty study groups: Facilitating mentoring for school-wide change. *Theory Into Practice, 39*(1), 43–48.

Lick, D. W. (2003). Keynote Address. *Developing learning teams.* Smaller Learning Communities Conference, Pinellas County Coalition of Smaller Learning Communities Schools, Pinellas Park, FL, July 28, 2003.

Little, J., Gearhart, M., Curry, M., and Kafka, J. (2003, November). Looking at student work for teacher learning, teacher community, and school reform. *Phi Delta Kappan.* pp. 185–192.

Little, J. (1993, Summer). Teachers' professional development in a climate of educational reform. *Educational Evaluation and Policy Analysis,* pp. 129–151.

Loucks-Horsley, S. (1998a). *Ideas that work: Mathematics professional development.* Washington, DC: Eisenhower National Clearinghouse for Mathematics and Science Education and USDE.

Loucks-Horsley, S. (1998b, Summer). *JSD forum. Journal of Staff Development* [pamphlet].

Louis, K. S., Kruse, S. D. & Associates (1995). *Professionalism and community perspectives on reforming urban schools.* Thousand Oaks, CA: Corwin.

Louis, K. S., Kruse, S. D., & Marks, H. M. (1996). Schoolwide professional community. In F. M. Newmann (Ed.), *Authentic achievement: Restructuring schools for intellectual quality.* San Francisco: Jossey-Bass.

Louis, K. S., Marks, K., & Kruse, S. (1996). Teachers professional community in restructuring schools. *American Research Journal, 33*(4), 757–798.

Louisiana Department of Education. December 2003. 2004-2005 Request for LINCS School Applications.

Lucas, B. A. (2000). *Whole-faculty study groups' impact on the professional community of schools.* Unpublished doctoral dissertation, University of Minnesota.

McDonald, J. P. (2002, October). Teachers studying student work: Why and how? *Phi Delta Kappan.* pp. 120–127.

McLaughlin, M., & Talbert, J. (2001). *Professional Communities and the Work of High School Teaching.* Chicago: University of Chicago Press.

Mullen, C. A., & Lick, D. W. (1999). *New directions in mentoring: Creating a culture of synergy.* London: Falmer.

Murphy, C. (1991a, October). Changing organizational culture through administrative study groups. *Newsletter of the National Staff Development Council, 1,* 4.

Murphy, C. U. (1991b). Lessons from a journey into change. *Educational Leadership, 48*(8), 63–67.

Murphy, C. U. (1992). Study groups foster school-wide learning. *Educational Leadership, 50*(3), 71–74.

Murphy, C. U. (1995). Whole-faculty study groups: Doing the seemingly undoable. *Journal of Staff Development, 16*(3), 37–44.

Murphy, C. U., & Lick, D. W. (1998). *Whole-faculty study groups: A powerful way to change schools and enhance learning.* Thousand Oaks: Corwin.

Murphy, C. U. (1999). Study groups. *Journal of Staff Development, 20*(3), 49–51.

Murray, J., & Hallinger, P. (1988). "Characteristics of instructionally effective districts," *Journal of Educational Research,* Vol.8, pp. 175–181.

National Staff Development Council (2003). *Standards for staff development.* Oxford, OH.

National Staff Development Council (2004). *RESULTS.* May, 2004.

Newmann, G., & Wehlage, G. (1995). *Successful school restructuring: A report to the public and educators by the center on organization and restructuring of schools.* Madison: Wisconsin Center for Education Research.

Richardson, J. (2001, May). Shared culture: A consensus of individual values. *Results.* NSDC.

Richardson, J. (1996, October). School culture: A key to improved student learning. *The School Team Innovator,* I, 4.

Richardson, Joan (2004). Lesson Study. *Tools for Schools.* NSDC. February/March 2004.

Riley, P. (1994). *The winner within.* Encino, CA: Berkeley Books.

Rosenholtz, S. (1989). *Teacher's workplace: The social organization of schools.* New York: Longman.

Roy, P. & Hord, S. (2003). *Moving NSDC's staff development standards into practice: Innovation configurations.* Oxford, Ohio: NSDC

Saphier, J., & Gower, R. (1997). *The skillful teacher: Building your teaching skills.* Acton, MA: Research for Better Teaching.

Saphier, J., & King, M. (1985, March). Good seeds grow in strong cultures. *Educational Leadership, 42*(6), 67–74.

Sarason, S. B. (1990). *The predictable failure of educational reform: Can we change schools before it's too late?* San Francisco: Jossey-Bass.

Schlechty, P. C. (1993). On the frontier of school reform with trailbrazers, pioneers, and settlers. *Journal of Staff Development, 14*(4), 46–51.

Sebring, P., & Bryk, A. (2000). School leadership and the bottom line in Chicago. *Phi Delta Kappan, 81,* 440–443.

Senge, P. (1990). *The fifth discipline: The art and practice of the learning organization.* New York: Currency.

Sergiovanni, T. J. (1999). *The lifeworld of leadership: Creating culture, community, and personal meaning in our schools.* San Francisco: Jossey-Bass.

Shelofsky, B. S. (1999, July). *A summative report on the whole-faculty study group process at the Jackson Elementary School, 1995–99.* Greeley, CO: Jackson Elementary School.

Showers, B. (1985). Teachers Coaching teachers. *Educational Leadership, 42* (7), 43–49.

Sizer, T., & Sizer, N. (1999). *The students are watching: Schools and the moral contract.* Boston: Beacon.

Southern Regional Education Board. (1998). *High schools that work: 1998 secondary school teacher survey.* Atlanta, GA: Author.

Sparks, D. (2003). Significant change begins with leaders. *Results.* NSDC. October 2003.

Sparks, G. (1983). Synthesis of research on staff development for effective teaching. *Educational Leadership, 41*(3), 65–72.

Spillane, J. P., Halverson, R., & Diamond, J. B. (1999). "Toward a Theory of Leadership Practice: A Distributed Perspective". Northwestern University. Institute for Policy Research Working Paper.

Spillane, J. P. (1996). "Districts matter: Local educational authorities and state instructional policy," *Educational Policy,* Vol. 10, pp. 63–87.

Vanzant, L. (1980). *Achievement motivation, sex-role acceptance, and mentor relationships of professional females.* Unpublished doctoral dissertation, East Texas State University.

Webster's new world dictionary (2nd ed.). (1986). New York: Prentice Hall.

Zemelman, S., Daniels, H., & Hyde, A. (1993). Best practice: New standards for teaching and learning in America's schools. Portsmouth, NH: Heinemann.

Index

CORWIN
PRESS

The Corwin Press logo—a raven striding across an open book—represents the union of courage and learning. Corwin Press is committed to improving education for all learners by publishing books and other professional development resources for those serving the field of K–12 education. By providing practical, hands-on materials, Corwin Press continues to carry out the promise of its motto: **"Helping Educators Do Their Work Better."**